Cellular neural networks and visual computing

Cellular Nonlinear/neural Network (CNN) technology is both a revolutionary concept and an experimentally proven new computing paradigm. Analogic cellular computers based on CNNs are set to change the way analog signals are processed and are paving the way to an entire new analog computing industry.

This unique undergraduate-level textbook includes many examples and exercises, including CNN simulator and development software accessible via the Internet. It is an ideal introduction to CNNs and analogic cellular computing for students, researchers, and engineers from a wide range of disciplines. Although its prime focus is on visual computing, the concepts and techniques described in the book will be of great interest to those working in other areas of research, including modeling of biological, chemical, and physical processes.

Leon Chua is a Professor of Electrical Engineering and Computer Science at the University of California, Berkeley where he coinvented the CNN in 1988 and holds several patents related to CNN Technology. He received the Neural Network Pioneer Award, 2000.

Tamás Roska is a Professor of Information Technology at the Pázmány P. Catholic University of Budapest and head of the Analogical and Neural Computing Laboratory of the Computer and Automation Research Institute of the Hungarian Academy of Sciences, Budapest and was an early pioneer of CNN technology and a coinventor of the CNN Universal Machine as an analogic supercomputer, He has also spent 12 years as a part-time visiting scholar at the University of California at Berkeley.

Cellular neural networks and visual computing

Foundation and applications

Leon O. Chua

and

Tamás Roska

CAMBRIDGE UNIVERSITY PRESS
Cambridge, New York, Melbourne, Madrid, Cape Town, Singapore, São Paulo

Cambridge University Press
The Edinburgh Building, Cambridge CB2 2RU, UK

Published in the United States of America by Cambridge University Press, New York

www.cambridge.org
Information on this title: www.cambridge.org/9780521652476

First published 2002
This digitally printed first paperback version 2005

A catalogue record for this publication is available from the British Library

Library of Congress Cataloguing in Publication data

Chua, Leon O., 1936–
Cellular neural networks: foundation and primer / Leon O. Chua and Tamás Roska.
    p.   cm.
Includes bibliographical references and index.
ISBN 0 521 65247 2
1. Neural networks (Computer Science) I. Roska, T. II. Title.
QA.76.87.C494 2002
006.3′2–dc21   2001025555

ISBN-13 978-0-521-65247-6 hardback
ISBN-10 0-521-65247-2 hardback

ISBN-13 978-0-521-01863-0 paperback
ISBN-10 0-521-01863-3 paperback

To our wives, Diana and Zsuzsa

Contents

An up-dated website, with the programs referred to in the text, as well as with other new material, is as follows: www.itk.ppke.hu/cnn-technology/

Acknowledgements

We started to teach a formal course devoted entirely to CNN only in 1996, in the Spring Semester, at Berkeley, and in the Autumn Semester in Budapest. Since then, several versions of Lecture Notes have been iterated. We are indebted to many of our former students – some of whom have become our coworkers – who have helped us in various forms we are thankful to all of them. Dr. Ákos Zarándy, Dr. Ken Crounse, Dr. Csaba Rekecky, Dr. Chai-Wah Wu, Dr. László Kék, Dr. László Nemes, Dr. András Radványi, and Dr. Péter Szolgay, as well as Tao Yang, An-Shan Huang, Dávid Bálya, Katalin Keserű, István Petrás and István Szatmári made special efforts to help us during the many years of forming the text to this present version. We are also grateful to Phil Meyler for his kind initiative to publish this textbook.

Leon O. Chua and Tamás Roska
Berkeley–Budapest, May 2000

1 Introduction

Scenario

Recent history of the electronic and computer industry can be viewed as three waves of revolutionary processes.[1] The first revolution, making cheap computing power available via microprocessors in the 1970s, led to the PC industry of the 1980s. The cheap laser and fiber optics, which resulted in cheap bandwidth at the end of the 1980s, led to the Internet industry of the 1990s. The third wave, the sensor revolution at the end of the 1990s, will also provide for a new industry. Sensor revolution means that cheap sensor and MEMS (micro-electro-mechanical system) arrays are proliferating in almost all the conceivable forms. Artificial eyes, nose, ears, taste, and somatosensory devices as well as sensing all physical, chemical, and biological parameters, together with microactuators, etc. are becoming commodities. Thousands and millions of generically analog signals are produced waiting for processing. A new computing paradigm is needed. The cited technology assessment[1] reads:

> The long-term consequence of the coming sensor revolution may be the emergence of a newer analog computing industry in which digital technology plays a mere supporting role, or in some instances plays no role at all.

For processing analog array signals, the revolutionary Analogic Cellular Computer paradigm is a major candidate. The core of this computer is a Cellular Nonlinear/neural network[2] (CNN), an array of analog dynamic processors or cells. The computer architecture is the CNN Universal Machine,[3] with its various physical implementations. At the same time, Analogic CNN computers mimic the anatomy and physiology of many sensory and processing organs with an additional capability of stored programmability. Recent studies on optical and nano-scale implementations open up new horizons on the atomic and molecular levels.

The CNN was invented by Leon O. Chua and Lin Yang in Berkeley in 1988. Unlike cellular automata, CNN host processors accepting and generating analog signals, the time is continuous, and the interaction values are also real values. Unlike lattice dynamics, the input of the CNN array plays an important role. Moreover, CNN becomes a rigorous framework for complex systems exhibiting emergent behavior and the various forms of emergent computations. The notion of the cloning template, the representation of the local interconnection pattern, is crucial. This allows not only modeling but also engineering of complex systems.

Stored programmability, invented by John von Neumann, was the key for endowing digital computers with an almost limitless capability within the digital universe of signals, *opening the door to human invention* via digital algorithms and software. Indeed, according to the Turing–Church thesis, any algorithms on integers conceived by humans can be represented by Recursive functions/Turing Machines/Grammars. The *CNN Universal Machine is universal* not only in a Turing sense but also on analog array signals. Due to stored programmability, it is *also open to human intelligence* with a practically limitless capability within the universe of analog array signals, via analogic spatio-temporal algorithms and software.

The new world opened by the Analogic CNN computing paradigm is nowadays a reality. There are operational focal plane visual microprocessors with 4096 or 16 000 processors, which are fully stored, programmable, and there are Walkman-size self-contained units with image supercomputer speed.

The CNN Universal Chip[4] highlighted on the cover of this book represents a milestone in information technology because it is the first operational, fully programmable industrial-size brain-like stored-program dynamic array computer in the world. This complete computer on a chip consists of an array of 64 × 64 0.5 micron CMOS cell processors, where each cell is endowed not only with a photo sensor for direct optical input of images and videos, but also with communication and control circuitries, as well as local analog and logic memories. Each CNN cell is interfaced with its nearest neighbors, as well as with the outside world. This massively parallel focal-plane array computer is capable of processing 3 trillion equivalent digital operations per second (in analog mode), a performance which can be matched only by supercomputers. In terms of the *SPA* (*speed, power, area*) measures, this CNN universal chip is far superior to any equivalent DSP implementation by at least three orders of magnitude in either *speed, power,* or *area.* In fact, by exploiting the state-of-the-art vertical packaging technologies, close to *peta* (10^{15}) OPS CNN universal cube can be fabricated with such universal chips, using 200 × 200 arrays.

There are many applications which call for TeraOPS or even PetaOPS in a Walkman-size device. Some of these applications include high-speed target recognition and tracking, real-time visual inspection of manufacturing processes, intelligent vision capable of recognizing context sensitive and moving scenes, as well as applications requiring real-time fusing of multiple modalities, such as multispectral images involving visible, infrared, long wave infrared, and polarized lights.

In addition to the immense image and video processing power of the CNN universal chip, we can exploit its unique brain-like architecture to implement brain-like information processing tasks which conventional digital computers have found wanting. Such brain-like processing operations will necessarily be *non-numeric* and *spatio-temporal* in nature, and will require no more than the accuracy of common neurons, which is less than eight bits. Since the computation is a non-iterative wave-like process, the input–output accuracy is not constrained by the iterative digital process. The CNN universal chip is therefore an ideal tool for developing and implementing brain-like information processing schemes. It is this vision of brain-like computing via the CNN universal chip that makes the publication of this textbook both a timely and historic event, the first undergraduate textbook on this new computing paradigm.

The textbook

Cellular Nonlinear/neural Networks (CNN) is an invention with rapid proliferation. After the publication of the cited original paper by Chua and Yang in 1988, several papers explored the rich dynamics inherent in this simple architecture. Indeed, many artificial, physical, chemical, as well as living (biological) systems and organs can be very conveniently modeled via CNN. Hence, the book is written in such a way that no electronic circuit knowledge is needed to understand the first 14 chapters of this book. Indeed, it is our teaching experience, at Berkeley and in Budapest, that undergraduate students from different backgrounds and with a modest knowledge of mathematics and physics taught in engineering, physics, and chemistry departments, as well as biology students from similar backgrounds can understand the book.

In Chapter 2, the basic notations, definitions, and mathematical foundation are presented. The standard CNN architecture is introduced. The cell, the interconnection structure, the local connectivity pattern, the canonical equations and some useful notations, and the biological motivation are described. The importance of the local interconnection "synaptic weight" pattern, the cloning template, or gene, is emphasized. Indeed, these templates, mostly defined by 19 parameters, define the complete array dynamics, which generate an output "image" from an input "image."

In Chapter 3, after two examples, a simple technique for determining array dynamics, based on cell dynamics, is introduced and explained. Next, 11 useful templates are shown with examples and rigorous mathematical analysis.

Chapter 4 is devoted to the digital computer simulation of CNN dynamics. Numerical integration algorithms, digital hardware accelerators, as well as the analog implementation are discussed. An accompanying simulator CANDY is provided in the Appendix.

In Chapter 5 the characterization of the simplest form of a CNN is explored and the binary input binary output case is described. It is quite surprising that even this very basic form with a 3×3 neighborhood template could implement $2^{512} \sim 10^{134}$ different local Boolean functions.

Uncoupled CNN templates constitute a simple class of CNN. Their unified theory and applications described in Chapter 6 provide a thorough understanding of this class of CNN.

In Chapter 7, we begin the introduction of the CNN computer represented by the CNN Universal Machine architecture. We emphasize the need for local analog and logic memory, a global clock and global wire, as well as a local logic unit. It is shown, for example, that every local Boolean function can be realized by using these simple elements in each cell processor.

In Chapter 8, "Back to Basics," the mathematical analysis of the stability of CNN in terms of cloning templates is presented. It turns out that, in most cases, simple conditions are available to test the templates defining completely stable CNN.

The complete architecture of the CNN Universal Machine is shown in Chapter 9. Moreover, the computational infrastructure consisting of a high-level language, a compiler, operating system, and a development system are introduced. An example describing all the elementary details uncovers the basic implementation techniques.

Chapter 10 presents template design and optimization algorithms. The use of a simple program TEMPO for template optimization and decomposition is prepared and provided in the Appendix.

Many two-dimensional linear filters can be represented by CNN. These techniques are shown in Chapter 11 which also introduces the discrete space Fourier transform.

Once we allow spatial coupling, the dynamics of the CNN becomes not only much richer, but also exotic. The coupled CNN is described in Chapter 12 with a design method for binary propagation problems. In particular, it turns out that the global connectivity problem, long considered impossible by locally connected arrays, can be solved by a quite simple coupled CNN.

Nonlinear and delay type synaptic weights and their use are introduced in Chapters 13 and 14, respectively. These types of CNN are typical in modeling living neural networks as well as in solving more complex image processing problems.

In Chapter 15, we show the basics of the CMOS analog and digital implementation of the CNN Universal Machine. Indeed, the first visual microprocessor and its computational infrastructure are described. A computing power comparison is really breathtaking: about three orders of magnitude speed advantage for complex spatio-temporal problems on the same area of silicon.

Finally, in Chapter 16, the surprising similarity between CNN architecture and models of the visual pathway is highlighted. Models and some measurements in living retina are compared.

In addition to the many examples in the text, exercises at the end of the book help both students as well as lecturers to make practical use of the textbook.

The Appendices, provided via the Internet, contain a CNN template library (TEMLIB), a simple yet efficient simulator (CANDY), and a template design and optimization tool (TEMPO/TEMMASTER). These design tools provide for a working environment for the interested reader as well as for the students to explore this new field of modeling and computing. The text can be taught, typically, as a one-semester course.

New developments

More than 1000 reviewed papers and books have been published since the seminal paper by Chua and Yang on CNN technology. Recently, the scope has started to broaden in many directions. Various new forms of physical implementations have started to emerge. Optical implementation is already emerging using molecular level analog optical memory (Bacteriorhodopsine or polymer materials) and atomic[5] and molecular[6] level implementation of the CNN array as well as of the CNN Universal Machine may become feasible; the Analogic Cellular Computer represents a new platform for computing. However, this notion of computing contains brand-new elements and techniques, partially reflecting some forms of nature-made information processing.

Nature-made information processing has several different manifestations. On the *molecular level* this means the protein structures or interacting molecules on a two- or three-dimensional grid; on the *neuronal level* it may mean the many sensory organs and subsequent neural processing. On the *functional neuronal level* it may mean the information representation in spatio-temporal memory, the functional laterality of the brain, as well as the parallel processing places and functional units learned via PET, NMR, fNMR, etc. On the *mathematical-physical level* it may mean several dynamic spatio-temporal processes and phenomena represented by different nonlinear partial differential equations (PDEs). Autowaves, spiral waves, trigger waves are just a few of these exotic waves.

In modern image processing, PDE-based techniques are becoming the most challenging and important new directions. For the analogic CNN computer these are the native, elementary instructions like the multiplication, addition, XOR, NAND, etc. in digital computers. A new understanding about computing itself is emerging. The striking intellectual and scientific challenge is how to combine these diverse phenomena in useful algorithms running on a standard spatio-temporal computer, based on the CNN Universal Machine.

The analogic cellular *visual microprocessors*, embedded in a complete programming environment,[7] offer surprising system performance. Two types of tasks are becoming tractable:

Class K: Kilo real-time [K r/t] frame rate class.
The frame rate of the process in this class is in the order of about a thousand times faster than the real-time video frame rate (30 frames per second). A typical experiment is where a pattern classification with more than 10,000 frames per second was tested (more than 0.33 K r/t). Using current CMOS technology, 1.5 K r/t, that is about 50,000 frame per second, is feasible.

In this Class K, the high frame rate is the key in the computation. Clearly, the sensing and computing tasks are to be physically integrated. In standard digital technology, there is no time for A to D conversion and to complete the calculation, all within a few microseconds.

Class T: TeraOPS equivalent computing power class.
Even if the frame rate is small, like real-time video (30 frames per second), the required computing power (per chip) is enormous. Indeed, a trillion operations per second are to be – and can be – achieved. These TeraOPS chips are capable of solving a nonlinear PDE on a grid in a few microseconds. The detection of a moving inner boundary of the left ventricle in an echocardiogram, via an analogic CNN algorithm combining several waves, local logic, and morphology operators, took only 250 microseconds on the ACE4K analogic Visual Microprocessor Chip made in Seville. These chips hosted 4096 cell processors on a chip. This means about 3.0 TeraOPS equivalent computing power, which is about a thousand times faster than the computing power of an advanced Pentium processor.

A major challenge, not yet solved by any existing technologies, is to build analogic adaptive sensor-computers,[8] where sensing and computing understanding are fully and functionally integrated on a chip. Adaptive tuning of the sensors, pixel by pixel, is performed based on the content and context of the dynamically changing scene under sensing.

2 Notation, definitions, and mathematical foundation

2.1 Basic notation and definitions

Definition 1: Standard CNN architecture

A *standard CNN architecture* consists of an $M \times N$ rectangular array of cells ($C(i, j)$) with Cartesian coordinates (i, j), $i = 1, 2, \ldots, M$, $j = 1, 2, \ldots, N$ (Fig. 2.1).

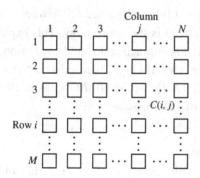

Fig. 2.1.

Remark:
There are applications where $M \neq N$. For example, a 5×512 CNN would be more appropriate for a scanner, fax machine, or copy machine.

Definition 2: Sphere of influence of cell $C(i, j)$

The *sphere of influence*, $S_r(i, j)$, of the radius r of cell $C(i, j)$ is defined to be the set of all the neighborhood cells satisfying the following property

$$S_r(i, j) = \{C(k, l) \mid \max_{1 \leq k \leq M, 1 \leq l \leq N} \{|k - i|, |l - j|\} \leq r\} \qquad (2.1)$$

where r is a positive integer.

7

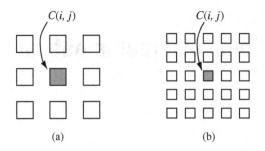

Fig. 2.2. (a) $r = 1$ (3×3 neighborhood), (b) $r = 2$ (5×5 neighborhood).

We will sometimes refer to $S_r(i, j)$ as a $(2r + 1) \times (2r + 1)$ neighborhood. For example, Fig. 2.2(a) shows an $r = 1$ (3×3) neighborhood. Fig. 2.2(b) shows an $r = 2$ (5×5) neighborhood.

Remarks:

1 In IC implementations, every cell is connected to all its neighbors in $S_r(i, j)$ via "*synaptic*" circuits.

2 When $r > N/2$, and $M = N$, we have a fully connected CNN where every cell is connected to every other cell and $S_r(i, j)$ is the entire array. This extreme case corresponds to the classic Hopfield Net. It is impractical to build any reasonable size (several thousand cells) Hopfield Net in a VLSI chip. There exists a "commercial" Hopfield-like chip by INTEL called "ETANN," type 80170 ($500 in 1995). This chip has 64 cells which makes it more of an expensive "toy."

Definition 3: Regular and boundary cells

A cell $C(i, j)$ is called a *regular cell* with respect to $S_r(i, j)$ if and only if all neighborhood cells $C(k, l) \in S_r(i, j)$ exist. Otherwise, $C(i, j)$ is called a *boundary cell* (Fig. 2.3).

Remark:

The outermost boundary cells are called **edge cells**. Not all boundary cells are edge cells if $r > 1$.

Definition 4: Standard CNN

A *class 1 $M \times N$ standard CNN* is defined by an $M \times N$ rectangular array of cells $C(i, j)$ located at site (i, j), $i = 1, 2, \ldots, M$, $j = 1, 2, \ldots, N$. Each cell $C(i, j)$ is defined mathematically by:

1 State equation

$$\dot{x}_{ij} = -x_{ij} + \sum_{C(k,l) \in S_r(i,j)} A(i, j; k, l) y_{kl} + \sum_{C(k,l) \in S_r(i,j)} B(i, j; k, l) u_{kl} + z_{ij} \qquad (2.2)$$

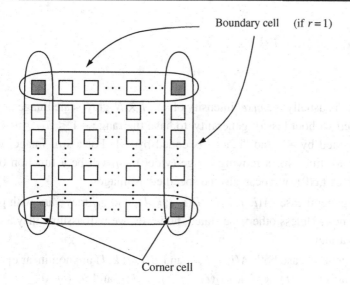

Boundary cell   (if $r = 1$)

Corner cell

Fig. 2.3.

where $x_{ij} \in R$, $y_{kl} \in R$, $u_{kl} \in R$, and $z_{ij} \in R$ are called **state**, **output**, **input**, and **threshold** of cell $C(i, j)$, respectively. $A(i, j; k, l)$ and $B(i, j; k, l)$ are called the **feedback** and the **input synaptic** operators to be defined below.

2 Output equation

$$y_{ij} = f(x_{ij}) = \frac{1}{2}|x_{ij} + 1| - \frac{1}{2}|x_{ij} - 1| \qquad (2.3)$$

This is called standard nonlinearity (Fig. 2.4).

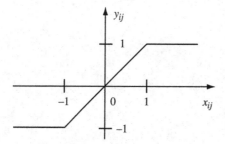

Fig. 2.4.

3 Boundary conditions

The boundary conditions are those specifying y_{kl} and u_{kl} for cells belonging to $S_r(i, j)$ of edge cells but lying outside of the $M \times N$ array.

4 Initial state

$$x_{ij}(0), \quad i = 1, \ldots, M, \quad j = 1, \ldots, N \tag{2.4}$$

Remarks:

1 The input u_{kl} is usually the *pixel* intensity of an $M \times N$ gray-scale image or picture
   P, normalized without loss of generality, to have the range $-1 \le u_{kl} \le +1$ where
   "white" is coded by -1 and "black" is coded by $+1$. For a *still* image, u_{kl} is a
   constant for all time, for a moving image (video) u_{kl} will be a function of time.
   Other variables $(x(0), y, z)$ can also be specified as images.

2 In the most general case, $A(i, j; k, l)$, $B(i, j; k, l)$, and z_{ij} may vary with position
   (i, j) and time t. Unless otherwise stated, however, we will assume they are space
   and time invariant.

3 In the most general case both $A(i, j; k, l)$ and $B(i, j; k, l)$ are nonlinear operators[1]
   which operate on $x_{kl}(t)$, $y_{kl}(t)$, $u_{kl}(t)$, $x_{ij}(t)$, $y_{ij}(t)$, and $u_{ij}(t)$, $0 \le t \le t_0$, to
   produce a scalar $(A(i, j; k, l) \circ y_{kl})(t_0)$ and $(B(i, j; k, l) \circ u_{kl})(t_0)$, $0 \le t \le t_0$.

4 We may also introduce synaptic laws depending on the states (C template) and on
   mixed variables (D template), respectively.
   That is $(C(i, j; k, l) \circ x_{kl})(t_0)$ and $(D(i, j; k, l) \circ (u_{kl}, x_{kl}, y_{kl})(t_0)$.

Unless otherwise stated, however, $A(i, j; k, l)y_{kl}$ and $B(i, j; k, l)u_{kl}$ will denote
ordinary multiplication with real coefficients where they may be nonlinear functions of
states, inputs, and outputs of cells $C(i, j)$, $C(k, l)$ and **may** involve some **time delays**
(i.e., they may contain a finite time history, as in the case of having a time delay).

The following are some space and time invariant nonlinear examples chosen from
the CNN catalog of applications (CNN Software Library). See some of them in
TEMLIB (Appendix A).

EXAMPLE 2.1:

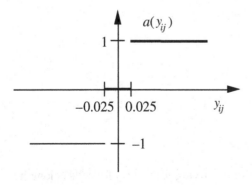

Fig. 2.5.

$A(i, j; k, l) = a(y_{ij})$: depends on output (from TEMPLATE *MajorityVoteTaker*) (Fig. 2.5).

EXAMPLE 2.2:

$C(i, j; k, l) = c(x_{ij})$: depends on state (from TEMPLATE LGTHTUNE) (Fig. 2.6).

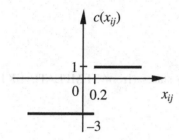

Fig. 2.6.

EXAMPLE 2.3:

$A(i, j; k, l) = a(u_{ij}, u_{kl})$ and $B(i, j; k, l) = b(u_{ij}, u_{kl})$: depends on two inputs (from TEMPLATE *GrayscaleLineDetector*) (Fig. 2.7).

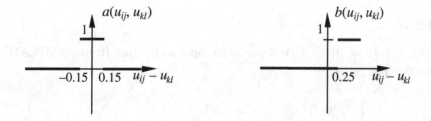

Fig. 2.7.

EXAMPLE 2.4:

$A(i, j; k, l) = a(y_{ij}, y_{kl})$: depends on two outputs (from TEMPLATE *GlobalMaximumFinder*) (Fig. 2.8).

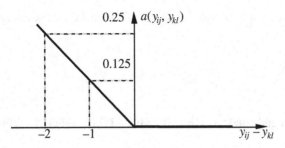

Fig. 2.8.

EXAMPLE 2.5:

$C(i, j; k, l) = c(x_{ij}, x_{kl})$: depends on two states (from TEMPLATE EXTREME) (Fig. 2.9).

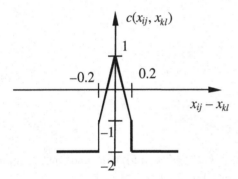

Fig. 2.9.

EXAMPLE 2.6:

$D(i, j; k, l) = d(u_{kl}, y_{ij})$: depends on input and output (from TEMPLATE EROSION) (Fig. 2.10).

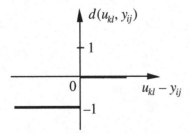

Fig. 2.10.

Some examples of *time-delay* operators:

EXAMPLE 2.7:

$(A(i, j; k, l)y_{kl})(t) = 0.68y_{kl}(t - 10)$: depends on the past of the output (from TEMPLATE *SpeedDetection*).

EXAMPLE 2.8:

$(B(i, j; k, l)u_{kl})(t) = -0.25u_{kl}(t - 10), (k, l) \neq (i, j)$: depends on the past of the input (from TEMPLATE *ImageDifferenceComputation*).

Remarks:

1 A gray-scale image can be represented pixelwise using a one-to-one map between a picture element (pixel) and a cell. The luminance value of the pixel would be coded as: black $\rightarrow +1$, white $\rightarrow -1$, gray $\rightarrow (-1, +1)$.

2 It is useful and correct to think of the triple $\{A(i, j; k, l), B(i, j; k, l), z_{ij}\}$ as an elementary **CNN instruction (macro)**, because they specify how an $M \times N$ input image **U** at $t = 0$ will be transformed to produce an $M \times N$ **output** image **Y**(t) for all $t \geq 0$.

Definition 5: Space-invariant or isotropic CNN

A CNN is space-invariant or isotropic if and only if both the synaptic operators $A(i, j; k, l)$, $B(i, j; k, l)$ and the threshold z_{ij} *do not* vary with space. In this case, we can write

$$\sum_{C(k,l) \in S_r(i,j)} A(i, j; k, l)y_{kl} = \sum_{|k-i| \leq r} \sum_{|l-j| \leq r} A(i - k, j - l)y_{kl}$$

$$\sum_{C(k,l) \in S_r(i,j)} B(i, j; k, l)u_{kl} = \sum_{|k-i| \leq r} \sum_{|l-j| \leq r} B(i - k, j - l)u_{kl}$$

$$z_{ij} = z \tag{2.5}$$

A *standard CNN* (with linear synaptic operators) has the following state equation (using the same notation as in (2.2)):

$$\dot{x}_{ij} = -x_{ij} + \sum_{C(k,l) \in S_r(i,j)} A(i, j; k, l)y_{kl} + \sum_{C(k,l) \in S_r(i,j)} B(i, j; k, l)u_{kl} + z_{ij}$$

$$+ \sum_{C(k,l) \in S_r(i,j)} C(i, j; k, l)x_{kl} + \sum_{C(k,l) \in S_r(i,j)} D(i, j; k, l)(u_{kl}, x_{kl}, y_{kl}) \tag{2.2*}$$

2.2   Mathematical foundations

2.2.1   Vector and matrix representation and boundary conditions

The system of $n = MN$ ordinary differential equations (ODE) defining a standard (not necessarily space-invariant) CNN can be recast in the form

$$\dot{x}_{ij} = h_{ij}(\tilde{\mathbf{x}}_{ij}, t), \quad i = 1, 2, \ldots, M, \quad j = 1, 2, \ldots, N \tag{2.6}$$

where

$$h_{ij}(\tilde{\mathbf{x}}_{ij}, t) = -x_{ij}(t) + \sum_{C(k,l) \in S_r(i,j)} A(i, j; k, l) y_{kl}(t) + s_{ij}(t)$$

where

$$y_{kl} = f(x_{kl})$$
$$s_{ij}(t) = \sum_{C(k,l) \in S_r(i,j)} B(i, j; k, l) u_{kl}(t) + z_{ij}(t)$$

$\tilde{\mathbf{x}}_{ij}$ is a vector of length $(2r + 1)^2$ whose components include all variables $x_{kl} \in S_r(i, j)$, i.e.

$$\{x_{kl} : |k - i| \le r, |l - j| \le r\}$$

We can cast Eq. (2.6) into the following $M \times N$ *matrix* differential equation which exhibits a one-to-one correspondence with the CNN architecture

$$
\begin{bmatrix}
\dot{x}_{11} & \dot{x}_{12} & \cdots & \dot{x}_{1N} \\
\dot{x}_{21} & \dot{x}_{22} & \cdots & \dot{x}_{2N} \\
\vdots & \vdots & & \vdots \\
\dot{x}_{M-1,1} & \dot{x}_{M-1,2} & \cdots & \dot{x}_{M-1,N} \\
\dot{x}_{M1} & \dot{x}_{M2} & \cdots & \dot{x}_{MN}
\end{bmatrix}
$$
$$
=
\begin{bmatrix}
h_{11}(\tilde{\mathbf{x}}_{11}) & h_{12}(\tilde{\mathbf{x}}_{12}) & \cdots & h_{1N}(\tilde{\mathbf{x}}_{1N}) \\
h_{21}(\tilde{\mathbf{x}}_{21}) & h_{22}(\tilde{\mathbf{x}}_{22}) & \cdots & h_{2N}(\tilde{\mathbf{x}}_{2N}) \\
\vdots & \vdots & & \vdots \\
h_{M-1,1}(\tilde{\mathbf{x}}_{M-1,1}) & h_{M-1,2}(\tilde{\mathbf{x}}_{M-1,2}) & \cdots & h_{M-1,N}(\tilde{\mathbf{x}}_{M-1,N}) \\
h_{M1}(\tilde{\mathbf{x}}_{M1}) & h_{M2}(\tilde{\mathbf{x}}_{M2}) & \cdots & h_{MN}(\tilde{\mathbf{x}}_{MN})
\end{bmatrix}
\tag{2.7}
$$

Definition 6: Virtual cells
Any cell $C(k, l)$, with $|k - i| \le r, |l - j| \le r$, and $k \notin \{1, 2, \ldots, M\}$ and/or $l \notin \{1, 2, \ldots, N\}$ is called a *virtual cell*, and the associated x_{kl}, y_{kl}, u_{kl}, and z_{kl} are called *virtual state*, *virtual output*, *virtual input*, and *virtual threshold*, respectively.

Boundary conditions

Any virtual variable in $\mathbf{x}_{ij}$ of Eq. (2.6) must be specified via various boundary conditions which are the most commonly used for a 3×3 neighborhood.

1 Fixed (Dirichlet) boundary conditions

Left virtual cells:	$y_{i,0} = \alpha_1,$	$u_{i,0} = \beta_1,$	$i = 1, 2, \ldots, M$
Right virtual cells:	$y_{i,N+1} = \alpha_2,$	$u_{i,N+1} = \beta_2,$	$i = 1, 2, \ldots, M$
Top virtual cells:	$y_{0,j} = \alpha_3,$	$u_{0,j} = \beta_3,$	$j = 1, 2, \ldots, N$
Bottom virtual cells:	$y_{M+1,j} = \alpha_4,$	$u_{M+1,j} = \beta_4,$	$j = 1, 2, \ldots, N$

where α_i and β_i are user prescribed constants (usually equal to zero).

Circuit interpretation: Add one row or column along the boundary and force each cell to have a fixed input and output by *batteries* (Fig. 2.11).

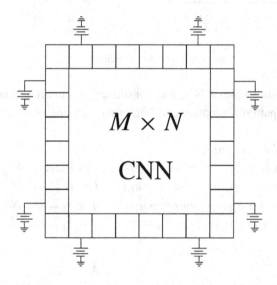

$M \times N$

CNN

Fig. 2.11. The circuit interpretation of the fixed (Dirichlet) boundary condition.

2 Zero-flux (Neumann) boundary conditions (Fig. 2.12)

Left virtual cells:	$y_{i,0} = y_{i,1},$	$u_{i,0} = u_{i,1},$	$i = 1, 2, \ldots, M$
Right virtual cells:	$y_{i,N+1} = y_{i,N},$	$u_{i,N+1} = u_{i,N},$	$i = 1, 2, \ldots, M$
Top virtual cells:	$y_{0,j} = y_{1,j},$	$u_{0,j} = u_{1,j},$	$j = 1, 2, \ldots, N$
Bottom virtual cells:	$y_{M+1,j} = y_{M,j},$	$u_{M+1,j} = u_{M,j},$	$j = 1, 2, \ldots, N.$

Remark:

This boundary condition usually applies to the case where there is no input, i.e., $u_{ij} = 0$ for all (i, j). Because any input would cause energy and/or material flow from the outside making the system an "open system" in the sense of thermodynamics, CNN

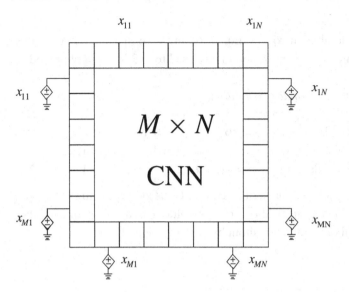

Fig. 2.12. The circuit interpretation of the Neumann boundary condition.

with *zero* input is called *autonomous* CNN, and constitutes an important class with widespread applications in pattern formation and "autowave" generation.

3 Periodic (Toroidal) boundary conditions

Left virtual cells: $y_{i,0} = y_{i,N}$, $u_{i,0} = u_{i,N}$, $i = 1, 2, \ldots, M$

Right virtual cells: $y_{i,N+1} = y_{i,1}$, $u_{i,N+1} = u_{i,1}$, $i = 1, 2, \ldots, M$

Top virtual cells: $y_{0,j} = y_{M,j}$, $u_{0,j} = u_{M,j}$, $j = 1, 2, \ldots, N$

Bottom virtual cells: $y_{M+1,j} = y_{1,j}$, $u_{M+1,j} = u_{1,j}$, $j = 1, 2, \ldots, N$.

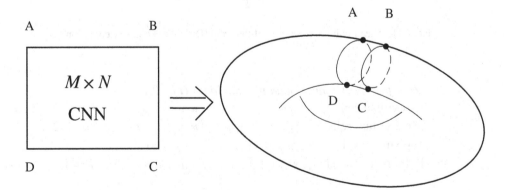

Fig. 2.13. The circuit interpretation of the Periodic (Toroidal) boundary condition.

Identify each cell from the top row with the corresponding cell in the bottom row, identify each cell from the left column with the corresponding cell in the right column.

This is equivalent to fabricating a CNN chip on a silicon torus as its substrate.

Vector differential equation

Since virtually all theorems and numerical techniques for solving systems of ODE are formulated in vector form, we must repack the $M \times N$ matrix ODE (2.6) into an $MN \times 1$ vector ODE. There are many ways to order the variables. We consider three typical orders:

1 Row-wise packing scheme
2 Diagonal packing scheme
3 Column-wise packing scheme

These packing schemes are shown in Figs 2.14(a), (b), and (c), respectively.

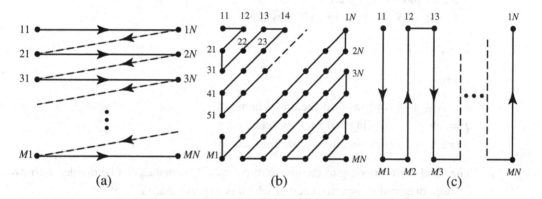

Fig. 2.14. Three (among many others) possible packing schemes.

After repacking, we obtain a system of $n = MN$ vector systems

$$\underbrace{\begin{bmatrix} \dot{\hat{x}}_1 \\ \dot{\hat{x}}_2 \\ \vdots \\ \dot{\hat{x}}_n \end{bmatrix}}_{\dot{\mathbf{x}}} = -\underbrace{\begin{bmatrix} \hat{x}_1 \\ \hat{x}_2 \\ \vdots \\ \hat{x}_n \end{bmatrix}}_{\mathbf{x}} + \underbrace{\begin{bmatrix} \quad \end{bmatrix}}_{\hat{\mathbf{A}}} \underbrace{\begin{bmatrix} \hat{y}_1 \\ \hat{y}_2 \\ \vdots \\ \hat{y}_n \end{bmatrix}}_{\mathbf{y}} + \underbrace{\begin{bmatrix} \quad \end{bmatrix}}_{\hat{\mathbf{B}}} \underbrace{\begin{bmatrix} \hat{u}_1 \\ \hat{u}_2 \\ \vdots \\ \hat{u}_n \end{bmatrix}}_{\mathbf{u}} + \underbrace{\begin{bmatrix} \hat{z}_1 \\ \hat{z}_2 \\ \vdots \\ \hat{z}_n \end{bmatrix}}_{\mathbf{z}}$$

or in vector form

$$\dot{\mathbf{x}} = -\mathbf{x} + \hat{\mathbf{A}}\mathbf{y} + \hat{\mathbf{B}}\mathbf{u}(t) + \mathbf{z}(t)$$
$$y_i = f(x_i) \tag{2.8}$$

where $\mathbf{x} = [\hat{x}_1, \hat{x}_2, \ldots, \hat{x}_n]^T$ is the state vector with the same order of state variables.

The two matrices $\hat{\mathbf{A}}$ and $\hat{\mathbf{B}}$ are $n \times n$ matrices whose nonzero entries are the synaptic weights $A(i, j; k, l)$ and $B(i, j; k, l)$, respectively, corresponding to the above three

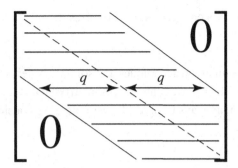

Fig. 2.15. The band structure of $\hat{\mathbf{A}}$ and $\hat{\mathbf{B}}$.

packing schemes. Each matrix is quite *sparse* (most entries are zero) with the *band* structure shown in Fig. 2.15.

For $M = N$, the band has a bandwidth

$$w = 2q + 1$$

where

$q = N + 1$ for row-wise packing schemes,
$q = 2N - 2$ for diagonal packing schemes,
$q = 2N - 1$ for column-wise packing schemes.

The band corresponding to the above three packing schemes can be divided into two or more diagonal sub-bands, each of which is a sparse matrix.

Remarks:
$\hat{\mathbf{A}}$ and $\hat{\mathbf{B}}$ are very large matrices, e.g., for $M = N = 1000$ (for HDTV applications), $n = 1,000,000$, $q = 1001$, $w = 2003$ for row-wise packing scheme, which is only 0.2% of $L = 10^6$ (L is the bandwidth of the full matrix). This shows $\hat{\mathbf{A}}$ and $\hat{\mathbf{B}}$ are very sparse matrices.

2.2.2   Existence and uniqueness of solutions

To motivate the importance of the questions of "existence and uniqueness of solutions" for a CNN, a question which has never been an issue in linear circuit and system theory, consider the following three simple nonlinear circuits.

Example 1

Consider the circuit shown in Fig. 2.16(a) whose state equation is given by

$$\dot{x} = -\frac{1}{2x}, \quad t \geq 0 \tag{2.9}$$

The characteristics of the right-hand side are shown in Fig. 2.16(b). The solution of Eq. (2.9) with initial condition $x(0) = x_0 > 0$ is given by

$$x(t) = \sqrt{x_0^2 - t}, \quad t \geq 0 \tag{2.10}$$

and sketched in Fig. 2.16(c). Observe that this circuit has *no* solution with any initial state $x_0 > 0$ for $t \geq T = x_0^2$.

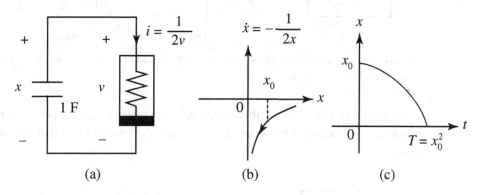

$$i = \frac{1}{2v}$$

$$\dot{x} = -\frac{1}{2x}$$

(a)   (b)   (c)

Fig. 2.16. Example of a circuit which has no solution after a finite time T.

Example 2

Consider the circuit shown in Fig. 2.17(a) whose state equation is given by

$$\dot{x} = \frac{3}{2}x^{1/3} \tag{2.11}$$

The characteristics of the right-hand side are shown in Fig. 2.17(b). The solution of Eq. (2.11) with initial condition $x(0) = 0$ is given by

$$x(t) = \begin{cases} 0, & 0 \leq t \leq T \\ (t - T)^{3/2}, & t > T \end{cases} \tag{2.12}$$

for *any* $T \in R$. This solution is shown in Fig. 2.17(c) for different choices of $T = T_1, T_2, \ldots, T_N$. Since T is arbitrary, this circuit has an *infinite* number of *distinct* solutions.

Example 3

Consider the circuit shown in Fig. 2.18(a) whose state equation is given by

$$\dot{x} = x^2 \tag{2.13}$$

The characteristics of the right-hand side are shown in Fig. 2.18(b). The solution of Eq. (2.13) with initial state $x(0) = 1$ is given by

$$x = \frac{1}{1 - t} \tag{2.14}$$

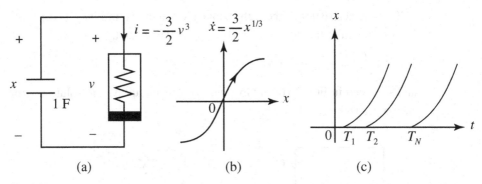

Fig. 2.17. Example of a circuit having infinitely many distinct solutions, all with the same initial state $x(0) = 0$.

As shown in Fig. 2.18(c), this circuit has a solution which cannot be continuous beyond $t \geq 1$ because it blows up at $t = 1$. This phenomenon is called a *finite escape time*.

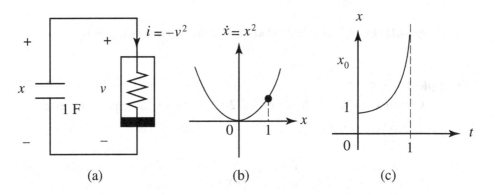

Fig. 2.18. Example of a circuit having a finite escape time.

The examples in Fig 2.18 show that even a simple two-element nonlinear circuit may not have a solution, and even if a solution exists it may not be unique, or may not be continued for all times $t \geq 0$. How do we determine whether a nonlinear circuit has a unique solution for all times $t \geq 0$. This is of fundamental importance for us since we will be concerned with asymptotic behavior as $t \to \infty$. There is no general method to answer this fundamental question since any method or theorem must exclude such simple equations as (2.9), (2.11), and (2.13)! Fortunately, for CNN, we can prove the following:

Theorem 1: Global existence and uniqueness theorem
Assume the standard CNN described by Eq. (2.2) satisfies the following three hypotheses:

H1: The synaptic operators are linear and memoryless, i.e., $A(i, j; k, l)y_{kl}$ and $B(i, j; k, l)u_{kl}$ are scalar multiplications, where $A(i, j; k, l)$ and $B(i, j; k, l)$ are real numbers.

H2: The input $u_{ij}(t)$ and threshold $z_{ij}(t)$ are *continuous* functions of time.

H3: The nonlinearity $f(x)$ is *Lipschitz continuous* in the sense that there exists a constant L such that for all $x', x'' \in R$

$$\|f(x') - f(x'')\| \le L\|x' - x''\| \tag{2.15}$$

(*Note*: for the scalar case, the norm is equivalent to the absolute value.)

Then for any initial state $x_{ij}(0) \in R$, the CNN has a *unique* solution for any $t \ge 0$ (see Fig. 2.19).

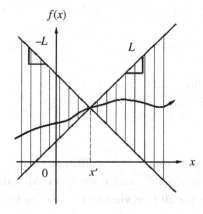

Fig. 2.19.

Remark:
The standard CNN satisfies all three hypotheses H1, H2, and H3.

Proof:
Hypotheses H1 implies we can recast Eq. (2.1) into the vector form

$$\dot{\mathbf{x}} = -\mathbf{x} + \hat{\mathbf{A}}\mathbf{y} + \hat{\mathbf{B}}\mathbf{u}(t) + \mathbf{z}(t) = \mathbf{h}(\mathbf{x}, t) \quad y_i = f(x_i) \tag{2.16}$$

We show first that $\mathbf{h}(\mathbf{x}, t)$ is Lipschitz continuous with respect to $\mathbf{x}$. Choose any $\mathbf{x}'$, $\mathbf{x}'' \in \mathbf{R}^n$, and let $\mathbf{y} = [f(x_1), \dots, f(x_n)]^T$, so that, $\mathbf{y}' = \mathbf{f}(\mathbf{x}')$ and $\mathbf{y}'' = \mathbf{f}(\mathbf{x}'')$.

$$\begin{aligned}
\|\mathbf{h}(\mathbf{x}', t) - \mathbf{h}(\mathbf{x}'', t)\| &= \|-\mathbf{x}' + \hat{\mathbf{A}}\mathbf{y}' + \mathbf{x}'' - \hat{\mathbf{A}}\mathbf{y}''\| \\
&= \|\mathbf{x}'' - \mathbf{x}' + \hat{\mathbf{A}}(\mathbf{y}' - \mathbf{y}'')\| \\
&\le \|\mathbf{x}'' - \mathbf{x}'\| + \|\hat{\mathbf{A}}\|\|\mathbf{y}' - \mathbf{y}''\|
\end{aligned} \tag{2.17}$$

Now

$$\|\mathbf{y}' - \mathbf{y}''\| = \left\| \begin{bmatrix} f(x_1') \\ f(x_2') \\ \vdots \\ f(x_n') \end{bmatrix} - \begin{bmatrix} f(x_1'') \\ f(x_2'') \\ \vdots \\ f(x_n'') \end{bmatrix} \right\|$$

$$= \sqrt{|f(x_1') - f(x_1'')|^2 + \cdots + |f(x_n') - f(x_n'')|^2}$$

$$\leq \sqrt{L^2|x_1' - x_1''|^2 + L^2|x_2' - x_2''|^2 + \cdots + L^2|x_n' - x_n''|^2}$$

(in view of hypothesis H3)

$$= L \left\| \begin{matrix} x_1' - x_1'' \\ x_2' - x_2'' \\ \vdots \\ x_n' - x_n'' \end{matrix} \right\|$$

$$= L \|\mathbf{x}' - \mathbf{x}''\| \tag{2.18}$$

Substituting equation (2.18) into equation (2.17), we obtain

$$\|\mathbf{h}(\mathbf{x}', t) - \mathbf{h}(\mathbf{x}'', t)\| \leq \left(1 + L\|\hat{A}\|\right)\|\mathbf{x}' - \mathbf{x}''\|$$
$$= \hat{L}\|\mathbf{x}' - \mathbf{x}''\| \tag{2.19}$$

where $\hat{L} \triangleq 1 + L\|\hat{\mathbf{A}}\|$ is a global Lipschitz constant, independent of $\mathbf{x}$ and t.

Hence, $\mathbf{h}(\mathbf{x}, t)$ is *uniformly* Lipschitz continuous with respect to $\mathbf{x}$. Moreover, since for each $\mathbf{x}_0 \in \mathbf{R}^n$, $\mathbf{h}(\mathbf{x}_0, t)$ is continuous for all t, in view of H2, we can find a bound $M_{x_0 t_0 a}$ (which in general depends on $\mathbf{x}_0$, t_0, and a) such that

$$\|\mathbf{h}(x_0, t)\| \leq M_{\mathbf{x}_0, t_0, a} \quad \forall\, t \in [t_0, t_0 + a]$$

Then for all $\mathbf{x}$, such that

$$\|\mathbf{x} - \mathbf{x}_0\| \leq b, \quad t \in [t0, t0 + a]$$
$$\|\mathbf{h}(x, t)\| \leq M_{x_0, t_0, a} + \hat{L}b$$

in view of the Lipschitz continuity of $\mathbf{h}(\mathbf{x}, t)$.

It follows from the *Picard–Lindelof Theorem*[2] that a *unique* solution exists for a time duration of

$$\min\left(a, \frac{b}{M_{x_0, t_0, a} + \hat{L}b}\right) \text{ second}$$

By choosing b large enough and $a > 1/\hat{L}$, one can see that a solution exists for approximately $1/\hat{L}$ seconds where $\hat{L}$ is *independent* of $\mathbf{x}_0$, t_0, a, and b. We can use *the same procedure* to show a unique solution exists for the next $1/\hat{L}$ seconds, etc. So, a unique solution exists for any time.   □

2.2.3   Boundedness of solutions

Theorem: Explicit solution bound

For all initial states, inputs, and thresholds satisfying

$$|x_{ij}(0)| \leq 1, \quad |u_{ij}(t)| \leq 1, \quad |z_{ij}(t)| \leq z_{max}$$

the solution $x_{ij}(t)$ of the standard CNN with linear memoryless synaptic operators $A(i, j; k, l)$ and $B(i, j; k, l)$ is uniformly bounded in the sense that there exists a constant x_{max} such that

$$|x_{ij}(t)| \leq x_{max} \quad \forall t \geq 0, \quad 1 \leq i \leq M, \quad 1 \leq j \leq N$$

where

$$x_{max} = 1 + z_{max} + \max_{\substack{1 \leq i \leq M \\ 1 \leq j \leq N}} \left[\sum_{C(k,l) \in S_r(i,j)} (|A(i, j; k, l)| + |B(i, j; k, l)|) \right] \tag{2.20}$$

Lemma 1 (Appendix 1)

The complete solution of

$$\dot{x} = -x + f(t)$$
$$x(0) = x_0$$

is given by

$$x(t) = x_0 e^{-t} + \int_0^t e^{-(t-\tau)} f(\tau) \, d\tau, \quad t \geq 0$$

In the special case where $f(\tau) = f_0$ where f_0 is a constant, we have

$$x(t) = x_0 e^{-t} + f_0(1 - e^{-t}), \quad t \geq 0$$

The equivalent electrical circuit is as shown in Fig. 2.20.

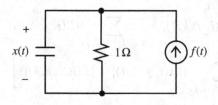

Fig. 2.20.

Proof of Theorem 2:

$$\dot{x}_{ij} = -x_{ij} + \underbrace{\underbrace{\sum_{C(k,l) \in S_r(i,j)} A(i,j;k,l)y_{kl}}_{\alpha_{ij}(t)} + \underbrace{\sum_{C(k,l) \in S_r(i,j)} B(i,j;k,l)u_{kl}}_{\beta_{ij}(u(t))} + z_{ij}}_{f(t)} \qquad (2.21)$$

where $\alpha_{ij}(t)$ and $\beta_{ij}(t)$ are defined for all $t \geq 0$ in view of Theorem 1. Applying Lemma 1,

$$x(t) = x_{ij}(0)\,e^{-t} + \int_0^t e^{-(t-\tau)}[\alpha_{ij}(\tau) + \beta_{ij}(u(\tau)) + z_{ij}(\tau)]\,d\tau \qquad (2.22)$$

Applying triangular inequality

$$x(t) \leq |x_{ij}(0)\,e^{-t}| + \int_0^t e^{-(t-\tau)}[|\alpha_{ij}(\tau)| + |\beta_{ij}(u(\tau))| + |z_{ij}(\tau)|]\,d\tau$$

$$\leq |x_{ij}(0)e^{-t}| + (\alpha_{\max} + \beta_{\max} + z_{\max}) \int_0^t e^{-(t-\tau)}\,d\tau \qquad (2.23)$$

where

$$\alpha_{\max} = \max_{t \geq 0} |\alpha_{ij}(t)| \leq \sum_{C(k,l) \in S_r(i,j)} |A(i,j;k,l)| \max_{t \geq 0} y_{kl}(t) \qquad (2.24)$$

$$\beta_{\max} = \max_u |\beta_{ij}(u)| \leq \sum_{C(k,l) \in S_r(i,j)} |B(i,j;k,l)| \max_u u_{kl}(t) \qquad (2.25)$$

But

$$\int_0^t e^{-(t-\tau)}\,d\tau = 1 - e^{-t} < 1, \quad t \geq 0 \qquad (2.26)$$

$$|u_{kl}(t)| \leq 1 \qquad (2.27)$$

$$|x_{ij}(0)| \leq 1 \qquad (2.28)$$

Hence, (2.21)–(2.28) imply

$$|x_{ij}(t)| \leq |x_{ij}(0)\,e^{-t}| + \alpha_{\max} + \beta_{\max} + z_{\max}$$

$$\leq 1 + z_{\max} + \sum_{C(k,l) \in S_r(i,j)} |A(i,j;k,l)| + \sum_{C(k,l) \in S_r(i,j)} |B(i,j;k,l)|$$

$$\leq 1 + z_{\max} + \max_{\substack{1 \leq i \leq M \\ 1 \leq j \leq N}} \left[\sum_{C(k,l) \in S_r(i,j)} (|A(i,j;k,l)| + |B(i,j;k,l)|) \right]$$

$$= x_{\max}$$

independent of (i,j). $\qquad\qquad\qquad\qquad\qquad\qquad\qquad\qquad\qquad\qquad\qquad\qquad$ □

Remarks:

1 For space-invariant CNN, $|x_{ij}(t)|$ is bounded by

$$\hat{x}_{\max} = 1 + z_{\max} + \sum_{1 \leq k \leq M} \sum_{1 \leq l \leq N} \left(|A_{kl}| + |B_{kl}| \right) \tag{2.29}$$

2 *Theorem 2* imposes a *minimum* power supply voltage for any CNN circuit implementation, and is fundamental for designing a CNN circuit.

2.2.4 Space-invariant CNN

Cloning template representation

Since the majority of all CNN applications use only space-invariant standard CNNs with a 3×3 neighborhood (sphere of influence $r = 1$), it will be extremely convenient to introduce some concise notations and terminologies for future analysis.

Consider a typical cell $C(i, j) \in S_r(i, j)$ as follows

$C(i-1, j-1)$	$C(i-1, j)$	$C(i-1, j+1)$
$C(i, j-1)$	$C(i, j)$	$C(i, j+1)$
$C(i+1, j-1)$	$C(i+1, j)$	$C(i+1, j+1)$

Let us examine the contributions from the two synaptic operators and the threshold items in (2.21).

1 Contributions from the feedback synaptic operator $A(i, j; k, l)$

In view of space-invariance, we can write

$$\sum_{C(k,l) \in S_r(i,j)} A(i, j; k, l) y_{kl} = \sum_{|k-i| \leq 1} \sum_{|l-j| \leq 1} A(k-i, l-j) y_{kl}$$

$$= a_{-1,-1} y_{i-1,j-1} + a_{-1,0} y_{i-1,j} + a_{-1,1} y_{i-1,j+1}$$

$$a_{0,-1} y_{i,j-1} + a_{0,0} y_{i,j} + a_{0,1} y_{i,j+1}$$

$$a_{1,-1} y_{i+1,j-1} + a_{1,0} y_{i+1,j} + a_{1,1} y_{i+1,j+1}$$

$$= \sum_{k=-1}^{1} \sum_{l=-1}^{1} a_{k,l} y_{i+k,j+l} \tag{2.30}$$

where $a_{mn} = A(m, n)$

$$\stackrel{\triangle}{=} \begin{array}{|c|c|c|} \hline a_{-1,-1} & a_{-1,0} & a_{-1,1} \\ \hline a_{0,-1} & a_{0,0} & a_{0,1} \\ \hline a_{1,-1} & a_{1,0} & a_{1,1} \\ \hline \end{array} \circledast \begin{array}{|c|c|c|} \hline y_{i-1,j-1} & y_{i-1,j} & y_{i-1,j+1} \\ \hline y_{i,j-1} & y_{i,j} & y_{i,j+1} \\ \hline y_{i+1,j-1} & y_{i+1,j} & y_{i+1,j+1} \\ \hline \end{array} = A \circledast Y_{ij} \tag{2.31}$$

where the 3×3 matrix **A** is called the *feedback cloning template*, and the symbol "$\circledast$" denotes the summation of dot products, henceforth called a *template dot product*. In discrete mathematics, this operation is called "spatial convolution." The 3×3 matrix Y_{ij} in (2.31) can be obtained by moving an opaque mask with a 3×3 window to position (i, j) of the $M \times N$ output image Y, henceforth called the *output image* at $C(i, j)$.

An element a_{kl} is called a center (resp., surround) element, weight, or coefficient, of the feedback template $\mathbf{A}$, if and only if $(k, l) = (0, 0)$ (resp., $(k, l) \neq (0, 0)$).

It is sometimes convenient to decompose the $\mathbf{A}$ template as follows

$$\mathbf{A} = \mathbf{A}^0 + \bar{\mathbf{A}} \tag{2.32}$$

$$\mathbf{A}^0 = \begin{array}{|c|c|c|} \hline 0 & 0 & 0 \\ \hline 0 & a_{0,0} & 0 \\ \hline 0 & 0 & 0 \\ \hline \end{array}$$

$$\bar{\mathbf{A}} = \begin{array}{|c|c|c|} \hline a_{-1,-1} & a_{-1,0} & a_{-1,1} \\ \hline a_{0,-1} & 0 & a_{0,1} \\ \hline a_{1,-1} & a_{1,0} & a_{1,1} \\ \hline \end{array}$$

where $\mathbf{A}^0$ and $\bar{\mathbf{A}}$ are called the *center* and *surround* component templates, respectively.

2 Contributions from the input synaptic operator $B(i, j; k, l)$
Following the above notation, we can write

$$\sum_{C(k,l) \in S_r(i,j)} B(i, j; k, l) y_{kl} = \sum_{|k-i| \leq 1} \sum_{|l-j| \leq 1} B(k - i, l - j) u_{kl}$$

$$= \sum_{k=-1}^{1} \sum_{l=-1}^{1} b_{kl} u_{i+k, j+l} \tag{2.33}$$

$$\stackrel{\Delta}{=} \begin{array}{|c|c|c|} \hline b_{-1,-1} & b_{-1,0} & b_{-1,1} \\ \hline b_{0,-1} & b_{0,0} & b_{0,1} \\ \hline b_{1,-1} & b_{1,0} & b_{1,1} \\ \hline \end{array} \circledast \begin{array}{|c|c|c|} \hline u_{i-1,j-1} & u_{i-1,j} & u_{i-1,j+1} \\ \hline u_{i,j-1} & u_{i,j} & u_{i,j+1} \\ \hline u_{i+1,j-1} & u_{i+1,j} & u_{i+1,j+1} \\ \hline \end{array} = B \circledast U_{ij} \tag{2.34}$$

where the 3×3 matrix B is called the *feedforward* or *input cloning template*, and $\mathbf{U}_{ij}$ is the translated masked input image.

Similarly, we can write

$$\mathbf{B} = \mathbf{B}^0 + \bar{\mathbf{B}} \tag{2.35}$$

$$\mathbf{B}^0 = \begin{array}{|c|c|c|} \hline 0 & 0 & 0 \\ \hline 0 & b_{0,0} & 0 \\ \hline 0 & 0 & 0 \\ \hline \end{array}$$

$$\bar{\mathbf{B}} = \begin{array}{|c|c|c|} \hline b_{-1,-1} & b_{-1,0} & b_{-1,1} \\ \hline b_{0,-1} & 0 & b_{0,1} \\ \hline b_{1,-1} & b_{1,0} & b_{1,1} \\ \hline \end{array}$$

where $\mathbf{B}^0$ and $\bar{\mathbf{B}}$ are called the *center* and *surround* feedforward template, respectively.

3 Contribution from the threshold terms

$$z_{ij} = z$$

Using the above notations, a *space-invariant CNN is completely described by*

$$\dot{x}_{ij} = -x_{ij} + \mathbf{A} \circledast \mathbf{Y}_{ij} + \mathbf{B} \circledast \mathbf{U}_{ij} + z \tag{2.36}$$

We will usually decompose (2.36) as follows

$$\dot{x}_{ij} = \underbrace{-x_{ij} + a_{00} f(x_{ij})}_{g(x_{ij})} + \underbrace{\bar{\mathbf{A}} \otimes \mathbf{Y}_{ij} + \mathbf{B} \otimes \mathbf{U}_{ij} + z}_{w_{ij}(t)} \tag{2.37}$$

where

$$h_{ij}(x_{ij}; w_{ij}) = g(x_{ij}) + w_{ij}(x_{ij}, t) \tag{2.38}$$

is called the *rate function*, $g(x_{ij})$ is called the driving-point (DP) component because it is closely related to a central concept from nonlinear circuit theory, and

$$w_{ij}(x_{ij}, t) = \bar{\mathbf{A}} \circledast \mathbf{Y}_{ij} + \mathbf{B} \circledast \mathbf{U}_{ij} + z$$

is called the *offset level*.

2.2.5   Three simple CNN classes

Each CNN is uniquely defined by three terms of the cloning templates $\{\mathbf{A}, \mathbf{B}, z\}$, which consist of 19 *real numbers* for a 3×3 neighborhood ($r = 1$). Since real numbers are uncountable, there are infinitely many distinct CNN templates, of which the following three subclasses are the simplest and hence mathematically tractable.

Definition 7: Excitatory and Inhibitory synaptic weights (Fig. 2.21)
A feedback synaptic weight a_{kl} is said to be excitatory (resp., inhibitory) if and only if it is positive (resp., negative).

A synaptic weight is "excitatory" (resp., inhibitory) because it makes the rate function $h_{ij}(x_{ij}, w_{ij})$ more positive (less positive) for a positive input, and hence increases (resp., decreases) $\dot{x}_{ij}$, namely the rate of growth of $x_{ij}(t)$.

Definition 8: Zero-feedback (feedforward) class $\mathcal{C}(0, \mathbf{B}, z)$ (Fig. 2.22)
A CNN belongs to the *zero-feedback* class $\mathcal{C}(0, \mathbf{B}, z)$ if and only if all feedback template elements are zero, i.e., $\mathbf{A} \equiv 0$.

Each cell of a zero-feedback CNN is described by

$$\dot{x}_{ij} = -x_{ij} + \mathbf{B} \circledast \mathbf{U}_{ij} + z \tag{2.39}$$

(a) $\mathcal{C}(\mathbf{A}, \mathbf{B}, z)$

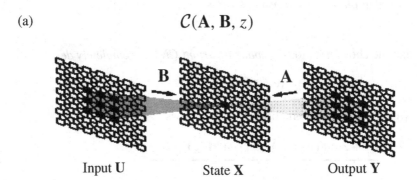

Input **U**   State **X**   Output **Y**

(b)

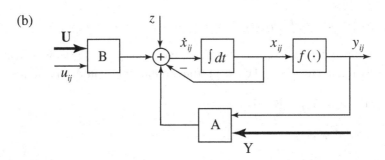

Fig. 2.21. A space-invariant CNN $\mathcal{C}(\mathbf{A}, \mathbf{B}, z)$ with a 3×3 neighborhood $S_1(i, j)$. (a) Signal flow structure of a CNN with a 3×3 neighborhood. The two shaded cones symbolize the weighted contributions of input and output voltages of cell $C(k, l) \in S_1(i, j)$ to the state voltage of the center cell $C(i, j)$. (b) System structure of a cell $C(i, j)$. Arrows printed in bold mark parallel data paths from the input and the output of the surround cells u_{kl} and y_{kl}, respectively. Arrows with thinner lines denote the threshold, input, state, and output, z, u_{ij}, x_{ij}, and y_{ij}, respectively.

Definition 9: Zero-input (Autonomous) class $\mathcal{C}(A, 0, z)$ (Fig. 2.23)

A CNN belongs to the *zero-input* class $\mathcal{C}(A, 0, z)$ if and only if all feedforward template elements are zero, i.e., $\mathbf{B} \equiv 0$.

Each cell of a zero-input CNN is described by

$$\dot{x}_{ij} = -x_{ij} + \mathbf{A} \circledast \mathbf{Y}_{ij} + z \tag{2.40}$$

Definition 10: Uncoupled (scalar) class $\mathcal{C}(\mathbf{A}^0, \mathbf{B}, z)$ (Fig. 2.24)

A CNN belongs to the *uncoupled* class $\mathcal{C}(\mathbf{A}^0, \mathbf{B}, z)$ if and only if $a_{ij} = 0$ except $i = j$, i.e., $\bar{\mathbf{A}} \equiv 0$.

Each cell of an *uncoupled* CNN is described by a *scalar* nonlinear ODE which is not coupled to its neighbors:

$$\dot{x}_{ij} = -x_{ij} + a_{00} f(x_{ij}) + \mathbf{B} \circledast \mathbf{U}_{ij} + z \tag{2.41}$$

(a)   Zero-feedback CNN: $\mathcal{C}(0, \mathbf{B}, z)$

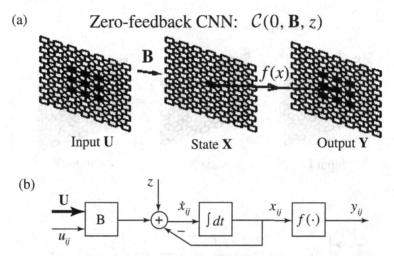

Input **U**   State **X**   Output **Y**

Fig. 2.22. Zero-feedback (feedforward) CNN $\in \mathcal{C}(0, \mathbf{B}, z)$. (a) Signal flow structure of a zero-feedback CNN with a 3×3 neighborhood. The cone symbolizes the weighted contributions of input voltages of cells $C(k, l) \in S_1(i, j)$ to the center cell $C(i, j)$. (b) System structure of a cell $C(i, j)$. Arrows printed in bold denotes the input signal from the surround cells. In this case, there is no self-feedback, and no couplings from the outputs of the surround cells.

(a)   Zero-input CNN: $\mathcal{C}(\mathbf{A}, 0, z)$

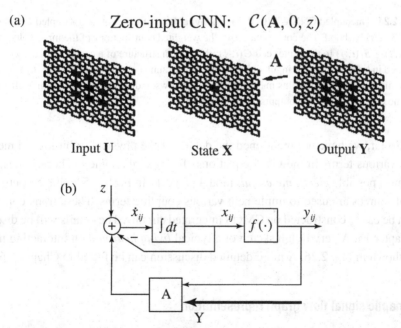

Input **U**   State **X**   Output **Y**

Fig. 2.23. Zero-input (Autonomous) CNN $\in \mathcal{C}(0, \mathbf{B}, z)$. (a) Signal flow structure of a zero-input CNN with a 3×3 neighborhood. The cone symbolizes the weighted contributions of the output voltage of cells $C(k, l) \in S_1(i, j)$ to the center cell $C(i, j)$. (b) System structure of a center cell $C(i, j)$. Arrow printed in bold denotes the signal fed-back from the outputs of the surround cells. In this case, there are no input signals.

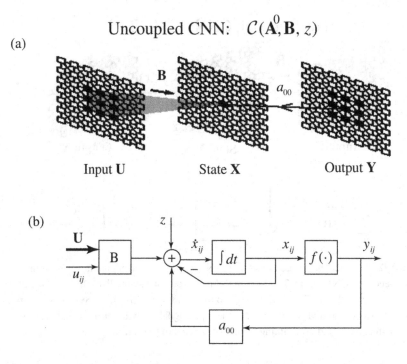

(a)

Uncoupled CNN: $\mathcal{C}(\overset{0}{\mathbf{A}}, \mathbf{B}, z)$

Input **U**   State **X**   Output **Y**

(b)

Fig. 2.24. Uncoupled CNN $\in \mathcal{C}(0, \mathbf{B}, z)$. (a) Signal flow structure of an uncoupled CNN with a 3×3 neighborhood. The cone symbolizes the weighted contributions of the input voltages of cells $C(k, l) \in S_1(i, j)$ to the center cell $C(i, j)$. (b) System structure of a center cell $C(i, j)$. Arrow printed in bold denotes the input signals from the surround cells. In this case, the data streams simplified into simple streams marked by thinner arrows, indicating only a "scalar" self-feedback, but no couplings from the outputs of the surround cells.

So far, we have not mentioned the details of the physical or biological meaning of the various terms in the CNN equations. To highlight some of these issues, next we show a possible *electronic circuit* model of a cell. In Fig. 2.25, voltage-controlled current sources are used to implement various coupling terms. These trans-conductances can be easily constructed on CMOS integrated circuits. The details will be discussed in Chapter 15. A very rough sketch of a typical *living neuron* with interacting neighbors is shown in Fig. 2.26. A more detailed discussion can be found in Chapter 16.

2.2.6   Synaptic signal flow graph representation

Sometimes it will be more convenient to use *a synaptic signal flow graph representation*[3] for both the **A** and the **B** templates as shown in Figs 2.27 and 2.28, respectively. These two flow graphs show *explicitly* the directions of the signal flows from neighboring cells and their associated *synaptic weights* a_{kl} and b_{kl}, respectively. Except for the symbols $\{a_{00}, a_{kl}\}$ for *the synaptic signal flow graph A*, and $\{b_{00}, b_{kl}\}$

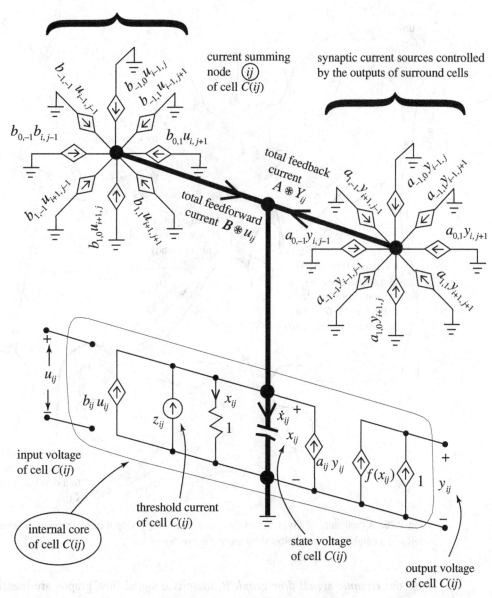

Fig. 2.25. Cell realization of a standard CNN cell $C(i, j)$. All diamond-shape symbols denote a voltage-controlled current source which injects a current proportional to the indicated controlling voltage u_{kl} or y_{kl}, weighted by b_{kl} or a_{kl}, respectively, except for the rightmost diamond $f(x_{ij})$ in the internal core which is a nonlinear voltage controlled current source, resulting in an output voltage $y_{ij} = f(x_{ij})$.

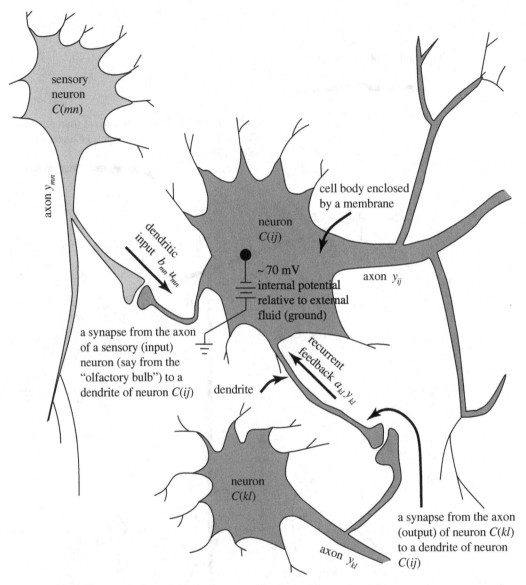

Fig. 2.26. A caricature of a typical neuron $C(i, j)$ receiving an input from a sensory neuron on the left and a neighbor neuron below through respective "synapses."

for the *synaptic signal flow graph B*, these two signal flow graphs are identical and hence easy to remember. Observe that the *bold heavy edges* indicate signal flowing *into* cell $C(i, j)$, whereas the *light edges* indicate signal flowing *out from* cell $C(i, j)$. Observe that each synaptic weight occurs exactly twice in each flow graph, and that they are always associated with a pair of edges, one bold edge and one light edge, with arrows *pointing in the same directions*. For example, the coefficient a_{-10} is associated with the two edges originating from the North (N) cell and terminating in the South (S)

(a)

$a_{-1,-1}$	$a_{-1,0}$	$a_{-1,1}$
$a_{0,-1}$	a_{00}	$a_{0,1}$
$a_{1,-1}$	$a_{1,0}$	$a_{1,1}$

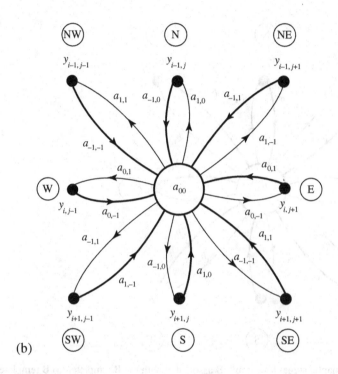

(b)

Fig. 2.27. Feedback synaptic signal flow graph A associated with the **A** template.[3] (a) The **A** template with self-feedback synaptic weight a_{00}, (b) Signal flow graph A.

cell. This is because the "top" cell $C(i-1, j)$ is *North* of the center cell $C(i, j)$, which is itself North of the "bottom" cell $C(i+1, j)$. The same observation applies to the horizontal pairs, and all diagonal pairs of similarly-directed bold-light edges. Observe also that for each *zero* coefficient $a_{kl} = 0$, or $b_{kl} = 0$, two corresponding edges will disappear from the corresponding signal flow graph. Hence, for templates with only a few non-zero entries, their associated synaptic signal flow graphs are particularly simple. It is in such situations where useful insights can be obtained, specially when two or more such synaptic signal flow graphs are interconnected to form a composite synaptic system graph.

(a)

$b_{-1,-1}$	$b_{-1,0}$	$b_{-1,1}$
$b_{0,-1}$	b_{00}	$b_{0,1}$
$b_{1,-1}$	$b_{1,0}$	$b_{1,1}$

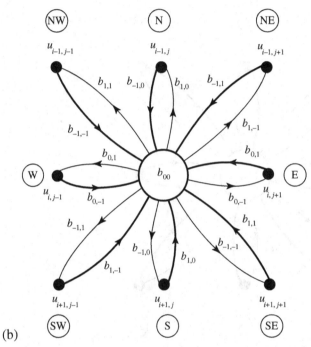

(b)

Fig. 2.28. Input synaptic signal flow graph B associated with the **B** template. (a) **B** template with self-input synaptic weight b_{00}. (b) Signal flow graph B.

3 Characteristics and analysis of simple CNN templates

3.1 Two case studies: the EDGE and EDGEGRAY templates

3.1.1 The EDGE CNN

EDGE: binary edge detection template

$$\mathbf{A} = \begin{array}{|c|c|c|} \hline 0 & 0 & 0 \\ \hline 0 & 0 & 0 \\ \hline 0 & 0 & 0 \\ \hline \end{array} \quad \mathbf{B} = \begin{array}{|c|c|c|} \hline -1 & -1 & -1 \\ \hline -1 & 8 & -1 \\ \hline -1 & -1 & -1 \\ \hline \end{array} \quad z = \boxed{-1}$$

I Global task

Given: static binary image **P**

Input: $\mathbf{U}(t) = \mathbf{P}$

Initial state: $\mathbf{X}(0) =$ Arbitrary (in the examples we choose $x_{ij}(0) = 0$)

Boundary conditions:[1] Fixed type, $u_{ij} = 0$, $y_{ij} = 0$ for all virtual cells, denoted by

$$[\mathbf{U}] = [\mathbf{Y}] = [0]$$

Output: $\mathbf{Y}(t) \Rightarrow \mathbf{Y}(\infty) =$ Binary image showing all edges of **P** in black.

Remark

The Edge CNN template is designed to work correctly for *binary* input images only. If **P** is a gray-scale image, $\mathbf{Y}(\infty)$ will in general be gray-scale where black pixels correspond to sharp edges, near-black pixels correspond to fuzzy edges, and near-white pixels correspond to noise.

II Local rules

static input $u_{ij} \rightarrow$ steady state output $y_{ij}(\infty)$

1 white pixel $\rightarrow$ white, independent of neighbors

2 black pixel $\rightarrow$ white, if all nearest neighbors are black

3 black pixel $\rightarrow$ black, if at least one nearest neighbor is white

4 black, gray or white pixel $\rightarrow$ gray, if nearest neighbors are gray

III Examples

EXAMPLE 3.1: Image size: 15×15 (see also Fig. 3.1)

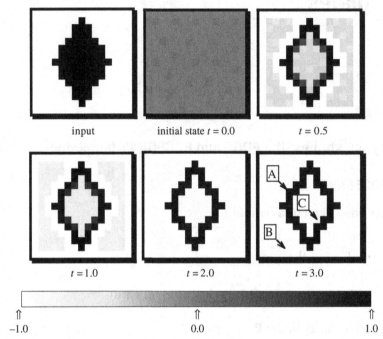

input   initial state $t = 0.0$ $t = 0.5$

$t = 1.0$ $t = 2.0$ $t = 3.0$

−1.0   0.0   1.0

Snapshots are shown in gray scale with 256 levels. Integration time step = 0.1.

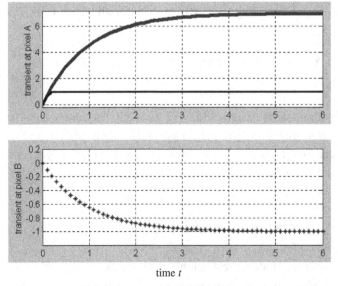

time t

Fig. 3.1. Cell transient at three different locations in image of example 3.1. ———: state variable x_{ij}; ———: output variable y_{ij}; ***: output and state are the same.

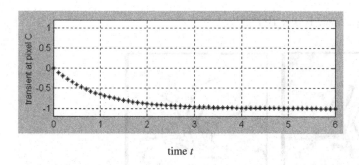

time t

Fig. 3.1. Continued.

EXAMPLE 3.2: Image size: 100×100

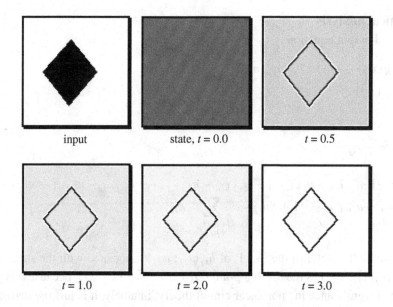

EXAMPLE 3.3: Image size: 100×100

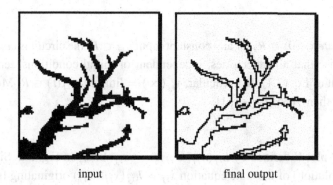

EXAMPLE 3.4: Image size: 100×100

input   final output

IV Mathematical analysis

State and output equation

$$\dot{x}_{ij} = g(x_{ij}) + w_{ij} = h_{ij}(x_{ij}, w_{ij})$$
$$y_{ij} = f(x_{ij}) \tag{3.1}$$

where

$$g(x_{ij}) = -x_{ij} \tag{3.2}$$

$$w_{ij} = -1 + 8u_{ij} - u_{i+1,j-1} - u_{i+1,j} - u_{i+1,j+1} - u_{i,j-1} - u_{i,j+1} - u_{i-1,j-1}$$
$$-u_{i-1,j} - u_{i-1,j+1} - 1 + 8u_{ij} - \sum_{\substack{kl \in S_1(i,j) \\ kl \neq ij}} u_{kl} \tag{3.3}$$

We will often refer to the loci Γ of $h_{ij}(x_{ij}; w_{ij})$ associated with the state equation $\dot{x}_{ij} = h_{ij}(x_{ij}; w_{ij})$ as the *driving-point (DP) plot* of cell $C(i, j)$, because this plot has a special significance in "nonlinear circuit theory"; namely, it is just the *driving-point characteristics* of the nonlinear resistive one-port N_R connected across the capacitor with the port current assumed to be directed away from N_R.

Property 1

For any *initial state* $x_{ij}(0) \in R$, for any constant input $u_{ij} \in R$, the circuit is *completely stable* in the sense that all trajectories, independent of initial conditions, tend to an equilibrium point of Eq. (3.1). In particular, $y_{ij}(\infty) = \lim_{t \to \infty} y_{ij}(t) \in R$. Moreover, if $u_{ij} \in \{-1, 1\}$, then $y(\infty) \in \{-1, 1\}$.

Proof:
Consider the DP plot Γ defined by $h_{ij}(x_{ij}; w_{ij}) = -x_{ij} + w_{ij}$ in Fig. 3.2. Since any *trajectory* (i.e. solution) of the state equation $\dot{x}_{ij} = h_{ij}(x_{ij}; w_{ij})$ originating from any

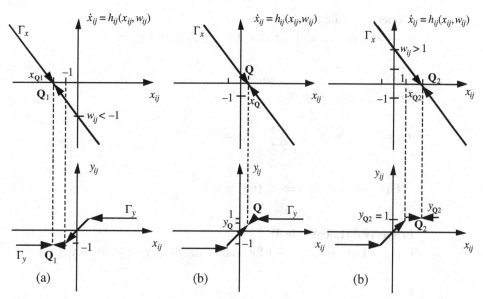

Fig. 3.2. The dynamic route corresponding to the edge detection template. (a) $w_{ij} \leq -1$; (b) $-1 < w_{ij} < 1$; (c) $w_{ij} \geq 1$.

initial state must move along Γ in accordance with the direction indicated, the directed loci Γ_x in Fig. 3.2 is called the *state dynamic route*. The intersection $\mathbf{Q}$ of Γ_x with the horizontal axis is called an *equilibrium point*. Observe from the three dynamic routes in Fig. 3.2 that all trajectories originating from *any* initial state tend to the equilibrium $x_{ij} = x_{\mathbf{Q}}$. The output y_{ij} can be obtained from the associated *output dynamic route* Γ_y. It follows from Γ_y that

$$y(\infty) = \begin{cases} w_{ij}, & \text{if } |w_{ij}| < 1 \\ 1, & \text{if } w_{ij} \geq 1 \\ -1, & \text{if } w_{ij} \leq -1 \end{cases} \qquad (3.4)$$

$\square$

Property 2 (Local rule 1)
If $u_{ij} = -1$, then $y_{ij}(\infty) = -1$, independent of $u_{kl} \in \{-1, 1\}, k, l \in S_1(i, j)$.

Proof:
Since $-8 \leq \sum_{\substack{kl \in S_1(i,j) \\ kl \neq ij}} u_{kl} \leq 8$, it follows that

$$w_{ij} = -1 + 8(-1) - \sum_{\substack{kl \in S_l(i,j) \\ kl \neq ij}} u_{kl} \leq -1 \qquad (3.5)$$

Eqs (3.4) and (3.5) $\Rightarrow y_{ij}(\infty) = -1$.

$\square$

Property 3 (Local rule 2)

If $u_{ij} = 1$ and $u_{kl} = 1$ for all $k, l \in S_1(i, j)$, then $y_{ij}(\infty) = -1$.

Proof:

Since $\sum_{\substack{kl \in S_1(i,j) \\ kl \neq ij}} u_{kl} = 8$

$$w_{ij} = -1 + 8(1) - \sum_{\substack{kl \in S_1(i,j) \\ kl \neq ij}} u_{kl} = -1 \tag{3.6}$$

Eqs (3.4) and (3.6) $\Rightarrow y_{ij}(\infty) = -1$. $\qquad\qquad\qquad\square$

Property 4 (Local rule 3)

If $u_{ij} = 1$ and if $u_{\alpha\beta} = -1$ for some $C(\alpha, \beta) \in S_1(i, j)$, then $y_{ij}(\infty) = 1$.

Proof:

Since $\sum_{\substack{kl \in S_1(i,j) \\ kl \neq ij}} u_{kl} \leq 6$

$$w_{ij} = -1 + 8(1) - \sum_{\substack{kl \in S_1(i,j) \\ kl \neq ij}} u_{kl} \geq 1 \tag{3.7}$$

Eqs (3.4) and (3.7) $\Rightarrow y_{ij}(\infty) = 1$. $\qquad\qquad\qquad\square$

Property 5 (Local rule 4)

If $u_{ij} \in [-1, 1]$ and $u_{kl} \in [-1, 1]$, $k, l \in S_1(i, j)$, then $y_{ij}(\infty) \in [1, 1]$.

Proof:

Since $\sum_{\substack{kl \in S_1(i,j) \\ kl \neq ij}} u_{kl} \in [-8, 8]$ and this sum is not an integer in general, it follows that $w_{ij} \in [-17, 15]$ and is in general not an integer. $\qquad\square$

3.1.2   The EDGEGRAY CNN

One objection to the Edge CNN template in Section 3.1.1 is that it works well only for *binary* input images. For gray-scale input images, the *output* may not be a *binary* image. Our next CNN template called Edgegray will overcome this problem by accepting *gray-scale* input images and always converging to a *binary* output image. Any imperfection in the input which we called "noise" will also converge to a binary output. One application of this CNN template is to convert gray-scale images into *binary* images, which can then be used as inputs to many image-processing tasks which require a binary input image. From an efficient information-processing point of view, gray-scale images contain too much redundancy and require many more "bits" than binary images. Consequently, in most image-processing systems, the gray-scale input image at the front end is quickly converted into a binary image which contains only the relevant information to be extracted, the most important of which being the binary edges.

EDGEGRAY: gray-scale edge detection template

$$
\mathbf{A} = \begin{array}{|c|c|c|} \hline 0 & 0 & 0 \\ \hline 0 & 2 & 0 \\ \hline 0 & 0 & 0 \\ \hline \end{array} \quad \mathbf{B} = \begin{array}{|c|c|c|} \hline -1 & -1 & -1 \\ \hline -1 & 8 & -1 \\ \hline -1 & -1 & -1 \\ \hline \end{array} \quad z = \boxed{-0.5}
$$

I Global task

Given: static gray-scale image $\mathbf{P}$

Input: $\mathbf{U}(t) = \mathbf{P}$

Initial state: $\mathbf{X}(0) = 0$

Output: $\mathbf{Y}(t) \Rightarrow \mathbf{Y}(\infty) =$ Binary image where the black pixels correspond to pixels lying on sharp edges of $\mathbf{P}$, or to fuzzy edges defined roughly to be the union of gray pixels of $\mathbf{P}$ which form one-dimensional (possibly short) line segments, or arcs, such that the intensity of pixels on one side of the arc differs significantly from the intensity of neighbor pixels on the other side of the arc.

Remarks

1 Some "edges" in the output may arise due to poor input image quality, or to artifacts introduced by sensors due to reflections and improper illuminations. Since the black pixels resulting from these situations are not edges, they must be regarded as *noise*.[3]

2 The above template $\mathbf{B}$ is an example of an important class of input templates, called a *Laplacian template*, having the properties that all "surround" input synaptic weights are inhibitory and identical, i.e., $b_{kl} = b < 0$, but the center synaptic weight is excitatory and the average of all input synaptic weights is zero; i.e., $\sum_{kl \neq 0} b_{kl} + b_{00} = 0$.

II Local rules

$\mathbf{U}_{ij}(0) \rightarrow y_{ij}(\infty)$

1 white pixel $\rightarrow$ white, independent of neighbors

2 black pixel $\rightarrow$ white, if all nearest neighbors are black

3 black pixel $\rightarrow$ black, if at least one nearest neighbor is white

4 gray pixel $\rightarrow$ black, if the Laplacian $\nabla^2 \mathbf{U}_{ij} \overset{\Delta}{=} B \circledast \mathbf{U}_{ij} > 0.5$ and $x_{ij}(0) = 0$

5 gray pixel $\rightarrow$ white, if the Laplacian $\nabla^2 \mathbf{U}_{ij} < 0.5$ and $x_{ij}(0) = 0$

$$6 \text{ gray pixel} \rightarrow \begin{cases} \text{black,} & \text{if the Laplacian} = 0.5 \text{ and } x(0) > 0 \\ \text{white,} & \text{if the Laplacian} = 0.5 \text{ and } x(0) < 0 \\ 0, & \begin{cases} \text{if the Laplacian} = 0.5 \text{ and } x(0) = 0 \\ \text{in this case, } y_{ij}(\infty) = 0 \text{ is unstable.} \end{cases} \end{cases}$$

III Examples

EXAMPLE 3.5: Image size: 15×15 (shows the transient waveforms at pixel A, B, and C)

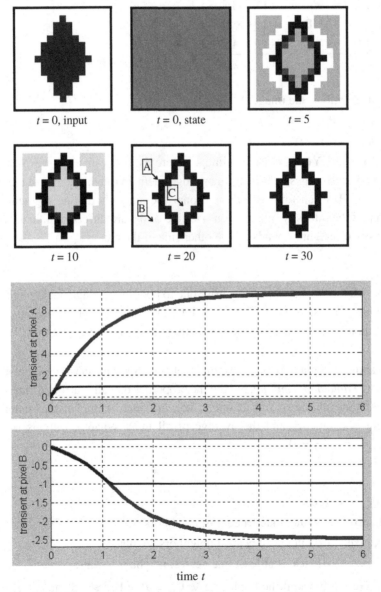

Fig. 3.3. Cell state and output transients for 30 steps at three different locations in the image of example 3.5 represented by bold and thinner lines, respectively.

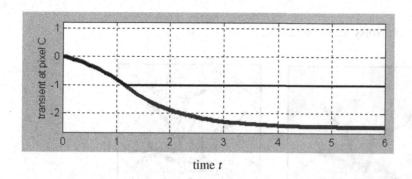

Fig. 3.3. Continued.

EXAMPLE 3.6: Image size: 100×100

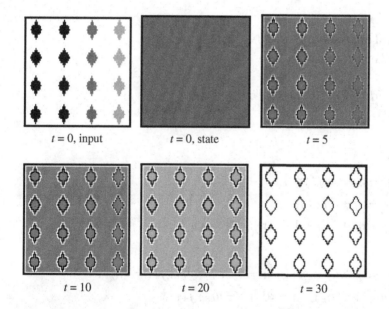

$t = 0$, input $t = 0$, state $t = 5$

$t = 10$ $t = 20$ $t = 30$

EXAMPLE 3.7: Image size: 100×100

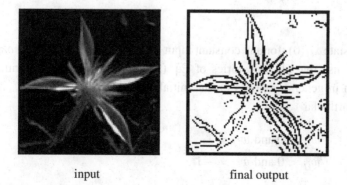

input   final output

EXAMPLE 3.8: Noisy image, image size: 100×100

input   final output

IV Mathematical analysis

State and output equations

$$\dot{x}_{ij} = g(x_{ij}) + w_{ij} = h_{ij}(x_{ij}; w_{ij})$$
$$y_{ij} = f(x_{ij}) \tag{3.8}$$

where

$$
\begin{aligned}
g(x_{ij}) &= -x_{ij} + a_{00} f(x_{ij}) \\
&= -x_{ij} + 2f(x_{ij}) \\
&= -x_{ij} + |x_{ij} + 1| - |x_{ij} - 1|
\end{aligned} \tag{3.9}
$$

$$
\begin{aligned}
w_{ij} &= -0.5 + 8u_{ij} - u_{i+1,j-1} - u_{i+1,j} - u_{i+1,j+1} - u_{i,j-1} \\
&\quad - u_{i,j+1} - u_{i-1,j-1} - u_{i-1,j} - u_{i-1,j+1} \\
&= -0.5 + 8u_{ij} - \sum_{\substack{kl \in S_1(i,j) \\ kl \neq ij}} u_{kl}
\end{aligned} \tag{3.10}
$$

Property 6

For any initial state $x_{ij}(0)$, for any constant input $u_{ij} \in [-1, 1]$, the CNN is *completely stable* in the sense that all trajectories of Eq. (3.1) tend to some equilibrium point whose location in general depends on the initial state $x_{ij}(0)$, $i = 1, 2, \ldots, M$, $j = 1, \ldots, N$. In particular

$$
\begin{aligned}
y_{ij}(\infty) &= 1, &&\text{if } w_{ij} > 0 \text{ and } w_{ij} \neq 1 \\
&= -1, &&\text{if } w_{ij} < 0 \text{ and } w_{ij} \neq -1
\end{aligned} \tag{3.11}
$$

1 if $w_{ij} = 0$, then

$$y_{ij}(\infty) = 1, \quad \text{if } x_{ij}(0) \in (-\infty, -2) \cup (0, 2]$$
$$y_{ij}(\infty) = -1, \quad \text{if } x_{ij}(0) \in [-2, 0) \cup (2, \infty)$$
$$= 0, \quad \text{if } x_{ij}(0) = 0 \tag{3.12}$$

In this case, the equilibrium point $\mathbf{Q}_-$ is unstable.

2 if $w_{ij} = 1$, then

$$\left.\begin{aligned} y_{ij}(\infty) = 1, \quad &\text{if } x_{ij}(0) > -1 \\ = -1, \quad &\text{if } x_{ij}(0) \leq -1 \end{aligned}\right\} \tag{3.13}$$

3 if $w_{ij} = -1$, then

$$\left.\begin{aligned} y_{ij}(\infty) = -1, \quad &\text{if } x_{ij}(0) < 1 \\ = 1, \quad &\text{if } x_{ij}(0) \geq 1 \end{aligned}\right\} \tag{3.14}$$

In this case, the equilibrium point $\mathbf{Q}_0$ is unstable.

Proof of Property 1 and Rules 4–6:
The first step is to examine the internal DP plot given by Eq. (3.2). Although this can be easily sketched directly from the explicit equation given in Eq. (3.2), it is instructive for our future analysis of more complicated CNNs to construct this curve graphically by adding the two components $-x_{ij}$ and $2f(x_{ij})$ as shown in the upper part of Fig. 3.4. Now since

$$w_{ij} = -0.5 + \mathbf{B} \circledast \mathbf{U}_{ij}$$

and assuming the *Laplacian*

$$\nabla^2 \mathbf{U}_{ij} \overset{\Delta}{=} \mathbf{B} \circledast \mathbf{U}_{ij} = 0.5$$

it follows that the offset level $w_{ij} = 0$ and hence

$$h_{ij}(x_{ij}; w_{ij}) = g_{ij}(x_{ij})$$

In this case, the state dynamic route Γ_x is identical to the internal DP plot $g_{ij}(x_{ij})$, except for the addition of arrowheads which indicate the *direction* a trajectory from any point on Γ_x must follow. It follows that of the three equilibrium points $\{\mathbf{Q}_-, \mathbf{Q}_0, \mathbf{Q}_+\}$, only $\mathbf{Q}_-$ and $\mathbf{Q}_+$ are locally *asymptotically stable*.

To determine the asymptotic output $y_{ij}(\infty) \overset{\Delta}{=} \lim_{t \to \infty} y_{ij}(t)$, we simply sketch the *output dynamic route* Γ_y directly below Γ_x with the vertical axes aligned with each other, as shown in Fig. 3.4.

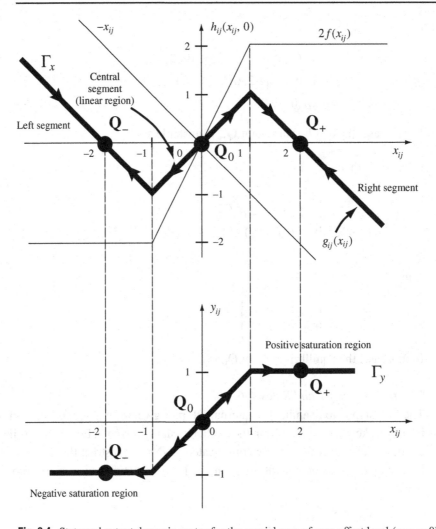

Fig. 3.4. State and output dynamic routes for the special case of zero offset level ($w_{ij} = 0$).

Since Γ_x in Fig. 3.4 corresponds to the case $\nabla^2 U_{ij} = 0.5$, *Local rule 6* follows directly from this dynamic route. For future analysis, it is crucial to note here that whenever the equilibrium point lies on the left segment, where $x_{ij} < -1$, or on the right segment, where $x_{ij} > 1$, the output *saturates* and is always equal to $y_{ij}(\infty) = -1$, or $y_{ij}(\infty) = +1$, respectively.

Now for $w_{ij} \neq 0$, the external DP plot defined by $h_{ij}(x_{ij}; w_{ij}) = g_{ij}(x_{ij}) + w_{ij}$ can be simply obtained by using the internal DP plot $g_{ij}(x_{ij})$ from Fig. 3.4 as a drafting template and translating it along the vertical direction upwards (resp., downwards) by an amount equal to the offset level w_{ij} if $w_{ij} > 0$ (resp., $w_{ij} < 0$). This geometrical interpretation is quite general and extremely useful – this is the reason for calling w_{ij} the *offset level*. Since $\dot{x}_{ij} = h_{ij}(x_{ij}; w_{ij})$, the dynamic route Γ_x associated with the

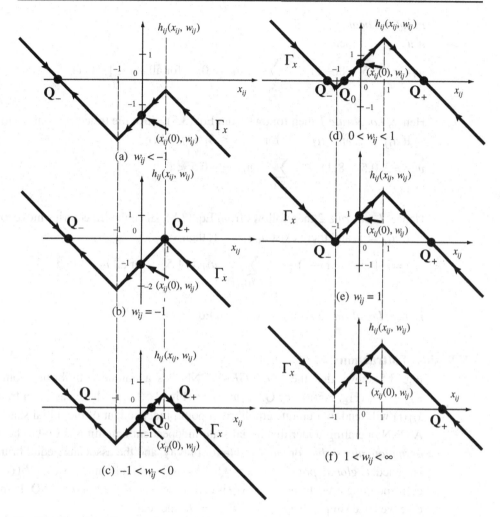

Fig. 3.5. State dynamic route for $w_{ij} \neq 0$.

rate function $h_{ij}(x_{ij}; w_{ij})$ for each of the six mutually exclusive cases (which covers the entire range of $w_{ij} \neq 0$) is shown in Figs 3.5(a)–(f), respectively.

Observe that any trajectory originating from any point on the upper (resp., lower) half plane must move towards right (resp., left) and settle on the right (resp., left) segment. Hence, at equilibrium the output is always binary: $y_{ij}(\infty) = +1$, or -1.

Now since $w_{ij} = -0.5 + \nabla^2 U_{ij} > 0$, if $\nabla^2 U_{ij} > 0.5$, then the associated state dynamic route is given by Figs 3.5(d)–(f), where all trajectories originating from $x_{ij}(0) = 0$ tend to $\mathbf{Q}_+$. Since $x_{ij}(\mathbf{Q}_+) > 1$, we have $y_{ij}(\infty) = 1$, which implies *Local rule 4*. Similarly, *Local rule 5* (which corresponds to $\nabla^2 U_{ij} < 0.5$, or equivalently $w_{ij} < 0$) follows from the state dynamic routes shown in Figs 3.5(a)–(c). $\square$

Proof of Local rules 1–3:

If $u_{ij} = -1$, then

$$w_{ij} = -0.5 + 8(-1) - \sum_{\substack{kl \in S_1(i,j) \\ kl \neq ij}} u_{kl} < 0, \quad \text{for all } u_{kl} \in [-1, 1].$$

Hence, *Local rule 1* then follows from Eq. (3.8), since the trajectories move to $\mathbf{Q}_-$.

If $u_{ij} = 1$, and $u_{kl} = 1$, for all $kl \in S_1(i, j)$, then

$$w_{ij} = -0.5 + 8(1) - \sum_{\substack{kl \in S_1(i,j) \\ kl \neq ij}} u_{kl} = -0.5 < 0$$

Hence, *Local rule 2* then follows from Eq. (3.8), since the trajectories move to $\mathbf{Q}_-$.

If $u_{ij} = 1$, and there exist $u_{\alpha\beta} = -1$, then

$$w_{ij} = -0.5 + 8(1) + 1 - \sum_{\substack{kl \in S_1(i,j) \\ kl \neq ij, kl \neq \alpha\beta}} u_{kl} \geq 1.5, \quad \text{for all } u_{kl} \in [-1, 1].$$

Hence, *Local rule 3* then follows from Eq. (3.4). ☐

V Basins of attraction

Fig. 3.5 shows that the *EDGEGRAY* CNN has a unique equilibrium point $\mathbf{Q}_-$ if $w_{ij} < -1$ (Fig. 3.5(a)), or $\mathbf{Q}_+$ if $w_{ij} > 1$ (Fig. 3.5(f)). In these cases, all trajectories $x_{ij}(t)$ will tend to a unique equilibrium point, independent of the initial states $x_{ij}(0)$. A CNN operating under this initial-state-independent condition is said to be *globally asymptotically stable*, or *monostable* for brevity, and the associated equilibrium point is called a *global point attractor* $\mathbf{Q}$. The union of all initial states $\mathcal{B}(Q)$ whose corresponding trajectories tend to $\mathbf{Q}$ is called the *Basin of attraction* of $\mathbf{Q}$. In the above case we have simply $\mathcal{B}(\mathbf{Q}_-) = \mathcal{B}(\mathbf{Q}_+) = R$, the real line.

Consider next the two typical cases $w_{ij} \in (-1, 0)$ and $w_{ij} \in (0, 1)$, as shown in Figs 3.5(c) and 3.5(d), where there are two *locally stable* equilibrium points $\mathbf{Q}_-$ and $\mathbf{Q}_+$, respectively. However, unlike the monostable case, which of the two equilibrium points the trajectory will converge to depends on the initial state $x_{ij}(0)$. In both Figs 3.5(c) and 3.5(d), the basin of attraction of $\mathbf{Q}_-$ is given by all points lying to the left of the *unstable* equilibrium point $\mathbf{Q}_0$; namely, $\mathcal{B}(\mathbf{Q}_-) = \{x_{ij} : -\infty < x_{ij} < x_{Q_0}\}$. Similarly, the basin of attraction of $\mathbf{Q}_+$ is given by $\mathcal{B}(\mathbf{Q}_+) = \{x_{ij} : x_{Q_0} < x_{ij} < \infty\}$. In this case, the *unstable* equilibrium point $\mathbf{Q}_0$ *separates* the set of all initial states $x_{ij}(0) \in R$ into two basins of attraction and the CNN is said to be *bistable*. Observe that the initial state $\mathbf{X}(0) = 0$ which we have prescribed for the EDGEGRAY CNN guarantees that the trajectories corresponding to any input gray-scale image will converge to the correct output image.

Finally, consider the two *singular* cases $w_{ij} = -1$ and $w_{ij} = 1$, as shown in Figs 3.5(b) and 3.5(e), where there are only two equilibrium points. In these cases, only one equilibrium point is locally stable; namely, $\mathbf{Q}_-$ in Fig. 3.5(b) with a basin of attraction $\mathcal{B}(\mathbf{Q}_-) = \{x_{ij} : -\infty < x_{ij} < x_{\mathbf{Q}_+}\}$ and $\mathbf{Q}_+$ in Fig. 3.5(e) with a basin of attraction $\mathcal{B}(\mathbf{Q}_+) = \{x_{ij} : x_{\mathbf{Q}_-} < x_{ij} < \infty\}$. The equilibrium points $\mathbf{Q}_+$ in Fig. 3.5(b) and $\mathbf{Q}_-$ in Fig. 3.5(e) are said to be *semi-stable* because they lie on the *boundaries* of these basins so that arbitrarily small perturbations will cause the trajectories to diverge away from the basins. Since "noise" is inevitable in any hardware realization, or computer simulation, these two semi-stable equilibrium points are *not observable* in practice and are, therefore, practically speaking, *unstable*.

3.2   Three quick steps for sketching the shifted DP plot

Since the most useful tool for studying the nonlinear dynamics of any *uncoupled* CNN is to analyze its state dynamic route Γ_x it is essential that we develop the skill to quickly sketch the *shifted* **DP plot** $\Gamma_x(w_{ij})$, which, in general, depends on both the *threshold* z_{ij} and the *inputs* $u_{kl} \in S_r(i, j)$ of all cells belonging to the sphere of influence $S_r(i, j)$. The following three simple steps are all that is needed:

Given: threshold z_{ij} and inputs $u_{kl} \in S_r(i, j)$.

Step 1: Calculate the slope of the middle segment $s_{00} = a_{00} - 1$ and the offset level $w_{ij} = z_{ij} + \mathbf{B} \circledast \mathbf{U}_{ij}$.

Step 2: Draw a straight-line segment with slope equal to s_{00} at the point $\dot{x}_{ij} = w_{ij}$ on the vertical axis and ends at $x_{ij} = -1$ and $x_{ij} = 1$, respectively. The two end points are the left and the right breakpoints of the *shifted* **DP plot**.

Step 3: Draw a half line with slope equal to -1 starting from each breakpoint, and tending to infinity in each direction.

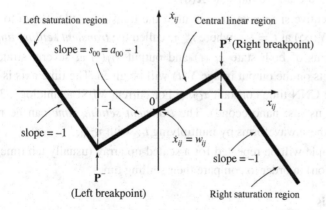

Fig. 3.6. A typical shifted DP plot $\Gamma_x(w_{ij})$.

3.3   Some other useful templates

Our object in this section is to select a gallery of CNN templates which can be analyzed mathematically and explained. Some are specially developed to illustrate a particular property – mainly for pedagogical values – and are not necessarily the best choice for the intended tasks. These templates will be analyzed in the order of their tractability and complexity. Each CNN is carefully chosen to illustrate either a new paradigm, mechanism, or application. For ease of reference, we will always follow a consistent style: each CNN will be identified by a *code name* (which may not be very meaningful) copied from the CNN template library, together with an expanded name which suggests the task it is designed to implement. This will be followed by a listing of $(\mathbf{A}, \mathbf{B}, z)$ templates, and the following standard sections:

I Global task

A non-technical description will be given of the input–output image transformation at the complete image level.

II Local rules

A precise recipe of how an input pixel transforms into an output pixel. Ideally, these local rules must be *complete* in the sense that each output pixel can be *uniquely* determined by applying these rules to the state and input of all pixels within that sphere of influence. The local rules may sometimes be *redundant* if they help to simplify the interpretation of the recipe, provided they are *consistent* (do not contradict each other).

The local rule may be more general than needed to specify the global task. For example, it may apply to a gray-scale input even if the global task specifies only binary inputs.

III Examples

Several examples will be given. The first example will include:
(a) The input picture $\mathbf{U}$ and initial state $\mathbf{X}(0)$.
(b) Several consecutive snapshots in time until the transient settles down to a static output image $\mathbf{Y}(\infty)$ at $t = t_\infty$, where t_∞ is called the *transient settling time*.
(c) Time waveforms of both state $x_{ij}(t)$ and output $y_{ij}(t)$ at several strategically identified points on the output image $\mathbf{Y}(t)$ will be given. The time axis is labeled in units of the CNN time constant τ_{CNN}. For current VLSI technology, 30 ns $\leq$ $\tau_{CNN} \leq$ 200 ns (ns: nanosecond). The *transient settling time* can be read off directly from these waveforms by multiplying t_∞ with τ_{CNN}.
(d) The first example will be repeated for a scaled-up array (usually ten times larger in each direction) in order to compare their settling times.

IV Mathematical analysis

Ideally, a rigorous mathematical proof will be given for each local rule. Whenever this is not available (either because a proof has not yet been developed, or the rules do not always hold and therefore need modification) an intuitive proof, often supplemented by various numerical studies, will be given.

3.3.1 CORNER: convex corner detection template

$$\mathbf{A} = \begin{array}{|c|c|c|} \hline 0 & 0 & 0 \\ \hline 0 & 2 & 0 \\ \hline 0 & 0 & 0 \\ \hline \end{array} \qquad \mathbf{B} = \begin{array}{|c|c|c|} \hline -1 & -1 & -1 \\ \hline -1 & 8 & -1 \\ \hline -1 & -1 & -1 \\ \hline \end{array} \qquad z = \boxed{-8.5}$$

I Global task

Given: static binary image $\mathbf{P}$

Input: $\mathbf{U}(t) = \mathbf{P}$

Initial state: $\mathbf{X}(0) = 0$

Output: $\mathbf{Y}(t) \Rightarrow \mathbf{Y}(\infty) =$ Binary image, where black pixels correspond to convex corners in $\mathbf{P}$ (where, roughly speaking, a black pixel is a convex corner if it is part of a convex boundary line of the input image).

II Local rules

$u_{ij}(0) \rightarrow y_{ij}(\infty)$

1 white pixel $\rightarrow$ white, independent of neighbors

2 black pixel $\rightarrow$ black, if and only if it has three or fewer black nearest neighbors (or equivalently five or more white nearest neighbors)

III Examples

EXAMPLE 3.9: Image size: 15×15

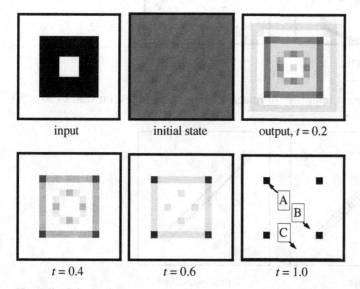

| input | initial state | output, $t = 0.2$ |

| $t = 0.4$ | $t = 0.6$ | $t = 1.0$ |

Normalized time unit $t_u = \tau_{\text{CNN}}$.

EXAMPLE 3.10: Image size: 100×100

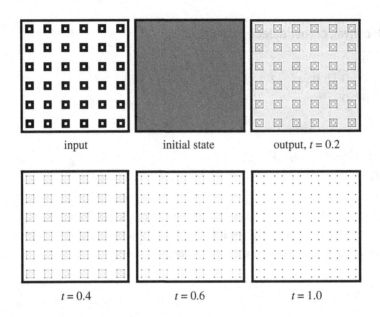

EXAMPLE 3.11: Realistic scene (100×100)

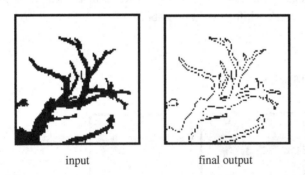

EXAMPLE 3.12: Corner template for image containing pixel level textures (50×50)

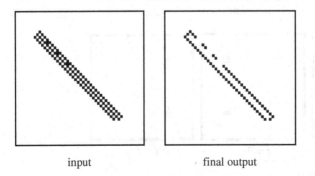

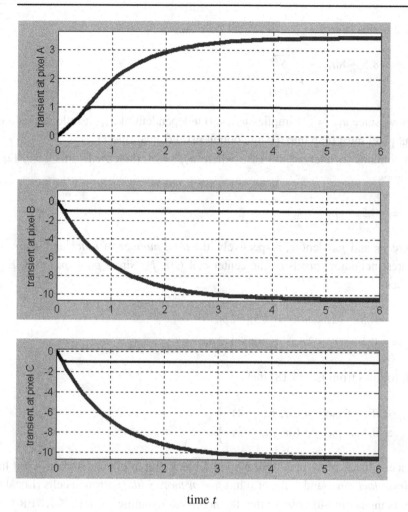

time t

Fig. 3.7. Cell state and output transients for 30 equidistant time steps at three different locations in the image of example 3.9. ——: state variable x_{ij}; ——: output variable y_{ij}.

IV Mathematical analysis

Since the EDGEGRAY and the CORNER CNN have the same **A** template, their internal DP plots $g_{ij}(x_{ij})$ are identical, as already derived earlier in Fig. 3.5(a) (for the EDGEGRAY template). Moreover, since they have the same **B** template, the output of the CORNER CNN is also given by Eq. (3.4) of the EDGEGRAY CNN; namely

$$
\begin{aligned}
y_{ij}(\infty) &= 1, &&\text{if } w_{ij} > 0 \text{ and } w_{ij} \neq 1 \\
&= -1, &&\text{if } w_{ij} < 0 \text{ and } w_{ij} \neq -1
\end{aligned}
\tag{3.15}
$$

where in this case

$$w_{ij} = -8.5 + 8u_{ij} - \sum_{\substack{kl \in S_1(i,j) \\ kl \neq ij}} u_{kl} \tag{3.16}$$

Now, since $u_{ij} = -1$ implies $w_{ij} < 0$ independent of u_{kl}, it follows that any white input pixel must map into a white output pixel (Local rule 1).

It remains to analyze the case where $u_{ij} = 1$ (black). In this case, Eq. (3.16) becomes

$$w_{ij} = -0.5 - (p_b - p_w) \tag{3.17}$$

where p_b and p_w denote, respectively, the *total number* of *black* and *white* surround (nearest neighbor) pixels of the center cell $C(i, j)$. Since $p_b + p_w = 8$, Eq. (3.17) implies

$$\begin{aligned} w_{ij} &= -0.5 - (2p_b - 8) = 7.5 - 2p_b \\ &= -0.5 - (8 - 2p_w) = -8.5 + 2p_w \end{aligned} \tag{3.18}$$

It follows from Eq. (3.18) that

$$\left. \begin{aligned} w_{ij} &< 0, \quad \text{if } p_b \geq 4 \ (\text{or, } p_w \leq 4) \\ &> 0, \quad \text{if } p_b \leq 3 \ (\text{or, } p_w \geq 5) \end{aligned} \right\} \tag{3.19}$$

Hence, a black input pixel will map to a black output pixel if and only if it has *three or less black* surround cells, or it has *five or more white* surround cells (Local rule 2).

It is interesting to observe that the nonlinear dynamics of the CORNER CNN tend to extract one pixel-wide horizontal and vertical edges which form the boundary of a square (e.g., see output image at $t = 0.4$). In other words, the CORNER CNN seems to exhibit some intelligence in self-organization by programming itself to carry out the prescribed global task in two steps: (1) extract horizontal and vertical edges at the perimeter of a square, and (2) extract the extreme "end" pixel of these edges. This fascinating self-programming phenomenon can be explained by examining carefully the time evolution of the *transient* process.

3.3.2 THRESHOLD: gray-scale to binary threshold template

$$\mathbf{A} = \begin{array}{|c|c|c|} \hline 0 & 0 & 0 \\ \hline 0 & 2 & 0 \\ \hline 0 & 0 & 0 \\ \hline \end{array} \quad \mathbf{B} = \begin{array}{|c|c|c|} \hline 0 & 0 & 0 \\ \hline 0 & 0 & 0 \\ \hline 0 & 0 & 0 \\ \hline \end{array} \quad z = \boxed{-z^*},$$

I Global task

Given: static gray-scale image **P** and threshold z^*

Input: $\mathbf{U}(t) =$ arbitrary or default to $\mathbf{U}(t) = 0$

Initial state: $\mathbf{X}(0) = \mathbf{P}$

Output: $\mathbf{Y}(t) \Rightarrow \mathbf{Y}(\infty) =$ binary image when all pixels **P** with gray-scale intensity $p_{ij} > z^*$ becomes black.

II Local rules

$$x_{ij}(0) \rightarrow y_{ij}(\infty)$$

1 $x_{ij}(0) < z^* \rightarrow$ white, independent of neighbors

2 $x_{ij}(0) > z^* \rightarrow$ black, independent of neighbors

3 $x_{ij}(0) = z^* \rightarrow z^*$, assuming zero noise

III Examples

EXAMPLE 3.13: Image size: 63×63

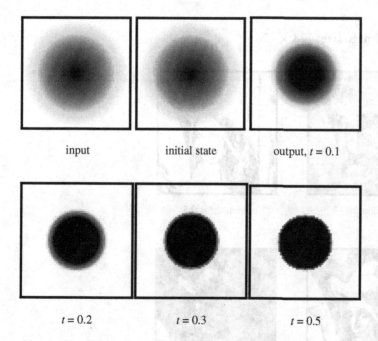

input   initial state   output, $t = 0.1$

$t = 0.2$ $t = 0.3$ $t = 0.5$

Normalized time unit $t_u = \tau_{\text{CNN}}$, $z^* = -0.4$.

EXAMPLE 3.14: Image size: 63×63

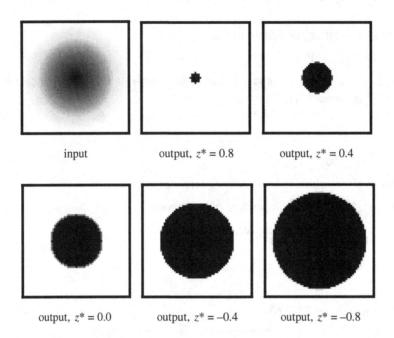

input   output, $z^* = 0.8$ output, $z^* = 0.4$

output, $z^* = 0.0$ output, $z^* = -0.4$ output, $z^* = -0.8$

EXAMPLE 3.15: Image size: 128×128

input   output, $z^* = 0.5$

output, $z^* = 0.0$ output, $z^* = -0.5$

EXAMPLE 3.16: Image size: 100×100

input	output, $z^* = 0.5$

output, $z^* = 0.0$	output, $z^* = -0.5$

Observe that the last two examples show that any image **P** can be transformed into a completely *black* image by a THRESHOLD template with $z^* = -4$, or a completely *white* image by choosing $z^* = 4$. Since these two transformations are quite useful for many image-processing tasks, we have recognized their importance by classifying them as separate CNNs in the CNN template Library under the names FILBLACK and FILWHITE, respectively, which we reproduce in Section 3.3.3.

IV Mathematical analysis (for THRESHOLD)

Since $b_{kl} = 0$, $w_{ij} = -z^*$, there is only one shifted DP plot for each threshold z^*, as shown in Fig. 3.8, independent of the inputs of the neighbors (which is arbitrary for this template).

It follows from the dynamic route shown in Fig. 3.8. that

$$y_{ij}(\infty) = -1, \quad \text{if } x_{ij}(0) < z^* \quad \text{(Local rule 1)}$$
$$= 1, \quad \text{if } x_{ij}(0) > z^* \quad \text{(Local rule 2)}$$
$$= z^*, \quad \text{if } x_{ij}(0) = z^* \quad \text{(Local rule 3)}$$

Observe that $y_{ij}(\infty) = z^*$ when $x_{ij}(0) = z^*$ because $x_{ij} = z^*$ in Fig. 3.8 is an equilibrium point ($\mathbf{Q}_0$). However, since $\mathbf{Q}_0$ is unstable, any "noise" Δx would eventually drive the "theoretical" gray-scale output to either *black* (if the noise

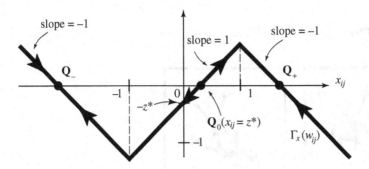

Fig. 3.8. Shifted DP plot $\Gamma_x(w_{ij})$ and its dynamic route.

$\Delta x_{ij}(0) > 0$), or *white* (if the noise $\Delta x_{ij}(0) < 0$). Hence, in practice, the above THRESHOLD CNN will always give a binary output image, assuming one waits long enough for the transients to settle down.

3.3.3   FILBLACK and FILWHITE templates

FILBLACK: Gray-scale to black CNN

$$\mathbf{A} = \begin{array}{|c|c|c|} \hline 0 & 0 & 0 \\ \hline 0 & 2 & 0 \\ \hline 0 & 0 & 0 \\ \hline \end{array} \quad \mathbf{B} = \begin{array}{|c|c|c|} \hline 0 & 0 & 0 \\ \hline 0 & 0 & 0 \\ \hline 0 & 0 & 0 \\ \hline \end{array} \quad z = \boxed{4}$$

I Global task

Given: static gray-scale image $\mathbf{P}$

Input: $\mathbf{U}(t) =$ arbitrary or default to $\mathbf{U}(t) = 0$

Initial state: $\mathbf{X}(0) = \mathbf{P}$

Output: $\mathbf{Y}(t) \Rightarrow \mathbf{Y}(\infty) =$ black image (all pixels are black)

II Local rules

$x_{ij}(0) \rightarrow y_{ij}(\infty)$

Arbitrary $x_{ij}(0) \in (-\infty, \infty) \rightarrow y_{ij}(\infty) = 1$

III Example

EXAMPLE 3.17: Image size 128×128

Input   Output, $z = 4.0$

FILWHITE: Gray-scale to white CNN

$$\mathbf{A} = \begin{array}{|c|c|c|} \hline 0 & 0 & 0 \\ \hline 0 & 2 & 0 \\ \hline 0 & 0 & 0 \\ \hline \end{array} \quad \mathbf{B} = \begin{array}{|c|c|c|} \hline 0 & 0 & 0 \\ \hline 0 & 0 & 0 \\ \hline 0 & 0 & 0 \\ \hline \end{array} \quad z = \boxed{-4}$$

I Global task

Given: static gray-scale image $\mathbf{P}$

Input: $\mathbf{U}(t) = $ arbitrary or default to $\mathbf{U}(t) = 0$

Initial state: $\mathbf{X}(0) = \mathbf{P}$

Output: $\mathbf{Y}(t) \Rightarrow \mathbf{Y}(\infty) = white$ image (all pixels are white)

II Local rules

$x_{ij}(0) \rightarrow y_{ij}(\infty)$

Arbitrary $x_{ij}(0) \in (-\infty, \infty) \rightarrow y_{ij}(\infty) = -1$

III Example

EXAMPLE 3.18: Image size 128×128

Input   Output, $z = -4.0$

3.3.4   LOGNOT: Logic NOT and set complementation ($P \rightarrow \bar{P} = P^c$) template

$$A = \begin{array}{|c|c|c|} \hline 0 & 0 & 0 \\ \hline 0 & 1 & 0 \\ \hline 0 & 0 & 0 \\ \hline \end{array} \quad B = \begin{array}{|c|c|c|} \hline 0 & 0 & 0 \\ \hline 0 & -2 & 0 \\ \hline 0 & 0 & 0 \\ \hline \end{array} \quad z = \boxed{0}$$

I Global task

Given: static binary image **P**

Input: $\mathbf{U}(t) = \mathbf{P}$

Initial state: $\mathbf{X}(0) = 0$

Output: $\mathbf{Y}(t) \Rightarrow \mathbf{Y}(\infty)$ = binary image where each black pixel in **P** becomes white, and vice versa. In set-theoretic or logic notation: $\mathbf{Y}(\infty) = \mathbf{P}^c = \bar{\mathbf{P}}$, where the bar denotes the "Complement" or "Negation" operator.

II Local rules

$$x_{ij}(0) \rightarrow y_{ij}(\infty)$$

1   black pixel $\rightarrow$ white pixel, independent of initial states

2   white pixel $\rightarrow$ black pixel, independent of initial states

III Example

EXAMPLE 3.19: Image size: 15×15

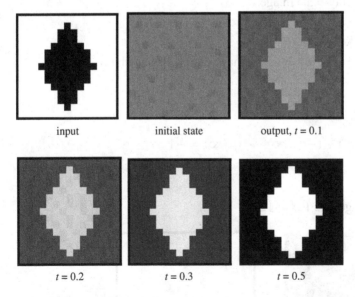

| input | initial state | output, $t = 0.1$ |

| $t = 0.2$ | $t = 0.3$ | $t = 0.5$ |

Normalized time unit $t_u = t_{\text{CNN}}$.

IV Mathematical analysis (for LOGNOT)

Since $s_{00} = a_{00} - 1 = 0$, and $w_{ij} = -2u_{ij}$, where $u_{ij} \in \{-1, 1\}$, only the two shifted DP plots shown in Figs 3.9(a) and 3.9(b) need to be considered. The above dynamic routes show that the LOGNOT template gives rise to a globally asymptotically stable

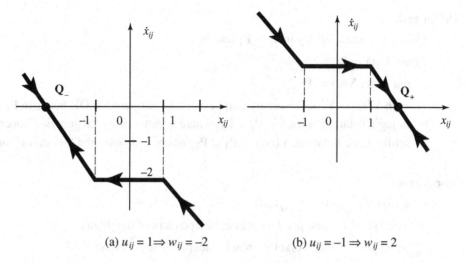

(a) $u_{ij} = 1 \Rightarrow w_{ij} = -2$ (b) $u_{ij} = -1 \Rightarrow w_{ij} = 2$

Fig. 3.9. Shifted DP plots for the cases $u_{ij} = 1$ and $u_{ij} = -1$.

(monostable) CNN provided the inputs are binary. Local rules 1 and 2 follow directly from Figs 3.9(a) and 3.9(b), respectively.

Remarks
Note that since the middle segment of the shifted DP plot in Figs 3.9 is horizontal, an ambiguous situation can occur if the inputs are not binary. In particular, when $u_{ij} = 0$, the horizontal segment coincides with the closed unit interval $[-1, 1]$ of the x_{ij}-axis, which implies that all points $x_{ij} \in [-1, 1]$ are equilibrium points. Moreover, this *continuum* of *non-isolated* equilibrium points possesses a weaker form of *stability* in the sense that if we perturb any equilibrium point on the interior of $[-1, 1]$ by a sufficiently small amount so that it remains within $[-1, 1]$, then the state of this CNN will assume this new position, unlike the previous semi-stable case where the trajectory eventually moves to another point outside of $[-1, 1]$. In other words, $y_{ij}(\infty)$ can assume any gray-scale value $-1 \leq y_{ij} \leq 1$.

Although the above singular situation rarely occurs in practical CNNs, the possibility of such weird phenomena can greatly complicate the derivation of a rigorous proof of many quite general mathematical properties. Even worse, it can make some such seemingly reasonable properties incorrect. Consequently, it will often be advisable, if not necessary, to add the reasonable hypothesis that the class of CNNs being considered for a rigorous mathematical proof has only isolated, and hence a *finite number*[1] of equilibrium points.

3.3.5   LOGOR: Logic OR and set union ∪ (disjunction ∨) template

$$\mathbf{A} = \begin{array}{|c|c|c|} \hline 0 & 0 & 0 \\ \hline 0 & 3 & 0 \\ \hline 0 & 0 & 0 \\ \hline \end{array} \quad \mathbf{B} = \begin{array}{|c|c|c|} \hline 0 & 0 & 0 \\ \hline 0 & 3 & 0 \\ \hline 0 & 0 & 0 \\ \hline \end{array} \quad z = \boxed{2}$$

I Global task

Given: two static binary images $\mathbf{P}_1$ and $\mathbf{P}_2$

Input: $\mathbf{U}(t) = \mathbf{P}_1$

Initial state: $\mathbf{X}(0) = \mathbf{P}_2$

Output: $\mathbf{Y}(t) \Rightarrow \mathbf{Y}(\infty) =$ binary output of the logic operation **OR** between $\mathbf{P}_1$ and $\mathbf{P}_2$. In logic notation, $\mathbf{Y}(\infty) = \mathbf{P}_1 \vee \mathbf{P}_2$, where $\vee$ denotes the "disjunction" operator. In set-theoretic notation, $\mathbf{Y}(\infty) = \mathbf{P}_1 \cup \mathbf{P}_2$, where $\cup$ denotes the "set union" operator.

II Local rules

$$u_{ij}(0) \qquad x_{ij}(0) \to y_{ij}(\infty)$$

1   white pixel   white pixel $\to$ white, independent of neighbors

2   white pixel   black pixel $\to$ black, independent of neighbors

3   black pixel   white pixel $\to$ black, independent of neighbors

4   black pixel   black pixel $\to$ black, independent of neighbors

III Examples

EXAMPLE 3.20: Image size: 15×15

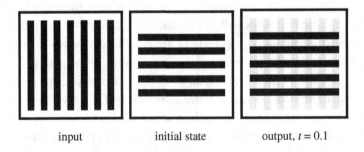

input   initial state   output, $t = 0.1$

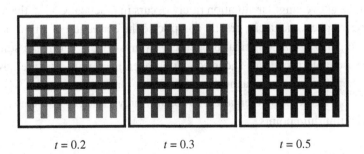

$t = 0.2$ $t = 0.3$ $t = 0.5$

Normalized time unit $t_u = t_{\text{CNN}}$.

EXAMPLE 3.21: Image size: 100×100

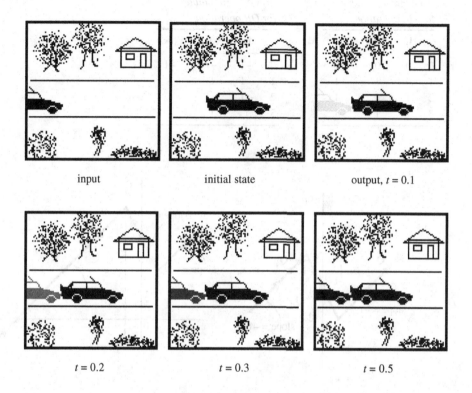

input	initial state	output, $t = 0.1$

$t = 0.2$	$t = 0.3$	$t = 0.5$

IV Mathematical analysis (for LOGOR)

Since this is our first template which belongs to the domain of "Boolean algebra," or "switching logic circuits," where the numbers $\{0, 1\}$ are used not in a numeric sense, but in a symbolic sense, it is particularly important to translate any logic truth table represented in Boolean variables into an equivalent CNN truth table represented in numerical values before any numerical calculation is made. The reason we will use both logic truth tables and CNN truth tables in this book is to avail ourselves of the large body of results in the literature on Boolean functions and their numerous combinatorial properties. To illustrate the importance of distinguishing these two equivalent truth table representations, let us consider the logic truth table 3.1(a) and its equivalent CNN truth table 3.1(b) for defining the LOGOR CNN.

Let us now derive the dynamic routes associated with the LOGOR templates. Since $s_{00} = a_{00} - 1 = 2$ and $w_{ij} = 2 + 3u_{ij}$, only the two shifted DP plots shown in Figs 3.10(a) and 3.10(b) are needed.

Consider first the case $u_{ij} = -1$ (white) so that the dynamic route is given by Fig. 3.10(a). In this case, if:

1 $x_{ij}(0) = -1$ (white), then $y_{ij}(\infty) = -1$ (white), which is *Local rule 1.*

Table 3.1. *Two equivalent representations of the LOGOR template.*
(a) Logic truth table   *(b) CNN truth table*
for OR operation.   *for OR operation.*

U	X(0)	Y(∞)		U	X(0)	Y(∞)
0	0	0	0		0	-1	-1	-1
1	0	1	1		1	-1	1	1
2	1	0	1		2	-1	-1	1
3	1	1	1		3	1	1	1

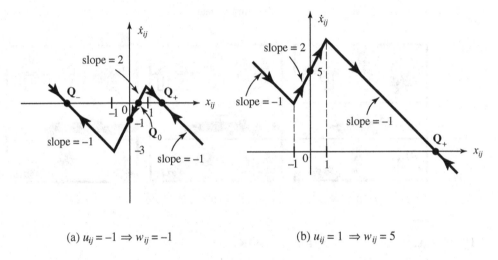

(a) $u_{ij} = -1 \Rightarrow w_{ij} = -1$ (b) $u_{ij} = 1 \Rightarrow w_{ij} = 5$

Fig. 3.10. Dynamic routes of the LOGOR CNN.

2 $x_{ij}(0) = 1$ (black), then $y_{ij}(\infty) = 1$ (black), which is *Local rule 2*.

Consider next the case $u_{ij} = 1$ (black) so that the dynamic route is given by Fig. 3.10(b). In this case the CNN is globally asymptotically stable and $y_{ij}(\infty) = 1$, regardless of the initial conditions, which implies *Local rule 3* and *Local rule 4*.

3.3.6   LOGAND: Logic AND and set intersection ∩ (conjunction ∨) template

$$\mathbf{A} = \begin{array}{|c|c|c|} \hline 0 & 0 & 0 \\ \hline 0 & 1.5 & 0 \\ \hline 0 & 0 & 0 \\ \hline \end{array} \quad \mathbf{B} = \begin{array}{|c|c|c|} \hline 0 & 0 & 0 \\ \hline 0 & 1.5 & 0 \\ \hline 0 & 0 & 0 \\ \hline \end{array} \quad z = \boxed{-1.5}$$

I Global task

Given: two static binary images $\mathbf{P}_1$ and $\mathbf{P}_2$

Input: $\mathbf{U}(t) = \mathbf{P}_1$

Initial state: $\mathbf{X}(0) = \mathbf{P}_2$

Output: $\mathbf{Y}(t) \Rightarrow \mathbf{Y}(\infty) =$ binary output of the logic operation "**AND**" between $\mathbf{P}_1$ and $\mathbf{P}_2$. In logic notation, $\mathbf{Y}(\infty) = \mathbf{P}_1 \wedge \mathbf{P}_2$, where $\wedge$ denotes the "conjunction" operator. In set-theoretic notation, $\mathbf{Y}(\infty) = \mathbf{P}_1 \cap \mathbf{P}_2$, where $\cap$ denotes the "intersection" operator.

II Local rules

$\quad u_{ij}(0) \qquad x_{ij}(0) \to y_{ij}(\infty)$

1 white pixel   white pixel $\to$ white, independent of neighbors

2 white pixel   black pixel $\to$ white, independent of neighbors

3 black pixel   white pixel $\to$ white, independent of neighbors

4 black pixel   black pixel $\to$ black, independent of neighbors

III Examples

EXAMPLE 3.22: Image size: 15×15

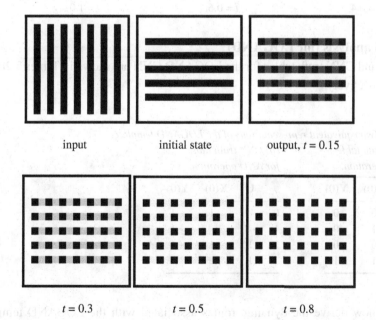

input   initial state   output, $t = 0.15$

$t = 0.3$ $t = 0.5$ $t = 0.8$

Normalized time unit $t_u = t_{\text{CNN}}$.

EXAMPLE 3.23: Image size: 100×100

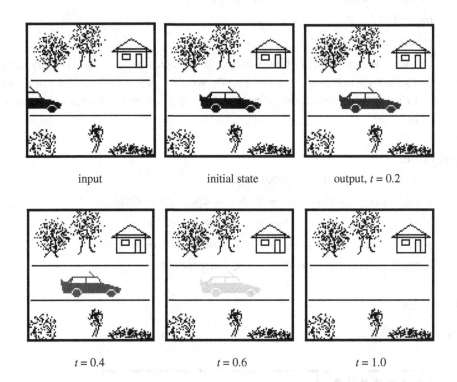

| input | initial state | output, $t = 0.2$ |

| $t = 0.4$ | $t = 0.6$ | $t = 1.0$ |

IV Mathematical analysis (for LOGAND)

The logic and CNN truth tables for the LOGAND CNN are shown in Tables 3.2(a) and 3.2(b), respectively.

Table 3.2. *Two equivalent representations of the LOGAND template.*
(a) Logic truth table   *(b) CNN truth table*
for AND operation.   *for AND operation.*

	U	X(0)	Y(0)			U	X(0)	Y(0)
0	0	0	0		0	-1	-1	-1
1	0	1	0		1	-1	1	-1
2	1	0	0		2	1	-1	-1
3	1	1	1		3	1	1	1

Let us now derive the dynamic routes associated with the LOGAND templates. Since $s_{00} = a_{00} - 1 = 0.5$ and $w_{ij} = -1.5 + 1.5u_{ij}$, only the two shifted DP plots shown in Figs 3.11(a) and 3.11(b) are needed.

Consider first the case $u_{ij} = -1$ (white) so that the dynamic route is given by

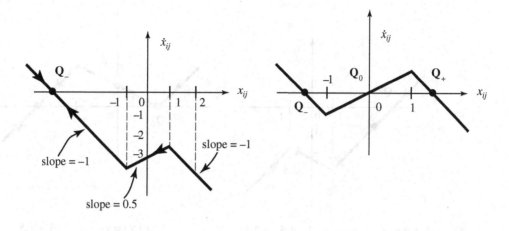

(a) $u_{ij} = -1 \Rightarrow w_{ij} = -1.5 - 1.5 = -3$ (b) $u_{ij} = 1 \Rightarrow w_{ij} = -1.5 + 1.5 = 0$

Fig. 3.11. Dynamic routes of the LOGAND CNN.

Fig. 3.11(a). In this case, the CNN is globally asymptotically stable, and $y_{ij}(\infty) = -1$ (white), regardless of the initial condition, which implies *Local rule 1* and *Local rule 2*.

Consider next the case $u_{ij} = 1$ (black) so that the dynamic route is given by Fig. 3.11(b). In this case, if:

(a) $x_{ij}(0) = -1$ (white), then $y_{ij}(\infty) = -1$ (white), which is *Local rule 3*.
(b) $x_{ij}(0) = 1$ (black), then $y_{ij}(\infty) = 1$ (black), which is *Local rule 4*.

Remark
In our original CNN template library, and previous publications, the threshold value for the LOGAND template was assigned the value $z = -1$. While both computer simulations and measurements made on an early version of the CNN universal chip[3] had verified the correct operation of this template, the dynamic routes shown in Fig. 3.12 corresponding to $z = -1$ show that this threshold value was a poor choice (see Fig. 3.12(b)), and could lead to incorrect operations in practice. In particular, if the initial state $x_{ij}(0) = -1$, then the output $y_{ij}(\infty)$ in Fig. 3.12(b) coincides with the *semi-stable* equilibrium point at $Q_-(x_{ij} = -1)$. The following two situations in practice could occur and lead to an incorrect output $y_{ij}(\infty) = 1$ (black), thereby violating *Local rule 3*. First, any positive perturbation in the state $\Delta x_{ij} > 0$ in Fig. 3.12(b) (to the right of Q_-) would cause the trajectory to move to Q_+ where $y_{ij}(\infty) = 1$. Second, due to manufacturing tolerance in the chip fabrication technology, it is virtually impossible to guarantee for the left breakpoint to be exactly located as shown in Fig. 3.12(b). If this breakpoint is slightly displaced upward so that only one equilibrium point (Q_+) remains, then the trajectory would converge to

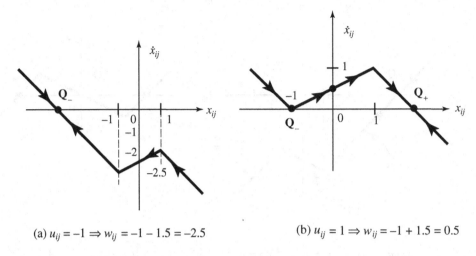

(a) $u_{ij} = -1 \Rightarrow w_{ij} = -1 - 1.5 = -2.5$ (b) $u_{ij} = 1 \Rightarrow w_{ij} = -1 + 1.5 = 0.5$

Fig. 3.12. Dynamic routes for the threshold value $z = -1$.

$\mathbf{Q}_+$. Since these two scenarios are quite common, it is astonishing to recall that our previous computer simulations *and* actual measurements on a physical chip based on this flaky design did not expose this potentially disastrous problem. One explanation could be that the perturbations due to the inevitable numerical or physical *noise* are small enough to require a *longer* "observation time" than had been given.

The above remark clearly points to the usefulness of our *dynamic route* approach for analyzing the validity and reliability of CNN templates, and for optimizing their reliability by finding more *robust* template coefficients.

3.3.7   LOGDIF: Logic difference and relative set complement ($\mathbf{P}_1 \setminus \mathbf{P}_2 = \mathbf{P}_1 - \mathbf{P}_2$) template

$$\mathbf{A} = \begin{array}{|c|c|c|} \hline 0 & 0 & 0 \\ \hline 0 & 1 & 0 \\ \hline 0 & 0 & 0 \\ \hline \end{array} \quad \mathbf{B} = \begin{array}{|c|c|c|} \hline 0 & 0 & 0 \\ \hline 0 & -1 & 0 \\ \hline 0 & 0 & 0 \\ \hline \end{array} \quad z = \boxed{-1}$$

I Global task

Given: two static binary input images $\mathbf{P}_1$ and $\mathbf{P}_2$

Input: $\mathbf{U}(t) = \mathbf{P}_2$

Initial state: $\mathbf{X}(0) = \mathbf{P}_1$

Output: $\mathbf{Y}(t) \Rightarrow \mathbf{Y}(\infty) =$ binary image representing the *set-theoretic*, or *logic complement* of $\mathbf{P}_2$ *relative to* $\mathbf{P}_1$. In set-theoretic or logic notation, $\mathbf{P}_1 \setminus \mathbf{P}_2 \overset{\Delta}{=} \mathbf{P}_1 - \mathbf{P}_2 \overset{\Delta}{=} \{x \in \mathbf{P}_1 : x \notin \mathbf{P}_2\}$, $\mathbf{Y}(\infty) = \mathbf{P}_1 \setminus \mathbf{P}_2$, or $\mathbf{Y}(\infty) = \mathbf{P}_1 - \mathbf{P}_2$, i.e., $\mathbf{P}_1$ *minus* $\mathbf{P}_2$.

II Local rules

$$u_{ij}(0) \qquad x_{ij}(0) \qquad \rightarrow y_{ij}(\infty)$$

1. white pixel $\in \mathbf{P}_2$ white pixel $\in \mathbf{P}_1 \rightarrow$ white
2. black pixel $\in \mathbf{P}_2$ white pixel $\in \mathbf{P}_1 \rightarrow$ white
3. black pixel $\in \mathbf{P}_2$ black pixel $\in \mathbf{P}_1 \rightarrow$ white
4. white pixel $\in \mathbf{P}_2$ black pixel $\in \mathbf{P}_1 \rightarrow$ black

III Examples

EXAMPLE 3.24: Image size: 15×15

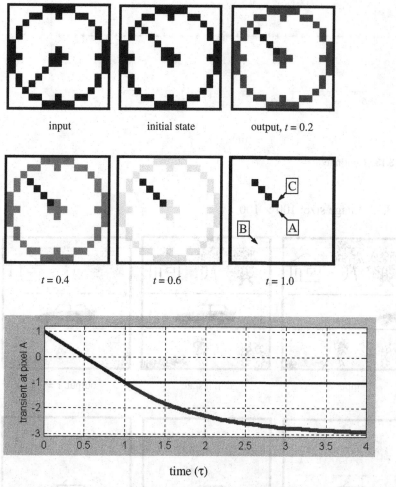

Fig. 3.13. Cell state and output transients for 40 equidistant time steps (0.1) at three different locations in the image of example 1. The origin $(0, 0)$ is the lower left corner. The pixel locations: $A(7, 7)$, $B(5, 3)$, $C(7, 8)$. Normalized time unit $t_u = t_{\text{CNN}}$. ——: state variable x_{ij}; ——: output variable y_{ij}; ***: output and state are the same.

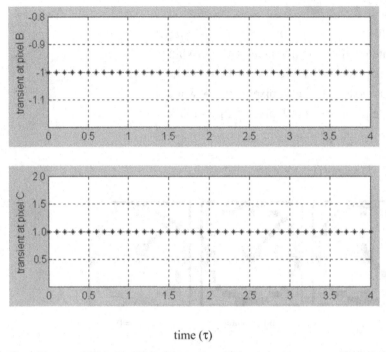

time (τ)

Fig. 3.13. Continued.

EXAMPLE 3.25: Image size: 100×100

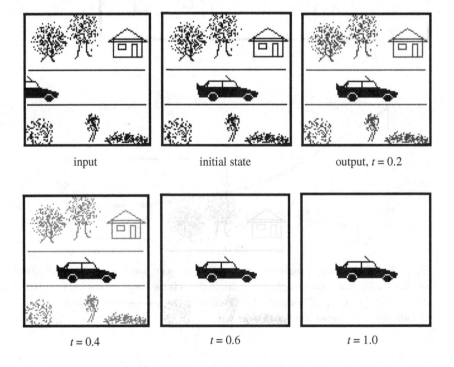

IV Mathematical analysis (for LOGDIF)

Since $s_{00} = a_{00} - 1 = 0$ and $w_{ij} = -1 - u_{ij}$, $u_{ij} \in \{-1, 1\}$, only the two shifted DP plots shown in Figs 3.14(a) and 3.14(b) need to be considered.

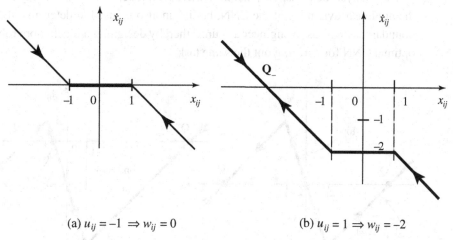

(a) $u_{ij} = -1 \Rightarrow w_{ij} = 0$ (b) $u_{ij} = 1 \Rightarrow w_{ij} = -2$

Fig. 3.14. Shifted DP plots for the LOGDIF CNN for $a_{00} = 1$ where $u_{ij} = -1$ and $u_{ij} = 1$, respectively.

Consider first the case when $u_{ij} = -1$ (i.e., pixel in P_2 is white). It follows from the dynamic route in Fig. 3.14(a) that if:

(a) $x_{ij}(0) = -1$ (white), then $y_{ij}(\infty) = -1$ (white), which is *Local rule 1*.
(b) $x_{ij}(0) = 1$ (black), then $y_{ij}(\infty) = 1$ (black), which is *Local rule 4*.

Consider next the case when $u_{ij} = 1$ (i.e., pixel in P_2 is black). It follows from the dynamic route in Fig. 3.14(b) that if:

(a) $x_{ij}(0) = -1$ (white), then $y_{ij}(\infty) = -1$ (white), which is *Local rule 2*.
(b) $x_{ij}(0) = 1$ (black), then $y_{ij}(\infty) = -1$ (white), which is *Local rule 3*.

Remarks
Unlike the preceding LOGNOT CNN where both equilibrium points are locally stable (for binary inputs) in the usual sense, the left equilibrium point $x_{ij} = -1$ in the LOGDIF CNN is locally stable in an "unusual" sense, even for binary inputs (in this case, for $u_{ij} = -1$). Here, any perturbation of the initial condition towards the origin will cause the output to be in gray scale (i.e., $-1 < y_{ij}(\infty) < 1$). This is because any point $x_{ij}(0)$ on the unit interval $[-1, 1]$ is an equilibrium point of this CNN when $u_{ij} = -1$, and will therefore remain dormant wherever the initial state $x_{ij}(0)$ lies, so long as $x_{ij}(0) \in (-1, 1)$.

To overcome this "sensitivity-to-initial-condition" drawback, we only need to enlarge the center feedback synaptic weight from $a_{00} = 1$ to any value satisfying

$1 < a_{00} < 3$. Observe that this CNN will not function correctly if $a_{00} > 3$ because in this case the shifted DP plots in Fig. 3.15, drawn for $a_{00} = 4.0$, would *violate Local rule 3*.

This analysis demonstrates that the shifted DP plot can be used not only for studying the nonlinear dynamics of the CNN, but it can also be used to determine its "failure" boundary, as well as to engineer a "cure," thereby designing a much more robust if not optimal CNN for carrying out the same task.

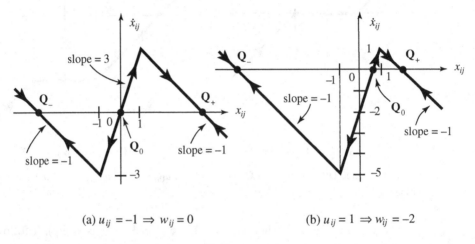

(a) $u_{ij} = -1 \Rightarrow w_{ij} = 0$ (b) $u_{ij} = 1 \Rightarrow w_{ij} = -2$

Fig. 3.15. Shifted DP plot for the case $a_{00} = 4$.

3.3.8   SHIFT: Translation (by 1 pixel-unit) template

$$
\mathbf{A} = \begin{array}{|c|c|c|} \hline 0 & 0 & 0 \\ \hline 0 & 1 & 0 \\ \hline 0 & 0 & 0 \\ \hline \end{array}
\quad
\mathbf{B} = \begin{array}{|c|c|c|} \hline b_{-1,-1} & b_{-1,0} & b_{-1,1} \\ \hline b_{0,-1} & b_{0,0} & b_{0,1} \\ \hline b_{1,-1} & b_{1,0} & b_{1,1} \\ \hline \end{array}
\quad
z = \boxed{0}
$$

where the input template $\mathbf{B}$ is chosen from one of eight possibilities corresponding to the eight compass directions shown in Fig. 3.16.

I Global task[3]

Given: static binary image $\mathbf{P}$

Input: $\mathbf{U}(t) = \mathbf{P}$

Initial state: $\mathbf{X}(0) = 0$

Boundary conditions: $y_{kl} = -1$, $u_{kl} = -1$ for all boundary "virtual" cells $C(k, l)$.

Output: $\mathbf{Y}(t) \to \mathbf{Y}(\infty) = \mathbf{P}(x - \alpha, y - \beta) =$ translation of the input image $\mathbf{P}$ by one pixel unit along one of eight compass directions (α, β), where $\alpha, \beta \in \{-1, 0, 1\}$, and (x, y) denotes the Cartesian coordinate of any pixel of $\mathbf{P}$.

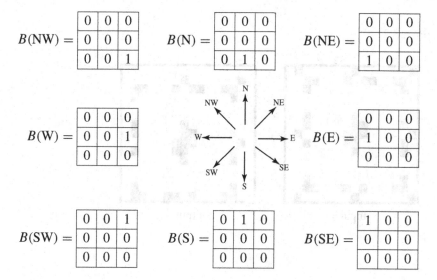

Fig. 3.16. Input templates for translating an image by one-pixel unit along the indicated directions.

II Local rules

$$u_{ij}(0) \rightarrow y_{ij}(\infty)$$

1   arbitrary $(-1$ or $1) \rightarrow 1$ (black) if $u_{i+\alpha, j+\beta} = 1$

2   arbitrary $(-1$ or $1) \rightarrow -1$ (white) if $u_{i+\alpha, j+\beta} = -1$.

III Examples

EXAMPLE 3.26: Image size: 15×15

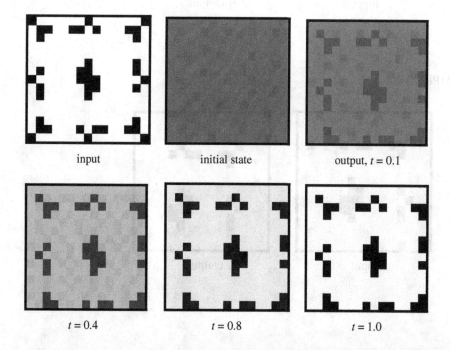

input   initial state   output, $t = 0.1$

$t = 0.4$ $t = 0.8$ $t = 1.0$

EXAMPLE 3.27:

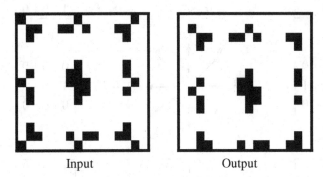

Input   Output

EXAMPLE 3.28:

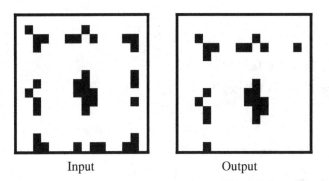

Input   Output

EXAMPLE 3.29:

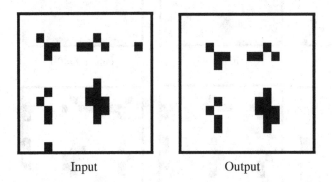

Input   Output

EXAMPLE 3.30:

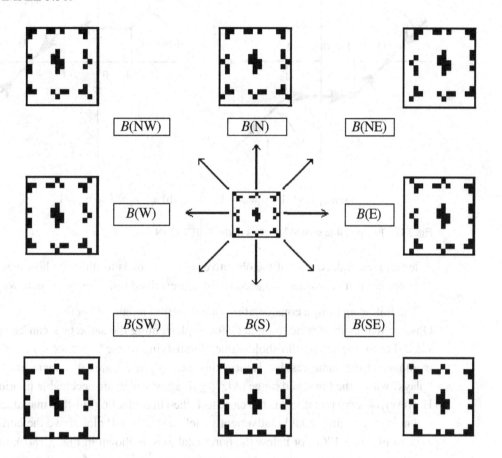

IV Mathematical analysis (for SHIFT template)

Observe that the middle segment of the shifted DP plot is horizontal because $s_{00} = a_{00} - 1 = 0$. Since $b_{kl} = 0$ except when $kl = i + \alpha, j + \beta$, we have

$$w_{ij} = 0 + \sum_{\substack{C(k,l) \in S_1(i,j) \\ kl \neq i+\alpha, j+\beta}} 0 \times u_{kl} + u_{i+\alpha, j+\beta} = u_{i+\alpha, j+\beta} \qquad (3.20)$$

Hence, for binary inputs, only the two shifted DP plots shown in Fig. 3.17 are possible. In Fig. 3.17(a), $y_{ij}(\infty) = -1$ (white) if $u_{i+\alpha, j+\beta} = -1$ (white), regardless of the neighborhood pixels (Local rule 2). Conversely, Fig. 3.17(b) shows that $y_{ij}(\infty) = 1$ (black) if $u_{i+\alpha, j+\beta} = 1$ (black) if $u_{i+\alpha, j+\beta} = 1$ (Local rule 1).

Remarks

1 For binary inputs, the SHIFT CNN will operate correctly for *arbitrary* initial states.

2 The eight templates in Fig. 3.16 are not found in the original template library. They were "synthesized" here for pedagogical purposes, using the shifted DP plot

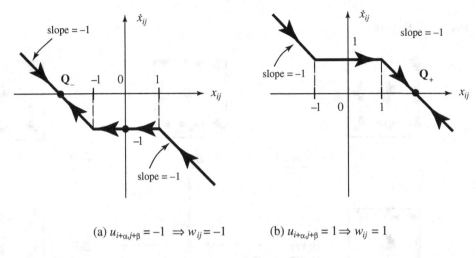

(a) $u_{i+\alpha, j+\beta} = -1 \Rightarrow w_{ij} = -1$ (b) $u_{i+\alpha, j+\beta} = 1 \Rightarrow w_{ij} = 1$

Fig. 3.17. Two possible shifted DP plots of the SHIFT CNN.

techniques. Indeed, one of the objectives of this book is to illustrate how new CNN templates can be invented to accomplish a prescribed task in a systematic way.

The following design considerations are therefore rather instructive.
Observe that many distinct templates for implementing the same task can be synthesized. For example, any threshold value z^* satisfying $0 < z^* \leq 1$, or $-1 < z^* < 0$, would yield the same results. Hence, this example illustrates that there are lots of "plays" within the threshold range of $|z^*| \leq 1$, all of which are acceptable in principle. However, observe that if $|z^*|$ is too close to 1, then imperfections in chip manufacturing technology, or aging, could inadvertently yield a shifted DP plot above the horizontal axis, as in Fig. 3.18(a), or below the horizontal axis as shown in Fig. 3.18(b), thereby resulting in operating failures. Consequently, our choice of $z^* = 0$ represents an optimal choice in so far as robustness with respect to variations in z is concerned.

Let us investigate next the robustness issue with respect to the value of the self-feedback synaptic weight a_{00}. Consider first the case where $a_{00} \leq 1$, as shown in Fig. 3.19(a) for $u_{i+\alpha, j+\beta} = -1$, and in Fig. 3.19(b) for $u_{i+\alpha, j+\beta} = 1$, respectively. Observe that the CNN will still operate correctly in the case where $0 < a_{00} \leq 1$. However, when $a_{00} < 0$, the left equilibrium point $\mathbf{Q}_-$ in Fig. 3.19(a), or the right equilibrium point $\mathbf{Q}_+$ in Fig. 3.19(b), lies inside the unit interval $(-1, 1)$, and hence the output is no longer binary since $|y_{ij}| = |x_{ij}| < 1$ in this case.

Consider next the shifted DP plots shown in Figs 3.20(a) and 3.20(b) where $a_{00} > 1$. In this case, the CNN will still operate correctly so long as $a_{00} < 2$. However, observe that when $a_{00} > 2$, the CNN becomes bistable and a spurious initial condition could cause the trajectory in Fig. 3.20(a) to switch to $\mathbf{Q}_+$, or in Fig. 3.20(b) to switch to $\mathbf{Q}_-$, thereby causing an incorrect operation in either case.

3 The 3×3 SHIFT CNN template in Fig. 3.16 can translate an input image by only

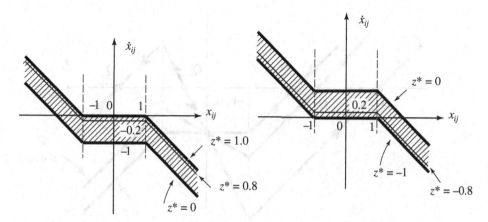

(a) Shifted DP plot for $z^* \in (0,1]$
lies inside the shaded area.

(b) Shifted DP plot for $z^* \in [-1,0)$
lies inside the shaded area.

Fig. 3.18. Shifted DP plots for $u_{i+\alpha,j+\beta} = -1$ and $u_{i+\alpha,j+\beta} = 1$.

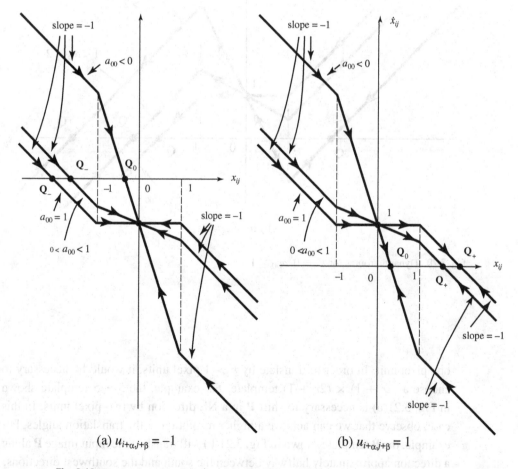

(a) $u_{i+\alpha,j+\beta} = -1$

(b) $u_{i+\alpha,j+\beta} = 1$

Fig. 3.19. Dynamic routes for $z^* = 0$, $a_{00} \leq 1$.

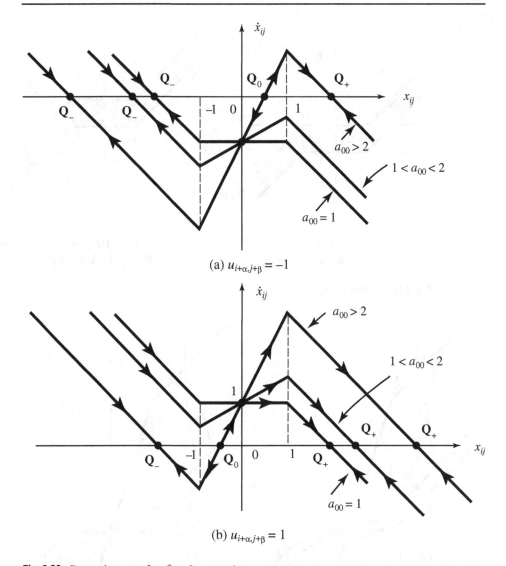

(a) $u_{i+\alpha,j+\beta} = -1$

(b) $u_{i+\alpha,j+\beta} = 1$

Fig. 3.20. Dynamic routes for $z^* = 0$, $a_{00} \geq 1$.

one pixel unit. In order to translate by $r > 1$ pixel units, it would be necessary to choose a $(2r + 1) \times (2r + 1)$ template. For example, the 5×5 template shown in Fig. 3.21(a) is necessary to shift **P** in a NE direction by two pixel units. In this case, observe that we can achieve a higher resolution in the translation angles. For example, the **B** template shown in Fig. 3.21(b) will translate the input image **P** along a direction approximately halfway between the south and the southwest directions.

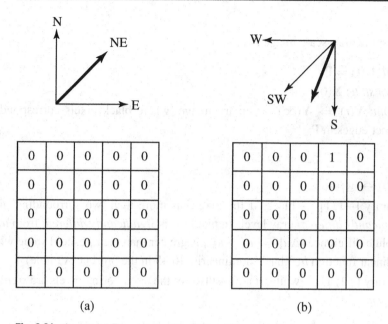

(a)   (b)

Fig. 3.21. Two 5 ×5 **B** templates for shifting **P** by two pixel units to north and west and by two pixel units to south and one pixel unit to west, respectively.

3.3.9   CONTOUR-1: Contour detection template

$$\mathbf{A} = \begin{array}{|c|c|c|} \hline 0 & 0 & 0 \\ \hline 0 & 2 & 0 \\ \hline 0 & 0 & 0 \\ \hline \end{array} \quad \mathbf{B} = \begin{array}{|c|c|c|} \hline b & b & b \\ \hline b & 0 & b \\ \hline b & b & b \\ \hline \end{array} \quad z = \boxed{4.7}$$

b is defined by the following nonlinear function $b(\cdot)$ of $\Delta u = u_{ij} - u_{kl}$ (due to symmetry of Δu we can write $u_{kl} - u_{ij}$ equivalently):

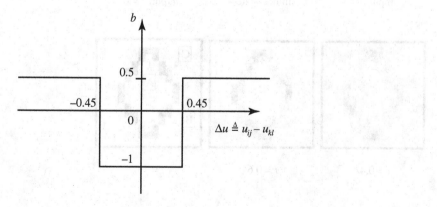

Fig. 3.22.

I Global task

Given: static gray-scale image **P**

Input: $\mathbf{U}(t) = \mathbf{P}$

Initial state: $\mathbf{X}(0) = 0$

Output: $\mathbf{Y}(t) \Rightarrow \mathbf{Y}(\infty) = $ binary image, where black pixels correspond to the sharper edges in **P**

II Local rules

$u_{ij}(0) \rightarrow y_{ij}(\infty)$

1 arbitrary $[-1, 1] \rightarrow$ black, if the pixel has more than two surrounding pixels of *significantly different* gray levels (a pixel u_{kl} is *significantly different* from u_{ij} if the absolute difference $|\Delta u| = |u_{ij} - u_{kl}|$ is greater than the threshold value where the nonlinear function $b(\cdot)$ has a nonlinearity (0.45 in the present example)

2 arbitrary $[-1, 1] \rightarrow$ white, if at most two of the neighboring pixels are *significantly different*

III Examples

EXAMPLE 3.31: Contour detection (image size: 15×15)

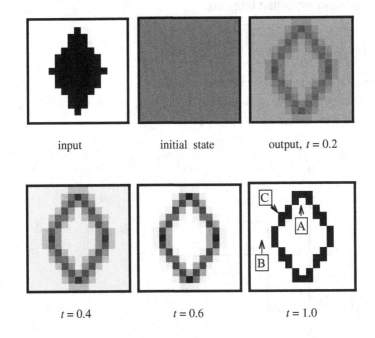

input   initial state   output, $t = 0.2$

$t = 0.4$ $t = 0.6$ $t = 1.0$

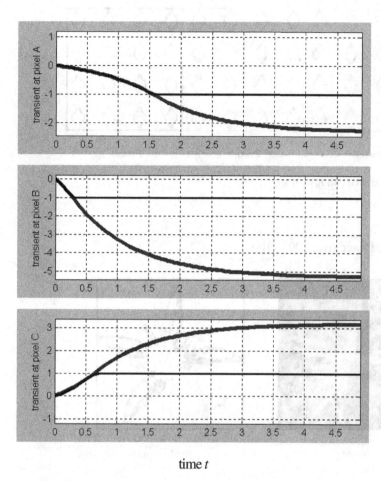

time t

Fig. 3.23. State and output transients for 50 equidistant time steps at three different locations in the image of example 3.31.

EXAMPLE 3.32: Image size: 100×100

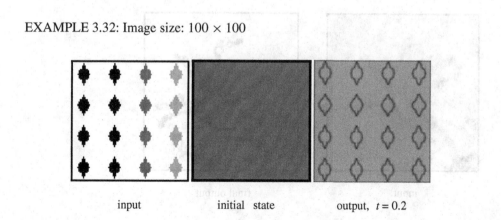

input   initial state   output, $t = 0.2$

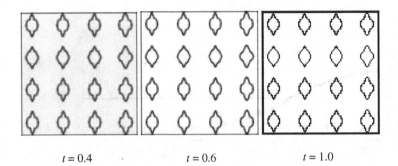

$$t = 0.4 \qquad\qquad t = 0.6 \qquad\qquad t = 1.0$$

Normalized time unit $t_u = \tau_{\text{CNN}}$.

EXAMPLE 3.33: Image size: 100×100

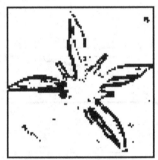

input   final output

EXAMPLE 3.34: Realistic scene

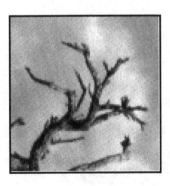

input   final output

IV Mathematical analysis (for CONTOUR-1 template)
State and output equation

$$\dot{x}_{ij} = g_{ij}(x_{ij}) + w_{ij} \stackrel{\Delta}{=} h_{ij}(x_{ij}; w_{ij})$$
$$w_{ij} = f(x_{ij})$$

where

$$g_{ij}(x_{ij}) = -x_{ij} + a_{00}f(x_{ij})$$
$$= -x_{ij} + 2f(x_{ij})$$
$$= -x_{ij} + |x_{ij} + 1| + |x_{ij} - 1|$$

$$w_{ij} = 4.7 + b(u_{ij} - u_{i+1,j-1}) + b(u_{ij} - u_{i+1,j}) + b(u_{ij} - u_{i+1,j+1})$$
$$+ b(u_{ij} - u_{i,j-1}) + b(u_{ij} - u_{i,j+1}) + b(u_{ij} - u_{i-1,j-1})$$
$$+ b(u_{ij} - u_{i-1,j}) + b(u_{ij} - u_{i-1,j+1})$$
$$= 4.7 - p_s + 0.5p_d$$
$$= 4.7 - (8 - p_d) + 0.5p_d$$

Hence

$$w_{ij} = -3.3 + 1.5p_d \qquad (3.21)$$

where

p_s = number of approximately similar pixels (i.e., $|\Delta u| \le 0.45$)

p_d = number of significantly different pixels (i.e., $|\Delta u| > 0.45$)

The shifted DP plots corresponding to the two most stringent situations are shown in Fig. 3.24. Since the shifted DP plot for the case of three or more significantly different

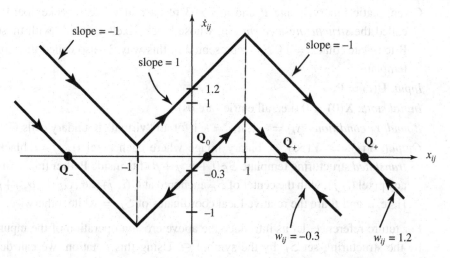

Fig. 3.24. Two shifted DP plots corresponding to $p_d = 3$ ($w_{ij} = 1.2$) and $p_d = 2$ ($w_{ij} = -0.3$).

gray pixels is obtained by simply translating the *upper* DP plot of Fig. 3.24 upwards, all trajectories must converge to the globally asymptotically stable equilibrium point $\mathbf{Q}_+$, thereby resulting in a *black* output pixel (Local rule 1). For two or less significantly different gray pixels, the shifted DP plot is obtained by translating the *lower* DP plot of Fig. 3.24 downwards. In this case, all trajectories originating from $x_{ij}(0) = 0$ must converge to the "left" equilibrium point $\mathbf{Q}_-$, thereby resulting in a *white* output pixel (Local rule 2).

Remarks:

A comparison of the output image from Example 3.34 (noisy image) with the output image obtained by our earlier *EDGE* template, or *EDGEGRAY* template (for the same input image) shows a significantly superior result with the *CONTOUR-1 template*. Observe that most of the annoying "noise" pixels from our earlier examples have been eliminated. Hence, the CONTOUR-1 CNN is capable of not only extracting the sharper edges from an image, but also simultaneously "filtering" out the "noisy" pixels. This is our first example which illustrates how "nonlinearity" can be used to achieve superior image-processing tasks found wanting by classical techniques.

3.3.10   EROSION: Peel-if-it-doesn't-fit Template

$$\mathbf{A} = \begin{array}{|c|c|c|} \hline 0 & 0 & 0 \\ \hline 0 & 2 & 0 \\ \hline 0 & 0 & 0 \\ \hline \end{array} \quad \mathbf{B} = \begin{array}{|c|c|c|} \hline b_{-1,-1} & b_{-1,0} & b_{-1,1} \\ \hline b_{0,-1} & b_{0,0} & b_{0,1} \\ \hline b_{1,-1} & b_{1,0} & b_{1,1} \\ \hline \end{array}$$

where $b_{kl} = 0$ or 1 (not all zeros), $z_E = 0.5 - p_1$, and $p_1 =$ total number of 1s in the **B** template, $p_1 > 0$.

I Global task

Given: static binary image **P** and a 3×3 black and white (checkerboard) pattern called the *structuring element* $\mathcal{S}_E$, whose black pixels coincide with those in the **B** template (black = 1). $\mathcal{S}_E$, represented in this way, is also called the structuring template

Input: $\mathbf{U}(t) = \mathbf{P}$

Initial state: $\mathbf{X}(0) = 0$ (i.e., all entries are 0s)

Boundary conditions: $y_{kl} = -1$, $u_{kl} = -1$ for all "virtual" boundary cells $C(k, l)$

Output: $\mathbf{Y}(t) \Rightarrow \mathbf{Y}(\infty) =$ binary image where each pixel $(i, j) =$ black, if the *translated* structuring template $\mathcal{S}_E(i + \alpha, j + \beta)$ fits inside **P** after translating $\mathcal{S}_E$ to any pixel (i, j), with the center of $\mathcal{S}_E$ anchored at $C(i, j)$ (i.e., $\mathcal{S}_E(i + \alpha, j + \beta) \subset \mathbf{P}$) Here, α and β are the relative local coordinates of $\mathcal{S}_E =$ white, otherwise.

For future reference, let us introduce the above erosion operation of the input picture by the structuring set $\mathcal{S}_E$ by the symbol $\ominus$. Using this notation, we can define the global task exactly via the following set-theoretic identity

$$\mathbf{Y}(\infty) = \mathbf{P} \ominus \mathcal{S}_E = \{x : \mathcal{S}_E + x \subset \mathbf{P}\} \tag{3.22}$$

where

$$\mathcal{S}_E + x = \{p + x : p \in \mathcal{S}_E\} \tag{3.23}$$

is the translation of the set $\mathcal{S}_E$ to $x \in \mathcal{S}_E$.

II Local rules

$$u_{ij}(0) \rightarrow y_{ij}(\infty)$$

1 arbitrary (black or white) $\rightarrow$ black if $\mathcal{S}_E(i + \alpha, j + \beta) \subset \mathbf{P}$

2 arbitrary (black or white) $\rightarrow$ white if $\mathcal{S}_E(i + \alpha, j + \beta) \not\subset \mathbf{P}$ (i.e., the translated structuring template does *not fit* completely inside $\mathbf{P}$)

III Examples

Since the input template **B** of the EROSION CNN is defined via the structuring template $\mathcal{S}_E$, and, since there are 2^9 distinct combinations of 3×3 Boolean (black-and-white) patterns, there are 2^9 distinct 3×3 structuring elements, and hence 2^9 distinct EROSION templates. Since many of the templates are quite useful for *morphological*[5] image-processing applications, we will give several such templates and illustrate their "sculpturing" properties. In particular (e.g., when the center pixel of $\mathcal{S}_E$ is black), the output image $\mathbf{Y}(\infty)$ of an EROSION CNN will be a proper subset of the input image $\mathbf{P}$, obtained by "peeling off" one or more black pixels (i.e., change black to white) located on the boundaries of $\mathbf{P}$. Which pixels to peel off are determined by "$\mathcal{S}_E$"; hence the reason for the name *structuring element*. Indeed, it is useful to think of $\mathcal{S}_E$ as a "scalpel" which can be used to "chip" away selected pixels of a given pattern, thereby changing its shape. It is this "scalping" property of the structuring template that makes the EROSION CNN a powerful morphological tool in nonlinear image processing. The following examples of EROSION **B** templates, coded by $\mathbf{B}[E_j]$ for future reference, constitute a basic scalping toolkit for morphological image sculptors.

EXAMPLE 3.35: Image size: 15×15

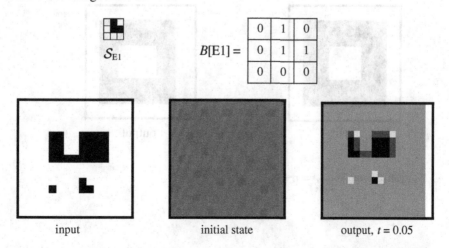

| input | initial state | output, $t = 0.05$ |

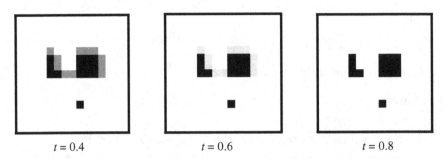

$t = 0.4$ $t = 0.6$ $t = 0.8$

Image size in the following examples: 15×15

EXAMPLE 3.36:

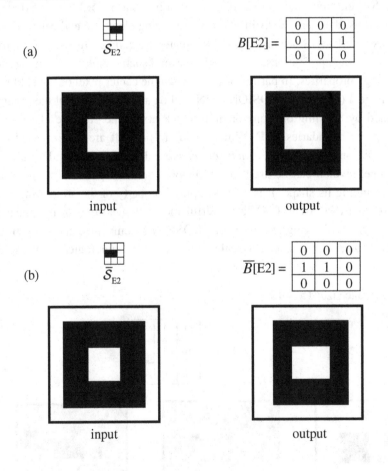

Normalized time unit $t_u = \tau_{\text{CNN}}$.

EXAMPLE 3.37:

$\mathcal{S}_{E3}$

$B[E3] =$

0	0	0
0	1	0
0	1	0

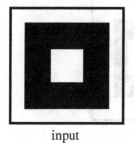

input

output

EXAMPLE 3.38:

$\mathcal{S}_{E4}$

$B[E4] =$

1	0	1
0	0	0
1	0	1

input

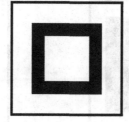

output

EXAMPLE 3.39:

$\mathcal{S}_{E5}$

$B[E5] =$

0	1	0
1	0	1
0	1	0

input

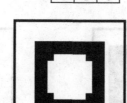

output

EXAMPLE 3.40:

$\mathcal{S}_{\text{E6}}$

$B[\text{E6}] =$

0	1	0
1	1	1
0	1	0

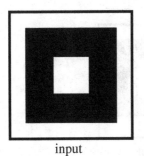
input

output

EXAMPLE 3.41:

$\mathcal{S}_{\text{E8}}$

$B[\text{E8}] =$

1	0	0
0	0	0
0	0	1

input

output

EXAMPLE 3.42:

$\mathcal{S}_{\text{E9}}$

$B[\text{E9}] =$

0	0	1
0	1	0
1	0	0

input

output

EXAMPLE 3.43:

(a)
$\mathcal{S}_{E10a}$

$B[\text{E}10a] =$

0	0	0
0	0	1
0	1	0

input

output

(b)
$\mathcal{S}_{E10b}$

$B[\text{E}10b] =$

0	0	0
0	1	1
0	1	0

input

output

EXAMPLE 3.44:

$\mathcal{S}_{E11}$

$B[\text{E}11] =$

0	0	0
0	0	1
0	0	0

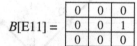

input

output

IV Mathematical analysis (for EROSION)

Observe first that since $s_{00} = a_{00} - 1 = 1$, the central segment of the shifted DP plot has a positive unit slope.

Consider the case when the set of black pixels in the 3×3 neighborhood of pixel $C(i, j)$ of the input image **P** contains all p_1 black pixels of the structuring template S_E as a subset. In this case

$$w_{ij} = z_E + \sum_{kl \in \{-1,0,1\}} b_{kl} u_{kl} = (0.5 - p_1) + 1(p_1) = 0.5$$

independent of the number p_1 of black pixels in S_E. The shifted DP plot in this case is shown by the upper curve in Fig. 3.25. It follows from the associated dynamic route that all trajectories starting from $x_{ij}(0) = 0$ must converge to $\mathbf{Q}_+$. Hence, $y_{ij}(\infty) = 1$ whenever the translated structuring template $S_E(i + \alpha, j + \beta)$ fits *inside* **P** (Local rule 1).

For the case when at least one black pixel of S_E coincides with the white pixel in **P** we have

$$w_{ij} = z_E + \sum_{kl \in \{-1,0,1\}} b_{kl} u_{kl} = (0.5 - p_1) + 1(p_b) - 1(\hat{p}_1) \leq -1.5$$

where p_b denotes the number of coincident black pixels in **P** and S_E, $\hat{p}_1$ is the number of coincident white pixels in **P** and S_E. Since $p_b < p_1$ in this case (by assumption) and $\hat{p}_1 \geq 1$, hence $p_b - p_1 \leq -1$ and for $1 \leq p_b \leq 9$, it follows that $w_{ij} \leq -1.5$. The lower dynamic route in Fig. 3.25 represents, therefore, the most stringent case that needs to be considered. Hence, we have $y_{ij}(\infty) = -1$ (Local rule 2).

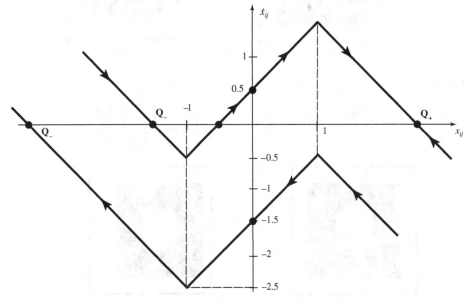

Fig. 3.25. Dynamic routes for the case $S_E(i + \alpha, j + \beta) \subset \mathbf{P}$ (upper curve) and the case $S_E(i + \alpha, j + \beta) \not\subset \mathbf{P}$ (lower curve).

For some values of p_1, p_b, and $\hat{p}_1$, we show the values of w_{ij} below in Table 3.3.

Table 3.3.

Number of black pixels in $\mathcal{S}_E$	Coincident pixels in **P** $\mathcal{S}_E$			Stable	
p_1	p_b	$\hat{p}_1$	w_{ij}	state Q	Local rule number
3	3	0	0.5	Q_+	1
	2	1	−1.5	Q_-	2
	1	2	−3.5	Q_-	2
	0	3	−5.5	Q_-	2
2	2	0	0.5	Q_+	1
	1	1	−1.5	Q_-	2
	0	2	−3.5	Q_-	2

3.3.11 DILATION: Grow-until-it-fits template

$$
\mathbf{A} = \begin{array}{|c|c|c|}
\hline
0 & 0 & 0 \\
\hline
0 & 2 & 0 \\
\hline
0 & 0 & 0 \\
\hline
\end{array}
\qquad
\mathbf{B} = \begin{array}{|c|c|c|}
\hline
b_{-1,-1} & b_{-1,0} & b_{-1,1} \\
\hline
b_{0,-1} & b_{0,0} & b_{0,1} \\
\hline
b_{1,-1} & b_{1,0} & b_{1,1} \\
\hline
\end{array}
\qquad
z = \boxed{z_D}
$$

where $b_{kl} = 0$ or 1, $z_D = p_1 - 0.5$, and $p_1 =$ total number of 1s in the **B** template, $p_1 > 0$.

I Global task

Given: static binary image **P** and a 3×3 black and white (checkerboard) pattern called the *structuring element* or its 0–1 representation of the structuring template $\mathcal{S}_D$. The structuring template is related to **B** by a $180°$ rotation with respect to the origin.

Input: $\mathbf{U}(t) = \mathbf{P}$

Initial state: $\mathbf{X}(0) = 0$ (i.e., all entries are 0s)

Boundary conditions: $y_{kl} = -1$, $u_{kl} = -1$ for all "virtual" boundary cells $C(k, l)$

Output: $\mathbf{Y}(t) \Rightarrow \mathbf{Y}(\infty) =$ binary image generated as follows:

step 1. To each *black* pixel $C_b(ij) \in \mathbf{P}$ located at coordinates (i, j) translate the structuring template $\mathcal{S}_D$ and anchor it at $C_b(ij)$. Denote this translated set of black pixels by $\mathcal{S}_D(ij)$.

step 2. Take the set-theoretic *union* of $\mathcal{S}_D(ij)$ over all *black* pixels $C_b(ij)$ of **P**:

$$
\mathbf{Y}(\infty) = \bigcup_{\substack{\text{all } (ij)\text{ such} \\ \text{that } u_{ij}=1}} \mathcal{S}_D(ij)
$$

Remarks 1:

For future references, let us denote the above *dilation* operation of the input picture **P** by the structuring set $\mathcal{S}_D$ by the symbol $\oplus$. Using this notation, we can define the global task via the following set-theoretic identity:

$$\mathbf{Y}(\infty) = P \oplus \mathcal{S}_D = \bigcup_{\text{over all } x \in P} \{\mathcal{S}_D + x : x \in P\} \tag{3.24}$$

where

$$\mathcal{S}_D + x = \{p + x : p \in \mathcal{S}_D\} \tag{3.25}$$

is the translation of the set $\mathcal{S}_D$ to $x \in \mathcal{S}_D$.

Observe that if we code the pixels of the set $\mathcal{S}_D$ by "black = 1" and "white = 0," then, having the structuring template $\mathcal{S}_D$, the resulting **B** template is a reflection of $\mathcal{S}_D$ with respect to the origin, i.e., by a 180° rotation. Hence $\mathcal{S}_D$ and **B** are related by a 180° rotation.

II Local rules

$$u_{ij}(0) \rightarrow y_{ij}(\infty)$$

1 black $\rightarrow$ black if all eight nearest neighbors of $C(i, j)$ are black

2 black $\rightarrow$ black if $b_{00} = 1$ (equivalently, if the central pixel of the structuring template $\mathcal{S}_D$ is black)

3 arbitrary $\rightarrow$ black, if there is at least one nearest neighbor $C(i + \alpha, j + \beta)$ of $(-1 \text{ or } 1)$ $C(i, j)$ whose color is black *and* if the color code of the corresponding pixel $b_{\alpha\beta}$ of the **B** template (at the same relative position (α, β)) is also black, i.e., $u_{i+\alpha, j+\beta} = 1$ *and* $b_{\alpha\beta} = 1$

4 arbitrary $\rightarrow$ white, if there is no nearest neighborhood of $(-1 \text{ or } 1)$ $C(ij)$ with the above property

III Examples

Image size in the following examples: 15×15.

EXAMPLE 3.45:

$\mathcal{S}_{D1}$

$B[D1] = \begin{array}{|c|c|c|} \hline 0 & 0 & 0 \\ \hline 1 & 1 & 0 \\ \hline 0 & 1 & 0 \\ \hline \end{array}$

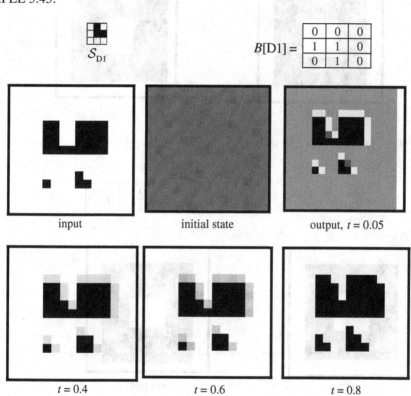

input   initial state   output, $t = 0.05$

$t = 0.4$ $t = 0.6$ $t = 0.8$

EXAMPLE 3.46:

(a)

$\mathcal{S}_{D2}$

$B[D2] = \begin{array}{|c|c|c|} \hline 0 & 0 & 0 \\ \hline 1 & 1 & 0 \\ \hline 0 & 0 & 0 \\ \hline \end{array}$

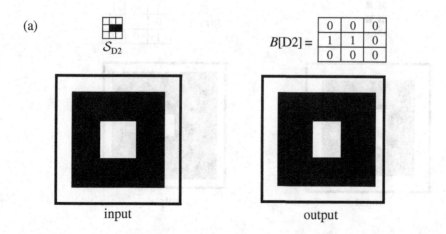

input   output

(b)

$\mathcal{S}_{\text{D2}}$

$B[\text{D2}] = \begin{array}{|c|c|c|} \hline 0 & 0 & 0 \\ \hline 0 & 1 & 1 \\ \hline 0 & 0 & 0 \\ \hline \end{array}$

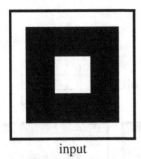

input

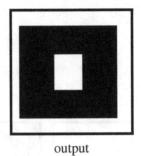

output

Normalized time unit $t_u = \tau_{\text{CNN}}$.

EXAMPLE 3.47:

$\mathcal{S}_{\text{D3}}$

$B[\text{D3}] = \begin{array}{|c|c|c|} \hline 0 & 1 & 0 \\ \hline 0 & 1 & 0 \\ \hline 0 & 0 & 0 \\ \hline \end{array}$

input

output

EXAMPLE 3.48:

$\mathcal{S}_{\text{D4}}$

$B[\text{D4}] = \begin{array}{|c|c|c|} \hline 1 & 0 & 1 \\ \hline 0 & 0 & 0 \\ \hline 1 & 0 & 1 \\ \hline \end{array}$

input

output

EXAMPLE 3.49:

$\mathcal{S}_{D5}$

$B[D5] = $

0	1	0
1	0	1
0	1	0

input

output

EXAMPLE 3.50:

$\mathcal{S}_{D6}$

$B[D6] = $

0	1	0
1	1	1
0	1	0

input

output

EXAMPLE 3.51:

$\mathcal{S}_{D7}$

$B[D7] = $

0	0	0
0	0	0
1	0	0

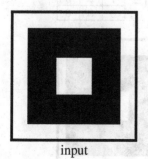

input

output

EXAMPLE 3.52:

$\mathcal{S}_{\text{D8}}$

$B[\text{D8}] =$

1	0	0
0	0	0
0	0	1

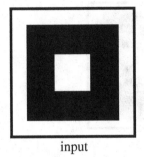

input

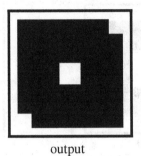

output

EXAMPLE 3.53:

$\mathcal{S}_{\text{D9}}$

$B[\text{D9}] =$

0	0	1
0	1	0
1	0	0

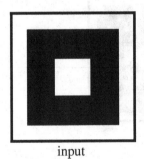

input

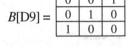

output

EXAMPLE 3.54:

(a)

$\mathcal{S}_{\text{D10a}}$

$B[\text{D10a}] =$

0	1	0
1	0	0
0	0	0

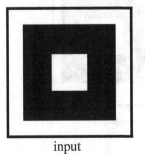

input

output

(b)

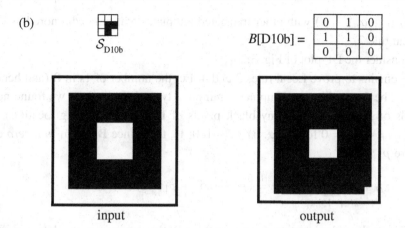

$$B[\text{D10b}] = \begin{array}{|c|c|c|} \hline 0 & 1 & 0 \\ \hline 1 & 1 & 0 \\ \hline 0 & 0 & 0 \\ \hline \end{array}$$

input   output

IV Mathematical analysis (for DILATION)

Observe first the central segment of the shifted DP plot has a positive unit slope.

If $u_{ij}(0) = 1$ and $u_{kl} = 1$ for all $kl \in \{-1, 0, 1\}$, then, since $p_1 > 0$ (by assumption), we have

$$w_{ij} = z_D + \sum_{kl \in \{-1,0,1\}} b_{kl} u_{kl} = (p_1 - 0.5) + \sum_{kl \in \{-1,0,1\}} b_{kl}$$
$$= (p_1 - 0.5) + p_1$$
$$= 2p_1 - 0.5 \geq 1.5$$

It follows from the dynamic route upper curve in Fig. 3.26 that $y_{ij}(\infty) = 1$ (Local rule 1).

If $u_{ij}(0) = 1$ and $b_{00} = 1$, i.e., both cell $C(ij)$ and the central pixel of $\mathcal{S}_D$ are black, then by anchoring $\mathcal{S}_D$ at cell $C(i, j)$, the translated set $\mathcal{S}_D(i + \alpha, j + \beta)$ has a black pixel at the location (i, j). Hence $y_{ij}(\infty) = 1$, since the set union operation

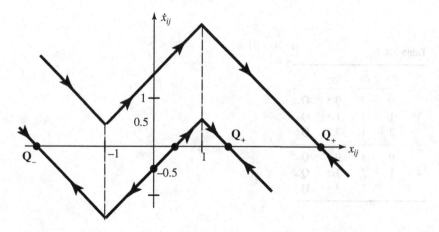

Fig. 3.26.

of $S_D(i + \alpha, j + \beta)$ with other translated templates will only add more black pixels (Local rule 2).

Consider the DP plot of Fig. 3.26.

It remains to prove Local rules 3 and 4. Let the number of 1s in **B** (and hence also in S_D) be denoted by p_1. If upon examining a typical **B** template, we found no black pixels of **P** coincide with any black pixels of **B** at corresponding locations, i.e., if $u_{i+\alpha, j+\beta} \cdot b_{\alpha\beta} = 0$ for all $(\alpha, \beta) \in \{-1, 0, 1\}$, then since **B** has p_1 *non-zero* entries, where $p_1 > 0$,

$$w_{ij} = z_D + \sum_{kl \in \{-1, 0, 1\}} b_{kl} u_{kl} = (p_1 - 0.5) + p_1(-1) = -0.5.$$

Hence, in this case, starting from $x_{ij}(0) = 0$, the dynamic route (lower shifted DP plot) shown in Fig. 3.26 must converge to $\mathbf{Q}_-$. Consequently, $C(ij)$ becomes white. This proves Local rule 4.

On the other hand, if there is at least one coincident black pixel in both **P** and **B** within the 3×3 neighborhood of $C(ij)$, then

$$w_{ij} = (p_1 - 0.5) + p_b + \hat{p}_1(-1)$$

where p_b denotes the number of coincident black pixels, $p_b \geq 1$, and $\hat{p}_1$ denotes the number of non-zero entries of **B** which do not have coincident black pixels in **P**. Clearly, since $\hat{p}_1 = p_1 - p_b$, we have

$$w_{ij} = (p_1 - 0.5) + p_b - p_1 + p_b = 2p_b - 0.5 \geq 1.5.$$

Now since $p_b \geq 1$, by assumption, the minimum of w_{ij} is 1.5, as is evident from Table 3.4 showing a few sample relationships among p_1, p_b, $\hat{p}_1$, w_{ij} and the equilibrium point where a trajectory originating from $x_{ij} = 0$ must converge.

Table 3.4.

p_1	p_b	$\hat{p}_1$	w_{ij}	**Q**
	0	3	−0.5	$\mathbf{Q}_-$
3	1	2	1.5	$\mathbf{Q}_+$
	2	1	3.5	$\mathbf{Q}_+$
	0	4	−0.5	$\mathbf{Q}_-$
4	1	3	1.5	$\mathbf{Q}_+$
	2	2	3.5	$\mathbf{Q}_+$

Observe that in all cases, we obtain $y_{ij}(\infty) = 1$, which implies *Local rule 3*.

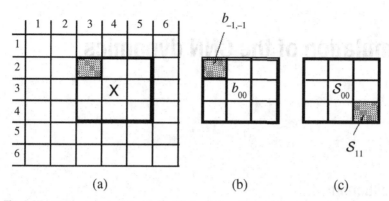

(a)   (b)   (c)

Fig. 3.27. (a) $\mathbf{P}_0$: a part of image $\mathbf{P}$; (b) the $\mathbf{B}$ template; (c) the structuring element. A typical situation satisfying Local rule 3.

Remarks 1:
Our above proof only shows that the Local rules 1–4 are a consequence of the dilation template. It is not obvious that the output image $\mathbf{Y}(\infty)$ generated by applying these local rules, or from the template directly by solving the associated ODEs, is identical to the original set-theoretic definition of the DILATION operation specified in the Global task. To show that they are indeed identical, let us consider the typical situation shown in Fig. 3.27, and pick a cell $C(ij)$, identified by "$\times$" in Fig. 3.27(a), located at $i = 3$, $j = 4$. Suppose now that there exists a nearest neighbor $(\alpha, \beta) \in \{-1, 0, +1\}$ such that $u_{i+\alpha, j+\beta} = 1$ and $b_{\alpha\beta} = 1$. A typical situation satisfying these conditions is shown in Fig. 3.27(a), where only a part $\mathbf{P}_0$ of the input image $\mathbf{P}$ is shown with the relevant rows and columns *relabeled* from 1–6 for ease of reference, and where the relevant black pixel at $(2, 3)$ is shown (the other pixels can be black or white). Here, $i = 3$, $j = 4$, $\alpha = -1$, $\beta = -1$, $u_{23} = u_{i-1, j-1} = 1$, and $b_{-1, -1} = 1$, as stipulated. Suppose the 3×3 input sub-pattern identified by rows $\{2, 3, 4\}$ and columns $\{3, 4, 5\}$ in Fig. 3.27(a) contains a black or white center pixel at location $(3, 4)$. Since $\mathbf{B}$ is obtained by a $180°$ rotation of the structuring template, and, since $b_{-1, -1} = 1$, the "reflected" pixel $\mathcal{S}_{11}$ shown in Fig. 3.27(c) must be black. Now since, by assumption, pixel $(2, 3)$ of $P_0 \subset P$ in Fig. 3.27(a) is black, we can anchor the central pixel $\mathcal{S}_{00}$ of the structuring template $\mathcal{S}_D$ of Fig. 3.27(c) at pixel location $(2, 3)$ in Fig. 3.27(a). This is redrawn in Fig. 3.27(c) as the "dash" window $\mathcal{S}_D(2, 3)$ overlapping a part of the 3×3 (shown in bold lines) input sub-pattern whose central element "$\times$" is located at position $(3, 4)$. Observe that in this case the "black" pixel $\mathcal{S}_{11}$ of $\mathcal{S}_D(2, 3)$ is located at the same position as the "black or white" center pixel $(3, 4)$ in Fig. 3.27(c). Hence, the "black or white" pixel "$\times$" must map into a "black" pixel after applying the dilation operation in view of its set "union" property, and the fact that pixel $\mathcal{S}_{11}$ of $\mathcal{S}_D$ is black.

Since the same proof above applies if the black pixel is located at any one of the seven other nearest neighbor positions, pixel $(3, 4)$ must map into black in each case (Local rule 3).

4 Simulation of the CNN dynamics

Introduction

There are many ways the CNN dynamics can be analyzed and simulated or solved:

- mathematical analysis of qualitative behavior and numerical methods to calculate the quantitative results, i.e. the signal values at well-defined time instances (usually at equidistant time sequences),
- software simulators using one of the numerical methods for solving the set of ODEs of CNN dynamics,
- multi-processor (DSP) digital emulators, hardware accelerator boards, to speed up the software simulators,
- continuous-time physical implementation of the CNN dynamics in the form of programmable analog VLSI chips,
- living organs which reflect the CNN dynamics (e.g. the retina or other parts of the retinotopic visual pathway).

In this chapter we will briefly review them, except the last area to be discussed in Chapter 16.

4.1 Integration of the standard CNN differential equation

The standard class 1 CNN dynamics with space-invariant templates is described by

$$\dot{x}_{ij} = -x_{ij} + \sum_{k=-r}^{r} \sum_{l=-r}^{r} a_{kl} y_{i+k,j+l} + \sum_{k=-r}^{r} \sum_{l=-r}^{r} b_{kl} u_{i+k,j+l} + z$$

$$y(x_{kl}) = f(x_{kl})$$

$$x_{ij}(0) = x_{ij0} \tag{4.1}$$

where a and b are the elements of the space invariant template matrices $\mathbf{A}$ and $\mathbf{B}$, respectively. We want to simulate the solution of these differential equations on a standard digital computer, like a PC with a Pentium microprocessor.

In general, a differential equation

$$\dot{x} = h(x; w)$$
$$x = x(t)$$
$$x(0) = x_0 \tag{4.2}$$

can be solved by standard numerical integration methods; the simplest one is the forward Euler formula which calculates the value of $x(t + \Delta t)$ from $x(t)$, Δt being the time step

$$x(t + \Delta t) \cong x(t) + \Delta t \dot{x}(t) = x(t) + \Delta t h(x(t); w) \tag{4.3}$$

(4.3) is qualitatively correct and accurate enough if we use a Δt time step small enough (in CNN we know in advance the range of dynamics of the state and its time derivatives as well).

Using (4.3) and (4.1), and using an equidistant time step sequence $0, \Delta t, 2\Delta t, \ldots,$ $m\Delta t, \ldots$ for $x(t)$ ($x(0), x(1), x(2), \ldots, x(m), \ldots$), we get from $x_{ij}(m)$ the next value $x_{ij}(m + 1)$.

$$x_{ij}((m + 1)\Delta t) \overset{\Delta}{=} x_{ij}(m + 1)$$

$$= (1 - \Delta t)x_{ij}(m) + \Delta t \sum_{k=-r}^{r} \sum_{l=-r}^{r} a_{kl} y_{i+k, j+l}(m)$$

$$+ \Delta t \sum_{k=-r}^{r} \sum_{l=-r}^{r} b_{kl} u_{i+k, j+k}(m) + \Delta t z$$

$$y(x_{kl}(m + 1)) = f(x_{kl}(m + 1)) \tag{4.4}$$

where Δt and t are defined in normalized time units, t_u; this time unit is τ_{CNN} (the "CNN time constant").

Observe that we extended the use of the integration formula (4.3) from the scalar case to the matrix case. This can easily be done since the CNN equations are very sparse. In general, a universal integration formula may not necessarily be accurate enough or even converge. Our CNN dynamics, in most practical cases, is very "mild," a $\Delta t \cong 0.1$ choice usually yields an accurate and convergent solution. In some complex cases, the "implicit" integration formula

$$x(t + \Delta t) \cong x(t) + \Delta t \dot{x}(t + \Delta t) \tag{4.5}$$

will always be stable.

4.2   Image input

There are several ways to input an image to the simulators. In case of the human eyes, each tiny cell has its own photoreceptor (light sensor). Similarly, in the cP400 CNN microprocessor chip (22 × 20 cells) each cell has its own light sensor. However, an electrical input is also provided (to interface to CCD cameras via a frame grabber, or a special on-chip interface). Using PCs or workstations, usually, the camera → frame grabber → software file is the way a given image is loaded on to a simulator.

In each case, we need a lens system to project the sharp image with appropriate illumination and size. Sometimes the transparency can directly be put on to the surface of the chip when illuminated by a lamp.

A pixel illumination level is coded in the following way: black is +1, white is −1, gray-scale values are in between. Hence, input, state, and output images can be coded.

4.3   Software simulation

The SimCNN[1] software simulator program (for multiple layers) running on a PC has *the following main functions*:

- calculates the CNN dynamics for a given template using (4.4),
- displays the input and output pictures, either by a gray-scale code or a color,
- simulates the CNN dynamics for a given sequence of templates (this option will be described later).

This simulator has its own

- template library (*.TEM files),
- subroutine library (*.CSD files), and
- picture library (*.BMP and *.IMG files).

EXAMPLE 4.1:

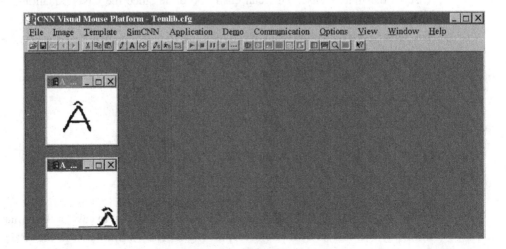

In addition to the main functions, several special services are available. SimCNN and other CNN design tools are used via the Visual Mouse Software Platform called VisMouse. VisMouse has a CNN specific window menu shown in Example 4.1. Input, state, output, and other images are shown in different windows; only one is active (highlighted) at a time (in Example 4.1, the one in the lower position).

To run a simulation using a single template placed in the template library, we have a simple, special way. We will illustrate this in the following examples.

Examples

We want to calculate the edges of a black and white image. Running the simulation for calculating the CNN dynamics for the EDGE template, first, we select the functions shown here in boxes. This means:

- we first download an image from a picture library;
- select a template from the template library;
- run the simulation with the well-defined parameters;
- show the resulting *input*, *state*, and *output* images at various time instants and at the end of the transients. These steps are shown sequentially on the display outputs shown in Examples 4.2–4.5.

EXAMPLE 4.2: The image "DIAMOND" is downloaded from the picture library.

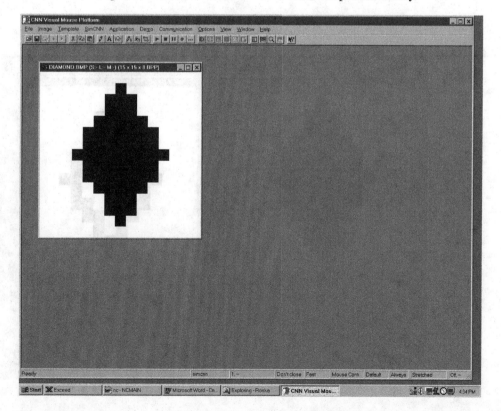

EXAMPLE 4.3: The output in the middle of the transient process (on the right-hand side).

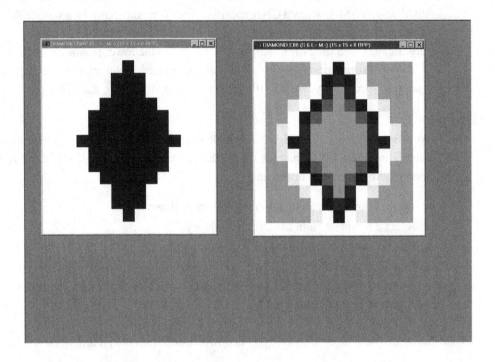

EXAMPLE 4.4: The output at the end ($t = 5$) of the transient.

EXAMPLE 4.5: The original downloaded image (left) and the input, state, output at the end of the transient (upper, middle, lower images on the right-hand side).

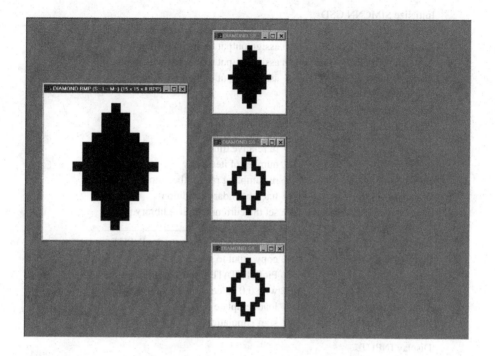

At the end of the simulation the sequence of the snapshots of the transient can be played back (and forth). The various signals can also be displayed graphically.

In these simulations the following default values are set: time step is 0.1 (forward Euler), time duration is 5.0 (50 steps), boundary is fixed at -1.0, and the initial STATE is the same as the INPUT.

If we want to change these default values or run a sequence of templates we have to write a CNN Script Description (CSD or simply Script language) program. A sample program showing the description of the above simulation is shown in Table 4.1. Reading the comments (right from the % sign), you can start writing your own program. Indeed, this sample program is stored as a default and you can just edit and save it.

The template activation is described in the part shown in a box. In our previous example for the EDGE template (in Chapter 3), we loaded different images to input and initial state. Here, we used the same input and initial state. If they are different, we can use the PicFill instruction as mentioned in the comment.

A few templates in the template library can be found in *Appendix A*. A more detailed summary of the use of SimCNN can be found in *Appendix B*.

Table 4.1. *The description of the simulation for the edge template in CSD (Script) language.*

{START: SimCNN}	% start SimCNN
Initialize SIMCNN CSD	
WinLayout 3	% number of windows to be displayed
AssignWinPart 1 INPUT	% assign output to the first window
AssignWinPart 2 STATE	% assign output to the first window
AssignWinPart 3 OUTPUT	% assign output to the first window
WinSetTitle 1 "INPUT"	
WinSetTitle 2 "STATE"	
WinSetTitle 3 "OUTPUT"	
TimeStep 0.1	% in relative time unit
IterNum 50	% number of iterations
OutputSampling 1	% re-sampling rate of the output
Boundary −1.0	% fixed boundary condition
TemplatePath PLATFORM	% set the current template library path
SendTo INPUT	% send the active image to the INPUT
PicCopy INPUT STATE	% copy input to state
	% PicFill STATE 0.0 would fill the state
	% with 0.0 values, this is not used here
TemLoad edge.tem	% load template
RunTem	% start simulation
Display INPUT	
Display STATE	
Display OUTPUT	% display the results
Terminate	% stop SimCNN
{STOP: SimCNN}	

Next we will show three examples to illustrate the role of choosing the correct time step (Δt), initial condition, and boundary condition. Unless otherwise stated the time step is set at a default value of 0.1.

Examples

In these examples, we show the role of the time step. We used a horizontal connected component detector template. The boundary condition (called also "frame" in the simulator) is fixed at [0] (default).

EXAMPLE 4.6: The input picture (far left) and the output and state pairs for three different time steps: 0.1 (upper pair), 0.2 (middle pair), 2.0 lower pair).

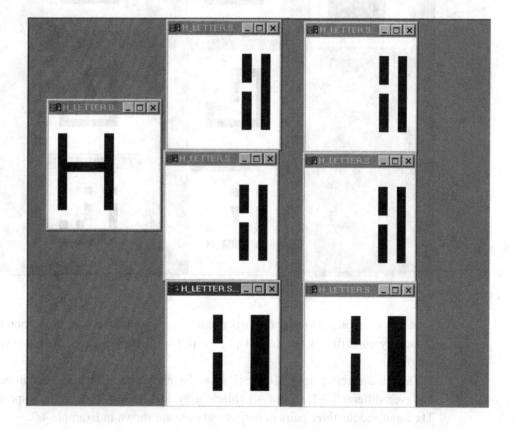

The input image is shown on the far left part in Example 4.6 (it is also placed on the initial state). Three pairs of images are shown on the right-hand side. The pairs are: the output (left) and the state (right) in Example 4.6. The three different results in the consecutive rows represent the final results at the end of the transients for three different time steps. In the case of the first two time step values, 0.1 and 0.2, correct results are calculated. For the third, the time step is 2.0, the result is wrong. Moreover, it starts to oscillate.

Generally, a time step smaller than 0.5 leads to correct results.

EXAMPLE 4.7: The results of a less robust edge detection template with various initial conditions ($+1, 0, -1$ at the top, middle, and lower rows, respectively).

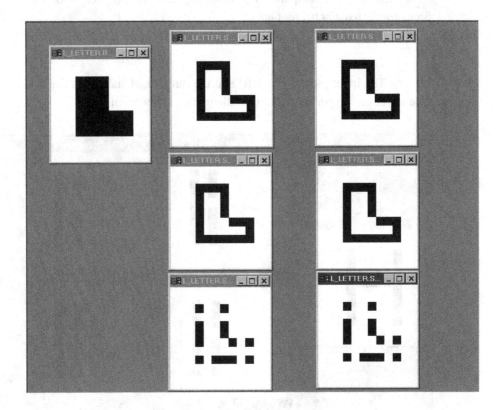

In this example, we show the dependence of the outputs on the initial conditions (boundary condition is the default $[\mathbf{Y}] = [\mathbf{U}] = [0]$). We used a less robust edge template.

The same pattern is applied three times as the input image. The initial conditions are, however, different, $+1, 0$, and -1 (black, gray, and white for all cells), respectively. The input and the three pairs of output and state are shown in Example 4.7.

Observe that the correct solution is calculated when the initial state is full black ($+1$) or zero. If the initial state is white (-1), then the output is wrong.

EXAMPLE 4.8: The effect of the boundary conditions. At different fixed values of boundary conditions, 0, −1, +1, the resulting output and state pairs are shown in the top, middle, and lower rows, respectively.

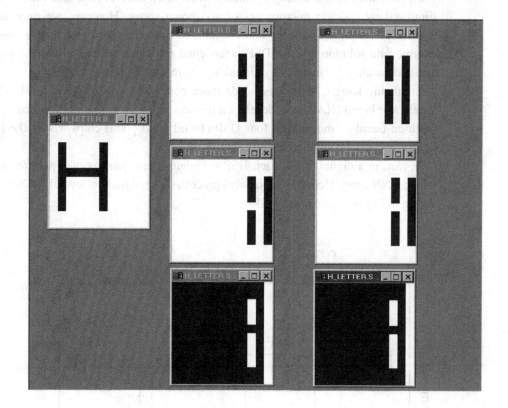

In this example, we show the role of the boundary conditions. The input image is placed on the initial state (far left on Example 4.8). A horizontal connected component detector template is used with three different boundary conditions. In the first case the boundary condition (frame) is fixed to zero, i.e. $[\mathbf{Y}] = [\mathbf{U}] = [0]$. The output and state are correct as shown on the upper image pair in Example 4.8. Next, the boundary conditions are set to −1.0 and 1.0. The results are shown in the middle and lower image pairs. In the latter case, the output is wrong. When the boundary conditions are set to zero flux or periodic, the results start propagating.

4.4   Digital hardware accelerators

The continuous valued analog dynamics when discretized in time and values can be simulated by a single microprocessor, as shown above. However, we may assign, in principle, a digital multiply-and-add unit to each cell. Next, we briefly show an intermediate solution when a DSP is assigned for a part of the cells. In a way we emulate the analog dynamics by digital hardware accelerators.

Emulating large CNN arrays needs more computing power. A special hardware accelerator board (HAB) was developed for simulating up to one-million-pixel arrays (with on-board memory) with four DSP (16 bit fixed point) chips. Using the HAB, large arrays can be simulated with cheap PCs.

In fact, in a digital HAB, each DSP calculates the dynamics of a partition of the whole CNN array. Hence, one physical processor is assigned to several CNN cells as shown in Fig. 4.1, using four DSPs.

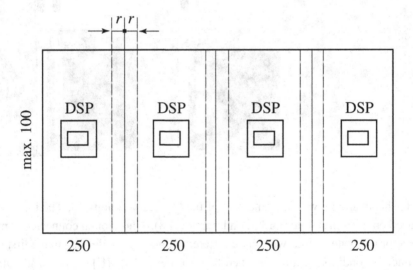

Fig. 4.1. The assignment of physical digital processors for many virtual CNN cells.

Actually, the DSP is a reduced instruction set (RISC) processor used for calculating CNN dynamics. Why do we use only four DSPs on a PC add-in-board? Because the board cannot host more due to area constraints. In a dedicated unit, in a PC-size box, 16–32 DSPs can be placed. New DSP packages host 4–8 DSP processors in a chip. Hence, the processor numbers are 4–8 times higher. Since for the calculation of the CNN dynamics a major part of the DSP is not used, special purpose chips have been developed (see the "CASTLE" architecture in Chapter 15).

4.5   Analog CNN implementations

In a CNN analog chip we can place more than 1000 processors (cells). This is because this special "analogic" (analogic: analog and logic) processor is much smaller than a DSP, and there is *no discretization in time and signal value.* Here, *physics does the "numerical integration" in time,* in a "single flow" (transient). There is *no iteration.* This implementation will be studied later in detail in Chapter 15.

To make a fair comparison, we have to define the equivalent computing power of an analog CNN chip related to the digital counterpart.

For the calculation of spatio-temporal dynamics, using a digital computer during *one time constant elapsed time*

- 10 time steps are taken and 20 multiply/add operations are to be performed (in a linear system, using forward Euler steps) per cell

This means 200 multiply/add operations per cell.

- Hence, for a 10,000 cell system, this means two million equivalent digital operations per one time constant elapsed time

In a CNN Universal chip, for a nonlinear array, using 0.5 micron single poly triple metal technology, the same task on a 100×100 cell chip could be implemented with a 100 ns time constant, hence, this means

- 20 trillion equivalent operations per second, i.e. 20 TeraOps
- *Present* operational chips: 22×20 cells, 30 mm^2, 280 ns, 0.8 micron, hence, 50×50 cells per 2 cm^2, i.e. 1 TeraOps

Table 4.2 shows some comparison of computing time for different simulators, emulators, and the first fully stored programmable analogic CNN Universal chip with optical input. It is obvious that for those problems which can be solved by the analog (analogic) chips, the analog array dynamics of the chip outperform all the software simulators and digital hardware emulators. Comparisons in running time of analogic CNN algorithms and more advanced CNN Universal chips can be found in Chapter 15.

It is important to emphasize that the analogic CNN technology is an emergent technology, complexity and speed is doubling sometimes within half a year.

Another type of comparison of the different architectures is shown in Table 4.3 (the emulated digital chip is not considered here). As a typical operation, an **A** template is considered (e.g. Laplace).

Although, the CNN Universal Machine architecture has not been formally introduced, we can say that it is a stored programmable array computer for implementing sequences of template operations with local analog and local logic memory.

Table 4.2. *Comparison of standard digital and analogic image processing technology. Computing time in* μs *(data transfer included) Image size:* 128 × 128.

	Pentium II (MMX) 0.25 μm, 233 MHz	TMS 320 6X 0.25 μm, 200 MHz 8 processors	CASTLE Emulated digital 0.5 μm, 66 MHz 12 processors	CNN chip 0.8 μm, τ_{CNN}: 250 ns 22 × 20 cells/ optical input
3 × 3 convolution				
B templates	1,000	427	32	$8/14.5^b$
$6\tau_{CNN}$ or 1 iteration		*2.34*	*31*	*125/69*
Erosion/dilation				
a_{00} + **B** templates	500	300	$2.7/32^a$	$8/14.5^b$
$6\tau_{CNN}$ or 1 iteration		*1.7*	*$185/16^a$*	*63/35*
Laplace				
A + **B** templates	15,000	6,414	480	$10.3/16.8^b$
$15\tau_{CNN}$ or 15 iterations		*2.3*	*31*	*1456/892*

Notes: [a]binary/gray-scale
[b]optical input and electrical output/electrical input and output.
Italic values indicate the speed advantage compared to the digital processors in the first two columns.
The first fully functional CNN Universal chip is considered only, more advanced CNN Universal chips are reviewed in Chapter 15.

Table 4.3.

"Hardware" /"wetware"	Number of processors /size	Discretization space	Discretization in time	Speed ns/cell*	Stored programable	Analog or digital
Pentium PC software	1	Y	Y	1,000	Y	D
DSP emulator	4–16	Y	Y	500– 2,000	Y	D
Intel 80170 neurochip	64	Y	feed-forward: N feed-back: Y	~20	N	A
CNNU chip cP 400 cP 4000	400–4,000 (10,000)	Y	N	2.5–0.1 (0.05)	Y	A
Human retina, single layer	10,000,000	Y	N	~1	Limited	A

Note: * calculated as: settling (computing) time/number of cells.

It is remarkable that a single operation of a single layer in the retina has, in this very simple model, the same computing power as the superfast analog chip.

4.6   Scaling the signals

We define an *input scale*:

white -1 +———+———+ 1 black
$\qquad\qquad 0$

an *output scale*:

white -1 +———+———+ 1 black
$\qquad\qquad 0$

and a *state scale*:

$-x_{max}$ +———+———+ x_{max}
$\qquad\quad 0$

where

$$x_{max} = 1 + |z| + \underbrace{\sum_{k=-r}^{r} \sum_{l=-r}^{r} |\mathbf{A}_{kl}| + |\mathbf{B}_{kl}|}_{M} \qquad (4.6)$$

For example, for the binary EDGE template

$$\mathbf{A} = \begin{array}{|c|c|c|} \hline 0 & 0 & 0 \\ \hline 0 & 0 & 0 \\ \hline 0 & 0 & 0 \\ \hline \end{array} \quad \mathbf{B} = \begin{array}{|c|c|c|} \hline -1 & -1 & -1 \\ \hline -1 & 8 & -1 \\ \hline -1 & -1 & -1 \\ \hline \end{array} \quad z = \boxed{-1}$$

$$x_{max} = 1 + 1 + 16 = 18$$
$$M = 16$$

We can also calculate the maximum values of $\dot{x}_{ij}$ (and $\ddot{x}_{ij}$)

$$\dot{x}_{max} = \underbrace{1 + |z| + M}_{x_{max}} + |z| + M = 1 + 2|z| + 2|M| \qquad (4.7)$$

For the binary EDGE it is 35.

The bounds can be used to design a fixed point simulator. A 16 bit fixed point representation is specially useful for many CNN analyses. The reason is this:

16 bit $\approx$ 64,000 values, i.e., $\pm$ 32,000 numerical units.

If the unit signal value (e.g., 1 v or 0.5 v) is represented by 1,000 numerical units (i.e., 1 mV or 0.5 mV resolution) then the allowed dynamic range (x_{max}) is 32 units of signal value. It means $x_{max} = 32$. This is a practically reasonable choice. Indeed, this is the reason why a cheap 16 bit fixed point DSP (Texas TMS 320C25) was used in the Hardware Accelerator Board.

4.7   Discrete-time CNN (DTCNN)

If we use $\Delta t = 1$ then we get from (4.4)

$$x_{ij}(m+1) = \sum_{k=-r}^{r} \sum_{l=-r}^{r} a_{kl} y_{i+k,j+l}(m) + \sum_{k=-r}^{r} \sum_{l=-r}^{r} b_{kl} u_{i+k,j+1}(m) + z$$
$$y_{kl}(m+1) = f(x_{kl}(m+1)) \tag{4.8}$$

This discrete-time recursive equation is called the discrete-time CNN (DTCNN) equation. If $f(\cdot)$ is not the standard nonlinear function (unity gain piecewise linear saturation function), but it is a so-called hard limiter $f_h(\cdot)$ (either between $+1/-1$ or $+1/0$, see Fig. 4.2) then equation (4.8) is a DTCNN with hard limiter.[2]

Let us emphasize that at $\Delta t = 1$ the DTCNN equation is not necessarily convergent. In principle if Δt is small enough, the discrete-time equation converges to the continuous-time solution. There are several different physical implementations for DTCNN, including software, digital hardware, and special purpose VLSI.

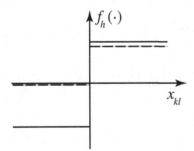

Fig. 4.2.

5 Binary CNN characterization via Boolean functions

5.1 Binary and universal CNN truth table

Our objective in this chapter is to show that every space-invariant *binary* (black-and-white) *CNN* belonging to the *uncoupled* class $C(\mathbf{A}^0, \mathbf{B}, z)$ with a 3×3 neighborhood ($r = 1$) which maps any static *binary* 3×3 input pattern $\mathbf{U}$ into a static binary 3×3 output pattern $\mathbf{Y}(\infty)$ can be *uniquely* defined by a *Boolean function* C of nine binary input variables[1]

$$\mathbf{u}_{ij} = [u_1, u_2, u_3, u_4, u_5, u_6, u_7, u_8, u_9]^T \tag{5.1}$$

where $u_i \in \{0, 1\}$ denotes one of the nine pixels within the sphere of influence of cell C_{ij} as shown in (a) below. Note that we have opted for a "single" rather than a "double" subscript notation to avoid clutter. Note also that $\mathbf{u}_{ij}$ has a *subscript* (ij) and is set in a *bold face* type in order to distinguish it from the input u_{ij} (set in light-face type) of cell C_{ij}. Although we can code the nine pixels $u_{kl}, kl \in \{-1, 0, 1\}$ by any combination of u_i, we have chosen the coding scheme shown in (b) below for pedagogical reasons that will be obvious later. A simple mnemonic to reconstruct this code is to remember the subscript "5" always refers to the input u_{00}, corresponding to the *center* cell C_{ij}, whereas the subscripts $\{8, 4, 2, 6\}$ refer to the surround cells in the N $\rightarrow$ E $\rightarrow$ S $\rightarrow$ W clockwise compass directions, and the remaining subscripts $\{7, 9, 1, 3\}$ refer to the surround cells in the NE $\rightarrow$ NW $\rightarrow$ SE $\rightarrow$ SW clockwise compass directions.

(a)

$u_{-1,-1}$	$u_{-1,0}$	$u_{-1,1}$
$u_{0,-1}$	$u_{0,0}$	$u_{0,1}$
$u_{1,-1}$	$u_{1,0}$	$u_{1,1}$

$\Rightarrow$

(b)

u_9	u_8	u_7
u_6	u_5	u_4
u_3	u_2	u_1

Now given any static binary input pattern $\mathbf{U}$, the color (black or white, since the CNN is *assumed* to be binary) of *any* output pixel is determined uniquely by only a small part of $\mathbf{U}$ exposed to a 3×3 transparent window centered at cell C_{ij}, because the sphere of influence $S_1(i, j)$ is *assumed* to be a 3×3 neighborhood. Hence the color $\{0, 1\}$ of the output pixel $y_{ij}(\infty)$ is uniquely determined by the binary value (0 or 1) of the nine pixels $u_1, u_2, \ldots, u_9$ exposed by the 3×3 window. This unique answer is obtained by solving the system of $M \times N$ ODE having the *prescribed* CNN templates $(\mathbf{A}^0, \mathbf{B}, z)$, and prescribed initial state $\mathbf{x}(0)$. Now even though there are *infinitely many* distinct templates (recall the coefficients of $\mathbf{A}^0$, $\mathbf{B}$, and z can be any *real* number, which is uncountable), there will be only a *finite* (albeit very large) number of distinct combinations of 3×3 "checkerboard" patterns of black and white cells, namely, $2^9 = 512$.

Fig. 5.1 shows how a single binary input is represented.

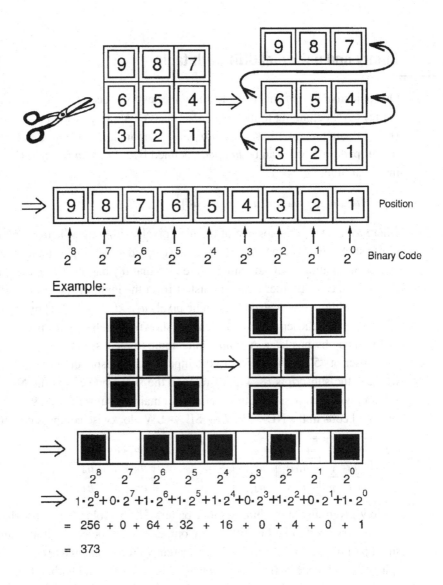

Fig. 5.1. Representing a single binary input.

CNN Program NAME	CNN Program Code													
	512	511	510	509	508	507	506	7	6	5	4	3	2	1
Fill White	0	0	0	0	0	0	0	0	0	0	0	0	0	0
1	0	0	0	0	0	0	0	0	0	0	0	0	0	1
2	0	0	0	0	0	0	0	0	0	0	0	0	1	0
3	0	0	0	0	0	0	0	0	0	0	0	0	1	1
4	0	0	0	0	0	0	0	0	0	0	0	1	0	0
5	0	0	0	0	0	0	0	0	0	0	0	1	0	1
6	0	0	0	0	0	0	0	0	0	0	0	1	1	0
Game of Life	0	0	0	1	0	1	0	0	0	0	0	0	0	1
Edge Detector	1	0	1	1	1	1	1	0	0	0	0	0	0	0
$2^{512}-3$	1	1	1	1	1	1	1	1	1	1	1	1	0	1
$2^{512}-2$	1	1	1	1	1	1	1	1	1	1	1	1	1	0
Fill Black	1	1	1	1	1	1	1	1	1	1	1	1	1	1

Total Number of Distinct CNN Programs = $2^{512} \approx 1.34078 \times 10^{154}$

Fig. 5.2. CNN program code of nine variable binary input.

Since each such pattern can map to either a "0" or a "1", there are exactly[2]

$$\Omega \overset{\Delta}{=} 2^{2^9} = 2^{512} \approx 1.3408 \times 10^{154} > 10^{154} \tag{5.2}$$

distinct Boolean maps of nine binary variables. These maps can be ordered in a table as shown in Fig. 5.2. Each row shows a different binary nine input one output map.

Let $\mathcal{C}_\Omega$ denote the universe of *all* such maps. Now since $\mathcal{C}_\Omega$ is the maximal set, by definition, the Boolean map generated by each member of the standard CNN universe $\mathcal{C}(\mathbf{A}^0, \mathbf{B}, z)$ must be a member of $\mathcal{C}_\Omega$.[3] Hence

$$\mathcal{C}(\mathbf{A}^0, \mathbf{B}, z) \subset \mathcal{C}_\Omega \tag{5.3}$$

We have just proved the following fundamental result:

Table 5.1. *Truth table for defining any Boolean functions of nine variables.*

Binary pattern number	Input variables									output $y_{ij}(\infty)$
	u_9	u_8	u_7	u_6	u_5	u_4	u_3	u_2	u_1	
0										
1										
⋮										
510										
511										

Theorem 1: Binary CNN truth table

Every binary standard CNN with template $(\mathbf{A}^0, \mathbf{B}, z)$ and prescribed initial state $\mathbf{X}(0)$ is a member of the universe $\mathcal{C}_\Omega$ of all Boolean functions of nine variables and is therefore uniquely characterized by the *CNN truth table* shown in Table 5.1, consisting of 512 *rows* (one for each distinct 3×3 checkerboard pattern), nine *input columns* (one for each binary input variable u_i), and one *output* column whose value (0 or 1) corresponds to $y_{ij}(\infty)$.

Theorem 1 gives us *the most rigorous* method for characterizing a space-invariant binary CNN, and is therefore of fundamental importance. Since this table will in general exceed the length of a typical page, let us divide it into 16 component truth tables each one containing 32 rows. For example, the 16 component truth tables which characterize the *Edge* templates are given in Examples 5.1(a)–(p). To clarify our notation, in the first component table shown in Example 5.1(a), each entry for the input variables is coded by a "0" or a "1", instead of our earlier notation of "-1" and "1", in order for us to exploit the extensive theory and literature on Boolean functions, which are almost universally couched in "zeros" and "ones." Observe that we have ordered the binary values in the truth table in the same order for enumerating the *binary number* $0, 1, 2, 3, \ldots, 511$, consecutively. Since it is usually more pleasing for the eye to decode a table of black-and-white cells than a table of "zeros" and "ones," we will henceforth code our CNN truth tables by black and white cells.

To construct the truth table for any binary CNN $\mathcal{C}(\mathbf{A}^0, \mathbf{B}, z)$ with the prescribed initial state $\mathbf{x}(0)$, simply solve the associated system of differential equations for each input of 512 distinct binary patterns listed in Table 5.1 and fill in the corresponding calculated output, either black (1) or white (0). Since the 512 binary patterns are fixed, each corresponding to a nine-bit binary expression of an integer N, $N = 0, 1, 2, \ldots, 511$, it is easy to write a computer program to generate the truth table automatically, given any templates $(\mathbf{A}^0, \mathbf{B}, z)$ and the prescribed initial condition $\mathbf{x}(0)$.

In particular, simply assume a 3×3 CNN array ($M = N = 3$) and find the solution of the *center cell* C_{00}.

The truth table for the edge CNN calculated by the above procedure is shown in Example 5.1, decomposed into 16 components. Clearly, except for displaying a few of these truth tables for analysis and pedagogical purposes, it is impractical to list the truth table of all useful CNNs. They can, however, easily be stored on a diskette, to be retrieved only when needed. Displaying the truth table on a computer screen has the advantage of showing a continuous table when any part of the table can be scrolled into entire view.

The alert reader will have already realized that the truth table format of Example 5.1 contains a great deal of redundancy. Indeed, in each of the 16 components shown

EXAMPLE 5.1: Edge CNN

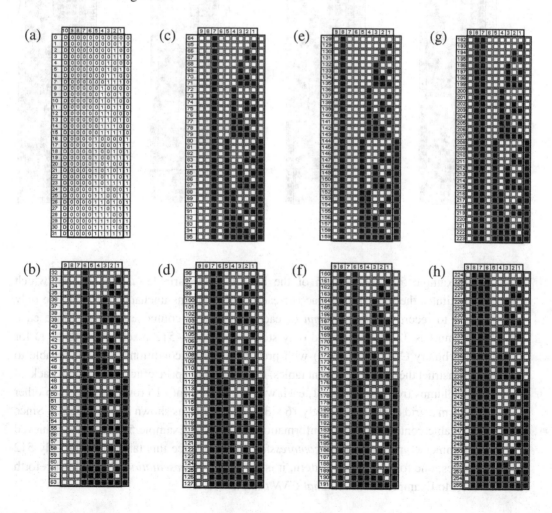

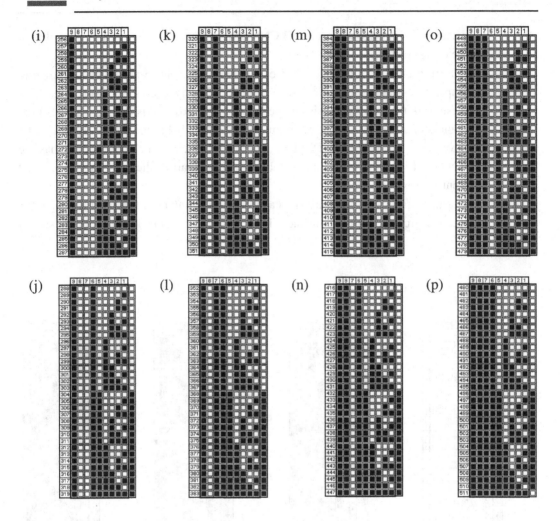

in Example 5.1, the domain of the binary input variables $u_1, u_2, \ldots, u_9$, which constitutes the bulk of the space of each table, remains unchanged. Hence, we only need to record *the last column* of each of these 16 component tables. Since each column has 32 cells, we need only store $16 \times 32 = 512$ pixel values (0 or 1) for each binary CNN $C(\mathbf{A}^0, \mathbf{B}, z)$ with prescribed initial conditions and will be able to reconstruct these 16 component tables. For maximum space efficiency, we can pack all 16 columns from Example 5.1, each with 32 entries, into 16 rows, next to each other to form a grid containing exactly $16 \times 32 = 512$ cells, as shown in Example 5.2. Since this table contains the same information as those of Example 5.1, we have achieved an immerse amount *of data compression*. Indeed, since this table contains only 512 entries, one for each input pattern, it is a *minimal representation*. We will henceforth refer to Example 5.2 *as minimal CNN truth table*.

Corollary to Theorem 1

Every space-invariant binary CNN with a 3×3 neighborhood and specified by templates $(\mathbf{A}^0, \mathbf{B}, z)$ and a prescribed initial state $\mathbf{X}(0)$ is associated with a unique minimal CNN truth table.

EXAMPLE 5.2: Minimal CNN truth table

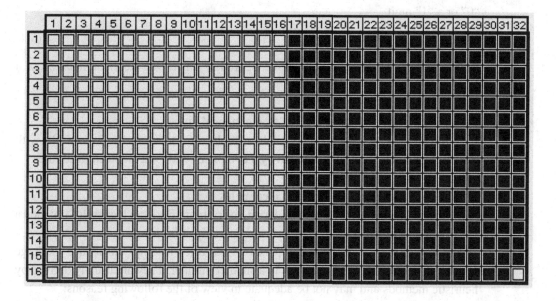

Remarks:

1 The *uniqueness* assertion in the above corollary is with respect to a given template $(\mathbf{A}^0, \mathbf{B}, z)$ *and* initial state $\mathbf{X}(0)$. It is not unique with respect to a given "global task" since a given task in general can be implemented by many distinct CNN templates (infinitely many indeed).

2 The above corollary only asserts that for every CNN template $(\mathbf{A}, \mathbf{B}, z)$ and initial state, there corresponds a minimal truth table, or equivalently, a Boolean function of nine variables. However, the converse is not true, i.e., given a Boolean function $\mathcal{B} \in C_\Omega$, or its associated minimal truth table, there may *not* exist a CNN template and an initial state $\mathbf{X}(0)$ which yields this truth table. However, we will prove later that every member of C_Ω, i.e., every Boolean function of nine variables, can be realized by a *CNN universal machine* to be studied in depth later. We will prove later that there are more than 10^{154} such Boolean functions of nine variables that can be programmed by a single CNN universal machine. This immensely large number is greater than the volume of the universe (10^{84} cm^3, calculated as a sphere with a diameter of 10 thousand million light years)!

5.2 Boolean and compressed local rules

Every CNN with a 3×3 neighborhood or its generalization, the *CNN universal machine*, to be presented later, which maps a static *binary input* image into a static *binary output* image, has a unique CNN truth table representation consisting of 512 rows, each one mapping a Boolean expression involving nine Boolean variables into a "0" or a "1" digit

$$(d_1, d_2, \ldots, d_9) \rightarrow \{0, 1\} \tag{5.4}$$

where $d_i \in \{0, 1\}$. We can now define rigorously our earlier heuristic notation of a local rule:

Definition 1: Complete set of CNN Boolean local rules
Each row of the CNN truth table is called a Boolean *CNN local rule*. Every CNN with 3×3 neighbors is rigorously defined by a complete set of 512 Boolean local rules.

Definition 2: Compressed Boolean local rules
Any other rule which can be used to derive one or more Boolean local rules is called a *compressed local rule*, or simple local rule if the usage is clear.

The motivation for devising compressed local rules is simply to reduce the large number (512) of Boolean local rules to a smaller number. They are usually derived by heuristic methods and may not be adequate in view of the following reasons:

1 While some local rule may correctly reproduce a large subset of Boolean local rules, it may contradict some others. In this case, we say it is an *inconsistent* local rule. If the inconsistency occurs only for a few rare input patterns, it may still be useful for pedagogical purposes, especially if the local rule compression ratio

   $$\gamma_{LR} \overset{\Delta}{=} \text{number of correctly reproduced}$$
   $$\text{Boolean local rules divided by 512}$$

   is sufficiently large, $\gamma_{LR} \leq 1$. In this case the errors may be acceptable for pedagogical reasons, especially if this local rule makes it possible to visualize or identify the main features of the input image that are to be extracted, modified, or transformed.
2 The set of compressed local rules are *incomplete* in the sense that some Boolean local rules *cannot* be deduced from them.

Definition 3: Complete set of compressed local rules
A set of compressed local rules is said to be *complete* if and only if no member of this set is inconsistent and if all 512 Boolean local rules can be deduced from this set.

Definition 4: Minimal set of compressed local rules

A complete set of compressed local rules is said to be *minimal* if no member of this set can be eliminated and still achieve completeness.

Computer-aided method for proving local rules

Given a CNN template $(\mathbf{A}^0, \mathbf{B}, z)$ and initial state $\mathbf{X}(0)$, there is presently no systematic algorithm to derive a *complete* set

$$\mathcal{S}_{LR} = \{\mathcal{S}_1, \mathcal{S}_2, \dots, \mathcal{S}_p\} \tag{5.5}$$

of local rules which are sufficient to map any binary input patterns into the prescribed output patterns obtained by solving the associated system of ODEs. In most cases, only a subset $\mathcal{S}_{LR}^- \subset \mathcal{S}_{LR}$ may be found. On rare occasions, a superset $\mathcal{S}_{LR}^+ \supset \mathcal{S}_{LR}$ may be found. On few occasions, some local rules may be *redundant*, in the sense that for *some* input patterns they predict the same output. It is also quite possible that two or more local rules may contradict each other's prediction and hence are said to be *inconsistent*. Finally, given a *complete* set of local rules, does there exist a proper subset which is also complete? If so, is it possible to find a complete set of local rules which are minimal in the sense that no other complete set exists which contains a fewer number of elementary local rules? We will now show that all of these questions, except the last one, can be easily resolved with the help of the CNN truth table, or equivalently, its associated minimal truth table. We will give a constructive solution to each question (except the last one) raised above in the form of an algorithm.

Algorithm 1: Checking whether a local rule candidate $\mathcal{S}_i$ is consistent

1 Use the prescribed template $(\mathbf{A}^0, \mathbf{B}, z)$ and initial state $\mathbf{X}(0)$ to derive the associated CNN truth table $\mathcal{T}$.

2 Apply the local rule $\mathcal{S}_1$ to *each* of the 512 input patterns. In general, $\mathcal{S}_1$ may *not* be *applicable* (NA) for some patterns (due to inadequate or overly simplistic assumptions). In this case, the output cell will be denoted by NA, or simply coded in gray scale. For those input patterns where $\mathcal{S}_1$ is applicable, there are three possibilities for the output cell: (i) Output is black (coded by Boolean number 1) and agrees with the corresponding output in the truth table. In this case, the output will be printed "black." (ii) Output is white (coded by Boolean number 0) and agrees with the corresponding output in the truth table. In this case, the output cell will be printed "white." (iii) The output is black (resp., white) but the corresponding cell in the truth table is white (resp., black). In this case, the output cell will be denoted by a cross $\boxtimes$, thereby indicating $\mathcal{S}_1$ is inconsistent and is not a valid local rule.

3 The local rule $\mathcal{S}_1$ is proved to be valid if and only if it is *not* inconsistent.

Algorithm 2: Checking whether a set $S = \{\mathcal{S}_1, \mathcal{S}_2, \dots, \mathcal{S}_k\}$ is complete

1 Derive the CNN truth table $\mathcal{T}$, as in Algorithm 1.

2 Apply *Algorithm 1* to each $\mathcal{S}_i \in \mathcal{S}$. If any $\mathcal{S}_i$ is inconsistent, stop. Otherwise, go to 3.

3 If *each* output cell is predicted to be either black or white by at least one local rule $\mathcal{S}_i \in \mathcal{S}$, then $\mathcal{S}$ is complete. In this case, we have a rigorous proof of the validity *and* completeness of the set of local rules.

Algorithm 3: Given a complete set $\mathcal{S}_{LR}$ of local rules, find a smallest proper subset which is also complete

1 Delete $\mathcal{S}_1$ from $\mathcal{S}_{LR}$ and apply Algorithm 2 to the remaining set. If it is complete, delete the first two elements $\mathcal{S}_1$ and $\mathcal{S}_2$ from $\mathcal{S}_{LR}$ and repeat Algorithm 2. Continue the same "pruning" procedure until the remaining set is no longer complete. In this case, the immediately preceding remaining set of local rules constitutes the *smallest* complete set with respect to the order where the elements of $\mathcal{S}_{LR}$ are deleted.

2 Repeat step 1 to all permutations of the ordering of the members of $\mathcal{S}_{LR}$.

3 Any complete set resulting from steps 1 and 2 having the smallest number of elements is a *minimal complete* set, relative to $\mathcal{S}_{LR}$.

Remarks:

1 The above choice of minimal complete set may not be unique, since there may exist several complete sets all containing the same smallest number of elements.

2 The "minimality" derived from Algorithm 3 may not be global in the sense that there may exist an entirely different set $\mathcal{S}_{LR}$ of complete rules in which Algorithm 3 would yield a minimal complete set having fewer elements than that determined from $\mathcal{S}_{LR}$. The difficulty in deriving a global minimal complete set is that there is no obvious algorithm to guarantee all distinct sets of complete local rules have been exhausted. A further difficulty lies in the criterion to be used for certifying which local rule is qualified as *elementary*. For otherwise, one could combine several local rules into a single but more complex local rule. Hence it is necessary to define "elementary" in the sense that no decomposition into two or more simpler local rules is possible. The algorithms are contained in the TEMPO program (Appendix C).

5.3   Optimizing the truth table

Recall that once a CNN template is specified a unique truth table can be easily generated by a simple computer program, say by solving a system of nine ODEs a total of 512 times, one for each distinct Boolean pattern of nine input variables, or by some explicit formula that applies only to some specific subclass of CNNs, e.g., the *uncoupled* class. One can examine each of the 512 3×3 binary input patterns and determine whether the output (black or white) of this CNN is "correct" from the user's perspective. The next tables (Examples 5.3–5.13) show the minimal truth tables, the truth tables and the window truth tables of the CORNER template. However, for example, among the 32 input patterns shown in Example 5.7 (corresponding to the Boolean local rules no 96–127) and the 32 input patterns shown in Example 5.8 (corresponding to the Boolean local rules no 160–191) for the CORNER CNN, we found the "black" output of this CNN for input patterns no 114, 116, 176, 177, 178, 180, and 184 to be "incorrect" in the sense that the center black pixel in each of these seven input patterns do *not look* like "corners," from the perspective of the human visual system. Similarly, we also disagree with this CNN's classification (white; i.e., *not* corner) of input pattern nos 115 and 121, because the black center pixel in these two patterns really look like "corners." Hence, we would consider these nine classifications made by the CORNER CNN to be "incorrect." It is important to note that this does *not* mean the CORNER truth table is incorrect, as *every truth table* is an exact and hence correct representation of the CNN having the prescribed template. Indeed, from the perspective of a *robot*, or some creatures having a different visual system, the above classifications may be completely acceptable.

From the human perspective, however, it would be desirable to reclassify the above nine Boolean local rules to obtain an optimized CNN truth table.[3] Once this is done, our next task is to design a CNN template (which may not exist) having this optimized truth table. If no such template exists, we will show later that a CNN universal machine can always be used to realize this optimized truth table, or any other truth table.

EXAMPLE 5.3: Minimal truth table of CORNER template

EXAMPLE 5.4:

EXAMPLE 5.5:

EXAMPLE 5.6: Tables of input–output patterns for CORNER template (1, 2)

EXAMPLE 5.7: Tables of input–output patterns for CORNER template (3, 4)

EXAMPLE 5.8: Tables of input–output patterns for CORNER template (5, 6)

EXAMPLE 5.9: Tables of input–output patterns for CORNER template (7, 8)

EXAMPLE 5.10: Tables of input–output patterns for CORNER template (9, 10)

EXAMPLE 5.11: Tables of input–output patterns for CORNER template (11, 12)

EXAMPLE 5.12: Tables of input–output patterns for CORNER template (13, 14)

EXAMPLE 5.13: Tables of input–output patterns for CORNER template (15, 16)

EXAMPLE 5.14: Corrected minimal truth table of CORNER template

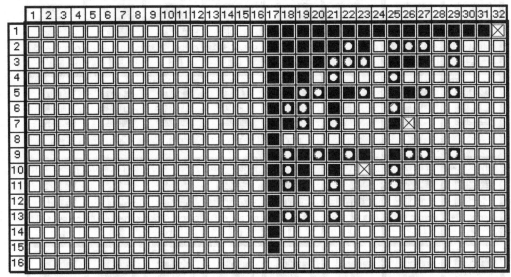

◖ squares correspond to corner misclassification (they should be white)
⊠ squares correspond to non-corner misclassification (they should be black)

EXAMPLE 5.15: Optimized minimal truth table of CORNER template

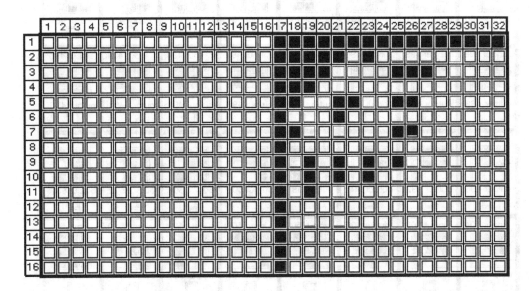

As an example, all misclassified input patterns by the CORNER CNN are designated in the minimal truth table shown in Example 5.14 by a white hole pixel if this pixel should be reclassified as white, and by a crossed pixel if this pixel should be reclassified as black. The resulting *optimized* CORNER CNN is shown in Example 5.15. Examples 5.16 and 5.17 show the binary and decimal code for the CORNER and optimized CORNER templates, respectively.

EXAMPLE 5.16: Binary code for **CORNER** template (512 bits)

00000000,00000000,00000000,00000000,00000000,00000001,00000000,00000000
,00000000,00000001,00000000,00000000,00000001,00010111,00000000,00000000
,00000000,00000001,00000000,00000000,00000001,00010111,00000000,00000000
,00000001,00010111,00000000,00000000,00010111,01111111,00000000,00000000
,00000000,00000001,00000000,00000000,00000001,00010111,00000000,00000000
,00000001,00010111,00000000,00000000,00010111,01111111,00000000,00000000
,00000001,00010111,00000000,00000000,00010111,01111111,00000000,00000000
,00010111,01111111,00000000,00000000,01111111,11111111,00000000,00000000

Decimal code for **CORNER** template (140 digits)

47,634,102,646,527,572,675,971
,460,498,910,645,354,219,674,273,748,634,236,474,670
,546,006,561,432,941,907,354,541,093,642,727,873,594
,350,604,011,030,198,552,062,948,695,326,343,495,680

EXAMPLE 5.17: Binary code for **optimized CORNER** template (512 bits)

,00000000,00000001,00000000,00000000,00000000,00000001,00000000,00000000
,00000000,00000001,00000000,00000000,00000000,00000001,00000000,00000000
,00000000,00000001,00000000,00000000,00000000,00000101,00000000,00000000
,00000000,01010101,00000000,00000000,00000001,01010101,00000000,00000000
,00000000,00000001,00000000,00000000,00000011,00000011,00000000,00000000
,00000000,00010001,00000000,00000000,00000011,00110011,00000000,00000000
,00000000,00000111,00000000,00000000,00000111,00001111,00000000,00000000
,00000000,01011111,00000000,00000000,11111111,11111111,00000000,00000000

Decimal code for **optimized CORNER** template (150 digits)

204,586,913,041,142, 969,522,351,928,009,830

,941,404, 290,185,269,210, 065,083,499,186,859,428,943

,804,165, 897,630,843,608,945,882,697, 576,708,597,045

,469,082,137,675,717, 688,639,024,082, 912,326,647,808

6 Uncoupled CNNs: unified theory and applications

6.1 The complete stability phenomenon

Our main objective in this section is to derive and prove a general theorem which unifies all of the CNN templates presented in the preceding chapter, and numerous others, under one umbrella. In particular, the mathematical analyses presented for all templates in Chapter 5 could be greatly simplified. We did not present this fundamental theorem earlier for pedagogical reasons: it is essential for the uninitiated students of CNN to understand and appreciate the fundamental notion and power of the *shifted DP plots* and their *dynamic routes*.

We have been thoroughly exposed to these rather simple concepts and have learned to exploit the dynamic routes not only for the analysis of the *nonlinear dynamics* (i.e., *transient* and *asymptotic* behaviors), but also as a highly intuitive and potent design tool for deriving optimum and robust CNN templates.

The alert students who have gone over the previous chapter would have recognized that, except for a degenerate case, no matter what the initial conditions are, the solution always converges to a globally *asymptotically stable* and hence unique equilibrium point (*monostable* case), or to one of two *locally stable* equilibrium points (*bistable* case). Although this latter "convergence" property is rather unusual for nonlinear dynamic circuits having multiple equilibria,[1] it is a gift that nature (i.e., the physical laws) has endowed upon an important class of CNNs on which all current nonlinear information processing applications are based. Let us first define this crucial CNN property which provides the *raison-d'etre* of its existence.

Definition 1: Completely stable (convergent) CNN

An $M \times N$ CNN $\mathcal{C}(\mathbf{A}, \mathbf{B}, z)$ is said to be *completely stable*, or *convergent*, iff every solution $\mathbf{x}(t; \mathbf{x}_0)$ with initial state $\mathbf{x}_0$ converges to an *equilibrium point* $\mathbf{Q}(\mathbf{x}_0)$, which in general depends on $\mathbf{x}_0 \in R^{M \times N}$.

6.2 Explicit CNN output formula

We are now ready to state and prove our long-awaited main theorem which holds for any *uncoupled* CNNs. Let $C(\mathbf{A}^0, \mathbf{B}, z)$ denote any space-invariant[2] CNN with a sphere of influence $S_r(ij)$, a feedback template $\mathbf{A}^0$ with all feedback synaptic weights $a_{ij} = 0$ except $i = j = 0$, an input (feedforward) template $\mathbf{B}$ with arbitrary input synaptic weights $b_{kl} \in R$, where $|k - i| \leq r$, $|l - j| \leq r$, and an arbitrary threshold $z \in R$.

Theorem 1: Completely stable CNN theorem

Every uncoupled CNN $C(\mathbf{A}^0, \mathbf{B}, z)$ with *static binary* inputs ($u_{kl} = -1$ or $u_{kl} = 1$) is *completely stable*. Moreover, the solution waveform $x_{ij}(t)$ *increases monotonically* to an equilibrium point $\mathbf{Q}$ if $x_{ij}(\mathbf{Q}) > 0$, or decreases monotonically to an equilibrium point $\mathbf{Q}$ if $x_{ij}(\mathbf{Q}) < 0$.

Moreover, except for two *degenerate* cases which correspond to a *semi-stable* or a *non-isolated* equilibrium, the *asymptotic* (i.e., *steady state*) *output* solution

$$y_{ij}(\infty) \stackrel{\Delta}{=} \lim_{t \to \infty} y_{ij}(t)$$

can be calculated by the following explicit algebraic formula which depends only on the *initial state* $x_{ij}(0)$, on the *offset* level

$$w_{ij} = z + \sum_{kl \in S_r(i,j)} b_{kl} u_{kl} \tag{6.1}$$

of *only* the neighbor cells $C(kl)$ within the sphere of influence $S_r(ij)$ of radius r of cell $C(ij)$, and on the value of the *self-feedback* synaptic weight a_{00}, of which there are four cases:

Case 1: Strong positive self-feedback case: $a_{00} > 1$

In this case, the CNN output is always equal to "1" or "−1" (i.e., *binary*) for arbitrary $u_{kl} \in R$, and is given by (assuming $|x_{ij}(0)| \leq 1$ and $|w_{ij}| \neq a_{00} - 1$)

$$y_{ij}(\infty) = \text{sgn}[(a_{00} - 1)x_{ij}(0) + w_{ij}] \tag{6.2}$$

where sgn($\cdot$) denotes the *signum* function.[3]

In addition, the CNN is

1 *bistable*, if $|w_{ij}| < a_{00} - 1$,
2 *monostable*,[4] if $|w_{ij}| > a_{00} - 1$,
3 *semi-stable*, if $|w_{ij}| = a_{00} - 1$.

In the semi-stable case, we have

$$y_{ij}(\infty) = 1, \qquad \text{if } x_{ij}(0) > -1 \text{ and } w_{ij} = a_{00} - 1 > 0$$
$$\text{or if } x_{ij}(0) \geq 1 \text{ and } w_{ij} = -(a_{00} - 1) < 0$$
$$= -1, \quad \text{if } x_{ij}(0) \leq 1 \text{ and } w_{ij} = -(a_{00} - 1) < 0$$
$$\text{or if } x_{ij}(0) \leq -1 \text{ and } w_{ij} = a_{00} - 1 > 0$$

Case 2: Unity-gain self-feedback case: $a_{00} = 1$
In this case, if $w_{ij} \neq 0$, then the CNN is *monostable* with a *binary* output which does not depend on $x_{ij}(0)$, and is given by

$$y_{ij}(\infty) = \text{sgn}[w_{ij}] \tag{6.3}$$

If $w_{ij} = 0$, we have the *degenerate* case of a non-isolated equilibrium where

$$y_{ij}(\infty) = x_{ij}(0) \tag{6.4}$$

Case 3: Weak positive self-feedback case: $0 < a_{00} < 1$
In this case the CNN is *monostable* whose output does not depend on $x_{ij}(0)$ and is given by:

1 If $|w_{ij}| > 1 - a_{00}$, then the output is binary and is given by

$$y_{ij}(\infty) = \text{sgn}[w_{ij} - (1 - a_{00})] \tag{6.5}$$

2 If $|w_{ij}| < 1 - a_{00}$, then the output is given in gray-scale value by

$$y_{ij}(\infty) = x_{ij}(\infty) = \frac{w_{ij}}{1 - a_{00}} \tag{6.6}$$

3 If $|w_{ij}| = 1 - a_{00}$, then

$$y_{ij}(\infty) = \text{sgn}[w_{ij}] \tag{6.7}$$

Case 4: Negative self-feedback case: $a_{00} < 0$
In this case the CNN is *monostable* and the output does not depend on $x_{ij}(0)$, and is given by

1 If $|w_{ij}| > 1 - a_{00}$, then the output is binary and is given by

$$y_{ij}(\infty) = \text{sgn}[w_{ij} - (1 - a_{00})] \tag{6.8}$$

2 If $|w_{ij}| < 1 - a_{00}$, then the output is given in gray-scale value by

$$y_{ij}(\infty) = x_{ij}(\infty) = \frac{w_{ij}}{1 - a_{00}} \tag{6.9}$$

3 If $|w_{ij}| = 1 - a_{00}$, then

$$y_{ij}(\infty) = \text{sgn}[w_{ij}] \tag{6.10}$$

6.3   Proof of completely stable CNN theorem

Since $a_{ij} = 0$ for all $(ij) \neq (0,0)$ in an *uncoupled* CNN, the associated state equation is given by

$$\dot{x}_{ij} = h_{ij}(x_{ij}; w_{ij}) \tag{6.11}$$

The rate function is defined by

$$h_{ij}(x_{ij}; w_{ij}) = g_{ij}(x_{ij}) + w_{ij} \tag{6.12}$$

where

$$\begin{aligned} g_{ij}(x_{ij}) &= -x_{ij} + a_{00}f(x_{ij}) \\ &= -x_{ij} + 0.5a_{00}|x_{ij} + 1| - 0.5a_{00}|x_{ij} - 1| \end{aligned} \tag{6.13}$$

is the internal DP plot, and

$$w_{ij} = z + \sum_{kl \in S_r(i,j)} b_{kl}u_{kl} \tag{6.14}$$

is the *offset level*. The dynamics of Eq. (6.11) is completely determined by the *shifted DP plot*

$$h_{ij}(x_{ij}; w_{ij}) = w_{ij} - x_{ij} + 0.5a_{00}|x_{ij} + 1| - 0.5a_{00}|x_{ij} - 1| \tag{6.15}$$

The equilibrium points of Eq. (6.11) are obtained by solving the piecewise-linear equation

$$w_{ij} - x_{ij} + 0.5a_{00}|x_{ij} + 1| - 0.5a_{00}|x_{ij} - 1| = 0 \tag{6.16}$$

Equation (6.16) can be solved by plotting the shifted DP plot $h_{ij}(x_{ij}; w_{ij})$ via the graphical method from the previous chapter and then finding its intersections with the horizontal axis. However, since a_{00} and w_{ij} are *parameters*, and not numerical values as in the previous chapter, let us solve Eq. (6.16) *algebraically* in each of the four linear regions – henceforth called the *piecewise-linear solution method*.

Region 1: $x_{ij} + 1 > 0$, $x_{ij} - 1 > 0$
In this region, Eq. (6.16) reduces to the linear equation

$$w_{ij} - x_{ij} + 0.5a_{00}(x_{ij} + 1) - 0.5a_{00}(x_{ij} - 1) = 0 \tag{6.17}$$

whose solution is

$$x_{ij} = w_{ij} + a_{00}, \quad \text{assuming } x_{ij} > -1 \text{ and } x_{ij} > 1 \tag{6.18}$$

Region 2: $x_{ij} + 1 < 0$, $x_{ij} - 1 < 0$
In this region, Eq. (6.16) reduces to the linear equation

$$w_{ij} - x_{ij} - 0.5a_{00}(x_{ij} + 1) + 0.5a_{00}(x_{ij} - 1) = 0 \tag{6.19}$$

whose solution is

$$x_{ij} = w_{ij} - a_{00}, \quad \text{assuming } x_{ij} < -1 \text{ and } x_{ij} < 1 \tag{6.20}$$

Region 3: $x_{ij} + 1 > 0$, $x_{ij} - 1 < 0$
In this region, Eq. (6.16) reduces to the linear equation

$$w_{ij} - x_{ij} + 0.5a_{00}(x_{ij} + 1) + 0.5a_{00}(x_{ij} - 1) = 0 \tag{6.21}$$

whose solution is

$$x_{ij} = \frac{-w_{ij}}{a_{00} - 1}, \quad \text{assuming } x_{ij} > -1 \text{ and } x_{ij} < 1 \tag{6.22}$$

Region 4: $x_{ij} + 1 < 0$, $x_{ij} - 1 > 0$
Since these two inequalities *cannot* be satisfied simultaneously, the region where a solution of Eq. (6.16) lies is the empty set.

Hence, Eq. (6.11) can have *at most* three equilibrium points whose locations are summarized in Table 6.1.

Table 6.1. *Possible equilibrium points of uncoupled CNNs.*

Region	Validating inequalities	Location	Equilibrium point
1	$x_{ij} > -1$ and $x_{ij} > 1$	$x_{ij} = w_{ij} + a_{00}$	$\mathbf{Q}_+$
2	$x_{ij} < -1$ and $x_{ij} < 1$	$x_{ij} = w_{ij} - a_{00}$	$\mathbf{Q}_-$
3	$x_{ij} > -1$ and $x_{ij} < 1$	$x_{ij} = \dfrac{-w_{ij}}{a_{00} - 1}$	$\mathbf{Q}_0$

It is important to observe that since the three equilibrium points in Table 6.1 are derived from Eqs (6.18), (6.20), and (6.22) by *assuming* first that a solution exists in the corresponding linear region, *it is necessary to check the validity of each of these solutions for a given numerical value of a_{00} and w_{ij}* via the two validating inequalities which each "candidate" solution must satisfy. If a particular equilibrium point $x_{ij}(\mathbf{Q})$ violates one of the inequalities, then $\mathbf{Q}$ is not a valid solution and will henceforth be called a *virtual equilibrium point*. To find the conditions that must be satisfied in order for a CNN to have three equilibrium points, simply substitute the expression for each equilibrium point $x_{ij} = x_{ij}(\mathbf{Q})$ at $\mathbf{Q} = \mathbf{Q}_+$, $\mathbf{Q}_-$, and $\mathbf{Q}_0$ from Table 6.1 into the two corresponding validating inequalities in column 2 and obtain the following results:

(a)$w_{ij} > -(a_{00} - 1)$ (6.23)

(b)$w_{ij} < a_{00} - 1$

Observe that if inequality (a) in Eq. (6.23) is violated so that $w_{ij} < -(a_{00} - 1)$, then inequality (b) would also be violated, and vice versa. Hence, for these two cases, the CNN has only one equilibrium point. There are two other possibilities where not all inequalities in Eq. (6.23) are satisfied, namely, when $w_{ij} = -(a_{00} - 1)$, or when $w_{ij} = (a_{00} - 1)$. In these two *degenerate* cases, the CNN has two equilibrium points.

Since Theorem 1 must hold *for all parameters* $a_{00} \in R$ and $w_{ij} \in R$, it is necessary for us to examine all possible combinations of a_{00} and w_{ij} which give rise to one, two, or three equilibrium points, and to investigate their local stability or instability.

A careful examination of all possibilities in the w_{ij}–a_{00} parameter plane reveals that there are only 21 regions in the w_{ij}–a_{00} parameter plane having *different* behaviors with respect to the *number* (3, 2, or 1), *qualitative nature* (locally stable, semi-stable, or unstable), and *robustness* of the equilibrium points, and therefore warrant a separate analysis. Since the values $a_{00} = 1$ and $a_{00} = 0$ are found to separate many regions having different behaviors, it is logical to arrange these 21 regions into four contiguous groups corresponding to $a_{00} > 1$, $a_{00} = 1$, $0 < a_{00} < 1$, and $a_{00} < 0$, respectively. Each of these groups can be further subdivided into regions separated by two straight lines $w_{ij} = a_{00} - 1$ and $w_{ij} = -(a_{00} - 1)$, respectively. Under these subdivisions the w_{ij}–a_{00} parameter plane is partitioned into 21 non-overlapping regions. We will show shortly that all *uncoupled* CNNs having their w_{ij}–a_{00} parameters belonging to any one region must have similar *dynamic routes*, and hence must exhibit the same qualitative dynamic behaviors. The following five tables (Tables 6.2–6.6) specify the area in the w_{ij}–a_{00} parameter plane corresponding to each of the 21 regions, along with a *figure number* which identifies which one among the following seven figures (Figs 6.1–6.7) contains the associated *dynamic routes*. These 21 regions partition the universe of all *uncoupled* CNNs into 21 subclasses of qualitatively similar CNNs, as shown in the sub-divided w_{ij}–a_{00} parameter plane Fig. 6.8.

Since all w_{ij}–a_{00} parameters are represented in Fig. 6.8(a) and (b), it follows that the qualitative behaviors of the universe of all uncoupled CNNs are completely characterized by the 21 dynamic routes shown in Figs 6.1–6.7. Since from any initial state $x_{ij}(0)$ the solution trajectory from $x_{ij}(0)$ must either flow in one and the same direction along the dynamic route until it arrives at an equilibrium point, or it must remain stationary if the initial state is itself an equilibrium point, it follows that every trajectory converges to an equilibrium point monotonically, i.e., using the jargon of engineers, there are no "ringings." This proves that every *uncoupled* CNN is completely stable.

It remains for us to derive the explicit formula (6.1)–(6.10) for the four cases listed in Theorem 6.1. Since the 21 regions in the subdivision diagram of Fig. 6.8 cover the entire w_{ij}–a_{00} parameter plane, it suffices for us to examine the corresponding

Table 6.2. *Parameter range:* $a_{00} > 1$.

Region	Dynamic route	Qualitative behavior
$0 < w_{ij} < a_{00} - 1$	Fig. 6.1(a)	Bistable at $\mathbf{Q}_-$ and $\mathbf{Q}_+$
$-(a_{00} - 1) < w_{ij} < 0$	Fig. 6.1(b)	Bistable at $\mathbf{Q}_-$ and $\mathbf{Q}_+$
$w_{ij} > a_{00} - 1 > 0$	Fig. 6.1(c)	Monostable at $\mathbf{Q}_+$
$w_{ij} < -(a_{00} - 1) < 0$	Fig. 6.1(d)	Monostable at $\mathbf{Q}_-$

Table 6.3. *Parameter range:* $a_{00} > 1$.

Region	Dynamic route	Qualitative behavior
$w_{ij} = a_{00} - 1$	Fig. 6.2(a)	Semi-stable at $\mathbf{Q}_-$
$w_{ij} = -(a_{00} - 1)$	Fig. 6.2(b)	Semi-stable at $\mathbf{Q}_+$

Table 6.4. *Parameter range:* $a_{00} = 1$.

Region	Dynamic route	Qualitative behavior
$w_{ij} > 0$	Fig. 6.3(a)	Monostable at $\mathbf{Q}_+$
$w_{ij} < 0$	Fig. 6.3(b)	Monostable at $\mathbf{Q}_-$
$w_{ij} = 0$	Fig. 6.3(c)	Continuum of equilibria: $-1 \leq x_{ij} \leq 1$

Table 6.5. *Parameter range:* $0 < a_{00} < 1$.

Region	Dynamic route	Qualitative behavior
$w_{ij} > 1 - a_{00} > 0$	Fig. 6.4(a)	Monostable at $\mathbf{Q}_+$
$w_{ij} < -(1 - a_{00})$	Fig. 6.4(b)	Monostable at $\mathbf{Q}_-$
$0 < w_{ij} < 1 - a_{00}$	Fig. 6.4(c)	Monostable and gray-scale: $0 < x_{ij} < 1$
$a_{00} - 1 < w_{ij} < 0$	Fig. 6.4(d)	Monostable and gray-scale: $-1 < x_{ij} < 0$
$w_{ij} = 1 - a_{00} > 0$	Fig. 6.5(a)	Monostable at $\mathbf{Q}_+$ ($x_{ij} = 1$); very sensitive
$w_{ij} = -(1 - a_{00}) < 0$	Fig. 6.5(b)	Monostable at $\mathbf{Q}_-$ ($x_{ij} = -1$); very sensitive

Table 6.6. *Parameter range:* $a_{00} < 0$.

Region	Dynamic route	Qualitative behavior
$w_{ij} > 1 - a_{00}$	Fig. 6.6(a)	Monostable at $\mathbf{Q}_+$
$w_{ij} < -(1 - a_{00}) < -1$	Fig. 6.6(b)	Monostable at $\mathbf{Q}_-$
$0 < w_{ij} < 1 - a_{00}$	Fig. 6.6(c)	Monostable and gray-scale: $0 < x_{ij} < 1$
$-(1 - a_{00}) < w_{ij}$	Fig. 6.6(d)	Monostable and gray-scale: $-1 < x_{ij} < 0$
$w_{ij} = 1 - a_{00} > 1$	Fig. 6.7(a)	Monostable at $\mathbf{Q}_+$ ($x_{ij} = 1$); very sensitive
$w_{ij} = -(1 - a_{00}) < -1$	Fig. 6.7(b)	Monostable at $\mathbf{Q}_-$ ($x_{ij} = -1$); very sensitive

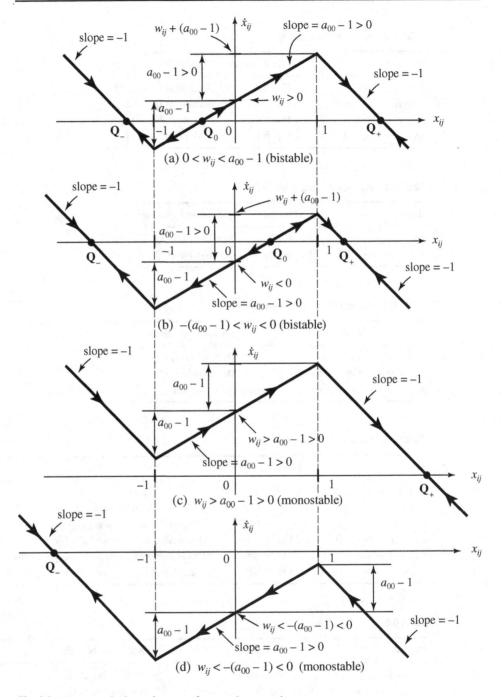

Fig. 6.1. Four generic dynamic routes for case 1: $a_{00} > 1$.

dynamic routes in Figs 6.1–6.7. Moreover, in view of our standing assumption that $|x_{ij}(0)| \leq 1$, all initial states are located on the central linear region $-1 \leq x_{ij} \leq 1$ and

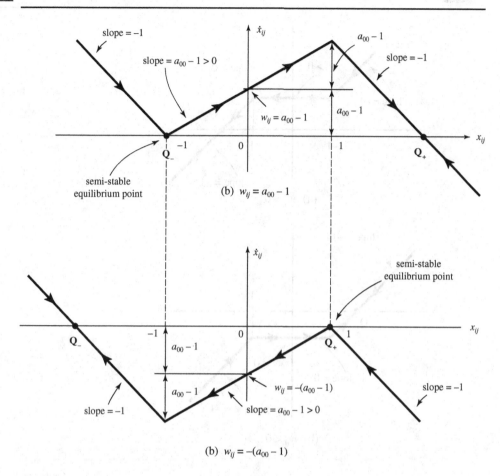

Fig. 6.2. Dynamic routes for two degenerate situations from case 1: $a_{00} > 1$.

hence we only need to examine the dynamics of a trajectory starting from *any* point on the middle segment of each shifted DP plot in Figs 6.1–6.7. This corresponds to *Region 3* whose associated *linear* differential equation can be obtained from Eq. (6.21)

$$\dot{x}_{ij} = w_{ij} - x_{ij} + a_{00}x_{ij} \tag{6.24}$$

Case 1: Strong positive self-feedback case: $a_{00} > 1$
It follows from Eq. (6.24) and the dynamic routes shown in Figs 6.1(a)–6.1(d) and in Fig. 6.2 that

$$(a_{00} - 1)x_{ij}(0) + w_{ij} > 0 \quad \Rightarrow \quad y_{ij}(t) \to \mathbf{Q}_+$$
$$(a_{00} - 1)x_{ij}(0) + w_{ij} < 0 \quad \Rightarrow \quad y_{ij}(t) \to \mathbf{Q}_- \tag{6.25}$$

provided $|x_{ij}(0)| \leq 1$ in Fig. 6.1 and $|x_{ij}(0)| < 1$ in Fig. 6.2. Since $x_{ij}(\mathbf{Q}_+) \geq 1$ and $x_{ij}(\mathbf{Q}_-) \leq 1$ in Figs 6.1 and 6.2, it follows from Eq. (6.25) that

$$(a_{00} - 1)x_{ij}(0) + w_{ij} > 0 \quad \Rightarrow \quad y_{ij}(t) \to 1$$

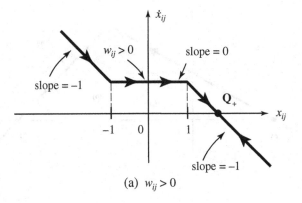

(a) $w_{ij} > 0$

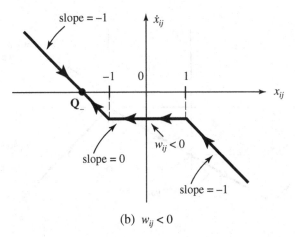

(b) $w_{ij} < 0$

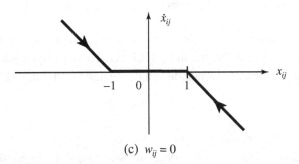

(c) $w_{ij} = 0$

Fig. 6.3. Two generic ($w_{ij} \neq 0$) dynamic routes and a degenerate ($w_{ij} = 0$) dynamic route from case 2: $a_{00} = 1$.

$$(a_{00} - 1)x_{ij}(0) + w_{ij} < 0 \quad \Rightarrow \quad y_{ij}(t) \rightarrow -1 \qquad (6.26)$$

Equation (6.26) can be recast into the explicit formula in Eq. (6.2), which holds not only for Figs 6.1(a)–6.1(d) when $|x_{ij}(0)| \leq 1$, but also for Figs 6.2(a) and 6.2(b) when $|x_{ij}(0)| < 1$.

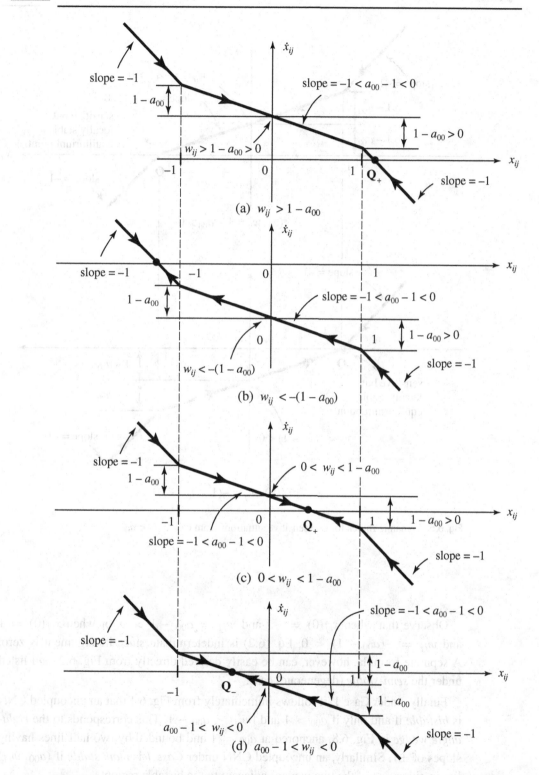

Fig. 6.4. Four generic dynamic routes from case 3: $0 < a_{00} < 1$.

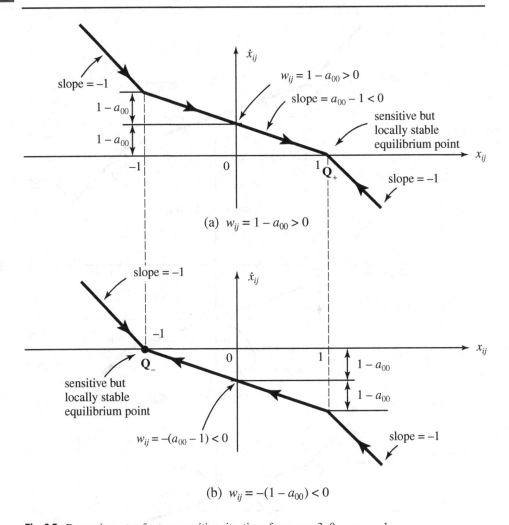

Fig. 6.5. Dynamic routes for two sensitive situations from case 3: $0 < a_{00} < 1$.

Observe that when $x_{ij}(0) = -1$ and $w_{ij} = a_{00} - 1 > 0$, or when $x_{ij}(0) = 1$ and $w_{ij} = -(a_{00} - 1) < 0$, Eq. (6.2) is indeterminate since its argument is zero. A separate formula, however, can be easily derived directly from Fig. 6.2, and listed under the *semi-stable* (degenerate) case.

Finally, under Case 1, it follows immediately from Fig. 6.1 that an uncoupled CNN is *bistable* if and only if $a_{00} > 1$ and $|w_{ij}| < a_{00} - 1$. This corresponds to the *right-angle wedge* in Fig. 6.8, anchored at $a_{00} = 1$ and bounded by two half lines having slopes of ± 1. Similarly, an uncoupled CNN under *Case 1* is *monostable* if (a_{00}, w_{ij}) lies in either one of the two wedges adjacent to the bistable region.

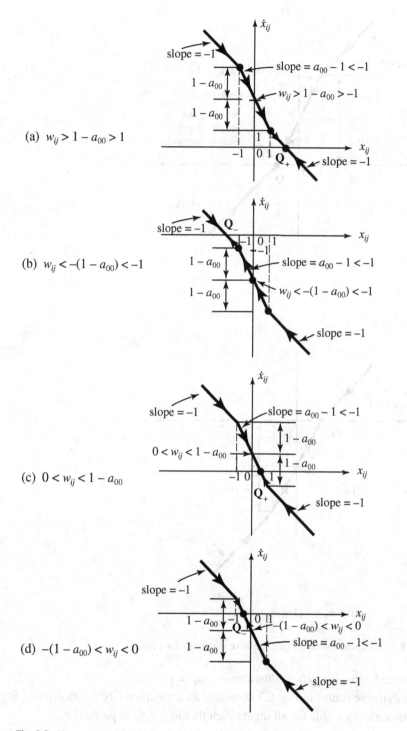

Fig. 6.6. Four generic dynamic routes for case 4: $a_{00} < 0$.

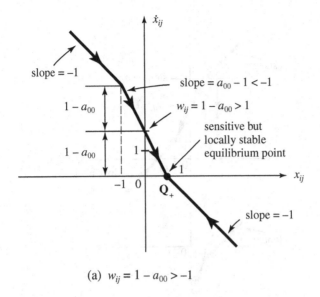

(a) $w_{ij} = 1 - a_{00} > -1$

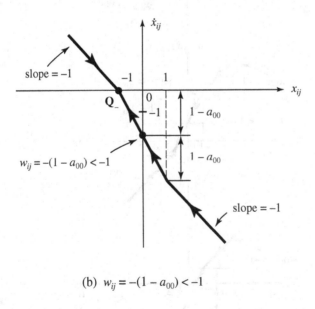

(b) $w_{ij} = -(1 - a_{00}) < -1$

Fig. 6.7. Dynamic routes for two sensitive situations for case 4.

Case 2: Unity-gain self-feedback case: $a_{00} = 1$
The dynamic routes in Fig. 6.3 show that an uncoupled CNN with $a_{00} = 1$ is globally asymptotically stable for all inputs such that $w_{ij} \neq 0$. In particular

$$x_{ij}(t) \rightarrow x_{ij}(\mathbf{Q_+}) > 1, \quad \text{if } w_{ij} > 0$$
$$x_{ij}(t) \rightarrow x_{ij}(\mathbf{Q_-}) < -1, \quad \text{if } w_{ij} < 0$$

(6.27)

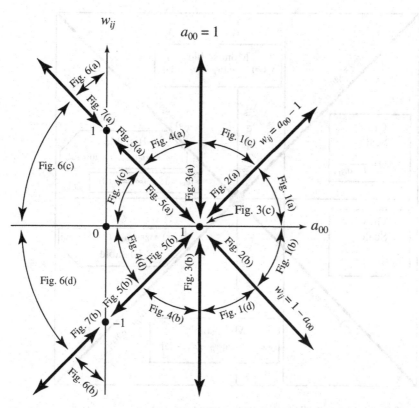

Fig. 6.8. (a) The primary CNN mosaic consists of a partitioning of the w_{ij}–a_{00} parameter plane into 21 distinct subclasses of qualitatively similar uncoupled CNNs.

independent of the initial state $x_{ij}(0)$. Eq. (6.3) then follows directly from Eq. (6.27).

For the *degenerate case* $w_{ij} = 0$, the dynamic route in Fig. 6.3(c) shows that every point $x_{ij} \in [-1, 1]$ is an equilibrium point. In this case, any initial state $x_{ij}(0) \in [-1, 1]$ gives rise to a *stationary* output

$$y_{ij}(\infty) = x_{ij}(0)$$

Such a CNN is still completely stable by definition. Observe that this degenerate uncoupled CNN corresponds to exactly one point, namely, $(a_{00}, w_{ij}) = (1, 0)$ in Fig. 6.8. This makes a lot of sense since this point is where all "wedges" of distinct dynamic behaviors intersect, a clearly *singular* situation!

Case 3: Weak positive self-feedback cases: $0 < a_{00} < 1$
Consider first the dynamic routes in Figs 6.4(a) and 6.4(b) corresponding to the cases $w_{ij} > 1 - a_{00}$ and $w_{ij} < -(1 - a_{00})$, respectively. Observe that

$$\begin{aligned} x_{ij}(t) &\to x_{ij}(\mathbf{Q}_+) > 1, &&\text{if } w_{ij} > 1 - a_{00} \\ x_{ij}(t) &\to x_{ij}(\mathbf{Q}_-) < -1, &&\text{if } w_{ij} < -(1 - a_{00}) \end{aligned} \qquad (6.28)$$

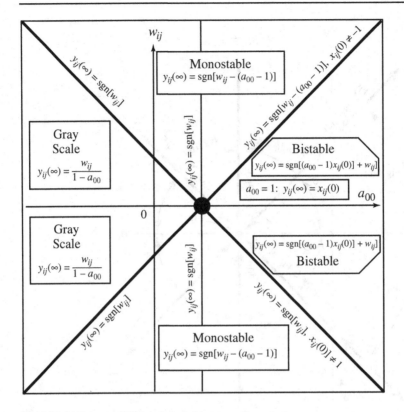

Fig. 6.8. (b) Primary CNN mosaic (with output formulas).

independent of the initial state $x_{ij}(0)$. Equation (6.5) then follows directly from Eq. (6.28).

Consider next the dynamic routes in Figs 6.4(c) and 6.4(d) corresponding to the cases $0 < w_{ij} < 1 - a_{00}$ and $a_{00} - 1 < w_{ij} < 0$, respectively. Observe that, in this case, the equilibrium point lies *inside* the middle segment, so that

$$\begin{aligned} x_{ij}(t) \to x_{ij}(\mathbf{Q}_+) < 1, \quad & \text{if } 0 < w_{ij} < 1 - a_{00} \\ x_{ij}(t) \to x_{ij}(\mathbf{Q}_-) > -1, \quad & \text{if } 1 - a_{00} < w_{ij} < 0 \end{aligned} \qquad (6.29)$$

where the coordinate of x_{ij} at $\mathbf{Q}_+$ or $\mathbf{Q}_-$ is given by Eq. (6.22); namely

$$\frac{w_{ij}}{1 - a_{00}} = \begin{cases} x_{ij}(\mathbf{Q}_+), & \text{if } 0 < w_{ij} < 1 - a_{00} \\ x_{ij}(\mathbf{Q}_-), & \text{if } a_{00} - 1 < w_{ij} < 0 \end{cases} \qquad (6.30)$$

Since $y_{ij} = x_{ij}$ when $|x_{ij}| \le 1$, Eq. (6.6) follows from Eq. (6.30). Observe that the output in this case is in *gray scale*, and not binary.

Finally, consider the dynamic routes shown in Fig. 6.5 corresponding to the limiting cases $w_{ij} = 1 - a_{00} > 0$ and $w_{ij} = -(1 - a_{00}) < 0$, respectively. In this limiting case, the gray-scale output tends to a binary output, as specified explicitly by Eq. (6.7).

Case 4: Negative self-feedback case: $a_{00} < 0$

Consider first the dynamic routes shown in Figs 6.6(a) and 6.6(b) corresponding to the cases $w_{ij} > 1 - a_{00} > 1$ and $w_{ij} < -(1 - a_{00}) < -1$. In this case we have *binary* outputs as specified by Eq. (6.8) as in *case 3*. When $0 < w_{ij} < (1 - a_{00})$, or $-(1 - a_{00}) < w_{ij} < 0$, the dynamic routes shown in Figs 6.6(c) and 6.6(d) show that the output is in gray scale and is given explicitly by Eq. (6.9). Finally, in the limiting cases where $w_{ij} > 1 - a_{00} > 1$, or $w_{ij} < -(1 - a_{00}) < -1$, the gray-scale output tends to a binary output specified by Eq. (6.10). This completes our proof of *Theorem 1*.

6.4   The primary CNN mosaic

Theorem 1 is truly fundamental not only because it yields *explicit* algebraic formulas for determining the output $y_{ij}(\infty)$ of any *uncoupled* CNN *without solving* the associated nonlinear differential equation, but also because it gives us a bonus in the form of a mosaic-like panel, where every wedge in the panel corresponds to a particular dynamic route, or qualitative behavior. In order to call attention to the fundamental significance of Fig. 6.8, as well as for ease of future reference, we will henceforth call this partitioned w_{ij}–a_{00} parameter plane *the primary CNN mosaic*. Each of the 21 regions in this mosaic will be called a *CNN mosaic wedge*, or simply a CNN "wedge." Each one-dimensional line segment which forms the boundary of two adjacent CNN wedges is called a *CNN mosaic spine*.

Observe that only wedges separated by *bold radial* spines in Fig. 6.8(a) differ significantly in their qualitative behaviors. For example, the two wedges corresponding to Figs 6.1(a) and 6.1(b) are separated by a thin spine because they both represent bistable CNNs. Observe that the primary CNN mosaic is made up of "12" two-dimensional "wedges" and "9" one-dimensional bold "radial spines."

It is sometimes instructive to lump together two or more adjacent wedges in the primary CNN mosaic which are not separated by a bold radial spine into a single CNN *sector* because all CNNs located on the wedges in the sector exhibit the same "functional," though not "dynamic," behaviors. For example, it is logical to combine the two *bistable* wedges into one bistable sector. Similarly, the four *gray-scale* wedges can be combined into one large gray-scale sector. Observe that the *bistable sector* and the *gray-scale sector* in the primary CNN mosaic are mirror images of each other. Observe also that two "bilateral" wedges which are mirror images of each other in the primary CNN mosaic tend to share some common features. For example, the wedges corresponding to Figs 6.1(d) and 6.4(a) both represent a monostable binary CNN having $\mathbf{Q}_+$ as their global asymptotically stable equilibrium point. Similarly, the two bilateral wedges corresponding to Figs 6.1(c) and 6.3(b) both represent a monostable binary CNN, having $\mathbf{Q}_-$ as their global asymptotically stable equilibrium point.

A closer examination of each of the 21 regions in the *primary CNN mosaic* and the associated formulas reveals the following general properties:

1 With the exception of the semi-stable case corresponding to the two dynamic routes shown in Figs 6.2(a) and 6.2(b), there are *only four distinct* output formulas for uncoupled CNNs:

Bistable output formula
$$y_{ij}(\infty) = \text{sgn}[(a_{00} - 1)x_{ij}(0) + w_{ij}]$$
Monostable output formula
$$y_{ij}(\infty) = \text{sgn}[w_{ij} - (a_{00} - 1)]$$
Gray-scale output formula
$$y_{ij}(\infty) = \frac{w_{ij}}{1 - a_{00}}$$
Co-dimension 1 output formula
$$y_{ij}(\infty) = \text{sgn}[w_{ij}]$$

(6.31)

The last formula pertains to all uncoupled CNNs having parameters lying on the six bold straight lines through the point $(1, 0)$ in the primary CNN mosaic. The term "co-dimension 1" is taken from "Bifurcation theory," and means the number of "*constraints*," or *equations* needed to specify a particular region. In our case, we have only one equation, either $w_{ij} = |a_{00} - 1|$ (corresponding to Figs 6.2(a), 6.2(b), 6.5(a), 6.5(b), 6.7(a), and 6.7(b)) or $a_{00} = 1$ (corresponding to Figs 6.3(a) and 6.3(b)). For future reference, we have redrawn the following primary CNN mosaic which emphasizes only these output formulas (Figures 6.8(a) and 6.8(b)).

2 The output formula for the semi-stable case (Figs 6.2(a) and 6.2(b)) reduces to $y_{ij}(\infty) = \text{sgn}[w_{ij}]$, provided $|x_{ij}(0)| \neq 1$.

3 The most degenerate case occurs at the point $(a_{00}, w_{ij}) = (1, 0)$ (Fig. 6.3(c)). This is a *co-dimension 2* bifurcation point because it is identified by two equations $a_{00} = 1$ and $w_{ij} = 0$. The output formula for this case is simply $y_{ij}(\infty) = x_{ij}(0)$.

6.5   Explicit formula for transient waveform and settling time

An inspection of the 21 cases shown in Figs 6.1–6.7 shows that, except for the degenerate cases shown in Figs 6.3(c), 6.5 and 6.7, all dynamic routes from any initial state $x_{ij}(0)$ starting from the central region contain two linear segments. Hence, except for the unity gain ($a_{00} = 1$) case, where the central region s_0 is horizontal, the state equation within each linear segment has the form

$$\dot{x}_{ij} = m_\mathbf{Q} x_{ij} + x_\mathbf{Q}$$

(6.32)

where $m_Q = m(s_-)$, $m(s_0)$, $m(s_+)$ denotes the slope of the left, central, or right segment, henceforth denoted by s_-, s_0, and s_+, respectively; namely

$$\left.\begin{array}{l} m(s_-) = -1 \\ m(s_0) = a_{00} - 1 \\ m(s_+) = -1 \end{array}\right\} \tag{6.33}$$

and x_Q denotes the coordinate of the three equilibrium points Q_-, Q_0, and Q_+ given in Table 6.1, namely

$$\left.\begin{array}{l} x_Q(s_-) = x(Q_-) = w_{ij} - a_{00} \\ x_Q(s_0) = x(Q_0) = \dfrac{-w_{ij}}{a_{00} - 1} \\ x_Q(s_+) = x(Q_+) = w_{ij} + a_{00} \end{array}\right\} \tag{6.34}$$

The solution of Eq. (6.32) is given by

$$x_{ij}(t) = x_Q + [x(t_j) - x_Q] e^{m_Q(t-t_j)}, \quad t \geq t_j \tag{6.35}$$

where x_Q is given by Eq. (6.34). This formula holds for each of the three segments s_-, s_0, and s_+, regardless of whether any of these segments intersect the horizontal axis. In other words, one or two equilibrium points may be *virtual* in the sense that they do *not* intersect the horizontal axis, as in Figs 6.1(c), 6.1(d), etc. Nevertheless, their *linear extension* will always intersect the horizontal axis at the coordinates given by Eq. (6.34). The time "t_j" in Eq. (6.35) denotes either the initial time $t_0 = 0$, or the time $t = t_+$ (resp., $t = t_-$) when the solution converges to the breakpoint at $x_{ij} = 1$ (resp., $x_{ij} = -1$), respectively. We can solve for t_+ and t_- from Eq. (6.35) upon substituting $t_j = 0$, $x(t_j) = x(0)$ and $x_{ij}(t) = 1$ or $x_{ij}(t) = -1$; namely

$$t_+ = \frac{1}{a_{00} - 1} \ln\left[\frac{1 - x(Q_+)}{x_{ij}(0) - x(Q_+)}\right] \tag{6.36a}$$

$$t_- = \frac{1}{a_{00} - 1} \ln\left[\frac{1 - x(Q_-)}{x_{ij}(0) - x(Q_-)}\right] \tag{6.36b}$$

Substituting Eqs (6.36a)–(6.36b) and (6.34) into Eq. (6.35), we obtain the following explicit formulas depending on whether the dynamic route moves to the right (i.e., $\dot{x}_{ij}(0) > 0$) or to the left (i.e., $\dot{x}_{ij}(0) < 0$).

Case 1: $x_{ij}(0) \to x(Q_+)$ *(i.e., $\dot{x}_{ij}(0) > 0$)*

$$x_{ij}(t) = x(Q_0) + [x_{ij}(0) - x(Q_0)] e^{(a_{00}-1)t} \quad 0 \leq t \leq t_+ \tag{6.37a}$$

$$x_{ij}(t) = x(Q_+) + [x_{ij}(0) - x(Q_+)] e^{-(t-t_+)} \quad t_+ \leq t < \infty \tag{6.37b}$$

The solution waveform corresponding to the dynamic route of Fig. 6.1(a) is shown in Fig. 6.9(a).

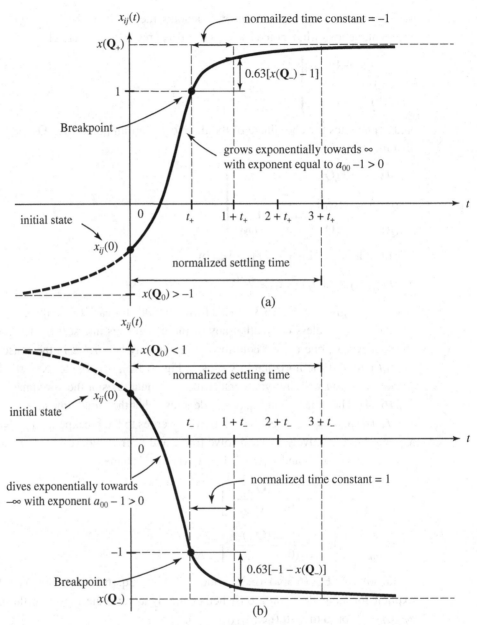

Fig. 6.9. Solution waveforms for $a_{00} > 1$ corresponding to the dynamic routes in Figs 6.1(a) and 6.1(b). Observe that over a time period equal to "one" normalized time constant, an exponential waveform rises by 63% of the distance between the breakpoint and the equilibrium value.

Case 2: $x_{ij}(0) \to x(\mathbf{Q}_-)$ (i.e., $\dot{x}_{ij}(0) < 0$)

$$x_{ij}(t) = x(\mathbf{Q}_0) + \left[x_{ij}(0) - x(\mathbf{Q}_0) \right] e^{(a_{00}-1)t} \quad 0 \le t \le t_- \tag{6.38a}$$

$$x_{ij}(t) = x(\mathbf{Q}_+) + \left[x_{ij}(0) - x(\mathbf{Q}_+) \right] e^{-(t-t_+)} \quad t_- \le t < \infty \tag{6.38b}$$

The solution waveform corresponding to the dynamic route of Fig. 6.1(b) is shown in Fig. 6.9(b).

Equations (6.37)–(6.38) hold for all cases except for the dynamic routes in Figs 6.3, 6.5, and 6.7, which are given separately as follows:

(a) Unity-gain case: $a_{00} = 1$

Case 1: $x_{ij}(0) \to x(\mathbf{Q}_+)$ *(i.e.,* $\dot{x}_{ij}(0) > 0$*)*
In this case, define

$$t'_+ = \frac{1 - x_{ij}(0)}{w_{ij}}, \quad |x_{ij}(0)| \le 1 \tag{6.39}$$

$$x_{ij}(t) = x_{ij}(0) + w_{ij}t, \qquad\qquad 0 \le t \le t'_+ \tag{6.40a}$$
$$x_{ij}(t) = x_{ij}(\mathbf{Q}_+) + [1 - x(\mathbf{Q}_+)]e^{-(t-t+)}, \quad t_+ \le t < \infty \tag{6.40b}$$

The solution waveform corresponding to the dynamic route of Fig. 6.3(a) is shown in Fig. 6.10(a).

Case 2: $x_{ij}(0) \to x(\mathbf{Q}_-)$ *(i.e.,* $\dot{x}_{ij}(0) < 0$*)*
In this case, define

$$t'_- = \frac{-1 - x_{ij}(0)}{w_{ij}}, \quad |x_{ij}(0)| \le 1$$

$$x_{ij}(t) = x_{ij}(0) + w_{ij}t, \qquad\qquad 0 \le t \le t'_- \tag{6.41a}$$
$$x_{ij}(t) = x(\mathbf{Q}_-) + [-1 - x(\mathbf{Q}_-)]e^{-(t-t_-)} \quad t_- \le t < \infty \tag{6.41b}$$

The solution waveform corresponding to the dynamic route of Fig. 6.3(b) is shown in Fig. 6.10(b).

(b) For the dynamic routes of Figs 6.5(a) and 6.7(a), the solution waveform consists of the single exponential

$$x_{ij}(t) = x(\mathbf{Q}_0) + \left[x_{ij}(0) - x(\mathbf{Q}_+)\right]e^{(a_{00}-1)t} \quad t \ge 0 \tag{6.42}$$

(c) For the dynamic routes of Figs 6.5(b) and 6.7(b), the solution waveform consists of the single exponential

$$x_{ij}(t) = x(\mathbf{Q}_0) + \left[x_{ij}(0) - x(\mathbf{Q}_-)\right]e^{(a_{00}-1)t} \quad t \ge 0 \tag{6.43}$$

Observe from Fig 6.10 that the "exponential" waveform starting from the breakpoint $x_{ij} = 1$, or $x_{ij} = -1$, tends to the equilibrium point $x(\mathbf{Q}_+)$, or $x(\mathbf{Q}_-)$, in approximately three "time constants," which in this case is equal to 3 since the

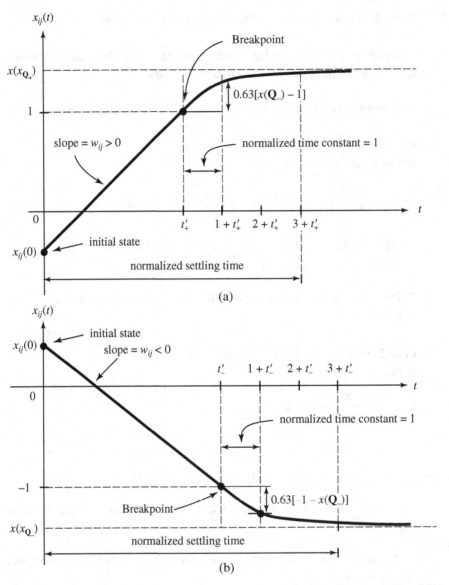

Fig. 6.10. Solution waveforms for $a_{00} = 1$ corresponding to the dynamic routes in Figs 6.3(a) and 6.3(b).

"normalized" *time constant* is assumed to be equal to unity throughout this book. Consequently, we can calculate the *normalized settling time* τ_s of an uncoupled CNN explicitly

$$\tau_s = 3 + t_1 \tag{6.44}$$

where $t_1 = t_+, t_-, t'_+,$ or t'_- corresponding to Eqs (6.37), (6.38), (6.40), and (6.41), respectively. Hence, *given the initial condition* $x_{ij}(0)$, the normalized settling time can be calculated directly from Eq. (6.44). The *actual* settling time is then simply obtained by multiplying the *circuit time constant* τ_{CNN} with the normalized settling time. We will see in Chapter 7 that the *actual settling time* is a crucial piece of information essential in the operation of a *CNN universal chip*.

6.6   Which local Boolean functions are realizable by uncoupled CNNs?

We have seen in the preceding chapter that there are $2^{2^9} = 2^{512}$ distinct Boolean functions of nine variables and that 2^{512} is an enormous number, larger than the volume of the universe. Since the class $\mathcal{C}(\mathbf{A}^0, \mathbf{B}, z)$ of uncoupled CNNs represented only a very small, albeit very powerful subclass of all CNNs, it is important to identify exactly the subset of these local Boolean functions[5] *which can be realized by an uncoupled CNN*. Since all input and output Boolean variables are binary (i.e., $\{-1, 1\}$ or its corresponding Boolean code $\{0, 1\}$), we can exclude the gray-scale sector made up of the four wedges in the primary CNN mosaic which correspond to Figs 6.4(c), 6.4(d), 6.6(c), and 6.6(d), and are represented by Eqs (6.6) and (6.9). Moreover, since the term $(a_{00} - 1)x_{ij}(0)$ in Eq. (6.2), or the term $(1 - a_{00})$ in Eqs (6.5) and (6.8), are *constants*, parameterized by a_{00} and/or $x_{ij}(0)$, they play the same role as the *threshold* z in Eq. (6.1). Hence, without loss of generality, for the purpose of this section, we can assume these constant terms to be zero. This assumption is automatically satisfied if we choose $a_{00} = 1$, which corresponds to the *unity-gain self-feedback case*. We have therefore just proved the following important result:

Theorem 2: Local Boolean function realization theorem
A local Boolean function $\beta(x_1, x_2, \ldots, x_9)$ of nine variables is realizable by *every* cell of an *uncoupled* CNN if and only if $\beta(\cdot)$ can be expressed explicitly by the formula

$$\beta = \text{sgn}[\langle \mathbf{a}, \mathbf{x} \rangle - b] \tag{6.45}$$

where $\langle \mathbf{a}, \mathbf{x} \rangle$ denotes the *dot product* between the vectors[6]

$$\mathbf{a} = [a_1, a_2, \ldots, a_9] \tag{6.46}$$

and

$$\mathbf{x} = [x_1, x_2, \ldots, x_9] \tag{6.47}$$

where $a_i \in R$ is any real number, $b \in R$ and $x_i \in \{-1, 1\}$ is the ith Boolean variable, $i = 1, 2, \ldots, 9$.

Proof of Theorem 2:
Without loss of generality, let us choose $a_{00} = 1$ so that the output of the CNN is given by Eq. (6.31) and which we rewrite as follows

$$y_{ij}(\infty) = \text{sgn}\left[\sum_{kl \in S_1(ij)} b_{kl}u_{kl} + z\right] \tag{6.48}$$

Observe that Eq. (6.48) is identical to Eq. (6.45) if we identify **a** by a vector whose components are b_{kl}, **x** by a vector whose components are u_{kl}, and $b = -z$.   □

Remarks:
We add the adjective *local* to *Theorem 2* in order to emphasize that our uncoupled CNN realizes *not only one* Boolean function, which could easily be done by standard logic circuits. Rather *every cell* of our *uncoupled* CNN will simultaneously implement the same Boolean function. For example, a 100×100 CNN array for implementing a local Boolean function would *simultaneously* implement 10,000 identical Boolean functions, each one taking its input only from its "local" neighbors located within its sphere of influence $S_r(ij)$, where $r = 1$ (3×3 neighborhood) in most cases.

Definition 2: Linearly separable class
The class of all Boolean functions which can be expressed by Eq. (6.45) is called the *linearly separable class.*

Corollary
The class $C(\mathbf{A}^0, \mathbf{B}, z)$ of all uncoupled CNNs *with binary inputs* and *binary outputs* is *identical* (with respect to Boolean input–output maps) to the *linearly separable class* of Boolean functions.

6.7 Geometrical interpretations

It is instructive to interpret the geometrical meaning of Eq. (6.45). For two Boolean variables, Eq. (6.45) can be rewritten in terms of the CNN input variables u_1 and u_2 and output variable y as follows

$$\left.\begin{array}{ll} y = 1, & \text{if } a_1 u_1 + a_2 u_2 > b \\ y = -1, & \text{if } a_1 u_1 + a_2 u_2 < b \end{array}\right\} \tag{6.49}$$

Since $u_1, u_2 \in \{-1, 1\}$, we can represent any one of the 16 *truth tables* associated with Eq. (6.49) by identifying the four "input combinations" $(-1, -1)$, $(-1, 1)$, $(1, -1)$, and $(1, 1)$ as the four "corners" of a *unit square*, and by coding the output $\beta = 1$ by a *black pixel*, and the output $\beta = -1$ by a *white pixel*, respectively.

u_1	u_2	y_1
-1	-1	-1
-1	1	1
1	-1	1
1	1	1

(a) CNN truth table for y_1

u_1	u_2	y_2
-1	-1	1
-1	1	-1
1	-1	1
1	1	1

(b) CNN truth table for y_2

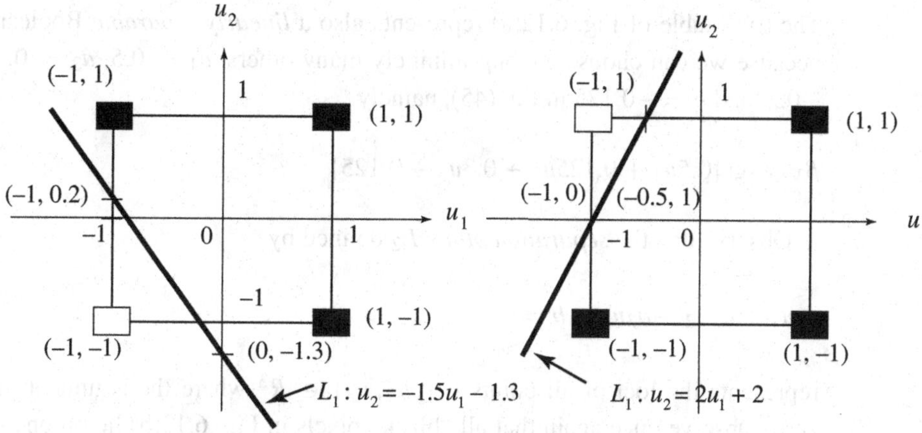

(c) $a_1 = 1.5$, $a_2 = 1$, $b = -1.3$

(d) $a_1 = 1.5$, $a_2 = 1$, $b = -1.3$

Fig. 6.11. Geometrical interpretation of two linearly separable Boolean functions of two variables.

For example, using this "corner coordinate" coding scheme, the two CNN truth tables shown in Figs 6.11(a) and 6.11(b) are coded in Figs 6.11(c) and 6.11(d), respectively.

Now observe that the Boolean function defined by the truth table in Fig. 6.11(a) belongs to the linearly separable class because we can choose, among infinitely many others, $a_1 = 1.5$, $a_2 = 1$, and $b = -1.3$ in Eq. (6.45) so that this Boolean function is expressed explicitly in the form of Eq. (6.45), namely

$$\beta_1 = \text{sgn}[1.5x_1 + x_2 + 1.3] \tag{6.50}$$

Similarly, by choosing $a_1 = -2$, $a_2 = 1$, and $b = -2$, the CNN truth table of Fig. 6.11(b) can be expressed by

$$\beta_2 = \text{sgn}[2x_1 + x_2 + 2] \tag{6.51}$$

Consequently, β_2 is also a linearly separable Boolean function.

Observe that the "separating" straight line L_1 defined by

$$a_1x_1 + a_2x_2 - b = 0 \tag{6.52}$$

represents the loci of all points $(x_1, x_2) \in R^2$ where the argument of the signum function sgn($\cdot$) is zero. Observe also that in Figs 6.11(c) and 6.11(d) all "black" pixels lie on one side of the separating straight line L_1, and all "white" pixels lie on the other side of L_1.

Consider next a Boolean function of three variables defined by the CNN truth table shown in Fig. 6.12(a). By identifying each corner of the unit cube in Fig. 6.12(b) as one of the eight combinations of (u_1, u_2, u_3), we can use the same corner coordinate coding scheme as in Fig. 6.11 to code this truth table in R^3, as shown in Fig. 6.12. The truth table of Fig. 6.12(a) represents also a *linearly separable* Boolean function because we can choose, among infinitely many others, $a_1 = 0.5$, $a_2 = 0.125$, $a_3 = -0.3$, and $b = -0.125$ in Eq. (45), namely

$$\beta_3 = \text{sgn}[0.5u_1 + 0.125u_2 - 0.3u_3 + 0.125] \tag{6.53}$$

Observe that the *separation plane* L_2 defined by

$$a_1u_1 + a_2u_2 + a_3u_3 - b = 0 \tag{6.54}$$

represents the loci of all points $(u_1, u_2, u_3) \in R^3$ where the argument of sgn($\cdot$) is zero. Observe once again that all "black" pixels in Fig. 6.12(b) lie on one side of the separating plane L_2 and all "white" pixels lie on the other side.

It should now be obvious that any Boolean function of "n" variables can be coded by placing "black" or "white" pixels at each corner of an n-dimensional *unit hypercube*, where each corner is identified by n coordinates $(u_1, u_2, \ldots, u_n)$, $u_i \in \{-1, 1\}$. Using this corner coordinate coding scheme, a Boolean function of n variables is linearly separable if and only if there exists an $(n-1)$-dimensional *hyperplane*

$$a_1u_1 + a_2u_2 + \cdots + a_nu_n - b = 0 \tag{6.55}$$

which separates all "black" corner pixels from the "white" corner pixels.

We close this section by showing a simple example of a Boolean function of two variables which is not linearly separable, and hence can not be realized by an uncoupled CNN. This example is the XOR (Exclusive OR) function whose CNN truth table is given in Fig. 6.13(a). The corresponding unit square representation is shown in Fig. 6.13(b). Observe that it is impossible to draw any straight line L_1 in the u_1–u_2 plane which would separate the "black" corner pixels from the "white" corner pixels.

This is equivalent to saying that the CNN truth table of Fig. 6.13(a) *cannot* be expressed by the explicit formula of Eq. (6.45). It follows from Theorem 2 that it is impossible to find an uncoupled CNN which implements the XOR Boolean function.[2] Fortunately, our next chapter will show that any one of the 2^{512} Boolean functions of nine variables can be realized by programming a *CNN universal chip*.

u_1	u_2	u_3	y_3
−1	−1	−1	−1
−1	−1	1	−1
−1	1	−1	1
−1	1	1	−1
1	−1	−1	1
1	−1	1	1
1	1	−1	1
1	1	1	1

(a)

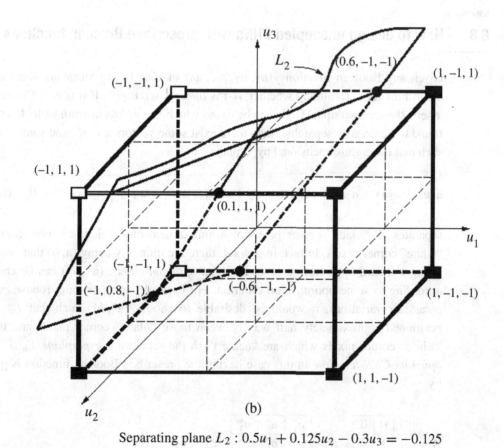

(b)

Separating plane $L_2 : 0.5u_1 + 0.125u_2 - 0.3u_3 = -0.125$

Fig. 6.12. Geometrical interpretation of a linearly separable Boolean function of three variables.

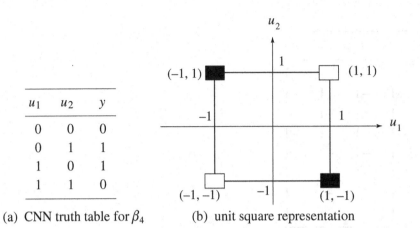

(a) CNN truth table for β_4 (b) unit square representation

Fig. 6.13. Geometrical interpretation of a Boolean function (XOR) which is *not* linearly separable.

6.8   How to design uncoupled CNNs with prescribed Boolean functions

Given any Boolean function $y(u_1, u_2, \ldots, u_9)$ of nine binary variables, there exist algorithms for determining whether $y(\cdot)$ is *linearly separable*. If it is not, *Theorem 2* asserts that no uncoupled CNN can be found which has $y(\cdot)$ as its truth table. If $y(\cdot)$ is found to be linearly separable, then there exist some vectors $\mathbf{a} \in R^9$ and some $b \in R$ such that the eight-dimensional hyperplane

$$a_1u_1 + a_2u_2 + a_3u_3 + a_4u_4 + a_5u_5 + a_6u_6 + a_7u_7 + a_8u_8 + a_9u_9 - b = 0 \quad (6.56)$$

separates all "black" corner pixels of a nine-dimensional unit *hypercube* from the "white" corner pixels. In fact, in general, there are infinitely many $(\mathbf{a}, b)$ that qualify. Using standard optimization procedures, an *optimum* choice $(\mathbf{a}^*, b^*)$ can be chosen according to some optimization criterion. For example, for maximum robustness to parameter variations, it would be desirable to choose $(\mathbf{a}^*, b^*)$ such that L_{n-1} is positioned approximately half way between those "black" corner pixels and those "white" corner pixels which are "nearest" to the separating *hyperplane* L_{n-1}. The *optimum CNN template* in this case having the prescribed Boolean function is given by

$$\mathbf{A} = \begin{array}{|c|c|c|} \hline 0 & 0 & 0 \\ \hline 0 & 1 & 0 \\ \hline 0 & 0 & 0 \\ \hline \end{array} \quad B = \begin{array}{|c|c|c|} \hline a_1^* & a_2^* & a_3^* \\ \hline a_4^* & a_5^* & a_6^* \\ \hline a_7^* & a_8^* & a_9^* \\ \hline \end{array} \quad z = \boxed{-b^*}$$

Observe that the above design procedure is based on a unity-gain self-feedback CNN ($a_{00} = 1$). From the perspective of robustness with respect to parameter variations, our choice of $a_{00} = 1$ is actually an optimum choice, as is clear from an inspection of the two dynamic routes in Figs 6.3(a) and 6.3(b) corresponding to $w_{ij} > 0$ and $w_{ij} < 0$, respectively. However, for other design criteria, say a minimum "transient settling time" criterion, a higher value of a_{00} should be chosen, as we will show in the next section. In fact, we will see that $a_{00} = 1$ is the "worst" choice if "speed" is our design criterion.

If we pick $a_{00} \neq 1$, then Eq. (6.2) must be used in our design; namely

$$y_{ij}(\infty) = \text{sgn}[(a_{00} - 1)x_{ij}(0) + w_{ij}] \tag{6.57}$$

In this case, the CNN must be parameterized by a prescribed value of $x_{ij}(0)$. We will usually choose $x_{ij}(0) = 0$ unless there are reasons to choose a non-zero value. The advantage for choosing $x_{ij}(0) = 0$ is that Eq. (6.57) then reduces to Eq. (6.48) and hence the same template given by Eq. (6.56) holds without modification. In this case, it is important to remember that, whereas an *arbitrary* initial state may be chosen for the $a_{00} = 1$ case, the *prescribed* initial state $x_{ij}(0)$ used in deriving the $(\mathbf{a}, b)$ vector must be used in actual operations in order to guarantee that the correct Boolean function is implemented.

One situation where it would be necessary to choose a non-zero value for $x_{ij}(0)$ is when the CNN is designed to implement a Boolean function of "10" variables or when each cell $C(ij)$ has two *external* self-inputs u_{ij} and u'_{ij}. This generalization is possible if we choose $x_{ij}(0) \in \{-1, 1\}$ to be the 10th Boolean variable. In this case, Eq. (6.56) becomes

$$\sum_{i=1}^{9} a_i x_i + a_{10} x_{10} - b = 0 \tag{6.58}$$

where $x_{10} \overset{\Delta}{=} x_{ij}(0)$ and $a_{10} = a_{00} - 1$. Hence, we must choose

$$a_{00} = a_{10} + 1 \tag{6.59}$$

as the self-feedback synaptic weight for the **A** template in Eq. (6.56), instead of $a_{00} = 1$, *assuming* that $a_{10} \geq 1$ for the hyperplane equation. If $a_{10} < 1$, then one must verify that the resulting CNN will *not* operate in the *gray-scale* sector in the *primary CNN mosaic*; namely, for all inputs $u_i \in \{-1, 1\}$, $i = 1, 2, \ldots, 9$, we must ensure that Eq. (6.6) of case 3 and Eq. (6.9) of case 4 cannot occur.[8] In particular the correct Boolean function will be implemented only if

$$|x_{ij}| = \sum_{kl \in S_1(ij)} b_{kl} u_{kl} + z > -a_{10} \tag{6.60}$$

is satisfied for all $u_i \in \{-1, 1\}$, $i = 1, 2, \ldots, 9$.

Let us now illustrate the above ideas by some actual design examples.

Design Example 1: Two self-input AND gate

x_1	x_2	β
0	0	0
0	1	0
1	0	0
1	1	1

(a) Boolean truth table for
Logic AND function

u_1	u_2	y
−1	−1	−1
−1	1	−1
1	−1	−1
1	1	1

(b) CNN truth table for
Logic AND function

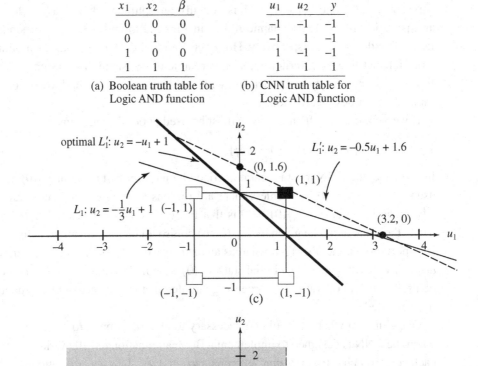

Fig. 6.14. Truth table and unit-square representation of Boolean AND function and acceptable candidate for separating lines.

Recall the LOGAND template presented in Chapter 5 for implementing the Boolean AND function of two variables. We will now apply the above systematic procedure to design an optimized CNN for performing the same task. Let us begin as always with our most basic representation; namely, the CNN truth table[9] (where YES = 1, NO = −1) corresponding to the Boolean truth table (where YES = 1, NO = 0), as shown in Figs 6.14(b) and 6.14(a), respectively. Using the corner coordinate coding scheme, the first three rows of the CNN truth table are coded by a "white" pixel at $(-1, -1)$, $(-1, 1)$, and $(1, -1)$, respectively. The 4th row is coded by a "black" pixel at $(1, 1)$.

To determine whether an *uncoupled* CNN can be designed to implement the logic AND function, one must find a *straight* line L_1 which separates the black pixels from the white pixels. Since we have already studied an earlier template (LOGAND) which realizes this function, we know such a straight line must exist (Theorem 2).

The equation of the separating straight line L_1 can be derived from the synaptic coefficients of the template LOGAND, which we reproduce below for convenience

$$\mathbf{A} = \begin{array}{|c|c|c|} \hline 0 & 0 & 0 \\ \hline 0 & 1.5 & 0 \\ \hline 0 & 0 & 0 \\ \hline \end{array} \quad \mathbf{B} = \begin{array}{|c|c|c|} \hline 0 & 0 & 0 \\ \hline 0 & 1.5 & 0 \\ \hline 0 & 0 & 0 \\ \hline \end{array} \quad z = \boxed{-1.5} \tag{6.61}$$

From Eq. (6.61), we identify $a_{00} = 1.5$, $b_{00} = 1.5$, and $z = -1.5$, from which we obtain

$$a_{00} - 1 = 0.5, \quad w_{ij} = z + b_{00}u_{ij} = -1.5 + 1.5u_{ij}$$

and

$$y_{ij}(\infty) = \text{sgn}[0.5x_{ij}(0) + 1.5u_{ij} - 1.5] \tag{6.62}$$

Let us choose (arbitrarily) $u_1 = x_{ij}(0)$ and $u_2 = u_{ij}$ as the two *self-inputs* to cell $C(ij)$. The equation of the separating line L_1 associated with Eq. (6.62) is therefore given by

$$0.5u_1 + 1.5u_2 - 1.5 = 0$$

or

$$u_2 = -\frac{1}{3}u_1 + 1 \tag{6.63}$$

This line passes through the points $(3.2, 0)$ and $(0, 1.6)$, as shown in Fig. 6.14(c). Note that L_1 indeed separates the black pixel from the white pixels, as expected. Observe, however, that L_1 is quite close to the black pixel so that a small perturbation of the slope and/or intercept of L_1 could fail to separate the points. For example, a 34% increase in the nominal designed values of $a_{00} = 1.5$ and $b_{00} = 1.5$ plus a 7% increase in the nominal designed value of $z = -1.5$ would result in the following perturbed template

$$\mathbf{A}' = \begin{array}{|c|c|c|} \hline 0 & 0 & 0 \\ \hline 0 & 2 & 0 \\ \hline 0 & 0 & 0 \\ \hline \end{array} \quad \mathbf{A}' = \begin{array}{|c|c|c|} \hline 0 & 0 & 0 \\ \hline 0 & 2 & 0 \\ \hline 0 & 0 & 0 \\ \hline \end{array} \quad z' = \boxed{-1.6} \tag{6.64}$$

The corresponding output equation and straight line L_1' are given by

$$y_{ij}(\infty) = \text{sgn}[x_i(0) + 2u_{ij} - 1.6] \tag{6.65}$$

and

$$u_2 = -\frac{1}{2}u_1 + 1.6 \tag{6.66}$$

The straight line corresponding to Eq. (6.66) is shown by the dashed line L_1' in Fig. 6.14(c). Observe that L_1' has moved above the black pixel and hence this CNN fails to operate correctly!

Since no template parameters can be realized exactly in practice, it is important that the CNN template be designed to be as robust as possible. Clearly, there are many other straight lines that are acceptable. Observe that the straight line in L_1' Fig. 6.14(c) does *not* have this "separation" property because part of L_1' overlaps with the nonshaded area above and to the right of the black pixel at $(1, 1)$. An analysis of the shape of the shaded area in Fig. 6.14(d) shows that *for maximum* robustness with respect to perturbations in the "slope" and "intercept" of the separation line L_1, we should choose L_1 to lie approximately half way between the nearest "black" and "white" pixels. The *optimal* line satisfying this "robustness" criterion in this case is the bold line L_1^* shown in Fig. 6.14(c), which is described by

$$u_2 = -u_1 + 1 \tag{6.67}$$

To implement the CNN truth table for the logic AND function, we must have

$$\left. \begin{array}{ll} x_{ij}(0) + u_{ij} - 1 > 0 & \Rightarrow \quad y_{ij}(\infty) = 1 \\ x_{ij}(0) + u_{ij} - 1 < 0 & \Rightarrow \quad y_{ij}(\infty) = -1 \end{array} \right\} \tag{6.68}$$

Equation (6.68) is equivalent to the single CNN output equation

$$y_{ij}(\infty) = \text{sgn}[x_{ij}(0) + u_{ij} - 1] \tag{6.69}$$

Comparing Eq. (6.69) with Eq. (6.57), we identify

$$a_{00} - 1 = 1 \quad \Rightarrow \quad a_{00} = 2 \tag{6.70a}$$

and

$$w_{ij} = z + b_{00}u_{ij} + \sum_{kl \neq (0,0)} b_{kl}u_{kl}$$

$$\Rightarrow \quad \left. \begin{array}{l} z = -1 \\ a_{00} = 2 \\ b_{00} = 1 \\ b_{kl} = 0 \quad kl \neq (0, 0) \end{array} \right\} \tag{6.70b}$$

It follows from Eqs (6.70a) and (6.70b) that the optimum CNN template for implementing a Boolean AND operation on two *self*-inputs $x_{ij}(0)$ and u_{ij} is given by

$$\mathbf{A}^* = \begin{array}{|c|c|c|} \hline 0 & 0 & 0 \\ \hline 0 & 2 & 0 \\ \hline 0 & 0 & 0 \\ \hline \end{array} \quad \mathbf{B}^* = \begin{array}{|c|c|c|} \hline 0 & 0 & 0 \\ \hline 0 & 1 & 0 \\ \hline 0 & 0 & 0 \\ \hline \end{array} \quad z^* = \begin{array}{|c|} \hline -1 \\ \hline \end{array} \tag{6.71}$$

This completes our Design Example 1.

Design Example 2: Two-neighbor input AND gate

Consider next the case where each cell $C(ij)$ has only one input u_{ij} and a logic AND operation is to be applied to the respective inputs either between cell $C(ij)$ and *one* neighbor $C(kl)$, or between two neighbors $C(kl)$ and $C(k'l')$. There are two cases to consider, each one involving several subclasses:

Case 1: $(u_1, u_2) = (u_{i+k,j+l}, u_{i+k',j+l'})$, kl and $k'l' \in \{-1, 1\}$ $\quad$ (6.72a)

Case 2: $(u_1, u_2) = (u_{ij}, u_{i+k,j+l})$, $kl \in \{-1, 1\}$ $\quad$ (6.72b)

Our optimal design follows directly from the preceding example upon choosing the corresponding input variables from Eq. (6.72a) or (6.72b) for u_1 and u_2. Since the initial state $x_{ij}(0)$ is *not* considered to be an input in this case, unlike that of the Example 1, we can set $x_{ij}(0) = 0$ and choose the same optimal template $\mathbf{A}^*$ and threshold z^* as in Eq. (6.71). The output equation corresponding to Eq. (69) is then given as follows

Case 1: $y_{ij}(\infty) = \text{sgn}[u_{i+k,j+l} + u_{i+k',j+l'} - 1]$, kl and $k'l' \in \{-1, 1\}$ $\quad$ (6.73a)

Case 2: $y_{ij}(\infty) = \text{sgn}[u_{ij} + u_{kl} - 1]$, $kl \in \{-1, 1\}$ $\quad$ (6.73b)

The optimal $\mathbf{B}^*$ templates corresponding to Eqs (6.73a) and (6.73b) are collected in Tables 6.7 and 6.8, respectively. In each table, the positions of the two non-zero entries in the $\mathbf{B}^*$ templates correspond to the two cells where the logic AND operation is to be applied to their inputs.

Table 6.7. *Optimal $\mathbf{B}^*$ template for case 1 (not an exhaustive list).*

$$\mathbf{B}_1^* = \begin{bmatrix} 0 & 0 & 0 \\ 1 & 0 & 1 \\ 0 & 0 & 0 \end{bmatrix} \quad \mathbf{B}_2^* = \begin{bmatrix} 0 & 1 & 0 \\ 0 & 0 & 0 \\ 0 & 1 & 0 \end{bmatrix} \quad \mathbf{B}_3^* = \begin{bmatrix} 1 & 0 & 0 \\ 0 & 0 & 0 \\ 0 & 0 & 1 \end{bmatrix} \quad \mathbf{B}_4^* = \begin{bmatrix} 0 & 0 & 1 \\ 0 & 0 & 0 \\ 1 & 0 & 0 \end{bmatrix}$$

Table 6.8. *Optimal $\mathbf{B}^*$ template for case 2.*

$$\mathbf{B}_5^* = \begin{bmatrix} 0 & 0 & 0 \\ 1 & 1 & 0 \\ 0 & 0 & 0 \end{bmatrix} \quad \mathbf{B}_6^* = \begin{bmatrix} 0 & 0 & 0 \\ 0 & 1 & 1 \\ 0 & 0 & 0 \end{bmatrix} \quad \mathbf{B}_7^* = \begin{bmatrix} 0 & 1 & 0 \\ 0 & 1 & 0 \\ 0 & 0 & 0 \end{bmatrix} \quad \mathbf{B}_8^* = \begin{bmatrix} 0 & 0 & 0 \\ 0 & 1 & 0 \\ 0 & 1 & 0 \end{bmatrix}$$

$$\mathbf{B}_9^* = \begin{bmatrix} 1 & 0 & 0 \\ 0 & 1 & 0 \\ 0 & 0 & 0 \end{bmatrix} \quad \mathbf{B}_{10}^* = \begin{bmatrix} 0 & 0 & 0 \\ 0 & 1 & 0 \\ 0 & 0 & 1 \end{bmatrix} \quad \mathbf{B}_{11}^* = \begin{bmatrix} 0 & 0 & 1 \\ 0 & 1 & 0 \\ 0 & 0 & 0 \end{bmatrix} \quad \mathbf{B}_{12}^* = \begin{bmatrix} 0 & 0 & 0 \\ 0 & 1 & 0 \\ 1 & 0 & 0 \end{bmatrix}$$

Design Example 3

Examples 1 and 2 show that once the optimal separating line L^* is found which separates the "black" pixels from the "white" pixels, the optimal CNN template follows trivially from *Theorem 2*. Hence, the *fundamental problem* in the design of an *optimal uncoupled CNN* to implement any prescribed *linearly separable* Boolean function is simply to find the equation of the optimal separating line L_1^*.

In the above examples, this equation is derived geometrically by placing the line L_1 into an optimal position which separates those "black" pixels nearest to L_1 by approximately equal distances to L_1. Unfortunately, when there are more than two inputs, the above geometric approach is no longer applicable and it would be necessary to develop a strictly *computational* approach based on methods for *solving systems of linear* inequalities. This is the classic *linear programming problem* in *operation research* where several effective computation algorithms for solving the problem are available.

In order to obtain some insights on how this can be done, let us return to the above examples and analyze the computational nature of the problem.

Suppose we wish to find the coefficients a_1, a_2, and b such that the CNN output

$$y_{ij}(\infty) = \text{sgn}[a_1 u_1 + a_2 u_2 + b] \tag{6.74}$$

would implement the CNN truth table for the Logic AND Boolean function given earlier in Fig. 6.14(b). Substituting the values of (u_1, u_2, y) from each row of this truth table, we obtain the following system of four linear inequalities

$$-a_1 - a_2 + b < 0 \tag{6.75a}$$

$$-a_1 + a_2 + b < 0 \tag{6.75b}$$

$$a_1 - a_2 + b < 0 \tag{6.75c}$$

$$a_1 + a_2 + b > 0 \tag{6.75d}$$

Our first goal is to find three numbers (a_1, a_2, b) which *simultaneously* satisfy the above four inequalities. If no such numbers are found to exist, the Boolean function is *not* linearly separable and we can conclude that no *uncoupled* CNN can solve the problem in view of *Theorem 2*. If a solution is found, however, there are in general *infinitely many* possible solutions. This brings up then the *second problem* on how to pick one solution which is *optimal* with respect to some prescribed criterion. If our criterion is to optimize the "robustness to parameter variations," then the optimal solution already derived above is $(a_1^*, a_2^*, b^*) = (1, 1, -1)$. For more than two inputs, however, a systematic algorithm must be developed. This would constitute a very good and useful project.

Without loss of generality, let us assume that either $a_{00} = 1$ or $x_{ij}(0) = 0$, so that the initial condition does not contribute anything to the outcome of the CNN output equation for a 3×3 neighborhood ($r = 1$):

$$y_{ij}(\infty) = \text{sgn}\left[(a_{00} - 1)x_{ij}(0) + \sum_{\substack{|k-i|\leq 1 \\ |l-j||\leq 1}} b_{kl}u_{kl} + b \right] \qquad (6.76)$$

In this case, our problem is simply to solve and to possibly optimize the following set of ten coefficients

$$\mathbf{a} = (a_1, a_2, \ldots, a_9) \overset{\Delta}{=} (b_{-1,-1}, b_{-1,0}, b_{-1,1}, b_{0,-1}, b_{0,0}, b_{0,1}, b_{1,-1}, b_{1,0}, b_{1,1})$$
$$b = z \qquad (6.77)$$

Since a Boolean truth table with ten variables contains 1024 distinct Boolean expressions (i.e., local rules), in the worst case,[10] we need to solve the following system of 1024 *linear* inequalities involving only "1," "−1," or "0" as coefficients

$$\alpha_{11}a_1 + \alpha_{12}a_2 + \cdots + \alpha_{19}a_9 + z > 0$$
$$\alpha_{21}a_1 + \alpha_{22}a_2 + \cdots + \alpha_{29}a_9 + z > 0$$
$$\vdots \qquad (6.78)$$
$$\alpha_{N1}a_1 + \alpha_{N2}a_2 + \cdots + \alpha_{N9}a_9 + z > 0$$

where $N = 2^{10} = 1024$, $\alpha_{ij} \in \{-1, 0, 1\}$.

We will henceforth refer to Eq. (6.78) as the *fundamental CNN inequalities*. There are several well-known algorithms and software packages for solving Eq. (6.78), the most widely used being the *simplex algorithm*. Typically, such software packages are designed for solving linear programming problems which frequently arise in *economics* and *operation research* problems where a very large number (greater than 100) of variables are to be solved. Fortunately, in our case, we have at most ten variables to solve. Consequently, it is relatively straightforward to solve Eq. (6.78) with a computer. Moreover, since the coefficients α_{ij} of Eq. (6.78) can only assume the value 1, −1, or 0, it is possible to develop special dedicated computer programs that are extremely efficient. It is therefore possible to derive *templates for all uncoupled* CNNs. Optimizing them remains an important yet untackled problem whose solution is also within reach, because of the low dimensional nature of the problem.

6.9   How to realize non-separable local Boolean functions?

We have already seen an example of a *Boolean function* which is *not* linearly separable; namely, the XOR function. It follows from Theorem 2 that it is impossible to implement this function using an *uncoupled* CNN. Although numerous non-separable local

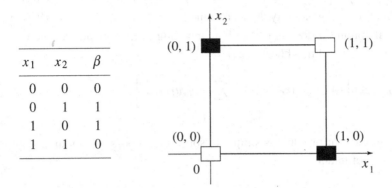

x_1	x_2	β
0	0	0
0	1	1
1	0	1
1	1	0

Fig. 6.15. Boolean truth table for the XOR function.

Boolean functions have been realized by CNNs having *non-zero feedback synaptic coefficients*, i.e., $a_{ij} \neq 0$ for at least one $i \neq j$, presently no theory exists which allows one to determine whether an arbitrary Boolean function is realizable by a CNN. However, if we are allowed to "hard wire" two or more CNNs so that the output of *each* cell $C(ij)$ of an uncoupled CNN $\mathcal{C}_a$ can be connected in parallel or in series to a corresponding cell $C(ij)$ of another uncoupled CNN $\mathcal{C}_b$, then any one of the $2^{2^9} = 2^{512}$ local Boolean functions can be realized. Before we prove this general assertion, we will present first a "constructive proof" which shows that the *non-separable* Exclusive OR (XOR) Boolean function presented earlier in Fig. 6.13, can be realized by applying first the input simultaneously (i.e., in parallel) to two elementary uncoupled CNNs $\mathcal{C}_a$ and $\mathcal{C}_b$ called *minterm CNNs* or *maxterm CNNs*, and then feeding their respective outputs simultaneously into a LOGOR CNN analyzed earlier in Chapter 5.

Consider the CNN truth table and its unit square representation for the XOR function presented earlier in Fig. 6.13 which we recast in Fig. 6.15 in terms of the Boolean variables $x_1, x_2 \in \{0, 1\}$. We revert to the Boolean variables $x_1, x_2 \in \{0, 1\}$ here because the *proofs* to be given in this section are based on some classic theorems from Boolean algebra which were invariably couched in Boolean variables ($x_i = 1$ (TRUE) or $x_i = 0$ (FALSE)) having no numerical significance. The reader should note that all "operations" in this section are Boolean operations involving the *complementation* (LOGNOT) operation $\bar{x}_i$ of x_i, the *conjunctive* (intersection, LOGAND) operation $x_1 \wedge x_2$ between x_1 and x_2, and the *disjunctive* (union, LOGOR) operation $x_1 \vee x_2$ between x_1 and x_2, respectively. In particular, no arithmetic or algebraic operations are involved.

We will show that the Boolean truth table of XOR in Fig. 6.15 can be realized as shown in Fig. 6.16 using only two elementary Boolean functions β_1 and β_2 and an OR operator; namely

$$\beta(x_1, x_2) = \beta_1(x_1, x_2) \vee \beta_2(x_1, x_2) \tag{6.79}$$

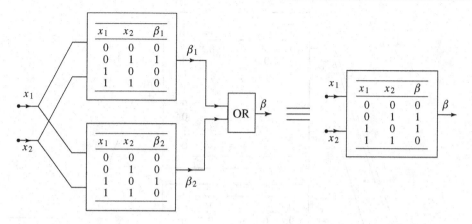

Fig. 6.16. Minterm realization of the XOR function.

Using the truth tables for β_1 and β_2 defined in Fig. 6.16, we obtain

$$\beta(0, 0) = \beta_1(0, 0) \vee \beta_2(0, 0) = 0 \vee 0 = 0$$
$$\beta(0, 1) = \beta_1(0, 1) \vee \beta_2(0, 1) = 1 \vee 0 = 1$$
$$\beta(1, 0) = \beta_1(1, 0) \vee \beta_2(1, 0) = 0 \vee 1 = 1$$
$$\beta(1, 1) = \beta_1(1, 1) \vee \beta_2(1, 1) = 0 \vee 0 = 0$$

(6.80)

which is precisely the truth table for XOR.

Observe that the two truth tables β_1 and β_2 in Fig. 6.16 have *only one* TRUE statement, i.e., their outputs are "0" except for one combination of x_1 and x_2. Such Boolean functions are examples of an elementary class defined as follows:

Definition 1: Minterm Boolean function
A Boolean function $\beta(x_1, x_2, \ldots, x_n)$ of n variables is said to be a *minterm* if its output column in the truth table consists of all "0"s except for one entry having a "1."

Definition 2: Minterm CNN
A CNN which implements a minterm Boolean function in each cell is called a minterm CNN.

Since there are 2^n rows in a truth table of "n" Boolean variables, there are $2^9 = 512$ distinct minterm Boolean functions of nine variables. For $n = 2$, there are only four minterm Boolean functions, two of which are defined by β_1 and β_2 in Fig. 6.16. In the context of information theory, a minterm Boolean function contains the *minimum* amount of information; namely, 1 "bit," hence the name "minterm."

Now consider an *arbitrary* Boolean function $\beta(x_1, x_2, \ldots, x_9)$ of nine variables where the output column in its truth table has exactly $N \leq 512$ *non-zero* entries (i.e., "1"). To each row of β having an output $\beta(x_1, x_2, \ldots, x_9) = 1$ we can define an

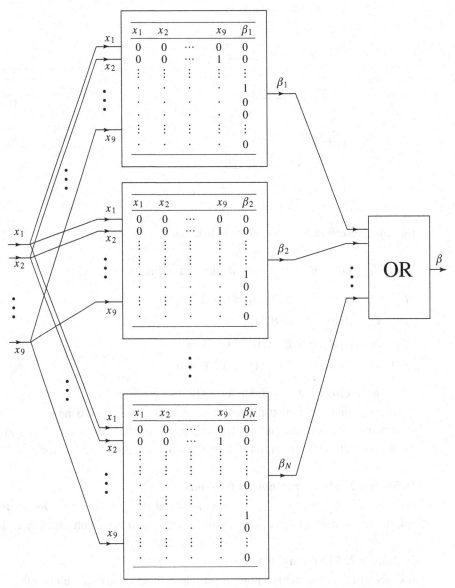

Fig. 6.17. Minterm realization of an arbitrary Boolean function of nine variables. Each of the $N \leq 512$ rows, nine inputs and one output. The OR operator has N inputs and one output.

associated *minterm* truth table. Hence, we can define uniquely N *minterm* Boolean functions $\beta_1, \beta_2, \ldots, \beta_N$.[11] ORing these N minterms, as shown in Fig. 6.17, we obtain

$$\beta(x_1, x_2, \ldots, x_9) = \beta_1 \vee \beta_2 \vee \beta_3 \vee \cdots \vee \beta_N \tag{6.81}$$

Observe that by construction, we have

$$\beta(x_1, x_2, \ldots, x_9) = 1, \quad \text{if } (x_1, x_2, \ldots, x_9) \text{ belongs to one}$$
$$\text{and only one, of the 512 rows of}$$
$$\beta_i, i = 1, 2, \ldots, N, \text{ whose output is ``1''}$$
$$= 0, \quad \text{otherwise}$$

which gives the prescribed truth table of β.

We are now ready to prove the following theorem:

Theorem 3: CNN minterm realization theorem

Every local Boolean function of nine variables can be realized by ORing at most 512 *uncoupled* CNNs.

Proof of Theorem 3:

It suffices for us to prove that *every minterm* Boolean function $\beta_i(x_1, x_2, \ldots, x_9)$, $i = 1, 2, \ldots, N \leq 512$, in Eq. (6.81) is linearly separable. To avoid clutter, let us first show that this is true for the two minterm Boolean functions associated with the XOR truth table in Fig. 6.16, since the generalization for any $n > 2$ will be obvious. In particular, we will show that each of the two minterms in Fig. 6.16 has an *explicit* "Boolean" output equation; namely

$$\beta_1(x_1, x_2) = \bar{x}_1 \wedge x_2 \tag{6.82}$$
$$\beta_2(x_1, x_2) = x_1 \wedge \bar{x}_2 \tag{6.83}$$

Substituting the $n^2 = 4$ combinations of $\{0, 1\}$, namely, $(0, 0)$, $(0, 1)$, $(1, 0)$, and $(1, 1)$, into Eqs (6.82) and (6.83), we obtain the corresponding truth tables shown in Tables 6.9 and 6.10, respectively, which are precisely the truth tables of β_1 and β_2 in Fig. 6.16. Substituting next Eqs (6.82) and (6.83) for β_1 and β_2 in Eq. (6.81) for $n = 2$, we obtain the following explicit Boolean output equation for the XOR truth table:

$$\beta = (\bar{x}_1 \wedge x_2) \vee (x_1 \wedge \bar{x}_2) \tag{6.84}$$

Table 6.9. *Truth table of $\beta_1 = \bar{x}_1 \wedge x_2$.*

x_1	x_2	$\bar{x}_1 \wedge x_2$	β_1
0	0	$\bar{0} \wedge 0 = 1 \wedge 0 = 0$	0
0	1	$\bar{0} \wedge 1 = 1 \wedge 1 = 1$	1
1	0	$\bar{1} \wedge 0 = 0 \wedge 0 = 0$	0
1	1	$\bar{1} \wedge 1 = 0 \wedge 1 = 0$	0

Table 6.10. *Truth table of $\beta_2 = x_1 \wedge \bar{x}_2$.*

x_1	x_2	$x_1 \wedge \bar{x}_2$	β_2
0	0	$0 \wedge \bar{0} = 0 \wedge 0 = 0$	0
0	1	$0 \wedge \bar{1} = 0 \wedge 0 = 1$	0
1	0	$1 \wedge \bar{0} = 1 \wedge 1 = 0$	1
1	1	$1 \wedge \bar{1} = 1 \wedge 0 = 0$	0

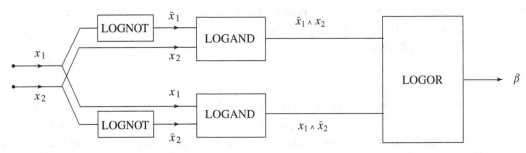

Fig. 6.18. Schematic diagram showing that the non-separable Boolean function XOR of two variables can be realized by hard-wiring two LOGNOT CNNs, two LOGAND CNNs, and one LOGOR CNN, all of them are linearly separable. The "interface circuitry" is not shown to avoid clutter.

Since Eq. (6.84) involves only the NOT, AND, and OR operations, it follows that we can realize Eq. (6.84) in hardware, as shown in Fig. 6.18, using only two LOGNOT CNNs, two LOGAND CNNs, and one LOGOR CNN.[12]

A careful analysis of Tables 6.9 and 6.10 shows that Eqs. (6.82) and (6.83) can be easily derived from each row "k" of the truth table of the Boolean function XOR having a non-zero output: simply apply the *complement* of the input variable associated with a "0" in row "k." Hence, since the values of input variables in row 2 of Fig. 6.15(a) are $(x_1, x_2) = (0, 1)$, we must choose $\bar{x}_1$ since the first variable is "0." Similarly, since the values of input variables in row 3 of Fig. 6.15(a) are $(x_1, x_2) = (1, 0)$, we must choose $\bar{x}_2$ since this time it is the second variable that is "0." Observe that this scheme will always result in an output term equal to $1 \wedge 1 = 1$ because the "0" in each relevant row has been changed to a "1."

By an obvious generalization of the above minterm decomposition method, it follows that every Boolean function of nine variables has the following explicit CNN minterm output equation.[13]

$$y(u_1, u_2, \ldots, u_9) = (u_1^{\alpha_{11}} \wedge u_2^{\alpha_{12}} \wedge \cdots \wedge u_9^{\alpha_{19}}) \vee (u_1^{\alpha_{21}} \wedge u_2^{\alpha_{22}} \wedge \cdots \wedge u_9^{\alpha_{29}})$$
$$\vee (u_1^{\alpha_{N1}} \wedge u_2^{\alpha_{N2}} \wedge \cdots \wedge u_9^{\alpha_{N9}}) \tag{6.85}$$

where $N \leq 512$, and

$$u_l^{\alpha_{kl}} = \bar{u}_l, \quad \text{if } x_l \text{ in the minterm input} = 0$$
$$= u_l, \quad \text{otherwise.}$$
(6.86)

Finally, observe that Eqs (6.85)–(6.86) can be realized by $N \leq 512$ LOGAND CNNs with nine inputs, one LOGOR CNN with N inputs, and one LOGNOT CNN for *each* input variable x_i in $(x_1, x_2, \ldots, x_9)$ with value $x_i = 0$ in each row of the truth table having an output equal to "1." This completes the proof of Theorem 3. □

Definition 3: Maxterm Boolean function

A Boolean function $\beta(x_1, x_2, \ldots, x_n)$ of n variables is said to be a *maxterm* iff its output column in the truth table consists of all "1"s except for one entry having a "0."

Definition 4: Maxterm CNN

A CNN which implements a maxterm Boolean function in each cell is called a maxterm CNN.

Since there are 2^n rows in a truth table of "n" Boolean variables, there are $2^9 = 512$ distinct maxterm Boolean functions of nine variables. For $n = 2$, there are only four maxterm Boolean functions, two of which are defined by β_1 and β_2 in Fig. 6.19. In the context of information theory, a maxterm Boolean function contains the *maximum* amount of information; namely, $2^n - 1$ "bits," hence the name "maxterm."

Now consider an *arbitrary* Boolean function $\beta(x_1, x_2, \ldots, x_9)$ of nine variables where the output column in its truth table has exactly $N \leq 512$ *zero* entries (i.e., "0"). To each row of β having an output $\beta(x_1, x_2, \ldots, x_9) = 0$ we can define an associated *maxterm* truth table. Hence, we can define uniquely N *maxterm* Boolean functions $\beta_1, \beta_2, \ldots, \beta_N$.[14] ANDing these N maxterms, we obtain

$$\beta(x_1, x_2, \ldots, x_9) = \beta_1 \wedge \beta_2 \wedge \beta_3 \wedge \cdots \wedge \beta_N$$
(6.87)

Observe that by construction, we have

$$\beta(x_1, x_2, \ldots, x_9) = 0, \quad \text{if } (x_1, x_2, \ldots, x_9) \text{ belongs to one}$$
$$\text{and only one, of the 512 rows of}$$
$$\beta_i, i = 1, 2, \ldots, N, \text{ whose output is "0"}$$
$$= 1, \quad \text{otherwise}$$

which gives the prescribed truth table of β.

We are now ready to prove the following theorem:

Theorem 4: CNN maxterm realization theorem

Every local Boolean function of nine variables can be realized by ANDing at most 512 *uncoupled* CNNs.

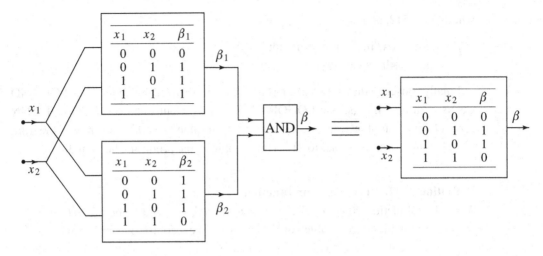

Fig. 6.19. Maxterm realization of the XOR function.

Proof of Theorem 4:

It suffices for us to prove that *every maxterm* Boolean function $\beta_i(x_1, x_2, \ldots, x_9)$, $i = 1, 2, \ldots, N \leq 512$, in Eq. (6.87) is linearly separable. To avoid clutter, let us first show that this is true for the two maxterm Boolean functions associated with the XOR truth table in Fig. 6.19, since the generalization for any $n > 2$ will be obvious. In particular, we will show that each of the two maxterms in Fig. 6.19 has an *explicit* "Boolean" output equation; namely

$$\beta_1(x_1, x_2) = x_1 \vee x_2 \tag{6.88}$$

$$\beta_2(x_1, x_2) = \bar{x}_1 \vee \bar{x}_2 \tag{6.89}$$

Substituting the $n^2 = 4$ combinations of $\{0, 1\}$, namely, $(0, 0)$, $(0, 1)$, $(1, 0)$, and $(1, 1)$, into Eqs (6.88) and (6.89), we obtain the corresponding truth tables shown in Tables 6.11 and 6.12, respectively, which are precisely the truth tables of β_1 and β_2 in Fig. 6.19. Substituting next Eqs (6.88) and (6.89) for β_1 and β_2 in Eq. (6.87) for $n = 2$, we obtain the following explicit Boolean output equation for the XOR truth table:

$$\beta = (x_1 \vee x_2) \wedge (\bar{x}_1 \vee \bar{x}_2) \tag{6.90}$$

Table 6.11. *Truth table of $\beta_1 = x_1 \vee x_2$.*

x_1	x_2	$x_1 \vee x_2$	β_1
0	0	$0 \vee 0 = 0$	0
0	1	$0 \vee 1 = 1$	1
1	0	$1 \vee 0 = 1$	1
1	1	$1 \vee 1 = 1$	1

Table 6.12. *Truth table of $\beta_2 = \bar{x}_1 \vee \bar{x}_2$.*

x_1	x_2	$\bar{x}_1 \vee \bar{x}_2$	β_2
0	0	$\bar{0} \vee \bar{0} = 1 \vee 1 = 1$	1
0	1	$\bar{0} \vee \bar{1} = 1 \vee 0 = 1$	1
1	0	$\bar{1} \vee \bar{0} = 0 \vee 1 = 1$	1
1	1	$\bar{1} \vee \bar{1} = 0 \vee 0 = 0$	0

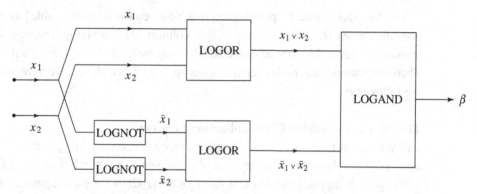

Fig. 6.20. Schematic diagram showing that the non-separable Boolean function XOR of two variables can be realized by hard-wiring two LOGNOT CNNs, two LOGOR CNNs, and one LOGAND CNN.

Since Eq. (6.90) involves only the NOT, AND, and OR operations, it follows that we can realize Eq. (6.90) in hardware, as shown in Fig. 6.20, using only two LOGNOT CNNs, two LOGOR CNNs, and one LOGAND CNN.

A careful analysis of Tables 6.3 and 6.4 shows that Eqs (6.88) and (6.89) can be easily derived from each row "k" of the truth table of the Boolean function XOR, having a zero output: simply apply the *complement* of the input variable associated with a "1" in row "k." Hence, since the values of input variables in row 1 of Fig. 6.15(a) are $(x_1, x_2) = (0, 0)$, we can choose x_1 and x_2. Similarly, since the values of input variables in row 4 of Fig. 6.15(a) are $(x_1, x_2) = (1, 1)$, we must choose $\bar{x}_1$ and $\bar{x}_2$ since this time both of the variables are "1." Observe that this scheme will always result in an output term equal to $0 \vee 0 = 0$ because the "1" in each relevant row has been changed to a "0."

By an obvious generalization of the above maxterm decomposition method, it follows that every Boolean function of nine variables has the following explicit CNN maxterm output equation

$$y(u_1, u_2, \ldots, u_9) = (u_1^{\alpha_{11}} \vee u_2^{\alpha_{12}} \vee \cdots \vee u_9^{\alpha_{19}})$$
$$\wedge (u_1^{\alpha_{21}} \vee u_2^{\alpha_{22}} \vee \cdots \vee u_9^{\alpha_{29}}) \wedge \cdots$$
$$\wedge (u_1^{\alpha_{N1}} \vee u_2^{\alpha_{N2}} \vee \cdots \vee u_9^{\alpha_{N9}}) \tag{6.91}$$

where $N \leq 512$, and

$$
\begin{aligned}
u_l^{\alpha_{kl}} &= \bar{u}_l, && \text{if } x_l \text{ in the maxterm input} = 1 \\
&= u_l, && \text{otherwise}
\end{aligned}
\tag{6.92}
$$

Finally, observe that Eqs (6.91)–(6.92) can be realized by $N \leq 512$ LOGOR CNNs with nine inputs, one LOGAND CNN with N inputs, and one LOGNOT CNN for *each* input variable x_i in $(x_1, x_2, \ldots, x_9)$ with value $x_i = 1$ in each row of the truth table having an output equal to "0." This completes the proof of Theorem 4. □

We close this chapter by pointing out that if a given Boolean truth table has $N > 256$ nonzero entries (i.e., "1"s) in the output column, then applying Theorem 4 would require less than 256 uncoupled CNNs. Conversely, if $N < 256$, then applying Theorem 3 would require less than 256 uncoupled CNNs. Hence, we have just proved the following:

Theorem 5: Uncoupled CNN realization theorem

Every Boolean function of nine variables can be realized by using at most $N = 256$ *uncoupled* CNNs having nine inputs and either one LOGOR CNN, or one LOGAND CNN, with N inputs, in addition to one LOGNOT CNN for each input variable x_i in $(x_1, x_2, \ldots, x_9)$ with value $x_i = 0$ in each row of the truth table having an output equal to "1," or with value $x_i = 1$ in each row having an output equal to "0."

Remarks:

Theorems 3–5 are mainly of theoretical interest. They prove that *every* local Boolean function of nine variables can be realized using *uncoupled* CNNs as building blocks. For each prescribed local Boolean function, we can usually derive much simpler realizations. No systematic procedure, however, is currently available for such realizations.

7 Introduction to the CNN Universal Machine

We have seen in Chapter 6 that not all tasks can be implemented by a single CNN template; the XOR function is a typical example.

There are many tasks which are solved by applying several templates, or by applying one template several times. If we consider a *template as an instruction* with well-defined input and output, we can define a *CNN subroutine* or *function* (as in C-like languages) when applying several templates. We can build up processes and complete programs from functions and other instructions.

We define a subroutine by specifying the following items:

- the input/output parameters,
- the global task,
- the informal description of the algorithm,
- the CNN implementation.

In this chapter the CNN implementation is given by three equivalent ways:

the *hardware schematics*, supposing each CNN template (placed in the CNN Software Library) is implemented by a separate device containing discrete hard-wired cells and additional local (cell by cell) and global devices.

a *flow diagram of the CNN algorithm*, and

a list of *consecutive instructions*, henceforth called a *program*, written in a simple vocabulary involving the CNN *analog* and *logic* operations, henceforth called an analogic CNN *language*, or simply "α" *language*.

An *Alpha Compiler* is supposed to exist to translate the code into executable programs on CNN chips. We will describe this process later in Chapter 9.

Indeed, we follow the theory and practice of digital computers. According to the classic Turing–Church thesis, each algorithm defined on integers or on a finite set of symbols (e.g., "yes" or "no") can be equivalently expressed by

- a Turing *machine*,
- a recursive function (an *algorithmic description* using a finite set of elementary operators), and
- a program defined on a computer using a *language*.

As to the α *language*, the key instruction is the CNN template operation defined as

TemplateName(InputImage, InitialStateImage, OutputImage, TimeInterval,

   BoundaryCond)

For example

EDGE(LLM1, LLM2, LLM3, 10, −1)

means that an edge detector template called EDGE is applied with input, initial state, and output images denoted by/stored in LLM1, LLM2, LLM3 images, the output is taken at time $t = 10$ (measured in the time constant of the CNN cell, τ_{NN}), and the fixed boundary value is −1.

7.1 Global clock and global wire

Definition
A component is called *global* if its output depends on all cells of the array or its output affects all cells of the array.

Like in any programmable system we need a clock. To emphasize that within one CNN template operation there is no clock, we will call our clock a *global clock* (GCL). This means that during one clock cycle an entire array of cells implements the same template instruction.

The global clock is used to control a set of switches (enabling, disabling, latching functions) which provide that at a given clock cycle only the prescribed signal route is open.

In many cases we have to decide whether any black pixels remain in the processed image, i.e. whether it is completely white or not. We call the operation GW(.) which tests this property (it is called "global white," "global wire," or "global line" in the literature).

GW($\cdot$) is defined as follows:
Given a binary image **P** containing $M \times N$ pixels

$$\mathrm{GW}(\mathbf{P}) = \begin{cases} 1(\text{Yes}) \text{ if all the pixels of } \mathbf{P} \text{ are white } (-1) \\ -1(\text{No}) \text{ if at least one pixel in } \mathbf{P} \text{ is black } (1) \end{cases}$$

In some implementations "NO" is represented by 0.

7.2 Set inclusion

We want to detect whether

$$S_1 \subset S_2$$

S_1 and S_2 are represented by pictures $\mathbf{P}_1$ and $\mathbf{P}_2$, respectively. A pixel is black if the corresponding element is included in the given set. $\mathbf{P}_1 \subset \mathbf{P}_2$ if and only if all black pixels defining $\mathbf{P}_1$ are elements of the black pixels representing $\mathbf{P}_2$.

Now we define the subroutine or function SUBSET $1(\cdot, \cdot, \cdot)$.

SUBSET $1(\mathbf{P}1, \mathbf{P}2, \mathbf{Y})$

$\mathbf{P}1, \mathbf{P}2$: binary images of size $M \times N$, the black pixels represent the relevant sets.

Y: logical value, Yes or No, represented by 1 and -1, respectively.

Global task

Determine whether a set $S2$ defined on a Euclidean plane is a subset of another set $S1$.

Algorithm

Given $\mathbf{P}_1$ and $\mathbf{P}_2$. The algorithm consists of three steps:

P3 := NOT(P1)

P1 := P3 AND P2

IF P1 contains only white pixels THEN
    Y := 1 (Yes)   ELSE Y := -1 (No)

Remark:

The NOT and AND operations are acting pixel by pixel.

EXAMPLE 7.1:

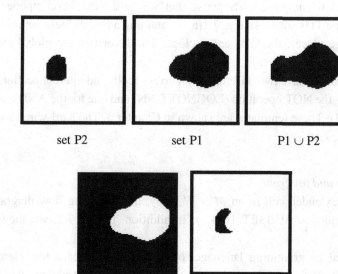

set P2   set P1   P1 ∪ P2

NOT P1   (NOT P1) AND P2

EXAMPLE 7.2:

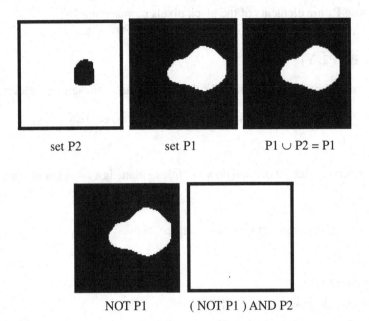

set P2   set P1   P1 ∪ P2 = P1

NOT P1   (NOT P1) AND P2

CNN implementation

1: Hardwired components

To implement this algorithm via CNN we need some additional components in each cell and two global components. Suppose that we hard-wire the components. An extended cell (type 1) is shown in Fig. 7.1(a), containing a (local) logic memory LLM with three storage places, the GW, and a clock. The latter two are global elements operating on the whole cell array.

We suppose that we have two different CNN arrays (cells and interconnections), one for implementing the NOT operation (LOGNOT CNN) and one for the AND operation (LOGAND CNN). These templates are shown in Chapter 3. The hard-wired solutions are shown in Fig. 7.1(b).

2: Flow diagram and program

If we place the extended cell in an $M \times N$ array, the following flow diagram will implement the function SUBSET $1(\cdot, \cdot, \cdot)$. In addition, in Fig. 7.2, we show the α program as well.

As in a digital programming language, our α language uses a few elementary instructions. Here, in addition to the template activation instruction, we use an

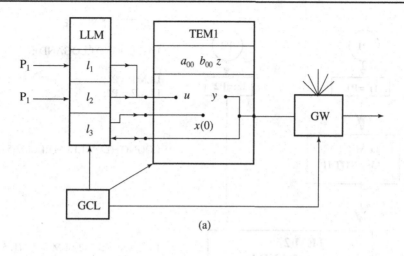

(a)

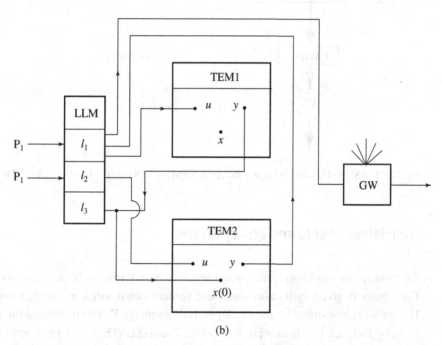

(b)

Fig. 7.1. (a) The extended cell 1. In addition to the CNN cell we have three new components: a local logic memory (LLM), a global white tester (GW) and a global clock (GCL); (b) the hard wired solution for SUBSET 1($\cdot$).

instruction for the GW($\cdot$) test and memory copying instructions. We declare the templates to be used in the function by listing them between the brackets of the USE declaration.

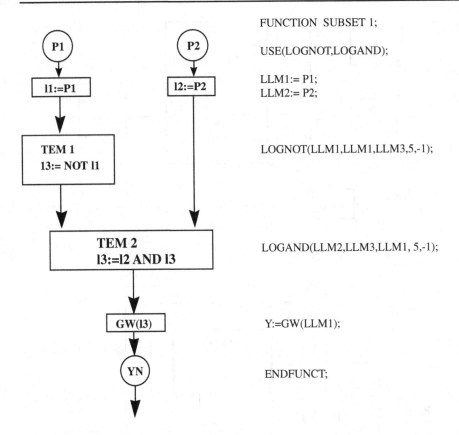

Fig. 7.2. The SUBSET subroutine as a function. TEM1 is LOGNOT, TEM2 is LOGAND.

7.3   Translation of sets and binary images

We want to translate two-dimensional sets and binary images by a prescribed vector. This vector is given by its horizontal and vertical coordinates, m and n, respectively. The set **S** is represented by the black pixels of an image **P**. The translated image **PT** is given by its black pixels as well. Subroutine TRANSLATE($\cdot$, $\cdot$, $\cdot$, $\cdot$) performs this task

TRANSLATE(P, PT, m, n)

P, **PT**: binary images of size $M \times N$; m, n: integers.

Global task

Translate image **P** by vector (m, n) (we suppose $m, n > 0$; if not, simple modifications can be applied).

Algorithm

Given **P**, m, and n. The algorithm is performed in an iteration (a program loop):

PT:=P
FOR i=1 STEP 1 TO m
  PT:=SHIFT(PT, EAST)
FOR j=1 STEP 1 TO n
  PT:=SHIFT(PT, NORTH)

Here, SHIFT(PT, EAST) and SHIFT(PT, NORTH) are the translating operators with one unit length to the directions EAST and NORTH, respectively.

EXAMPLE 7.3:

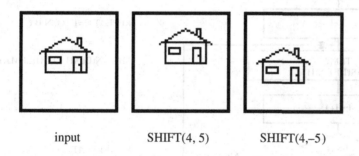

input   SHIFT(4, 5)   SHIFT(4,–5)

CNN implementation

1: hardware components

For the implementation of this algorithm we do not need more components than we used in the preceding subroutine (SUBSET 1). The controlling mechanism, however, is more sophisticated. We have to check when to stop the iteration after m and n steps. This means we need a global control unit which controls the switches and stops/starts the iteration.

Again, we suppose that we have two different CNN cells (and arrays), one for the SHIFT to north, one for the SHIFT to east. However, now we need m and n samples of each CNN component, or we use these two components with a sophisticated control unit.

2: Flow diagram and program

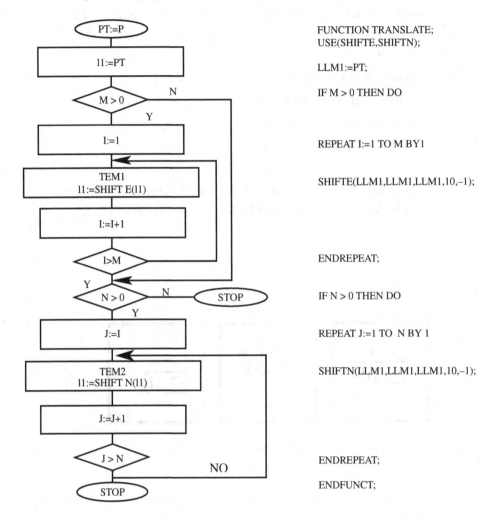

Fig. 7.3. The function TRANSLATE.

7.4   Opening and closing and implementing any morphological operator

Two frequently used morphological operators are the opening and closing.

Opening is defined as: first erosion then dilation.

Closing is defined as: first dilation then erosion.

The difference is in the sequence of the two elementary templates.

We will show here the subroutine CLOSE(P, S, PC) where P is the original image, S is the structuring element, and PC is the result.

CLOSE(P, B, PC)

P, PC: binary images of size $M \times N$

S: 3×3 structuring element represented in a **B** template for erosion, the 3×3 feedforward template **B** defined by the structuring element with 1 (black) and 0 (white) for dilation, reflect **B** (centrally) to get B1 as the feedforward template.

Global task

Given **P**, first apply a dilation, then an erosion with structuring element represented by **B**, defined above.

Algorithm

Given **P** and **S(B)**. The algorithm has four steps:

P1 := P
P2 := DILATION(P1,B1)
P3 := EROSION(P2,B)
PC := P3

EXAMPLE 7.4:

input   output of DILATION operation

EXAMPLE 7.5:

input = output of DILATION operation   output of EROSION operation

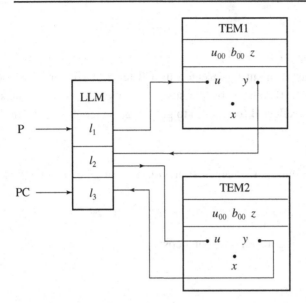

Fig. 7.4.

CNN implementation

1: hardwired components

The hardwired schematic is very simple. Figure 7.4 shows it: we have two CNN components.

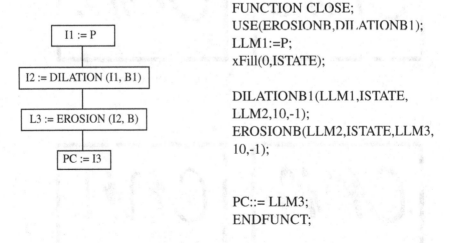

FUNCTION CLOSE;
USE(EROSIONB,DILATIONB1);
LLM1:=P;
xFill(0,ISTATE);

DILATIONB1(LLM1,ISTATE,
LLM2,10,-1);
EROSIONB(LLM2,ISTATE,LLM3,
10,-1);

PC::= LLM3;
ENDFUNCT;

Fig. 7.5. The flow diagram and program of CLOSE.

2: Flow diagram and program

Mathematical morphology has a calculus. Its deep mathematical foundations are well documented in textbooks.[1]

Opening of an image **A** by structuring element **B** is denoted by

$$\mathbf{A} \circ \mathbf{B} = (\mathbf{A} \bigcirc \mathbf{B}) \oplus B$$

where erosion is denoted by $\bigcirc$ and dilation by $\oplus$, respectively.

Closing, denoted by $\circ$, is defined by

$$\mathbf{A} \circ \mathbf{B} = (\mathbf{A} \oplus \mathbf{B}) \bigcirc \mathbf{B}$$

opening and closing are dual operators.

$$\mathbf{A} \circ \mathbf{B} = (\mathbf{A}^c \circ \mathbf{B})^c$$

where ^{c} means complement. Hence, replacing **A** by $\mathbf{A}^c$ and complementing the result we get

$$\mathbf{A} \circ \mathbf{B} = (\mathbf{A}^c \bigcirc \mathbf{B})^c$$

We can implement this calculus by using a sequence of templates. Next we show a few examples. An image **P** is modified by a structuring element $\mathcal{S}$.

EXAMPLE 7.6: Erosion

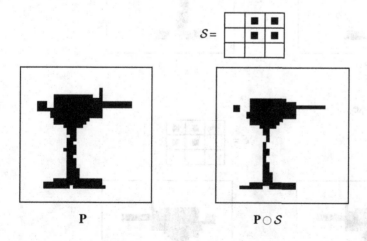

P   P$\bigcirc\mathcal{S}$

A *fundamental theorem of mathematical morphology*, the so-called Matheron representation, asserts that a very large class of morphological operators can be decomposed into a union of erosions with a basis set of structuring elements. The art is to find the basis.

EXAMPLE 7.7: Dilation

$\mathcal{S}=$

P

$P \oplus \mathcal{S}$

EXAMPLE 7.8: Open

$\mathcal{S}=$

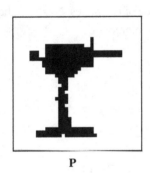

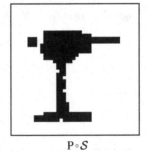

P

$P \circ \mathcal{S}$

EXAMPLE 7.9: Close

$\mathcal{S}=$

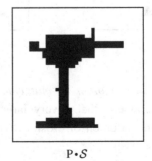

P

$P \bullet \mathcal{S}$

7.5 Implementing any prescribed Boolean transition function by not more than 256 templates

We have seen in Section 6.6 that the XOR Boolean function cannot be realized by a simple CNN template: it is not linearly separable. On the other hand, we can realize it by applying several templates. The truth table is shown in Table 7.1.

Table 7.1.

Term	Input u_1	Output u_2	y
1	-1	-1	-1
2	1	1	-1
3	1	-1	1
4	-1	1	1

Note: -1: false; 1: true

Using the minterm/maxterm notion, we can group the last two rows for generating the minterms by selecting those input combinations which yield outputs of logic 1

$m(u)$: $u_1 \bar{u}_2 + u_2 \bar{u}_1$

i.e., if one of the (now two) minterms is true, the output $y = F(u_1, u_2)$ will be true. Similarly, for the terms with output of logic 0, the maxterms $(M(u))$ are given by the first two rows

$M(u)$: $(u_1 + u_2)(\bar{u}_1 + \bar{u}_2)$

i.e., if one of the maxterms is false, the output $y = F(u_1, u_2)$ will be false.

Hence, we can generate the XOR truth table by the sequential applications of two minterms, combining them with an OR function. Since the minterms contain AND and NOT functions, what we need, altogether, are the building blocks for AND, OR, and NOT functions. We have shown already the CNN templates for these three Boolean functions. Therefore, applying CNN operations, with different templates, iteratively, we can generate the XOR function.

There is a *systematic general procedure* for implementing any local Boolean function by the iterative application of different templates. For the CNN logic representation, we will use the convention: TRUE = 1, FALSE = -1.

Having nine inputs $(u_1, u_2, \ldots, u_9)$ and one output we have $2^9 = 512$ output values $(1, -1)$ for all the 512 input combinations. This means that we can generate *any* local Boolean function of nine input/one output variables, i.e. a binary truth table by at most 512 applications of different minterms, each one implemented by a CNN

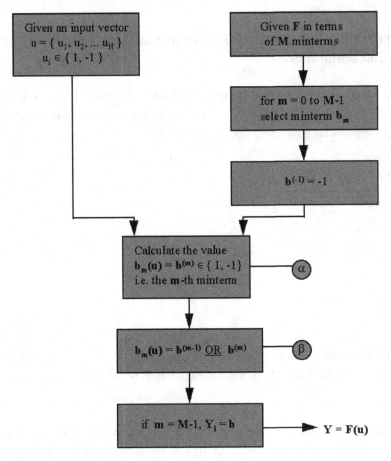

Fig. 7.6.

template. Next, we show a simple, extended CNN cell which can be used to implement this procedure. Before, however, let us describe this procedure in an elementary flow diagram.

Suppose we want to calculate the output y_{ij} of nine input Boolean function $Y = F(u_1, u_2, \ldots, u_9), u_1, u_2, \ldots, u_9$ are the nine binary values of the cells in the neighborhood of cell $C(ij)$.

F is given by the minterms, $b_0, b_1, \ldots, b_M$ ($M \leq 512$). In our simple XOR example: $M = 2, b_0$ and b_1 are the terms, $u_1 \bar{u}_2$ and $\bar{u}_1 u_2$, respectively. These minterms can be coded as $[1, -1]$ and $[-1, 1]$ and the procedure is shown in Fig. 7.6.

In words, it means that we calculate the results of all the minterms at the given u (phase α) and make the ORing (phase β). To implement this flow diagram using our CNN templates we need the following building blocks:

- a logical storage for the given cell's input u_{ij},
- the CNN templates ($\mathbf{A}, \mathbf{B}, z$) for the minterms,
- an OR logic unit, and

- another two-place logical storage (memory) with a shift (shift register).

This means that we need an extended CNN cell with the above units, in addition to the core CNN cell.

The extended CNN cell ij with its neighbors is shown in Fig. 7.7.

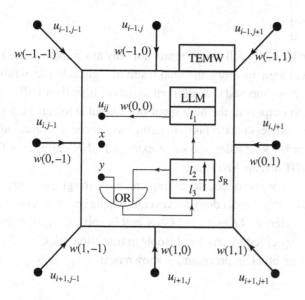

Fig. 7.7.

In the CNN cell we have an additional local logic unit (LLU): the OR gate. Suppose the nine Boolean variables $(u_1, u_2, \ldots, u_9)$ are placed on the inputs of all cells in the sphere of influence $S_r(ij)$. We have to find the template $(\mathbf{A}, \mathbf{B}, z)$ for a given minterm, then we can solve the problem. Next we will show this process.

A minterm is a linearly separable Boolean function. Referring to our earlier analysis, it can be shown (as an exercise) that the value of a minterm b_m at a given $(u_1, u_2, \ldots, u_9)$ combination, $u_i \in \{-1, 1\}$ can be calculated by the following CNN template.

$$
\mathbf{A} = \begin{array}{|c|c|c|} \hline 0 & 0 & 0 \\ \hline 0 & 1 & 0 \\ \hline 0 & 0 & 0 \\ \hline \end{array}
\quad
\mathbf{B}_m = \begin{array}{|c|c|c|} \hline w_{-1,-1} & w_{-1,0} & w_{-1,1} \\ \hline w_{0,-1} & w_{0,0} & w_{0,1} \\ \hline w_{1,-1} & w_{1,0} & w_{1,1} \\ \hline \end{array}
\quad z = -8
$$

$$
\begin{bmatrix} u_9 & u_8 & u_7 \\ u_6 & u_5 & u_4 \\ u_3 & u_2 & u_1 \end{bmatrix}
$$

where the **B** template is coded using the minterm b_m in the following way. If in minterm b_m a variable is presented with its TRUE value, then the corresponding term is $\mathbf{B}_m(k, l) = 1$, if it is FALSE, $\mathbf{B}_m(k, l) = -1$, if a variable does not exist, $\mathbf{B}_m(k, l) = 0$.

This unit can be called the restricted-weight threshold unit since the weights can take values from a finite limited set of values.

For example, minterm $u_1\bar{u}_2 u_3\bar{u}_4\bar{u}_5$ is coded by a template

$$\mathbf{B}_m = \begin{bmatrix} 0 & 0 & 0 \\ 0 & -1 & -1 \\ 1 & -1 & 1 \end{bmatrix}$$

Observe that one extended CNN cell can generate not only any minterm but, using the local logic unit and local logic memory, the final result of a given Boolean function of nine variables as well. It is supposed that all input variables have their buffers.

If the number of zero outputs in the nine input one output Boolean truth table are less than 256, then there are less maxterms than minterms. Hence it is practical to code the maxterms. This can be done using the same extended CNN cell except the local cell logic contains a NOT and an AND gate.

There are more efficient ways, of course, of implementing the given binary Boolean function using CNN. The above procedure, however, is simple and works in case of *any local Boolean function*. Hence, the extended CNN cell is universal for implementing any cellular automaton specified by any local Boolean transition rules.

A more complex, more efficient procedure is shown next.

7.6 Minimizing the number of templates when implementing any possible Boolean transition function

The next procedure shows a more efficient, slightly more complex procedure. The number of templates to be used are generally much smaller than the brute force method described in the previous section.

We use again a restricted-weight threshold unit, however, with more possible weight variables[2] in the bias/threshold term z (indeed $z = -8, -7, \ldots, -1, 0, 1, 2, \ldots, 8$) and use any specified two-input logic function Θ, instead of a single one (OR or AND).

Suppose again the state transition rule to be implemented is the neighborhood Boolean function $\mathbf{Y}$

$$\mathbf{Y} = F(u_1, u_2, u_3, \ldots, u_9)$$

i.e., F is a Boolean function of nine variables: it can be defined by the 512 bits (as we have shown).

We are looking for the solution as a sequence of "ballterms" $b^{(k)}$, $k = 0, 1, 2, \ldots, M$, implemented with restricted-weight threshold logic (i.e., equivalent templates) and corresponding two-input logic operations Θ^k which will generate F in M steps. All the Boolean functions can be defined by a 2^N-tuple as a response (TRUE or FALSE) to all possible N-tuple inputs. In our case $N = 9$. Hence, F is defined as a

512-tuple (there are $2^{512} \approx 10^{154}$ such 512-tuples, hence, different Boolean functions F).

F is generated as follows

$$f^{(0)} := b^{(0)}$$
$$f^{(1)} := f^{(0)} \Theta^{(1)} b^{(1)}$$
$$f^{(2)} := f^{(1)} \Theta^{(2)} b^{(2)}$$
$$\vdots$$
$$f^{(M)} := f^{(M-1)} \Theta^{(M)} b^{(M)}$$

where $\Theta^{(k)} \in L$ (one of the 16 two-input, one-output logic functions).

To calculate the consecutive terms $b^{(k)} \Theta(k)$ (and here $f^{(k)}$) we need *a distance calculation unit* of two N-tuples (u and v) where the distance is calculated as follows

$$\text{dist}(u, v) = \sum_{i=0}^{N-1} u_i \oplus v_i$$

where $\oplus$ denotes the XOR operation.

Clearly, using an XOR local logical unit and a few local logic memory units in a cell, this distance ($\text{dist}(u, v)$) calculation can be computed in about N steps.

The distance of two Boolean functions, f and g, of N variables can be calculated similarly

$$\text{dist}_F(f, g) = \sum_{u=0}^{2^N-1} f(u) \oplus g(u); \quad f, g \in F$$

where 2^N XOR operations ($N = 9 \rightarrow 2^N = 512$) are needed.

The greedy algorithm defined by the flow chart in Fig. 7.8 calculates the consecutive $b^{(k)} \Theta(k)$ functions. $b^{(k)}$ are chosen from the set **B**. Set **B** contains all the Boolean functions which can be implemented with the restricted weight values. If $N = 9$, there are $118\,098 = 3^9 \times 6$ elements of **B** (we choose six z values between -8 and $+8$).

A ballterm b is represented by the nine feedforward template element values and the z value, denoted by

$$b(b_1 b_2 b_3 b_4 b_5 b_6 b_7 b_8 b_9), z$$

where the last value is the bias value and the order is the same as shown before (the **A** template has a central nonzero element of 1).

The reasoning behind the algorithm is as follows (search algorithms are denoted by ■ in Fig. 7.8).

- In the first search algorithm, we find $b^{(0)}$ of minimum distance from the prescribed F.

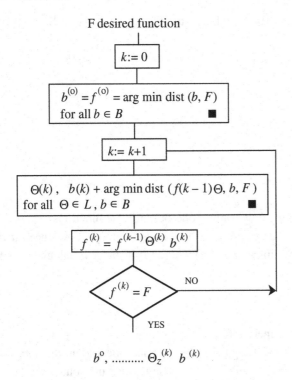

F desired function

$k := 0$

$b^{(0)} = f^{(0)} = \arg \min \mathrm{dist}\,(b, F)$
for all $b \in B$ ∎

$k := k+1$

$\Theta(k)\,,\quad b(k) + \arg \min \mathrm{dist}\,(f(k-1)\Theta, b, F)$
for all $\Theta \in L\,, b \in B$ ∎

$f^{(k)} = f^{(k-1)}\,\Theta^{(k)}\,b^{(k)}$

$f^{(k)} = F$ NO

YES

$b^{0},\,\ldots\ldots\ldots\,\Theta_z^{(k)}\,b^{(k)}$

Fig. 7.8.

- In the next iterative search algorithm, we test all the possible combinations of the restricted weight functions ($\in$ **B**) and the two-input one-output logic function ($\in$ L) to find the best combination: it will modify the previously composed function $f^{(k-1)}$ to $f^{(k)}$ which will be of minimal distance to F.

It is possible to prove that this algorithm converges and, in the worst case, will not result in more terms than the minterm (or maxterm) algorithm shown in the previous section.[3]

Example: game of life

This famous problem, with a single Boolean output value, is a linearly non-separable problem. Hence, it cannot be implemented by a single template. The algorithm in Fig. 7.8 results in just two terms

$$b^{(0)} = b(-1, -1, -1, -1, 0, -1, -1, -1, -1), +1$$
$$b^{(1)} = b(+1, +1, +1, +1, +1, +1, +1, +1, +1), -4$$
$$\Theta^{(1)} = \mathrm{AND}$$

Hence, we can implement the game of life with a cell of Fig. 7.7 containing an AND local logical unit, and the two templates which implement the "ballterms" $b^{(0)}$ and $b^{(1)}$

are

$$\mathbf{A} = \begin{bmatrix} 0 & 0 & 0 \\ 0 & 1 & 0 \\ 0 & 0 & 0 \end{bmatrix}; \quad \mathbf{B}^{(0)} = \begin{bmatrix} -1 & -1 & -1 \\ -1 & 0 & -1 \\ -1 & -1 & -1 \end{bmatrix}; \quad z = +1$$

and

$$\mathbf{A} = \begin{bmatrix} 0 & 0 & 0 \\ 0 & 1 & 0 \\ 0 & 0 & 0 \end{bmatrix}; \quad \mathbf{B}^{(1)} = \begin{bmatrix} +1 & +1 & +1 \\ +1 & +1 & +1 \\ +1 & +1 & +1 \end{bmatrix}; \quad z = -4$$

respectively.

7.7   Analog-to-digital array converter

SUBROUTINE ADARRAY$(\cdot, \cdot, \cdot)$

ADARRAY$(\mathbf{P}, n, \mathbf{B}[0, n - 1])$

$\mathbf{P}$: positive image $0 \le p_{ij} \le 1$

n: integer, number of bits

$\mathbf{B}[0, n - 1]$: $\mathbf{B}_{ij}[k]$: The value of the kth bit $\in \{0, 1\}$,

$k = 0, 1, 2, \ldots, n - 1$

Global task: array-type analog to digital converter

Given a signal array $\mathbf{P}$ at a given time instant t_0, i.e., $P = P(t)|_{t=t_0}$.

$$\mathbf{P} = [p_{ij}], \quad i = 1, 2, \ldots, M; \quad j = 1, 2, \ldots, N, \quad 0 \le p_{ij} \le 1.$$

Compute the representation of the real (analog) values

$$p_{ij}: B_{ij}[k], \quad k = 0, 1, 2, \ldots, n - 1$$

The algorithm

The algorithm (a well-known method) is given for a single cell, all cells are computing fully parallel, without interaction.

Given: $p, 0 \le p_{ij} \le 1$ real and n, integer, r: real, b: binary,

let: $r(-1) := p$ and $b(-1) := 1$

FOR $i := 0$ step 1 until $i < n$ DO

begin

$$r(i) := 2r(i - 1) - b(i - 1)$$

$$b(i) := \text{sgn}(r(i))$$

$$B(i) := \text{bconvert}(b(i))$$

end

where "bconvert" (binary converter) is a function with input $\{-1, +1\}$ and output $\{0, 1\}$ which represent logic LOW and HIGH. $B(i)$ are the sequence of the output bits.

Example

Convert the value $p = 0.6875 = \frac{1}{2} + \frac{1}{4} + \frac{1}{8} + \frac{1}{16}$ (i.e., the code $B()$ is: 1011). The consecutive steps of the algorithm are as follows

$$r(-1) = 0.6875; \quad b(-1) = 1$$

$i = 0$

begin $r(0) = 2 \times 0.6875 - 1 = 0.375$

$\qquad b(0) = \text{sgn}(0.375) = 1$

$\qquad B(0) = \text{bconvert}(1) = \boxed{1}$

end

$i = 1$

begin $r(1) = 2 \times 0.375 - 1 = -0.25$

$\qquad b(1) = \text{sgn}(-0.25) = -1$

$\qquad B(1) = \text{bconvert}(-1) = \boxed{0}$

end

$i = 2$

begin $r(2) = 2 \times (-0.25) + 1 = 0.5$

$\qquad b(2) = \text{sgn}(0.5) = 1$

$\qquad B(2) = \text{bconvert}(1) = \boxed{1}$

end

$i = 3$

begin $r(3) = 2 \times 0.5 - 1 = 0$

$\qquad b(3) = \text{sgn}(0) = 1$

$\qquad B(3) = \text{bconvert}(1) = \boxed{1}$

end

CNN implementation

1: hardwired components

To implement this algorithm via CNN we need some additional components in each cell. For the time being, we suppose that each template is implemented by a single CNN standard cell, as a component, and the whole array is hardwired from the components. An extended cell (type 2) is shown in Fig. 7.9.

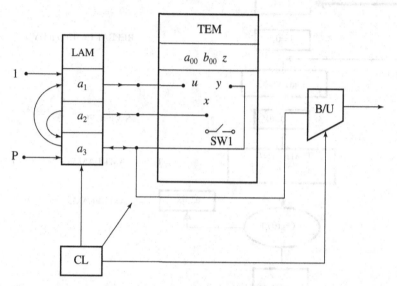

Fig. 7.9. The extended cell 2. In addition to the CNN cell which may have a switch, we have two new components: an analog storage device, a local analog memory (LAM) and a bipolar to unipolar converter (B/U).

The new components in the extended cell 2 are:

- in some CNN standard cells (type 2), for the time being we consider them as separate components, there is a *switch* SW1 which, if it is OFF, sets the value of the standard nonlinearity of the cell to zero, i.e., if SW1: OFF then $f(\cdot) = 0$; we suppose that if SW1 $=$ OFF then the input and output of the cell can be specified and the value at the state will be the outcome,

- an analog memory unit LAM (*local analog memory*), in this case with three storage places,

- a binary converter B/U (denoted by $b$convert$(\cdot)$), converting a bipolar $\{-1, 1\}$ analog signal into a unipolar $\{0, 1\} - \{$LOW, HIGH$\}$ logic bit.

Suppose we place the extended cell 2 in a CNN array, then we can design the flow diagram of the A/D algorithm. This flow diagram is shown in Fig. 7.10. On the same figure we show, in parallel, the program of the algorithm implementing our A/DARRAY$(\cdot)$ subroutine, for a single cell.

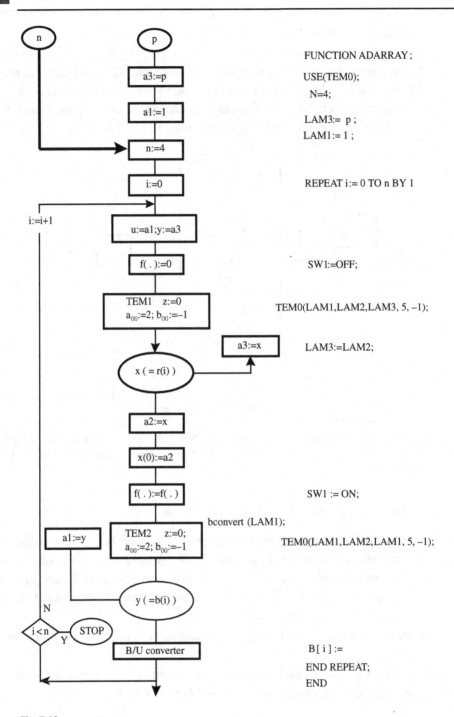

Fig. 7.10.

Here we suppose that this program is hardwired, i.e., the clock signals activate the subsequent units according to a predefined sequence.

8 Back to basics: Nonlinear dynamics and complete stability

8.1 A glimpse of things to come

All CNN templates we have investigated so far share the common property that regardless of the inputs, initial states, and boundary conditions, all transient dynamics eventually converge to some *dc* equilibrium state after some *settling time* $k\tau_{CNN}$, where τ_{CNN} is the time constant of a single cell, and $k \approx 5$–10. Such CNNs are said to be completely stable and represent the workhorse of most current CNN applications. Indeed, almost all current CNN analogic programs are developed under the assumption that all CNN templates (instructions) called for in the program are completely stable. However, we will see in the following sections that *not all* CNNs are completely stable. Indeed, some CNN templates will give rise to an *oscillatory periodic* steady state behavior. Others can even exhibit an eternally transient (not periodic) phenomenon called *chaos*.

While the majority of current CNN applications require *constant* dc (gray-scale) outputs, future applications will no doubt exploit the immense potentials of the relatively unexplored terrains of oscillatory and chaotic operating regions. In this chapter, we will derive several general mathematical criteria for complete stability. To appreciate the need for such criteria, we will present first a simple example of an *oscillatory* CNN in Section 8.2, and a *chaotic* CNN in Section 8.3.

8.2 An oscillatory CNN with only two cells

Consider a two-cell CNN characterized by zero boundary conditions and the following templates:

$$
\mathbf{A} = \begin{array}{|c|c|c|}
\hline
0 & 0 & 0 \\
\hline
\beta & \alpha & -\beta \\
\hline
0 & 0 & 0 \\
\hline
\end{array}
\quad
\mathbf{B} = \begin{array}{|c|c|c|}
\hline
0 & 0 & 0 \\
\hline
0 & 0 & 0 \\
\hline
0 & 0 & 0 \\
\hline
\end{array}
\quad
z = \boxed{0}
$$

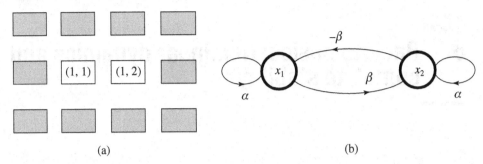

(a)　　　　　　　　　　　　　　　　　　　　　　(b)

Fig. 8.1. (a) A 1×2 CNN whose virtual boundary cells (shown blank) are clamped to a zero potential: $y_{0,0} = y_{0,1} = y_{0,2} = y_{0,3} = y_{1,0} = y_{1,3} = y_{2,0} = y_{2,1} = y_{2,2} = y_{2,3} = 0$. (b) Corresponding signal flow graph.

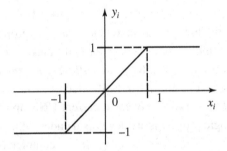

Fig. 8.2. The standard CNN piecewise-linear output characteristic.

Using our earlier notations from Section 2.2.6, this $M \times N = 1 \times 2$ CNN with feedback synaptic weights $a_{0,-1} = \beta$, $a_{0,0} = \alpha$, and $a_{0,1} = \beta$ can be represented by the signal flow graph shown in Fig. 8.1.

The state equation for this CNN is given by

$$\dot{x}_1 = -x_1 + \alpha y_1 - \beta y_2$$
$$\dot{x}_2 = -x_2 + \alpha y_2 + \beta y_1$$

(8.1)

where we neglect the row index for simplicity. Here, the output y_i is related to the state x_i by the standard nonlinearity

$$y_i = f(x_i) = 0.5|x_i + 1| - 0.5|x_i - 1|$$

(8.2)

which is shown graphically in Fig. 8.2 for convenience.

The solution waveforms of Eq. (8.1) corresponding to $\alpha = 2$, $\beta = 2$, and initial condition $x_1(0) = 0.1$ and $x_2(0) = 0.1$ are shown in Examples 8.1(a) and 8.1(b). Observe that instead of converging to a dc equilibrium point as in all of our previous examples, the state variables x_1 and x_2 converge to a *periodic* waveform, which is more clearly seen by plotting the associated *trajectory* on the x_1–x_2 plane, as shown in Example 8.1(c). Each point along the trajectory, which starts from $(x_1, x_2) =$

(0.1, 0.1) at $t = 0$ in Example 8.1(c), is parameterized by time but is not shown in the figure because here we are interested only in the relationship between $x_1(t)$ and $x_2(t)$ as $t \to \infty$, namely a *closed contour* called a *limit cycle*. Since the trajectory from (0.1, 0.1) does not converge to an equilibrium (x_{1Q}, x_{2Q}), this CNN is *not* completely stable.

EXAMPLE 8.1: Periodic solution waveforms of $x_1(t)$ and $x_2(t)$ and the corresponding trajectory for $\alpha = 2$, $\beta = 2$, $x_1(0) = 0.1$ and $x_2(0) = 0.1$.

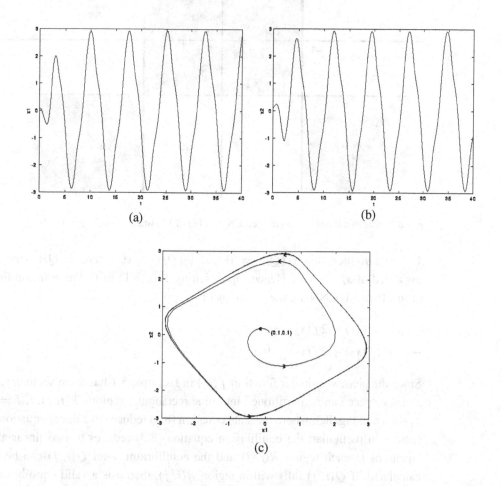

(a)

(b)

(c)

For this simple example, we can prove that all trajectories starting from any initial state except the origin will converge to a limit cycle. We will present the details of this proof in order to introduce the uninitiated reader to some elementary aspects of *nonlinear qualitative analysis*. The first step in analyzing the dynamics of an *autonomous* CNN (i.e., where the time variable t does not appear on the right-hand side of the state equation) is to find the location of all equilibrium points Q_i, $i =$

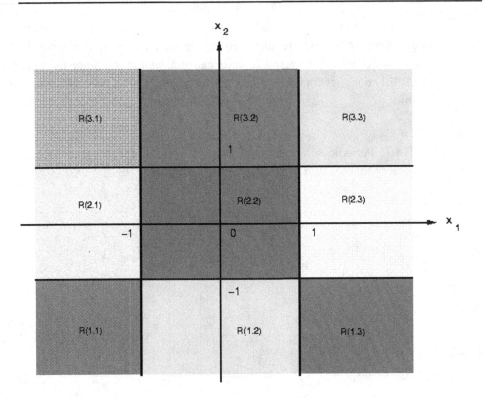

Fig. 8.3. The dynamics of the two-cell CNN in Fig. 8.1 is linear in each region $R(i, j)$.

$1, 2, \ldots, q$, such that $\dot{x}_1(Q_i) = 0$ and $\dot{x}_2(Q_i) = 0$, where $\dot{x}_j(Q_i)$ denotes $\dot{x}_j(t)$ evaluated at $x_i = x_{Q_i}$. Hence, upon setting Eq. (8.1) to 0, the equilibrium points of this two-cell CNN are the solutions of

$$-x_1 + 2f(x_1) - 2f(x_2) = 0 \tag{8.3a}$$
$$-x_2 + 2f(x_2) + 2f(x_1) = 0 \tag{8.3b}$$

Since the piecewise-linear function $f(x_i)$ in Example 8.1 has three segments, the x_1–x_2 state space can be partitioned into nine rectangular regions $R(i, j)$, $i, j = 1, 2, 3$, as shown in Fig. 8.3, where the state equation (8.1) reduces to a linear equation in each region. In particular, the equilibrium equation (8.3) reduces to two linear algebraic equations in each region $R(i, j)$ and the equilibrium point $Q(i, j)$ can be trivially calculated. If $Q(i, j)$ falls within region $R(i, j)$, then it is a valid equilibrium point. If $Q(i, j)$ falls outside of $R(i, j)$, it is a "virtual" equilibrium point and is simply discarded. The above "brute-force" procedure can be easily programmed to find all equilibrium points of any $M \times N$ CNN. However, the computation time would grow exponentially with MN so that it becomes impractical when MN is large.

In view of the simplicity of Eq. (8.3), the *following algebraic analysis* can be made to determine first those regions in Fig. 8.3 which have valid equilibrium points:

Step 1: Central strip $|x_1| < 1$ (regions $R(1, 2)$, $R(2, 2)$, and $R(3, 2)$ in Fig. 8.3)
In the strip $|x_1| < 1$, we can write $f(x_1) = x_1$ so that Eq. (8.3a) becomes $-x_1 + 2x_1 - 2f(x_2) = 0$. Consequently, $|f(x_2)| = |x_1|/2 < 0.5$ and hence $f(x_2) = x_2$. Equation (8.3) reduces in this case to

$$-x_1 + 2x_1 - 2x_2 = 0$$
$$-x_2 + 2x_2 + 2x_1 = 0 \qquad\qquad (8.4)$$

Since $(x_1, x_2) = (0, 0)$ is the *unique* solution of Eq. (8.4), only region $R(2, 2)$ in the central strip has an equilibrium point; namely, the origin.

Step 2: Left strip $x_1 < -1$ (regions $R(1, 1)$, $R(2, 1)$, and $R(3, 1)$ in Fig. 8.3)
In the strip $x_1 < -1$, we can write $f(x_1) = -1$ so that Eq. (8.3b) becomes $-x_2 + 2f(x_2) - 2 = 0$. Solving this equation for x_2, we find $x_2 = -4$ for region $R(1, 1)$ the only solution of Eq. (8.3b) (the other two solutions $x_2 = 2$ for region $R(2, 1)$ and $x_2 = 0$ for region $R(3, 1)$ are both *virtual* solutions). But $x_2 = -4$ implies $f(x_2) = -1$ so that Eq. (8.3a) in the left strip gives $-x_1 - 2 + 2 = 0$, or $x_1 = 0$, which is outside of the left strip. Hence $x_2 = -4$ is a virtual solution for Eq. (8.3). It follows that *there are no equilibrium points in the left strip $x_1 < -1$.*

Step 3: Right strip $x_1 > 1$ (regions $R(1, 3)$, $R(2, 3)$, and $R(3, 3)$ in Fig. 8.3)
In the strip $x_1 > 1$, we can write $f(x_1) = 1$ so that Eq. (8.3b) becomes $-x_2 + 2f(x_2) + 2 = 0$. Solving this equation for x_2, we find $x_2 = 4$ for region $R(3, 3)$ is the only solution of Eq. (8.3b) (the other two solutions $x_2 = -2$ for region $R(2, 3)$ and $x_2 = 0$ for region $R(1, 3)$ are both *virtual* solutions). But $x_2 = 4$ implies $f(x_2) = 1$ so that Eq. (8.3a) in the *right strip* gives $-x_1 + 2 - 2 = 0$, or $x_1 = 0$, which is outside of the right strip. Hence $x_2 = 4$ is a virtual solution for Eq. (8.3). It follows that *there are no equilibrium points in the right strip $x_1 > 1$.*

Steps 1–3 show that Eq. (8.1) has only one equilibrium point; namely, the origin. To determine the dynamical behavior near the origin, we examine the associated linear equation

$$\dot{x}_1 = x_1 - 2x_2$$
$$\dot{x}_2 = 2x_1 + x_2 \qquad\qquad (8.5)$$

obtained by setting $f(x_1) = x_1$ and $f(x_2) = x_2$ in Eq. (8.1). Since the eigenvalues of the above matrix are given by $\lambda_1 = 1 + j2$ and $\lambda_2 = 1 - j2$, the solution of Eq. (8.5) has the form

$$x_1(t) = ke^t \cos(2t + \theta)$$
$$x_2(t) = ke^t \sin(2t + \theta) \qquad\qquad (8.6)$$

where the constants k and θ depend on the initial condition $x_1(0)$ and $x_2(0)$. Since the trajectory associated with Eq. (8.6) is an "expanding" spiral, as shown in Example 8.1(b), and since all solutions of Eq. (8.1) are *bounded* (in view of Theorem 2 of *Chapter 2*), this expanding spiral must necessarily converge to some limiting *closed contour*, for otherwise the trajectory would intersect itself since there is no room for maneuvering on the x_1–x_2 plane. But no trajectory of an autonomous system of differential equations can intersect itself in view of the *uniqueness* property (Theorem 1 of Chapter 2) – otherwise we can choose the self-intersection point as our initial condition and obtain two different trajectories originating from this point. The above reasoning can be given a formal rigorous proof and the result is called the *Poincaré–Bendixon* theorem, which is a classic result from the theory of differential equations.[1]

8.3   A chaotic CNN with only two cells and one sinusoidal input

Suppose we apply a sinusoidal input $u_{11}(t) = 4.04 \sin(\frac{\pi}{2}t)$ to cell $C(1,1)$ of the two-cell CNN shown in Fig. 8.1 and choose $\alpha = 2$ and $\beta = 1.2$ as its parameters. In this case, under the same "zero" boundary conditions as before, the state equation (8.1) generalizes to the following non-autonomous system of two nonlinear differential equations

$$\dot{x}_1 = -x_1 + 2y_1 - 1.2y_2 + 4.04 \sin\left(\frac{\pi}{2}t\right)$$
$$\dot{x}_2 = -x_2 + 1.2y_1 + 2y_2 \tag{8.7}$$

where $y_i = f(x_i)$ is defined by Eq. (8.2). Equation (8.7) is the state equation of a 1×2 CNN with templates

$$\mathbf{A} = \begin{array}{|c|c|c|} \hline 0 & 0 & 0 \\ \hline 1.2 & 2 & -1.2 \\ \hline 0 & 0 & 0 \\ \hline \end{array} \quad \mathbf{B} = \begin{array}{|c|c|c|} \hline 0 & 0 & 0 \\ \hline 0 & 1 & 0 \\ \hline 0 & 0 & 0 \\ \hline \end{array} \quad z = \boxed{0}$$

zero boundary conditions, a sinusoidal input $u_{11}(t)$ to cell $C(1,1)$, and a zero input $u_{12} = 0$ to cell $C(1,2)$. The solution waveforms $x_1(t)$ and $x_2(t)$ corresponding to the initial condition $x_1(0) = 0.1$ and $x_2(0) = 0.1$ are shown in Figs 8.2(a) and 8.2(b), respectively. Observe that, unlike the periodic waveforms shown earlier in Example 8.1, these two waveforms do *not* converge to a periodic waveform as $t \to \infty$. The non-periodic nature of $x_1(t)$ and $x_2(t)$ is more clearly seen by examining the associated trajectory shown in Example 8.2(c). Observe that the trajectory looks like a never-ending tangle of yarn. To emphasize the non-periodic nature of $x_1(t)$ and $x_2(t)$, Examples 8.3(a) and 8.3(b) show the numerically calculated power spectra $X_1(\omega)$ of $x_1(t)$ and $X_2(\omega)$ of $x_2(t)$ have a *broadband, continuous, noise-like character*, which is quite different from that of a periodic signal, which consists of discrete lines corresponding to the harmonic components of its Fourier series expansion. From the theory of the nonlinear dynamics, the noise-like waveforms in Examples 8.2(a) and 8.2(b) are said to be *chaotic*, and the associated trajectory is called a *strange attractor* because other solutions corresponding to nearby initial conditions will all be "attracted" and converge to the same trajectory.

EXAMPLE 8.2: Chaotic solution waveforms of $x_1(t)$ and $x_2(t)$ and the corresponding trajectory for $\alpha = 2$, $\beta = 1.2$, $x_1(0) = 0.1$ and $x_2(0) = 0.1$.

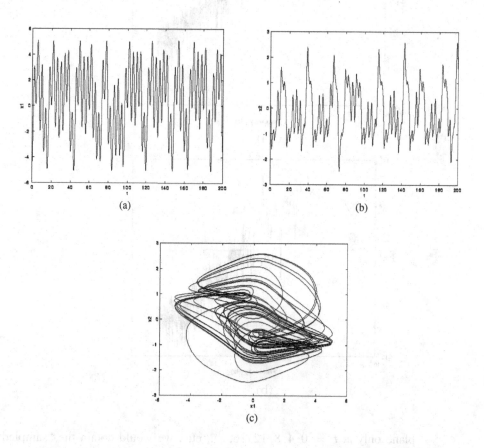

(a)

(b)

(c)

Even though the strange attractor in Example 8.2(c) looks extremely messy, it does possess some orderly geometrical structure, which, in the case of a periodic input, is best seen by sampling only the points on the trajectory once every period of the input waveform. The resulting set of points is called a Poincaré cross section, or by an abuse of language, simply a *Poincaré map* because it was first introduced by the famous French physicist and mathematician Poincaré. In this example, the period of the sinusoidal input is $T = 4$. Consequently, if we plot $(x_1(t), x_2(t))$ on the x_1–x_2

EXAMPLE 8.3: Frequency power spectra calculated numerically from the chaotic waveforms $x_1(t)$ and $x_2(t)$ in Example 8.2.

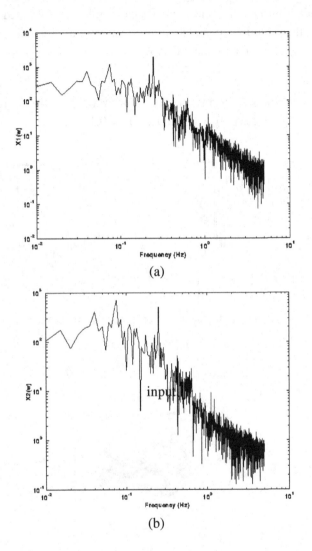

(a)

(b)

plane only at $t = 0, 4, 8, 12, 16, \ldots$, etc., we would obtain the "sampled" strange attractor in Example 8.4, which is often referred to as a Lady's shoe attractor.[2]

A discrete op-amp circuit[3] for simulating Eq. (8.7) is shown in Figure 8.4. The experimentally observed strange attractor corresponding to Example 8.2(c) is shown in Example 8.5(a). The corresponding Poincaré map obtained experimentally by "blanking" out the oscilloscope beam except at regular intervals of T is shown in Example 8.5(b). It is sometimes instructive to interpret such Poincaré maps as "strobing" the strange attractor by a stroboscope.

EXAMPLE 8.4: The Poincaré map extracted from the strange attractor in Example 8.2(c) is called the "Lady's shoe attractor" in view of its striking resemblance to a high-heel lady's pump.

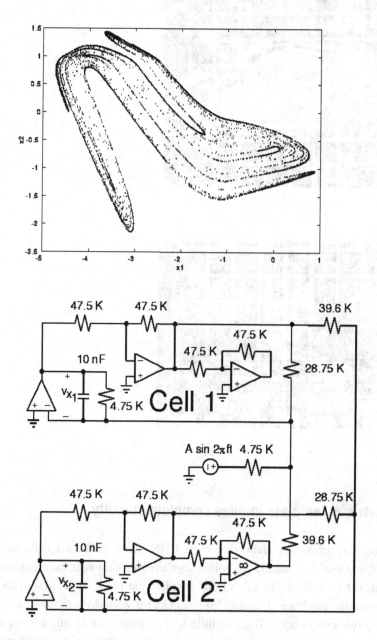

Fig. 8.4. A two-cell CNN circuit driven by a sinusoidal signal.

EXAMPLE 8.5: (a) Strange attractor obtained experimentally from the circuit in Fig 8.4. (b) The "Lady's shoe" Poincaré map extracted experimentally from the attractor in (a).

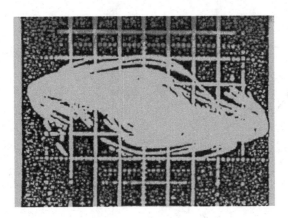

(a)

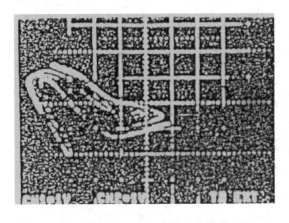

(b)

8.4   Symmetric A template implies complete stability

The preceding examples show that even CNNs with only two cells may not be completely stable. Fortunately, the following theorem guarantees the complete stability of an important subclass of CNNs. To simplify the proof of this theorem, we will assume that the nonlinear function $y_{ij} = f(x_{ij})$ is *bounded*, *differentiable*, and has *positive slope* everywhere. There is little loss of generality in this assumption since our original piecewise-linear function can be approximated arbitrarily closely by such a smooth function. In fact, any physical realization of $f(x_{ij})$ will be "smooth" rather than piece-wise linear so that this assumption is actually more consistent with reality.

Complete Stability Theorem 1

Any $M \times N$ space-invariant CNN of arbitrary neighborhood size with *constant inputs* and *constant threshold* is *completely stable* if the following three hypotheses are satisfied:

1 The **A** template is symmetric

$$A(i, j; k, l) = A(k, l; i, j) \tag{8.8}$$

2 The nonlinear function $y_{ij} = f(x_{ij})$ is *differentiable, bounded,* and

$$f'(x_{ij}) > 0, \quad \text{for all } -\infty < x_{ij} < \infty \tag{8.9}$$

3 All equilibrium points are *isolated.*[4]

Proof:

Consider the CNN state equation (2.8) from Chapter 2 for *constant* input **u** and threshold **z**:

$$\dot{\mathbf{x}} = -\mathbf{x} + \hat{\mathbf{A}}\mathbf{y} + \hat{\mathbf{B}}\mathbf{u} + \mathbf{z} \tag{8.10}$$

$$y_i = f(x_i), \quad i = 1, 2, \ldots, n = MN \tag{8.11}$$

Here, $\hat{\mathbf{A}}$ and $\hat{\mathbf{B}}$ are $n \times n$ matrices whose nonzero entries are the synaptic weights $A(i, j; k, l)$ and $B(i, j; k, l)$, respectively. Observe that hypothesis (8.8) and space invariance imply that

$$\hat{\mathbf{A}} = \hat{\mathbf{A}}^T \tag{8.12}$$

independent of the packing scheme.

Now, hypothesis (8.9) implies that $f(\cdot)$ is a one-to-one (injective) function and therefore has an *inverse* function

$$x_i = f^{-1}(y_i) \tag{8.13}$$

defined for all y_i over the range of $f(x_i)$, $x_i \in (-\infty, \infty)$. Define the *scalar function*

$$V(\mathbf{x}) = -\frac{1}{2}\mathbf{y}^T\hat{\mathbf{A}}\mathbf{y} + \sum_{i=1}^{n}\left[\int_{\theta}^{y_i} f^{-1}(v)dv\right] - \mathbf{y}^T\hat{\mathbf{B}}\mathbf{u} - \mathbf{y}^T\mathbf{z} \tag{8.14}$$

where θ is any number such that $f(-\infty) < \theta < f(\infty)$.[5]

A scalar function $V(\mathbf{x})$ is called a *Lyapunov function* if its time derivative along any trajectory is non-positive, i.e.,

$$\dot{V}(\mathbf{x}) \triangleq \frac{dV(\mathbf{x})}{dt} = \sum_{i=1}^{n}\frac{\partial V(\mathbf{x})}{\partial x_i}\dot{x}i \le 0.$$

Our first goal is to prove that Eq. (8.14) defines a Lyapunov function.

Observe that the right-hand side of Eq. (8.14) is a *scalar* function of $\mathbf{x} = [x_1, x_2, \ldots, x_n]^T$ since $y_i = f(x_i)$ via Eq. (8.11). Taking the *time* derivative of both sides of Eq. (8.14) we obtain

$$\dot{V}(\mathbf{x}) = -\frac{1}{2}(\dot{\mathbf{y}}^T \hat{\mathbf{A}} \mathbf{y} + \mathbf{y}^T \hat{\mathbf{A}} \dot{\mathbf{y}}) + \left(\sum_{i=1}^{n} f^{-1}(y_i) \cdot \dot{y}_i \right) - \dot{\mathbf{y}}^T \hat{\mathbf{B}} \mathbf{u} - \dot{\mathbf{y}}^T \mathbf{z} \qquad (8.15)$$

Now since $\mathbf{y}^T \hat{\mathbf{A}} \dot{\mathbf{y}}$ is a scalar and $\hat{\mathbf{A}} = \hat{\mathbf{A}}^T$ in view of Eq. (8.12), we can write

$$\mathbf{y}^T \hat{\mathbf{A}} \dot{\mathbf{y}} = (\mathbf{y}^T \hat{\mathbf{A}} \dot{\mathbf{y}})^T = \dot{\mathbf{y}}^T \hat{\mathbf{A}}^T \mathbf{y} = \dot{\mathbf{y}}^T \hat{\mathbf{A}} \mathbf{y} \qquad (8.16)$$

Substituting Eqs (8.13) and (8.16) into Eq. (8.15) and making use of Eq. (8.10), we obtain

$$\begin{aligned} \dot{V}(\mathbf{x}) &= -\dot{\mathbf{y}}^T \hat{\mathbf{A}} \mathbf{y} + \sum_{i=1}^{n} x_i \dot{y}_i - \dot{\mathbf{y}}^T \hat{\mathbf{B}} \mathbf{u} - \dot{\mathbf{y}}^T \mathbf{z} \\ &= -\dot{\mathbf{y}}^T (\hat{\mathbf{A}} \mathbf{y} + \hat{\mathbf{B}} \mathbf{u} - \mathbf{x} + \mathbf{z}) \\ &= -\dot{\mathbf{y}}^T \dot{\mathbf{x}} \end{aligned} \qquad (8.17)$$

Observe next that

$$\dot{\mathbf{y}} = \begin{bmatrix} \dfrac{dy_1}{dt} \\ \dfrac{dy_2}{dt} \\ \vdots \\ \dfrac{dy_n}{dt} \end{bmatrix} = \underbrace{\begin{bmatrix} f'(x_1) & & & \\ & f'(x_2) & & \\ & & \ddots & \\ & & & f'(x_n) \end{bmatrix}}_{\mathbf{Df(x)}} \begin{bmatrix} \dot{x}_1 \\ \dot{x}_2 \\ \vdots \\ \dot{x}_n \end{bmatrix} = \mathbf{Df(x)}\dot{\mathbf{x}} \qquad (8.18)$$

Substituting Eq. (8.18) into Eq. (8.17) and noting that $\mathbf{Df(x)}$ is symmetric, we obtain

$$\begin{aligned} \dot{V}(\mathbf{x}) &= -[\mathbf{Df(x)}\dot{\mathbf{x}}]^T \dot{\mathbf{x}} \\ &= -(\dot{\mathbf{x}}^T \mathbf{Df(x)} \dot{\mathbf{x}}) \\ &= -\sum_{i=1}^{n} f'(x_i)\dot{x}_i^2 \le 0 \end{aligned} \qquad (8.19)$$

Hence, $V(\mathbf{x})$ in Eq. (8.14) is a Lyapunov function. Let M denote the set of all points $\mathbf{x} \in R^n$ where $\dot{V}(\mathbf{x}) = 0$, i.e.,

$$M = \{\mathbf{x} : \dot{V}(\mathbf{x}) = 0\} \qquad (8.20)$$

Since $f'(x_i) > 0$ (hypothesis 2), Eq. (8.19) implies $\dot{V}(\mathbf{x}) = 0$ if, and only if, $\dot{x}_i = 0$, $i = 1, 2, \ldots, n$. It follows that M in Eq. (8.20) consists of the set of all equilibrium points of Eq. (8.10). Hence

$$\dot{V}(\mathbf{x}) < 0 \quad \text{for all } \mathbf{x} \in R^n \text{ except at equilibrium points} \qquad (8.21)$$

Now since $\mathbf{x}(t)$ is *bounded* in view of *Theorem 2* from Chapter 2, we can apply the *LaSalle invariant principle*[6] to conclude that *all trajectories* of Eq. (8.10) must converge to the *invariant set*[7] M of equilibrium points.

Now since all equilibrium points of Eq. (8.10) are isolated (hypothesis 3), it follows that all trajectories of Eq. (8.10) must converge to an equilibrium point.

Remarks

1 If the equilibrium points in M are not isolated,[8] then our theorem can be relaxed to assert only that all trajectories must converge to the set M of equilibrium points. Strictly speaking, this assertion does not imply that every trajectory will converge to an equilibrium point since there exist (admittedly highly pathological and rare) situations where every trajectory will approach M at an arbitrarily small rate so that $\dot{\mathbf{x}}_i \to 0$ and yet the trajectory never converges to any particular equilibrium point.

2 To visualize the geometrical ideas behind the above proof, consider the hypothetical surface $V(x_1, x_2)$ shown in Fig. 8.5. Notice that this surface has five local minima $\{Q_1, Q_3, Q_5, Q_7, Q_9\}$. Imagine the inside of the surface V as the surface of a rugged narrow mountain crevice and a small ball is coasting down the surface. One such hypothetical trajectory Γ representing the "track" made by the ball is shown in Fig. 8.5. Notice that, due to gravity, a ball originating from any point other than an extremum point must keep falling down along the steep slope until it settles down at a local minimum; i.e.

$$\dot{V}(x_1, x_2) = \frac{d}{dt} V(x_1(t), x_2(t)) < 0 \tag{8.22}$$

for all $(x_1, x_2) \neq (x_1(Q_i), x_2(Q_i))$.

An n-dimensional *scalar* function

$$V(x_1, x_2, \ldots, x_n) : R^n \to R^1 \tag{8.23}$$

is called a *Lyapunov function* associated with an *autonomous* system of differential equations

$$\dot{\mathbf{x}}_i = f_i(x_1, x_2, \ldots, x_n), \quad i = 1, 2, \ldots, n \tag{8.24}$$

if and only if, corresponding to *any* trajectory

$$(x_1, x_2, \ldots, x_n) = (\gamma_1(t), \gamma_2(t), \ldots, \gamma_n(t)) \tag{8.25}$$

of Eq. (8.24), the corresponding scalar function of time

$$V(t) \overset{\Delta}{=} V(\gamma_1(t), \gamma_2(t), \ldots, \gamma_n(t)) \tag{8.26}$$

decreases monotonically with time, i.e., $\dot{V}(t) \leq 0$. In particular, if $\dot{V}(t) = 0$ *only* at equilibrium points, then it follows that all trajectories must land at an equilibrium

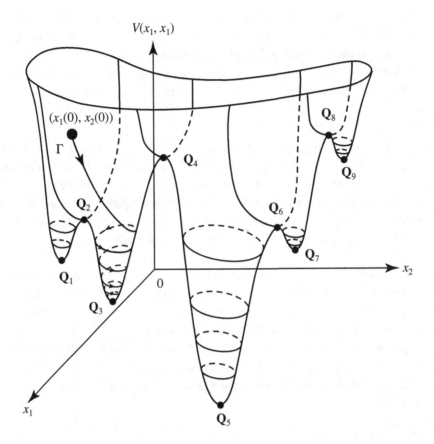

Fig. 8.5. A hypothetical Lyapunov function $V(x_1, x_2)$ with five local extrema $\mathbf{Q}_1, \mathbf{Q}_3, \mathbf{Q}_5, \mathbf{Q}_7, \mathbf{Q}_9$, and a hypothetical trajectory Γ converging toward the local minimum $\mathbf{Q}_3$.

point $\mathbf{Q}_i$ and the set $\mathcal{B}(\mathbf{Q}_i)$ of all initial conditions such that corresponding trajectories converge to $\mathbf{Q}_i$ is the *basin of attraction* of $\mathbf{Q}_i$. It follows from the above geometrical insights that one method to prove Eq. (8.24) is completely stable is to find a scalar function $V(x_1, x_2, \ldots, x_n)$ which possesses the above properties.[9] Unfortunately, no systematic procedure is presently available for finding such a scalar function, partly because solutions of most *nonlinear* systems of differential equations, such as Eq. (8.24), can*not* be found by analytical methods.

Now that the degree of difficulty for proving complete stability of Eq. (8.24) is understood, the reader would no doubt appreciate how lucky we are in being able to invent the scalar function $V(\mathbf{x})$ in Eq. (8.14) and prove that it qualifies as a Lyapunov function.

8.5   Positive and sign-symmetric A template implies complete stability

In this section we will present another complete stability criterion which depends only on the "sign," and *not* the "value," of the elements of the **A** template.

Definition 1: Sign symmetric A template
Let $\mathbf{A}_{180°}$ denote the template obtained by rotating an **A** template by $180°$ with respect to the center of the template. Let a_{ij} and a'_{ij} denote the corresponding ijth elements of **A** and $\mathbf{A}_{180°}$. We say a $(2r + 1) \times (2r + 1)$ **A** template, where r is the radius of the sphere of influence $S_r(ij)$, is *sign symmetric* if and only if a_{ij} and a'_{ij} are *both positive, both negative*, or *both zero*, for all $i, j = 1, 2, \ldots, 2r + 1$.

The above definition is equivalent to the condition that a_{ij} and $a_{-i,-j}$ are *both positive*, or *both negative*, or *both zero*, for all $(i, j) \neq (0, 0)$, where the double subscripts correspond to a Cartesian coordinate system the origin of which is located at the center of the template. As an illustrative example, consider the 5×5 **A** template shown in Fig. 8.6(a). To determine whether this template is *sign symmetric*, we first rotate "**A**" by $180°$ (always with respect to the center of the template) to obtain the associated $\mathbf{A}_{180°}$ template shown in Fig. 8.6(b). We then construct the corresponding "sign" templates, denoted by sgn[**A**] and sgn[$\mathbf{A}_{180°}$], respectively, by assigning the symbol $+$, $-$, or 0 to each entry a_{ij}, where $a_{ij} > 0$, $a_{ij} < 0$ and $a_{ij} = 0$ in **A** and $\mathbf{A}_{180°}$, respectively.

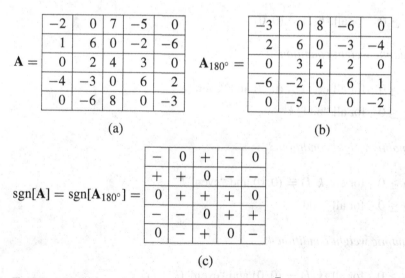

(a)

(b)

(c)

Fig. 8.6. (a) A non-symmetric 5×5 **A** template ($A \neq A^T$). (b) $\mathbf{A}_{180°}$ obtained by rotating the **A** template $180°$ with respect to the center of the template. (c) The "sign" of corresponding coefficients of **A** and $\mathbf{A}_{180°}$ are identical as depicted in this "sign" template sgn[**A**] whose entries consist of $+$, $-$, and 0's.

Then the **A** template is sign symmetric if and only if

$$\text{sgn}[\mathbf{A}] = \text{sgn}[\mathbf{A}_{180°}] \tag{8.27}$$

Since Eq. (8.27) is satisfied as shown in Fig. 8.6(c), we conclude that the **A** template in Fig. 8.6 is sign symmetric. Observe that this template is not symmetric with respect to the center, i.e., a sign-symmetric **A** template is, in general, not symmetric, but a symmetric **A** template is always sign symmetric.

Each of the following conditions concerning the relative signs of the *synaptic weights* a_{ij} of a $(2r + 1) \times (2r + 1)$ **A** template

$$\mathbf{A} = \begin{matrix}
a_{-r,-r} & \cdots & a_{-r,-1} & a_{-r,0} & a_{-r,1} & \cdots & a_{-r,r} \\
a_{-r+1,-r} & \cdots & a_{-r+1,-1} & a_{-r+1,0} & a_{-r+1,1} & \cdots & a_{-r+1,r} \\
\vdots & & & & & & \\
a_{0,-r} & \cdots & a_{0,-1} & \boxed{a_{0,0}} & a_{0,1} & \cdots & a_{0,r} \\
\vdots & & & & & & \\
a_{r-1,-r} & \cdots & a_{r-1,-1} & a_{r-1,0} & a_{r-1,1} & \cdots & a_{r-1,r} \\
a_{r,-r} & \cdots & a_{r,-1} & a_{r,0} & a_{r,1} & \cdots & a_{r,r}
\end{matrix}$$

is called a *synaptic weight condition*:

Definition 2: Synaptic weight conditions

Synaptic weight condition 1:

$$a_{kl} \geq 0 \quad \text{for all } (k, l) \neq (0, 0) \tag{8.28}$$

Synaptic weight condition 2:

$$\begin{aligned}
a_{kl} &\geq 0 \quad \text{for all } (k, l) \neq (0, 0) \text{ and "even" } k \\
a_{kl} &\leq 0 \quad \text{for all "odd" } k
\end{aligned} \tag{8.29}$$

Synaptic weight condition 3:

$$\begin{aligned}
a_{kl} &\geq 0 \quad \text{for all } (k, l) \neq (0, 0) \text{ and "even" } l \\
a_{kl} &\leq 0 \quad \text{for all "odd" } l
\end{aligned} \tag{8.30}$$

Synaptic weight condition 4:

$$\begin{aligned}
a_{kl} &\geq 0 \quad \text{for all } (k, l) \neq (0, 0) \text{ and "even" } (k + l) \\
a_{kl} &\leq 0 \quad \text{for all "odd" } (k + l)
\end{aligned} \tag{8.31}$$

We are now ready to state our next theorem.

Complete Stability Theorem 2[10]

An $M \times N$ CNN with a $(2r+1) \times (2r+1)$ **A** template is *completely stable*, for arbitrary **B** template and arbitrary *threshold z*, if the following three conditions are satisfied:

1 The **A** template is *sign symmetric*.
2 The template satisfies any one of the four *synaptic weight conditions*.
3 All the equilibrium points are isolated.

The proof of a special case of this theorem will be given in the next section.

Remark

Note that the synaptic weight condition 1 corresponds to an **A** template with non-negative coefficients (except possibly the center). Hence the title of this section is a *Corollary* of the above theorem.

Corollary to Complete Stability Theorem 2

An $M \times N$ CNN with a 3×3 **A** template, for arbitrary **B** *template* and arbitrary *threshold z*, is *completely stable* if the following three conditions are satisfied:

1 The **A** template is *sign symmetric*.
2 The **A** template possesses *any one* of the six synaptic weight patterns shown in Fig. 8.7
   where

   0 denotes a "zero" synaptic weight,
   ⊕ denotes a "positive" *or* "zero" synaptic weight,
   ⊖ denotes a "negative" *or* "zero" synaptic weight,
   × may assume *any* value.

3 All the equilibrium points are isolated.

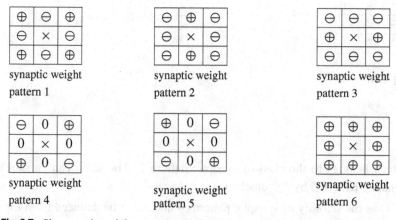

synaptic weight
pattern 1

synaptic weight
pattern 2

synaptic weight
pattern 3

synaptic weight
pattern 4

synaptic weight
pattern 5

synaptic weight
pattern 6

Fig. 8.7. Six synaptic weight patterns which satisfy condition 2 of the *Complete Stability Theorem 2*.

Proof:

This corollary follows directly from the above theorem since each of the synaptic weight patterns 1–3 and 6 satisfies one of the four synaptic weight conditions in (8.28)–(8.31).

Synaptic patterns 4 and 5 are trickier and we give the following sketch of the argument. If we rotate synaptic pattern 4 by 45°, counterclockwise, we obtain the pattern

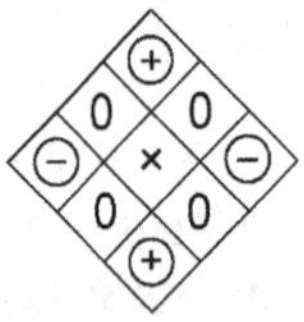

Fig. 8.8.

Looking at the nonzero entries, the center element is connected only to the top, down, left, and right neighbors. It can be shown that this is similar to the template

0	⊕	0
⊖	×	⊖
0	⊕	0

Fig. 8.9.

which belongs to the class of synaptic pattern 2. The same can be said by rotating synaptic pattern 5 by 45° clockwise.

Thus the stability of synaptic patterns 4 and 5 can be deduced from the stability of synaptic pattern 2.

To illustrate the properties of the synaptic weight patterns in Fig. 8.7, consider the following set of 12 hypothetical templates:

$$
A_1 = \begin{array}{|c|c|c|} \hline 0 & -2 & 0 \\ \hline 2 & 7 & 4 \\ \hline 0 & 0 & 0 \\ \hline \end{array}, \quad
A_2 = \begin{array}{|c|c|c|} \hline 0 & -2 & 7 \\ \hline -4 & 7 & -3 \\ \hline 7 & -1 & 0 \\ \hline \end{array}, \quad
A_3 = \begin{array}{|c|c|c|} \hline 0 & 0 & 0 \\ \hline -2 & 9 & -1 \\ \hline 0 & 0 & 0 \\ \hline \end{array}
$$

$$
A_4 = \begin{array}{|c|c|c|} \hline 7 & 0 & -1 \\ \hline 0 & 8 & 0 \\ \hline 0 & 0 & 0 \\ \hline \end{array}, \quad
A_5 = \begin{array}{|c|c|c|} \hline -7 & 0 & 0 \\ \hline 0 & 2 & 0 \\ \hline 2 & 0 & -6 \\ \hline \end{array}, \quad
A_6 = \begin{array}{|c|c|c|} \hline 0 & 1 & 2 \\ \hline -3 & 4 & -5 \\ \hline 0 & 0 & 0 \\ \hline \end{array}
$$

$$
A_7 = \begin{array}{|c|c|c|} \hline 0 & 0 & 1 \\ \hline 2 & 3 & 4 \\ \hline 5 & 6 & 0 \\ \hline \end{array}, \quad
A_8 = \begin{array}{|c|c|c|} \hline 0 & 0 & 0 \\ \hline -1 & -2 & -3 \\ \hline 0 & -5 & 0 \\ \hline \end{array}, \quad
A_9 = \begin{array}{|c|c|c|} \hline -1 & -2 & -3 \\ \hline 4 & 5 & 0 \\ \hline 0 & -7 & 0 \\ \hline \end{array}
$$

$$
A_{10} = \begin{array}{|c|c|c|} \hline -1 & 0 & -2 \\ \hline 0 & 7 & 0 \\ \hline -3 & 0 & 0 \\ \hline \end{array}, \quad
A_{11} = \begin{array}{|c|c|c|} \hline 1 & -4 & 5 \\ \hline 7 & 0 & 8 \\ \hline 6 & 2 & 0 \\ \hline \end{array}, \quad
A_{12} = \begin{array}{|c|c|c|} \hline -2 & -1 & 4 \\ \hline 2 & 3 & 1 \\ \hline 1 & -5 & -7 \\ \hline \end{array}
$$

Table 8.2 summarizes the properties of these templates.

Table 8.1.

Template	Is template A_i sign-symmetric?	Synaptic weight pattern possessed by template A_I
A_1	no	3
A_2	yes	1
A_3	yes	1, 2
A_4	no	5
A_5	no	4
A_6	no	none
A_7	no	6
A_8	no	1
A_9	no	3
A_{10}	no	2
A_{11}	no	none
A_{12}	yes	none

Observe that since none of the above 12 templates are symmetric, we cannot make use of the *Complete Stability Theorem 1*. However, applying the Corollary to *Complete Stability Theorem 2*, we can assert that templates A_2 and A_3 are completely stable.

8.6 Positive and cell-linking A template implies complete stability

In this section we will present yet another complete stability criterion, which substitutes the "sign symmetry" condition from Theorem 2 by a certain condition on the signal flow graph $\mathcal{G}_A(M \times N)$ associated with an $M \times N$ CNN, where $\mathcal{G}_A(M \times N)$ denotes a *directed* graph obtained by associating *each cell* $C(i, j)$ of the CNN with a *node* (i, j) and where *each* node is connected to its neighbors via the signal flow graph $\mathcal{G}_A$ associated with the **A** template defined in Fig. 2.17.

Definition 3: CNN signal flow graph $\mathcal{G}_A(M \times N)$

For each $M \times N$ CNN, we construct a *directed graph* $\mathcal{G}_A(M \times N)$ corresponding to an **A** template as follows:

1 Draw the signal flow graph $\mathcal{G}_A$ associated with the **A** template. For each non-zero and non-central synaptic weight $a_{kl} \neq 0$ ($k \neq i, l \neq j$) in **A**, draw a *directed* branch *from* node (k, l) *to* the center node (i, j), and a *similarly directed* branch from the center node (i, j) to the *reflected* node $(\bar{k}, \bar{l})$; i.e., node $(\bar{k}, \bar{l})$ is related to node (k, l) by a 180° rotation with respect to the center node (i, j).[11]
    See Figs 8.10(a) and 8.10(b) for an example.

2 To each cell $C(k, l)$ in an $M \times N$ CNN, draw a corresponding node (k, l), $k = 1, 2 \ldots, M, l = 1, 2, \ldots, N$ (see Figs 8.10(c) and 8.10(d) for a 4×4 CNN).

3 Duplicate the signal flow graph $\mathcal{G}_A$ (delete the coefficients a_{kl} and the self-loop) from *step 1* at each node (k, l) from *step 2*. All branches connected to "virtual" boundary nodes are deleted. The resulting directed graph is called the reduced CNN *signal flow graph* $\mathcal{G}_A(M \times N)$. For the 4×4 CNN shown in Fig. 8.10(c), we obtain the 16-node directed graph $\mathcal{G}_A(4 \times 4)$ shown in Fig. 8.10(d).

Definition 4: Cell-linking CNN

Let $\mathcal{G}_A(M \times N)$ be the signal flow graph of an $M \times N$ CNN associated with an **A** template. Then the CNN is said to be *cell-linking* if and only if for *every* two distinct nodes (k_1, l_1) and (k_2, l_2) in $\mathcal{G}_A(M \times N)$, there is a *similarly directed path*[12] in $\mathcal{G}_A(M \times N)$ from node (k_1, l_1) to node (k_2, l_2), *and a similarly directed return path* from node (k_2, l_2) to node (k_1, l_1).

For example, the 4×4 CNN shown in Fig. 8.10(c) is *not* cell-linking because there is at least one pair of nodes (e.g., from node $(2, 1)$ to node $(1, 1)$) where no similarly directed path exists. On the other hand, the 4×5 CNN shown in Fig. 8.11 is cell-linking as the reader can verify that there is a similarly directed path from any node (k_1, l_1) in the signal flow graph $\mathcal{G}_A(4 \times 5)$ to any other node (k_2, l_2). For example, to go from node $(2, 2)$ to node $(3, 4)$, we would travel along the similarly directed path $(2, 2) \rightarrow (3, 2) \rightarrow (2, 3) \rightarrow (3, 3) \rightarrow (4, 3) \rightarrow (3, 4)$.

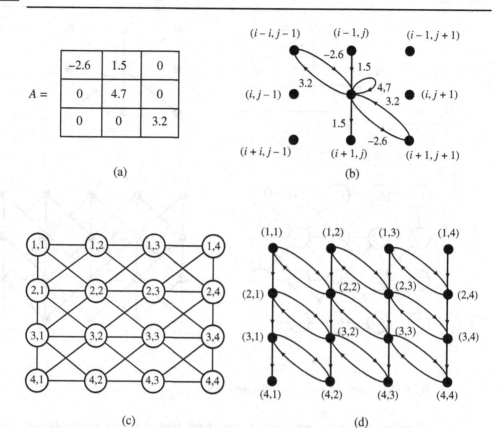

Fig. 8.10. Steps for constructing the signal flow graph $\mathcal{G}_A(M \times N)$ of an $M \times N$ CNN: (a) specify the **A** template; (b) draw the signal flow graph $\mathcal{G}_A$ associated with the **A** template. Note that for each non-zero synaptic weight $a_{kl} \neq 0$, $k \neq l$, there correspond two branches in $\mathcal{G}_A$. (c) A 4×4 ($M = N = 4$) CNN. (d) The reduced signal flow graph $\mathcal{G}_A(4 \times 4)$ associated with the **A** template.

Observe that before one can certify that a particular CNN is cell-linking, Definition 4 requires that one must examine *all possible combinations* of *initial* and *terminal* node pairs and in each case produce a similarly directed path. This would be a tedious task unless a computer program is written to do the checking. Fortunately, the following three *cell-linking tests* can be used to certify quickly, often by inspection, a large class of $N \times N$ CNNs to be cell-linking.

Cell-linking test 1

An $N \times N$ CNN, where N is an odd integer, is *cell-linking* if and only if there is a *similarly directed path* from the *center node*[13] of the associated signal flow graph $\mathcal{G}_A(N \times N)$ *to every other node* of $\mathcal{G}_A(N \times N)$.

Example 1

Consider the 3×3 CNN obtained by deleting row 4 and column 4 from the 4×4 CNN in Fig. 8.10(c). The corresponding signal flow graph $\mathcal{G}_A(3 \times 3)$ is obtained by deleting

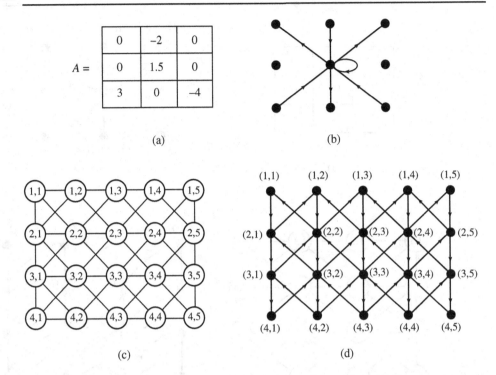

Fig. 8.11. Example of a 4 × 5 cell-linking CNN.

all nodes, and the branches attached to them, from the last row and the last column in Fig. 8.10(d). In this case, node $(2, 2)$ is the *center node* of the associated signal flow graph $\mathcal{G}_A(3 \times 3)$. Since there is no *similarly directed* path going from node $(2, 2)$ to node $(1, 3)$ in $\mathcal{G}_A(3 \times 3)$, we conclude that this 3×3 CNN is *not* cell-linking.

Example 2

Consider the 3×3 CNN obtained by deleting row 4 and columns 4, 5 from the 4×5 CNN in Fig. 8.11(c). The corresponding signal flow graph $\mathcal{G}_A(3 \times 3)$ is obtained by deleting all the nodes, and the branches attached to them, from the last row and the last two columns in Fig. 8.11(d). In this case, node $(2, 2)$ is the *center node* of the associated signal flow graph $\mathcal{G}_A(3 \times 3)$. Observe that there is a *similarly directed path* from node $(2, 2)$ to every other node of $\mathcal{G}_A(3 \times 3)$:

$(2, 2) \rightarrow (1, 1)$,

$(2, 2) \rightarrow (1, 3) \rightarrow (2, 3) \rightarrow (1, 2)$,

$(2, 2) \rightarrow (1, 3)$,

$(2, 2) \rightarrow (3, 2) \rightarrow (2, 1)$,

$(2, 2) \rightarrow (1, 3) \rightarrow (2, 3)$,

$(2, 2) \rightarrow (3, 2) \rightarrow (2, 1) \rightarrow (3, 1)$,

$(2, 2) \rightarrow (3, 2),$

$(2, 2) \rightarrow (3, 2) \rightarrow (2, 3) \rightarrow (3, 3).$

It follows from the *cell-linking test 1* that this 3×3 CNN is cell-linking.

Proof of cell-linking test 1:
The proof of this test follows from the proof of the following cell-linking test 2, since the center cell is rotationally symmetric with respect to itself.   □

Definition 5: Symmetric node-pair
If "a" is a node of the signal flow graph $\mathcal{G}_A(M \times N)$ let a^* denote the corresponding node which is $180°$ rotationally symmetric (about the center) with respect to a.

Lemma 1
There is a similarly directed path from node a to node b in $\mathcal{G}_A$ if, and only if, there is a similarly directed path from node b^* to node a^*.

Proof:
We will prove this Lemma by *mathematical induction* on the length n of the path as follows:

$n = 1$: if there is a branch from node a to b then there is a branch from b^* to a^* in view of the space-invariance of the templates, as shown in Fig. 8.12.

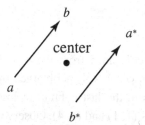

Fig. 8.12. A branch from a to b implies that a branch exists from b^* to a^*, and vice versa.

A directed path of length $n = k + 1$ from a to b contains a path of length k from a to c and a branch from c to b. By the induction hypothesis, there is a path of length k from c^* to a^* and a branch from b^* to c^*. So there is a path of length $k + 1$ from b^* to a^*. See Fig. 8.13.   □

Cell-linking test 2
An $M \times N$ CNN is cell-linking if and only if there is a pair of *rotationally symmetric* nodes[14] (k, l) and $(\bar{k}, \bar{l})$ such that there is a similarly directed path from node (k, l)

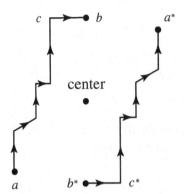

Fig. 8.13. A directed path from a to b implies that a directed path exists from b^* to a^*, and vice versa.

to *every other node* of $\mathcal{G}_A(M \times N)$, *and a similarly directed path* from node $(\bar{k}, \bar{l})$ to *every other node* of $\mathcal{G}_A(M \times N)$.

Example 3

Consider the 4×4 CNN shown in Fig. 8.10(c) and its associated signal flow graph $\mathcal{G}_A(4 \times 4)$ in Fig. 8.10(d). Observe that *for every pair* of rotationally symmetric nodes (k, l) and $(\bar{k}, \bar{l})$, of which there are many (e.g., (1, 1) and (4, 4), (3, 2) and (2, 3), (2, 1) and (3, 4), etc.), in $\mathcal{G}_A(4 \times 4)$, we cannot find a pair (k, l) and $(\bar{k}, \bar{l})$ such that there exists a *similarly directed* path from node (k, l) (resp., $(\bar{k}, \bar{l})$) to every other node of $\mathcal{G}_A(4 \times 4)$. It follows from *cell-linking test 2* that the 4×4 CNN of Fig. 8.10 is *not* cell-linking.

Example 4

Consider the 4×4 CNN obtained by deleting column 5 from the 4×5 CNN in Fig. 8.11(c). The corresponding signal flow graph $\mathcal{G}_A(4 \times 4)$ is obtained by deleting all nodes, and the branches attached to them, from the last column in Fig. 8.11(d). Consider the rotationally symmetric pairs of nodes (1, 1) and (4, 4). Observe that there is a *similarly directed* path from node (1, 1) to *every other node* of $\mathcal{G}_A(4 \times 4)$:

$(1, 1) \rightarrow (2, 1)$,

$(1, 1) \rightarrow (2, 1) \rightarrow (3, 1)$,

$(1, 1) \rightarrow (2, 1) \rightarrow (3, 1) \rightarrow (4, 1)$,

$(1, 1) \rightarrow (2, 1) \rightarrow (1, 2)$,

$(1, 1) \rightarrow (2, 1) \rightarrow (1, 2) \rightarrow (2, 2)$,

$(1, 1) \rightarrow (2, 1) \rightarrow (1, 2) \rightarrow (2, 2) \rightarrow (3, 2)$,

$(1, 1) \rightarrow (2, 1) \rightarrow (1, 2) \rightarrow (2, 2) \rightarrow (3, 2) \rightarrow (4, 2)$,

$(1, 1) \rightarrow (2, 1) \rightarrow (1, 2) \rightarrow (2, 2) \rightarrow (1, 3)$,

$$(1, 1) \to (2, 1) \to (1, 2) \to (2, 2) \to (1, 3) \to (2, 3),$$
$$(1, 1) \to (2, 1) \to (1, 2) \to (2, 2) \to (1, 3) \to (2, 3) \to (3, 3),$$
$$(1, 1) \to (2, 1) \to (1, 2) \to (2, 2) \to (1, 3) \to (2, 3) \to (3, 3) \to (4, 3),$$
$$(1, 1) \to (2, 1) \to (1, 2) \to (2, 2) \to (1, 3) \to (2, 3) \to (1, 4),$$
$$(1, 1) \to (2, 1) \to (1, 2) \to (2, 2) \to (1, 3) \to (2, 3) \to (1, 4) \to (2, 4),$$
$$(1, 1) \to (2, 1) \to (1, 2) \to (2, 2) \to (1, 3) \to (2, 3) \to (1, 4) \to (2, 4) \to (3, 4),$$
$$(1, 1) \to (2, 1) \to (1, 2) \to (2, 2) \to (1, 3) \to (2, 3)$$
$$\to (1, 4) \to (2, 4) \to (3, 4) \to (4, 4).$$

A *similarly directed path* can also be found from node $(4, 4)$ to every other node of $\mathcal{G}_A(4 \times 4)$. It follows from *cell-linking test 2* that this 4×4 CNN is cell-linking.

Proof of cell-linking test 2:
If the template is cell-linking, then by definition a and a^* have similarly directed paths to every other cell. Suppose both a and a^* have similarly directed paths to every other cell. Consider cell c different from a. Then cell c^* is different from a^*. So there is a path from a^* to c^*. By Lemma 1, there is a path from c to a. Since there is a path from a to everywhere else, c has a path to everywhere else too. $\qquad\square$

Cell-linking test 3
Let $C(M_1 \times N_1)$ denote any CNN subset of an $M \times N$ CNN, where $M_1 < M$ and $N_1 < N$. Suppose $N_1 > 1$ and $M_1 > 1$. If $C(M_1 \times N_1)$ is cell-linking, then so is its associated $M \times N$ CNN.

Example 5

Consider the 4×5 CNN shown in Fig. 8.11. Since *Example 4* shows that the 4×4 CNN subset is cell-linking, it follows from the *cell-linking test 3* that the associated 4×5 CNN is also cell-linking.

Proof of cell-linking test 3:
The proof is trivial by noting that the signal flow graph of an $M_1 \times N_1$ CNN can be obtained from the signal flow graph of an $M \times N$ CNN ($M \geq M_1, N \geq N_1$) by deleting some nodes and the branches connected to them. Thus a path in the smaller graph is also a valid path in the bigger graph. $\qquad\square$

We are now ready to state our next complete stability criterion.

Complete Stability Theorem 3
An $M \times N$ CNN with a $(2r + 1) \times (2r + 1)$ **A** template is *completely stable*, for *arbitrary* **B** *templates* and *arbitrary threshold z*, if the following three conditions are

satisfied:

1 The CNN is *cell-linking*.
2 Any one of the four *synaptic weight conditions* given by Eqs (8.28)–(8.31) is met.
3 All the equilibrium points are isolated.

Corollary *to Complete Stability Theorem 3*

An $N \times N$ CNN with a 3×3 **A** template, an *arbitrary* **B** *template*, and an *arbitrary threshold z*, is *completely stable* if the following three conditions are satisfied:

1 The CNN is *cell-linking*.
2 The **A** template possesses *any one* of the six *synaptic weight patterns* given in Fig. 8.7.
3 All the equilibrium points are isolated.

Proof:
We will only sketch the proof of this corollary.[15]

   Let us first prove the above corollary for the synaptic weight pattern 6. The state equation is

$$\dot{\mathbf{x}} = -\mathbf{x} + \hat{\mathbf{A}} f(\mathbf{x}) + \hat{\mathbf{B}}\mathbf{u} + \mathbf{z}$$

   The Jacobian matrix of the system is

$$(-I + \hat{\mathbf{A}}J)$$

where I is the identity matrix and

$$J = \begin{bmatrix} f'(x_1) & & \\ & \ddots & \\ & & f'(x_n) \end{bmatrix}$$

The off-diagonal elements of $\hat{\mathbf{A}}$ are the off-center elements of the **A** template which are nonnegative. Cell-linking implies the *irreducibility*[16] of the matrix $\hat{\mathbf{A}}$ and hence $-I + \hat{\mathbf{A}}J$ is also irreducible. Since the trajectories are bounded and the equilibrium points are isolated, the conclusion follows from Theorem A.1 in the Appendix of this chapter.

   By using Theorem A.2 in the Appendix, the synaptic weight patterns 1–3 can be transformed into the synaptic pattern 6. Since "stability" and "irreducibility" are preserved under these transformations, the corollary is proved.   □

Remarks
1 Complete Stability Theorem 3 can be used to prove Complete Stability Theorem 2 since for sign-symmetric templates the signal flow graph can be decomposed into cell-linking components.

2 The "connected component detector (CCD)" template

$$A = \boxed{\begin{array}{c|c|c} 1 & 2 & -1 \end{array}}$$

to be presented in Chapter 12 does not belong to any of the above classes.

To understand the elusiveness of this template, observe that the preceding stability criteria only make use of the "sign" of the template entries, not the actual values. In the following section, we will show that by changing the template entries of the CCD CNN by an arbitrarily small amount we can make it unstable. Consequently, any stability criterion capable of predicting the stability of the CCD template must include conditions involving the synaptic weights of the **A** template.

8.7   Stability of some sign-antisymmetric CNNs

We have already given an intuitive reason on why the stability of the CCD CNN is very difficult to prove. Numerical simulations have shown that the trajectories associated with the CCD template always converge to an equilibrium point. But, if we change the template values slightly, the system will oscillate.

In fact, computer simulations show that the parameters of the CCD template

$$A = \boxed{\begin{array}{c|c|c} 1 & 2 & -1 \end{array}}$$

lie on a *stability boundary* in the parameter space. In particular, the slightly perturbed **A** template

$$A = \boxed{\begin{array}{c|c|c} 1.01 & 2 & -1.01 \end{array}}$$

is found to be unstable. This is illustrated in Examples 8.6(a) and 8.6(b).

These templates belong to the class of templates

$$A = \boxed{\begin{array}{c|c|c} a^* & 2 & a \end{array}} , \quad B = \boxed{\begin{array}{c|c|c} 0 & 0 & 0 \end{array}} , \quad z = \boxed{\begin{array}{c} 0 \end{array}}$$

When the parameters a and a^* are varied, the corresponding CNN exhibit different behaviors. The a–a^* parameter plane can be partitioned into eight pairs of symmetrically spread regions which exhibit the same qualitative behavior.

We have shown earlier that if a and a^* are both positive, or both negative, then the CNN is stable (almost everywhere).

The following theorems can be proved:

Theorem 4

The CNNs in region 1 of the parameter plane in Fig. 8.14 do *not* possess any stable equilibrium point and are therefore *not stable*.

EXAMPLE 8.6: (a) Stable output waveforms corresponding to template

$$\mathbf{A} = \boxed{\begin{array}{c|c|c} 0.99 & 2 & -0.99 \end{array}}$$

in Region 4 with $x_1(0) = x_2(0) = 0.1$.
(b) Oscillating output waveforms corresponding to template

$$\mathbf{A} = \boxed{\begin{array}{c|c|c} 1.01 & 2 & -1.01 \end{array}}$$

in Region 1 with $x_1(0) = x_2(0) = 0.1$.

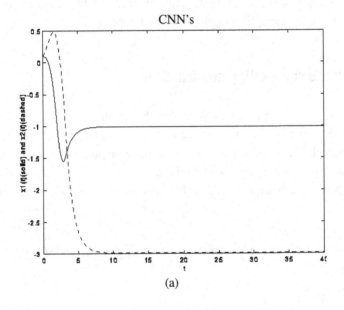

(a)

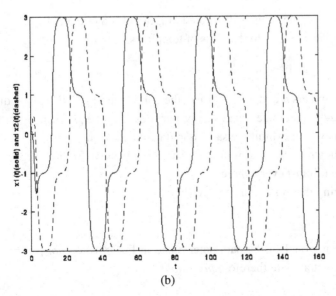

(b)

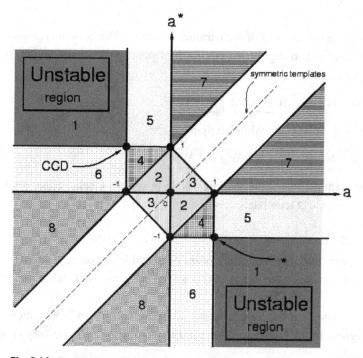

Fig. 8.14. Partitioning of the a–a^* parameter plane into 16 regions. See text for the behaviors of the CNNs in each region. The CNN at the point "*" is related to the CCD template $\mathbf{A} = \boxed{1 \mid 2 \mid -1}$ by a 180° rotation and shares the same functionality as the CCD template except that all pixels move in the other direction (see Chapter 12).

Theorem 5

The CNNs in regions 2 and 3 of the parameter plane in Fig. 8.14 are *completely stable* and any binary one-dimensional pattern corresponds to the output of a stable equilibrium point.

Theorem 6

The CNNs in regions 5 and 7 of the parameter plane in Fig. 8.14 are *completely stable* and all trajectories converge to an equilibrium point with a homogeneous "white" output for all cells

W	W	W	W	W	W	W	W	W	W

where "W" denotes a "white" output, or a homogeneous "black" output for all cells

B	B	B	B	B	B	B	B	B	B

where "B" denotes a "black" output.

Theorem 7

The CNNs in regions 6 and 8 of the parameter plane in Fig. 8.14 are *completely stable* and all trajectories converge to an equilibrium point with an alternating "white and black" output

W	B	W	B	W	B	W	B	W	B

or an alternating "black and white" output

B	W	B	W	B	W	B	W	B	W

Computer simulations show that all CNNs in region 4 behave like a CCD CNN. Observe that the CCD template

$$\mathbf{A} = \boxed{\begin{array}{c|c|c} 1 & 2 & -1 \end{array}}$$

lies at the common corner boundary point of unstable region 1, stable regions 5 and 6 (everything converges to one of two possible patterns), and stable region 4 (CCD behavior).

Let us examine next the trajectories of the following two CNNs which lie in two different regions in the parameter space in Fig. 8.14, but which are very close to each other:

Observe that the CNN in Example 8.6(a) is stable while the other in Example 8.6(b) is unstable.

Proof of Theorem 4:
Without loss of generality, let us assume $a < -1$ and $a^* > 1$. Suppose there is an equilibrium point such that $|x_i| \geq 1$ for all i. Assume $x_1 \geq 1$, then

$$\dot{\mathbf{x}}_1 = -x_1 + 2y_1 + ay_2 = -x_1 + 2 + ay_2 = 0$$

Since $2 - x_1 \leq 1$, we have $ay_2 = -(2 - x_1) \geq -1$. If $y_2 = 1$ then $ay_2 < -1$, which leads to a contradiction. Hence, $y_2 = -1$, i.e., $x_2 \leq -1$

Similarly

$$\dot{\mathbf{x}}_2 = -x_2 + 2y_2 + a^*y_1 + ay_3 = -x_2 - 2 + a^* + ay_3 = 0$$
$$-x_2 - 2 + a^* \geq 1 - 2 + 1 = 0 \quad \Rightarrow \quad ay_3 \leq 0$$

If $y_3 = -1$ then $ay_3 > 1$, which yields a contradiction. So, $y_3 = 1$ and $x_3 \geq 1$. Similarly, we find $x_4 \leq -1$, $x_5 \geq 1$, etc.

So, we have two possibilities:

$$x_{n-2} \leq -1, \quad x_{n-1} \geq 1, \quad x_n \leq -1$$

or

$$x_{n-2} \geq 1, \quad x_{n-1} \leq -1, \quad x_n \geq 1$$

In the first case

$$\dot{x}_n = -x_n + 2y_n + a^* y_{n-1} = -x_n - 2 + a^* = 0$$
$$x_n = a^* - 2 > -1, \text{ which leads to a contradiction.}$$

A similar proof applies for the second case.

So, the equilibrium point for this system with $|x_i| \geq 1$ for all i does not exist. Hence, an equilibrium point for this system must satisfy $|x_i| < 1$ for some i. It can be shown that such an equilibrium point is unstable. $\square$

Sketch of proof of Theorem 5

We will only show that any binary pattern is the output of some *stable* equilibrium point. Consider a binary output $\{b_1, b_2, \ldots, b_n\}$ where $b_i \in \{-1, 1\}$. We need to show that there exists an equilibrium point $(x_1, \ldots, x_n)$ such that $f(x_i) = b_i$. Stability follows from the fact that the Jacobian matrix at this equilibrium point is

$$
\begin{bmatrix}
-1 & & & \\
 & \ddots & & 0 \\
 & & \ddots & \\
0 & & & -1
\end{bmatrix}
$$

Since $b_i \in \{-1, 1\}$, this means that $|x_i| \geq 1$. In this case the state equation can be written as

$$\dot{x}_1 = -x_1 + 2y_1 + ay_2 = -x_1 + 2b_1 + ab_2 = 0$$
$$x_1 = 2b_1 + ab_2$$

$$\dot{x}_i = -x_i + 2y_i + a^* y_{i-1} + ay_{i+1}$$
$$\quad = -x_i + 2b_i + a^* b_{i-1} + ab_{i+1} = 0$$
$$x_i = 2b_i + a^* b_{i-1} + ab_{i+1}, \quad \text{for } 2 \leq i \leq n-1.$$

$$\dot{x}_n = -x_n + 2y_n + a^* y_{n-1}$$
$$\quad = -x_n + 2b_n + a^* b_{n-1} = 0$$
$$x_n = 2b_n + a^* b_{n-1}$$

Now we need to show that $f(x_i) = b_i$.

If $b_1 = 1$ then $x_1 = 2 + ab_2$. Since $|a| < 1 \Rightarrow |ab_2| < 1$, it follows that $x_1 \geq 1$.
If $b_1 = -1$ then $x_1 = -2 + ab_2 \leq -1$. Hence, $f(x_1) = b_1$.

Consider next $2 \leq i \leq n-1$. If $b_i = 1$ then $x_i = 2 + a^* b_{i-1} + ab_{i+1}$. Since $|a| + |a^*| \leq 1$, we have $|a^* b_{i-1} + ab_{i+1}| \leq |a| + |a^*| \leq 1$, and hence $x_i \geq 1$.

Similarly, if $b_i = -1$ then $x_i \leq -1$. Consequently $f(x_i) = b_i$. We can also show $f(x_n) = b_n$ so we have found such an equilibrium point which outputs the binary pattern b_i.

Proof of Theorem 6:
We will only prove the case in region 7 where $a > 1$. Suppose $a > 1$ and $a^* > 0$. Since the template is sign symmetric, we can apply the Complete Stability Theorem 2 to show that it is stable. It remains to show that there are only two stable equilibrium points, whose output is either

W	W	W	W	W	W	W	W	W	W

or

B	B	B	B	B	B	B	B	B	B

We know that a stable equilibrium point must satisfy $|x_i| \geq 1$ for all i.

$$\dot{x}_1 = -x_1 + 2y_1 + ay_2 = 0$$

Since $a > 1$ it is easy to show that if $y_2 = 1$ then $x_1 > 1$. If $y_2 = -1$ then $x_2 < -1$, so $y_1 = y_2$.

$$\dot{x}_2 = -x_2 + 2y_2 + a^*y_1 + ay_3$$
$$= -x_2 + (2 + a^*)y_2 + ay_3 = 0$$

Again it is easy to show that $y_2 = y_3$, so we must have $y_1 = y_2 = y_3 = y_4 = \cdots = y_n$. It follows that

W	W	W	W	W	W	W	W	W	W

and

B	B	B	B	B	B	B	B	B	B

are the output of the only two *stable* equilibrium points.   □

The *proof of Theorem 7* is similar to that of Theorem 6.

The Venn diagram in Fig. 8.15 illustrates the relationship between the various classes of templates we have discussed so far.

A   Appendix to Chapter 8

The theorems in this section rely on the convergence results of Hirsch and the equivalent transformation results of Chua and Roska[17] and Chua and Wu.[18]

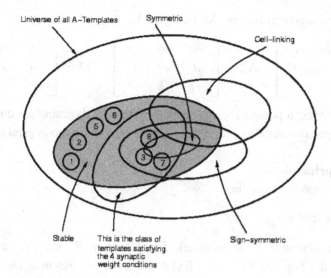

Fig. 8.15. Venn diagram illustrating the relationship between classes of templates. The number corresponds to the regions in Fig. 8.14.

Theorem A.1:[1][19]

Consider the system

$$\dot{\mathbf{x}} = \mathbf{F}(\mathbf{x})$$

Assume that for each $\mathbf{x}$ the Jacobian matrix $D\mathbf{F}$ is *irreducible*[20] and its off-diagonal elements are nonnegative. Suppose all trajectories remain bounded. Then, for all initial conditions in a full measure set, the corresponding trajectories approach the set of equilibrium points.

Theorem A.2:[2][18]

Consider a CNN with time-invariant input and bias

$$\dot{\mathbf{x}} = -\mathbf{x} + \hat{\mathbf{A}} f(\mathbf{x}) + \hat{\mathbf{B}}\mathbf{u} + \mathbf{z} \tag{A8.1}$$

Let

$$\mathbf{A} = \begin{bmatrix} a & b & c \\ d & e & f \\ g & h & i \end{bmatrix}$$

Then there exist $\hat{\mathbf{B}}_1, \hat{\mathbf{B}}_2, \hat{\mathbf{B}}_3$ and $\mathbf{z}_1, \mathbf{z}_2, \mathbf{z}_3$ such that each of the following three systems

$$\dot{\mathbf{x}} = -\mathbf{x} + \hat{\mathbf{A}}_1 f(\mathbf{x}) + \hat{\mathbf{B}}_1 \mathbf{u} + \mathbf{z}_1$$
$$\dot{\mathbf{x}} = -\mathbf{x} + \hat{\mathbf{A}}_2 f(\mathbf{x}) + \hat{\mathbf{B}}_2 \mathbf{u} + \mathbf{z}_2$$
$$\dot{\mathbf{x}} = -\mathbf{x} + \hat{\mathbf{A}}_3 f(\mathbf{x}) + \hat{\mathbf{B}}_3 \mathbf{u} + \mathbf{z}_3$$

is *topological conjugate* to system (A8.1), where $\hat{\mathbf{A}}_1$, $\hat{\mathbf{A}}_2$, and $\hat{\mathbf{A}}_3$ are given by:

$$
\mathbf{A}1 = \begin{bmatrix} -a & b & -c \\ -d & e & -f \\ -g & h & -i \end{bmatrix} \quad \mathbf{A}2 = \begin{bmatrix} -a & -b & -c \\ d & e & f \\ -g & -h & -i \end{bmatrix} \quad \mathbf{A}3 = \begin{bmatrix} a & -b & c \\ -d & e & -f \\ g & -h & i \end{bmatrix}
$$

Roughly speaking, topological conjugacy means that the dynamics are qualitatively the same. In particular, stability properties are preserved under topological conjugacy.

LaSalle's invariance principle

Consider the autonomous system

$$\dot{\mathbf{x}} = \mathbf{f}(\mathbf{x}), \quad \mathbf{x} \in R^n$$

Let $V(\mathbf{x})$ be a continuously differentiable function from R^n into R. Let S be an arbitrary set in R^n. Suppose $\dot{V} = \nabla V \cdot \mathbf{f}(\mathbf{x})$ does not change sign in S. Define

$$E = \{\mathbf{x} : \dot{V}(\mathbf{x}) = 0, \mathbf{x} \in \bar{S}\}$$

where $\bar{S}$ denotes the closure of S. Let M be the largest invariant set in E. Then M is a *closed* set, and for all solutions remaining in S for all $t \geq 0$, $x(t)$ approaches the closed invariant set M, or "∞," i.e., $M \cup \{\infty\}$, where "$\cup$" denotes "set union" and $\{\infty\}$ denotes the point at ∞.

9 The CNN Universal Machine (CNN-UM)

In Chapter 7, we have shown a couple of generic examples which can be solved by a sequence of CNN templates. The hardwired CNN implementation using different CNN components or different templates is, however, totally impractical. In this chapter we show the architecture of the first spatio-temporal analogic array computer, the CNN Universal Machine (CNN-UM).

In the examples mentioned above, and in many other examples including physiologically faithful models of various parts of the nervous system, especially vision, the following two completely different types of operations are used to solve a complex task:

- continuous-time, continuous valued spatio-temporal nonlinear array dynamics (2D and 3D arrays);
- local and global logic.

Hence, analog (continuous) and logic operations are mixed and *embedded* in the array computer. Therefore we call this type of array computing: *analogic*.

The CNN-UM architecture, shown subsequently:

- contains a *minimum number* of component types,
- provides *stored programmable* spatio-temporal array computing, and
- is universal in two senses:

    as *spatial logic*, it is equivalent to a Turing Machine and as a local logic it may implement any *local Boolean function*;

    as a *nonlinear dynamic operator*, it can realize any local operator of fading memory,[1] i.e., practically all reasonable operators. Indeed, the CNN-UM is a common computational paradigm for as diverse fields of spatio-temporal computing as, for example, retinal models, reaction diffusion equations, mathematical morphology, etc.

Remarks:

1 The stored program, as a sequence of templates, could be considered as a genetic code for the CNN-UM. The elementary genes are the templates; in case of $r = 1$ it

is a 19 real-number code. This, in a way is a minimal representation of a complex spatio-temporal dynamics.

2 In the nervous system, the consecutive templates are placed in space as subsequent layers.

9.1   The architecture

9.1.1   The extended standard CNN universal cell

Actually, in Chapter 7, we have shown almost all of the various components we need in the extended standard universal cell, shown schematically in Fig. 9.1.

We have two elements not yet introduced in Chapter 7.

The *local analog output unit* (LAOU) is a multiple-input single output analog device. It has the same function for continuous signal values as the local logic unit (LLU) for logic values – namely, it combines local (stored) analog values into a single output. We may have used it for analog addition in Section 7.6, instead of using the CNN cell for addition.

The *local communication and control unit* (LCCU) receives the programming instructions, in each cell, from the *global analogic programming unit* (GAPU), namely:

- the analog template values ($\mathbf{A}$, $\mathbf{B}$, and z),
- the logic function codes for the local logic unit, and
- the switch configuration of the cell specifying the signal paths and some settings in the functional units (e.g., $f(\cdot)$, LAOU, GW$(\cdot)$).

This means, at the same time, that we need registers (storage elements) in the GAPU for these three types of information, namely:

- an analog program register (APR) for the CNN templates,
- a logic program register (LPR) for the LLU functions, and
- a switch configuration register (SCR).

In Fig. 9.1(b) the analog part of a circuit schematic of the cell is shown. We are keeping in mind an electronic or a physiological model, although, except for a capacitor, no implementation-dependent elements are shown. An electronic integrated circuit (VLSI) implementation of these elements will be discussed in Chapter 15.

We assigned separate local analog memory places for the input (u), initial state ($x(0)$), threshold (z), and a sequence of outputs ($y^{(n)}$), however a single local analog memory with a few places can also be used for all of these signals/data.

In Fig. 9.1(c) we show the logic part. We have introduced the elements already in Chapter 7. The "global wire" (GW$(\cdot)$) operator receives inputs from all cells, their cell logic outputs are $Y_{ij} := Y_{ij}^{(k)}$, k: specified.

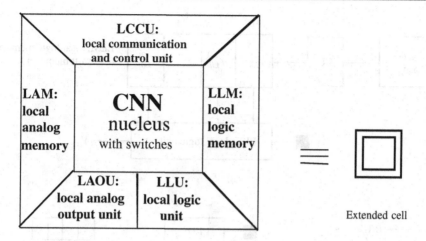

(a) The main components in the extended cell

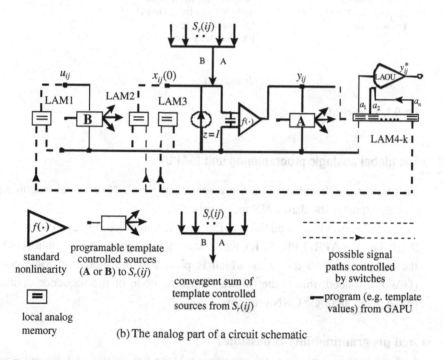

(b) The analog part of a circuit schematic

Fig. 9.1. The extended standard CNN universal cell.

Remarks:

There are other, very useful possibilities related to a "global wire." For example, weighted analog outputs of each row may be calculated and added for the whole array.

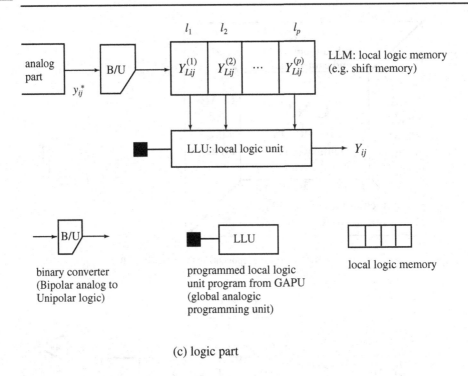

(c) logic part

Fig. 9.1. Continued.

9.1.2   The global analogic programming unit (GAPU)

This unit is the "conductor" of the whole analogic CNN universal machine it directs all the extended standard CNN universal cells.

Fig. 9.2 shows that, in addition to the three registers we already discussed in Section 9.1.1 (i.e., the APR, LPR, SCR), the global analogic programming unit (GAPU) hosts the main control of the array which is placed in the global analogic control unit (GACU). Indeed, this is the (digital) machine code of the sequence of instructions of the given analogic CNN program.

Why stored programmability is possible?

In digital computers, we tacitly assume and take for granted that, for any sequence of instructions:

(i)   all the transients decay within a specified clock cycle, and

(ii) all the signals remain within a prescribed range of dynamics (including dissipation, slope, etc.).

These conditions are not trivial in digital implementations either. Think about what would happen if a 75 MHz Pentium processor had a clock speed of 100 MHz. Clearly

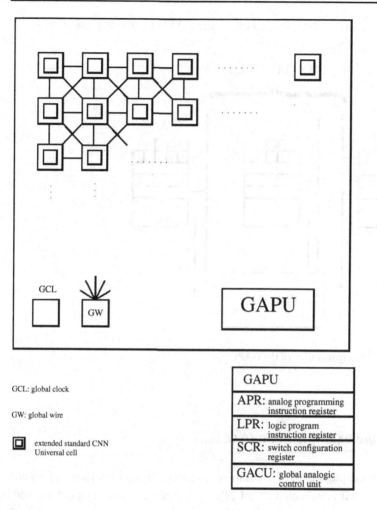

GCL: global clock

GW: global wire

extended standard CNN Universal cell

GAPU	
APR:	analog programming instruction register
LPR:	logic program instruction register
SCR:	switch configuration register
GACU:	global analogic control unit

Fig. 9.2. The structure of the CNN universal machine.

it would not work because of violating the first condition above. It may even destroy it due to violating the second condition.

A unique feature of the CNN dynamics and the CNN-UM architecture is that we can assure conditions (i) and (ii) as well. It is much less trivial here than in the digital case. Our main elementary instructions are the CNN templates and the local logic operations. But the CNN templates may induce the most exotic dynamics. The global clock (GCL) has a faster clock cycle for the logic part than for the analog part.

The global analogic control unit stores, in digital form, the sequence of instructions. Each instruction contains the operation code (template or logic), the selection code for the parameters of the operation (the code for the 19 values: **A, B**, z; or the code of the local logic function), and the switch configuration. The parameters are stored in the registers (APR, LPR, SCR).

Fig. 9.3 shows the arrangement of the GAPU from this point of view.

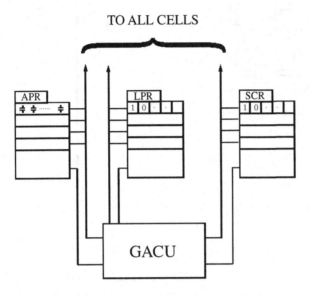

Fig. 9.3. The organization of the GAPU.

9.2 A simple example in more detail

In this example we show a complete sequence of various forms of an analogic CNN program as it is executed on a CNN Universal Machine. The outline and description of such a program contains the following information.

- *Global task.*
- The *flow diagram* of the algorithm.
- The description of the algorithm in high level α language (*analogic CNN language*) or in an assembler (the analogic machine code, AMC).
- The result of an α compiler in the form of *an analogic machine code (AMC)* as a sequence of *macro instructions* and its *binary form (optional)*.

The physical code generated by the CNN operating system and the controlling CNN chip "platform" is not shown here.

This example, called Bars-Up, is interesting in itself. The *global task* is shown in Fig. 9.4. We have to detect all objects which have bars pointing upwards, and a continuous (to this bar) middle segment (many animals are responding to these objects by firing some neurons in their infero-temporal cortex).

The flow diagram of the analogic CNN algorithm is shown in Fig. 9.5 with the intermediate results. The α language description (version 2.1) is shown in Table 9.1. We will show later the other codes generated by the α compiler.

The global task is: detect those objects which have bars pointing upwards. A typical input $\rightarrow$ output image pair is shown below. The original image is called BarsUpTest, the output is RESULT.

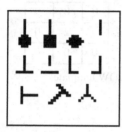 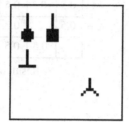

Fig. 9.4. The global task.

Remarks:

Here, we have a 5×5 template. Its actual physical implementation is not considered here. There are several ways to realize this "large neighborhood" CNN template, for example, to decompose it into several 3×3 templates.

Table 9.1. *Visual feature detection (α-language, version 2.1).*

```
        FUNCTION BARS-UP;
xLoad  (LLM1, BarsUpTest);
        LLM3:= LLM1;
        HOLLOW(LLM1,LLM1,LLM2,10,−1);
        LOGXOR(LLM2,LLM3,LLM1,10,−1);
        HORDIST(LLM1,LLM1,LLM2,10,−1);
        RECALL(LLM2,LLM3,LLM1,10,−1);
xSAVE(RESULT,LLM1);
        ENDFUNCT;
```

Here, in this function description, we have used two new α instructions:

xLOAD(local memory, file name) and

xSAVE(file name, local memory)

These are the input and output instructions from and to the digital environment.

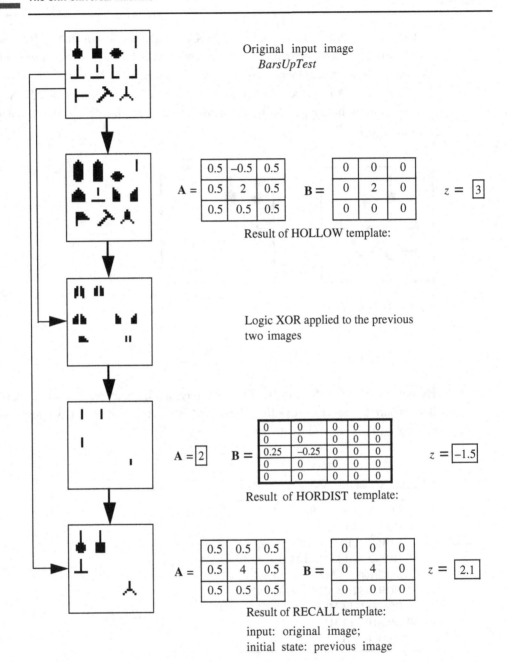

Original input image
BarsUpTest

$$A = \begin{array}{|c|c|c|} \hline 0.5 & -0.5 & 0.5 \\ \hline 0.5 & 2 & 0.5 \\ \hline 0.5 & 0.5 & 0.5 \\ \hline \end{array} \quad B = \begin{array}{|c|c|c|} \hline 0 & 0 & 0 \\ \hline 0 & 2 & 0 \\ \hline 0 & 0 & 0 \\ \hline \end{array} \quad z = \boxed{3}$$

Result of HOLLOW template:

Logic XOR applied to the previous
two images

$$A = \boxed{2} \quad B = \begin{array}{|c|c|c|c|c|} \hline 0 & 0 & 0 & 0 & 0 \\ \hline 0 & 0 & 0 & 0 & 0 \\ \hline 0.25 & -0.25 & 0 & 0 & 0 \\ \hline 0 & 0 & 0 & 0 & 0 \\ \hline 0 & 0 & 0 & 0 & 0 \\ \hline \end{array} \quad z = \boxed{-1.5}$$

Result of HORDIST template:

$$A = \begin{array}{|c|c|c|} \hline 0.5 & 0.5 & 0.5 \\ \hline 0.5 & 4 & 0.5 \\ \hline 0.5 & 0.5 & 0.5 \\ \hline \end{array} \quad B = \begin{array}{|c|c|c|} \hline 0 & 0 & 0 \\ \hline 0 & 4 & 0 \\ \hline 0 & 0 & 0 \\ \hline \end{array} \quad z = \boxed{2.1}$$

Result of RECALL template:
input: original image;
initial state: previous image

Fig. 9.5.

9.3   A very simple example on the circuit level

In the following example, we will explain the functional details of the CNN-UM
operation on the functional circuit level. Even though the example is very simple, it

contains the micro steps. At the same time, it is not a transistor level description. Some transistor level implementation details will be described in Chapter 15.

The task

Detect the horizontal intensity changes on a black and white image (Fig. 9.6 shows an example).

The steps of the solution

- detect those white pixels which have a black pixel on their direct right-hand side (detection means to put the detected pixel to the black value, i.e. +1),
- detect those black pixels which have a white pixel on their direct right-hand side,
- apply a pixel by pixel logic OR function.

The flow diagram of the algorithm and the templates

The first step is performed by a template TEM1 and the second step by TEM2. The two results are combined with a local logic OR operation.

The flow diagram with image fragments representing input, output, and intermediate results is shown in Fig. 9.6.

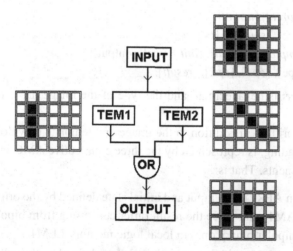

Fig. 9.6. The flow diagram of the analogic CNN algorithm. Operation is illustrated on a simple test image fragment.

The templates used in the CNN algorithm are as follows:

$$\text{TEM1 (white to black):} \quad \mathbf{A} = \begin{bmatrix} 0 & 0 & 0 \\ 0 & 2 & 0 \\ 0 & 0 & 0 \end{bmatrix}, \quad \mathbf{B} = \begin{bmatrix} 0 & 0 & 0 \\ -2 & 2 & 0 \\ 0 & 0 & 0 \end{bmatrix}, \quad I = -1.5$$

$$\text{TEM2 (black to white):} \quad \mathbf{A} = \begin{bmatrix} 0 & 0 & 0 \\ 0 & 2 & 0 \\ 0 & 0 & 0 \end{bmatrix}, \quad \mathbf{B} = \begin{bmatrix} 0 & 0 & 0 \\ 0 & 2 & -2 \\ 0 & 0 & 0 \end{bmatrix}, \quad I = -1.5$$

The macro code of the algorithm

As an example of the analogic macro code (AMC) description, we show the description of our very simple algorithm:

LOADTEM	>FF80, APR1	; loading template (TEM1)
LOADTEM	>FF60, APR2	; loading template (TEM2)
COPY	A_M2C, >FF40, LAM1	; copy Analog image from ; Memory to Chip
RUNTEM	APR1, LAM1, LAM1, LLM1	; *run TEM1 template operation*
RUNTEM	APR2, LAM1, LAM1, LLM2	; *run TEM2 template operation*
RUNLOG	OR, LLM1, LLM2, LLM3	; *run local logic operation OR*
COPY	L_C2M, LLM3, >FF00	; copy binary (Logic) image ; from Chip to Memory
END		

The syntax of the AMC instructions are simple:

LOADTEM	[*source*], [*target*];
COPY	[*type*], [*source*], [*target*];
RUNTEM	[*template*], [*input*], [*init. state*], [*output*];
RUNLOG	[*type*], [*op1*], [*op2*], [*result*].

The memory address is hexadecimal, and the type of the image has a mnemonic name.

The core of the algorithm, in addition to the image and template downloading and the output image uploading, is represented by the three consecutive AMC instructions denoted by italic comments. That is:

- run TEM1 (stored in APR1) with input and initial state defined by the original input image (stored in LAM1) and place the result (after converting from bipolar analog representation to unipolar binary one) in local logic memory LLM1
- run TEM2 (stored in APR2) with input and initial state defined by the original input image (stored in LAM1) and place the result (after converting from bipolar analog representation to unipolar binary one) in local logic memory LLM2
- apply the local logic unit (LLU) with a logic OR operation on the two intermediate results stored in local logic memories LLM1 and LLM2 and place the result in LLM3

These three macro instructions will be converted into a series of elementary machine micro instructions, as shown later.

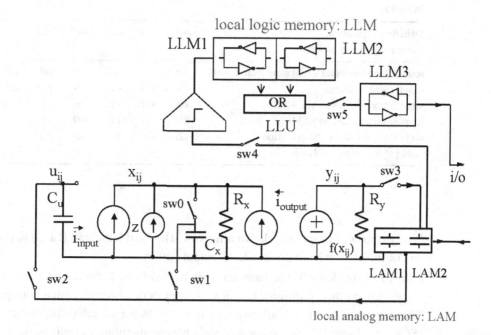

Fig. 9.7. A very simple extended cell with the six switches, sw0, sw1, sw2, sw3, sw4, sw5 and the logic output (at the output of LLM3). It is supposed that the input image has been downloaded to LAM1.

We will not go into the details of how the CNN operating system (COS) generates the machine micro code to be put into the GACU of the CNN Universal Chip (and how to fill the registers of the GAPU); however we want to show the functional circuit-level operation of an extended CNN cell. We will show the operations generated by the machine-level micro instructions in detail. First, we show an extended cell.

The functional circuit level schematics of an extended cell

An extended cell is shown in Fig. 9.7.

The local analog memory (LAM) has two places, LAM1 and LAM2. The analog cell contains two auxiliary storage capacitors at the input and at the state, respectively. The i_{input} and i_{output} values represent the weighted sums (as currents) from the inputs (**B** template) and from the outputs (**A** template) of the neighbor cells.

The local logic memory has three places, LLM1, LLM2, and LLM3. LLM1 and LLM2 is implemented as a shift register, the input is stored on LLM1 and every new input shifts the content by one place to the right (from LLM1 to LLM2, etc.). If we want to store a LAM value in (LLM1, LLM2), an automatic bipolar analog to unipolar

Table 9.2.

Switch configuration; and corresponding action	sw0	sw1	sw2	sw3	sw4	sw5
sconf0; load input and initial state from LAM1	off	on	on	off	off	off
sconf1; start transient	on	off	off	off	off	off
sconf2; store the result in LAM2	on	off	off	on	off	off
sconf3; store LAM2 in LLM	off	off	off	off	on	off
sconf4; activate the logic operation and put the result in LLM3	off	off	off	off	off	on

binary converter is applied, shown after sw4. The local logic unit (LLU) in this cell is an OR function. It has a direct LLM3 output buffer.

In this extended cell we have six switches: sw0, sw1, sw2, sw3, sw4, and sw5. Depending on their positions, ON or OFF, they code different switch configurations. The sequence of switch configurations is stored in the switch configuration register (SCR). In Table 9.2, we show five switch configurations (sconf0, sconf1, sconf2, sconf3, sconf4) which define five actions in each and all cells (fully parallel).

The content of the global analogic programming unit (GAPU)

First we specify the registers. Part of the content of the switch configuration register (SCR) has already been defined. This will be enough for running the three consecutive core macro instructions defined above.

The analog program instruction register (APR) contains two templates, i.e. the two sets of the 19 numbers defined by TEM1 and TEM2, coded some appropriate way in APR1 and APR2. The logic program instruction register (LPR) contains the codes for the logic operations of the local logic unit (LLU). Here we need only the OR operation. It is stored, and coded in an appropriate way, in LPR.

The sequence of the actions in the CNN Universal Machine with our simple extended cell, and the registers defined right now, is coded in the Global Analogic Control Unit (GACU). In our example, for the three macro instructions defined above, for implementing the core of our algorithms (running the two consecutive templates and the logic OR operation with the appropriate storage of the intermediate results), the sequence of macro instructions of the GACU are as follows.

Here, we suppose that the templates, the local logic operator, and the input image are loaded (TEM1 and TEM2 in APR1 and APR2, respectively, the OR operation in LPR1, and the input image, pixel by pixel, in the LAM1 place of each extended cell). Then the next sequence is applied:

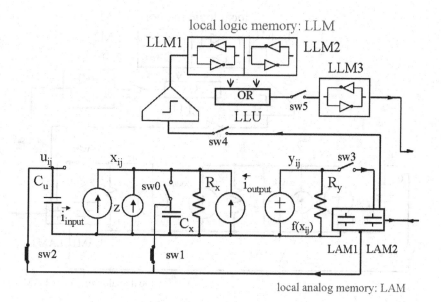

Fig. 9.8. Sconf0; load input and initial state from LAM1.

Action code	Comment
sconf0;	load input and initial state from LAM1
select APR1;	tune the template element values defined by TEM1
sconf1;	start the analog spatio-temporal transient
sconf2;	store the result in LAM2
sconf3;	store LAM2 in LLM1
sconf0;	load input and initial state from LAM1
select APR2;	tune the template element values defined by TEM2
sconf1;	start the analog spatio-temporal transient
sconf2;	store the result in LAM2
sconf3;	store LAM2 in LLM1 (the former LLM1 value will be automatically shifted to LLM2)
select LPR1;	tune to the local logic operation OR
sconf4;	calculate the OR operation and store the result in LLM3

In the first two action groups, the first two actions are also parallel.

The five extended cell configurations corresponding to sconf0, sconf1, sconf2, sconf3, and sconf4 are shown on Figs 9.8, 9.9, 9.10, 9.11, and 9.12, respectively. The comments are referring to the last two action groups (activating TEM2 and OR). The closed switches are shown in bold. Hence, it is easy to detect the active parts of the circuit.

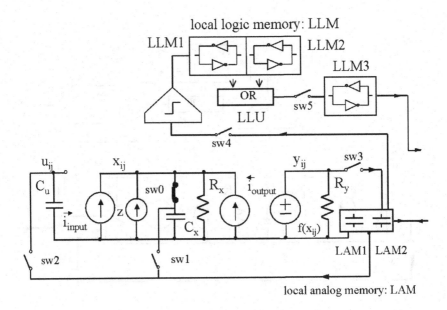

Fig. 9.9. Sconf1; start transient.

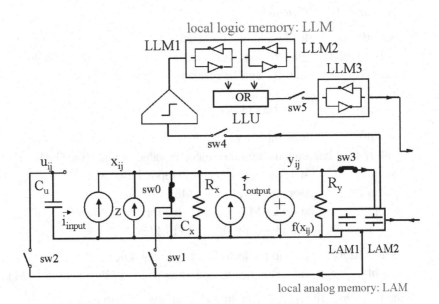

Fig. 9.10. Sconf2; store the result in LAM2.

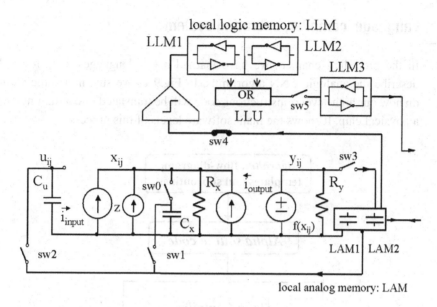

Fig. 9.11. Sconf3; store LAM2 in LLM.

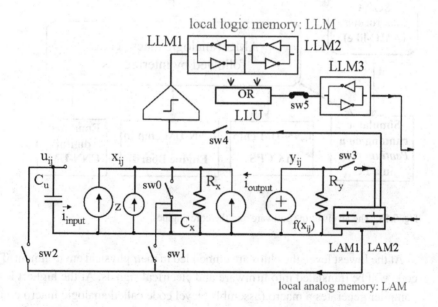

Fig. 9.12. Sconf4; activate the logic operation and put the result in LLM3.

9.4   Language, compiler, operating system

In the preceding chapters we have learned a few languages of different levels to describe the analogic CNN algorithms. In Fig.9.13 we summarize the various steps on how our high-level α instructions code will be translated into a running program on a physical chip. It shows the main software levels of this process.

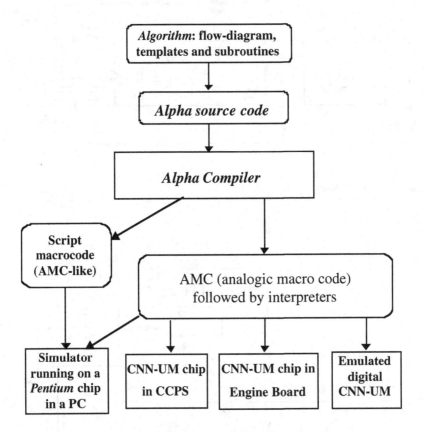

Fig. 9.13. The levels of the software and the core engines.

At the lowest level, the chips are embedded in their physical environment. The AMC code will be translated into firmware and electrical signals. At the highest level, the α compiler generates a macro (assembly) level code called analogic macro code, AMC. The input of the α compiler is the description of the flow diagram of the algorithm using the α language.

The AMC-like CNN Script Description (CSD) code is used for the software simulations to control the different parameters of the simulation as well as to specify the graphical demonstration of the results, as we have shown in Chapter 4. Here, the

Table 9.3. *Analogic macro code (AMC) description of BARS-UP.*

COPY	B2C_L2L, >FFC0, 1	* board to chip copy (to LAM1)
LOADT	>FFA0, 1	* load template1
LOADT	>FF80, 2	* load template2
LOADT	>FF60, 3	* load template3
RUNA	1, 1, 1, 2	* run template1
RUNTL	CXOR, 2, 2, 2	* logic XOR
RUNA	2, 2, 2, 2	* run template2
RUNA	3, 2, 1, 2	* run template3
COPY	C2C_L2L, 2, >FFC0	* chip to board copy (from LAM2)

syntax:

COPY	[type], [source], [destination]
LOADT	[source], [destination]
RUNA	[template], [input], [init. state], [output]
RUNL	[type], [op1], [op2], [output]

All the parameters are chip or board memory addresses, except the [type] parameters.

physical processor is the Pentium microprocessor, controlled by the physical code running under an operating system (like WINDOWS or UNIX). The simulator can also be used directly from the α source code via the compiler and the AMC (with default operating and graphical parameters).

As an example, for an AMC code in assembly format and in hexadecimal format, these codes for the program example BARS-UP, described in Section 9.2, are shown in Tables 9.3 and 9.4, respectively.

Consider now the CNN Universal Machine Chip, called CNN-UM chip. We need the appropriate software levels and a hardware-software environment. This is the CNN Chip Prototyping System (CCPS). In the CCPS we may also use the AMC code as the input. In Fig. 9.14 we show the flow diagram of the whole process down to the physical chip.

In this chip prototyping system the CNN-UM chip is hosted in a separate platform, connected to a PC. A special purpose add-in board, the Chip Prototyping System Board (CPS board) is serving as the hardware environment for the CNN Operating System (COS).

To make the whole CNN computer self-contained we need a CNN Universal Chip set[2] and to implement it on an Engine Board.

In single-board or single-chip solutions the CPS board and its software are integrated into the CNN-UM chip or board.

We stop here, not to explain more details. Our aim is to show that when writing analogic CNN programs in high-level languages (like the α language), the rest of the familiar computing infrastructure is ready to execute these programs in different

Table 9.4. *Compiled analogic macro code (in hexadecimal format).*

hexa	binary	code
12h	0000 0000 0001 0010	COPY
8h	0000 0000 0000 1000	B2C_L2L
FFC0h	1111 1111 1100 0000	>FFC0
1h	0000 0000 0000 0001	1
62h	0000 0000 0001 0010	LOADT
FFA0h	1111 1111 1010 0000	>FFA0
1h	0000 0000 0000 0001	1
62h	0000 0000 0001 0010	LOADT
FF80h	1111 1111 1010 0000	>FF80
2h	0000 0000 0000 0010	2
62h	0000 0000 0001 0010	LOADT
FF60h	1111 1111 1010 0000	>FF60
3h	0000 0000 0000 0011	3
61h	0000 0000 0001 0001	RUNA
1h	0000 0000 0000 0001	1
1h	0000 0000 0000 0001	1
1h	0000 0000 0000 0001	1
2h	0000 0000 0000 0010	2
61h	0000 0000 0001 0001	RUNL
5h	0000 0000 0000 0101	5
5h	0000 0000 0000 0101	5
5h	0000 0000 0000 0101	5
2h	0000 0000 0000 0010	2

formats and physical implementations. As to the latter, Chapter 15 will describe the main types and parameters of the physical implementations.

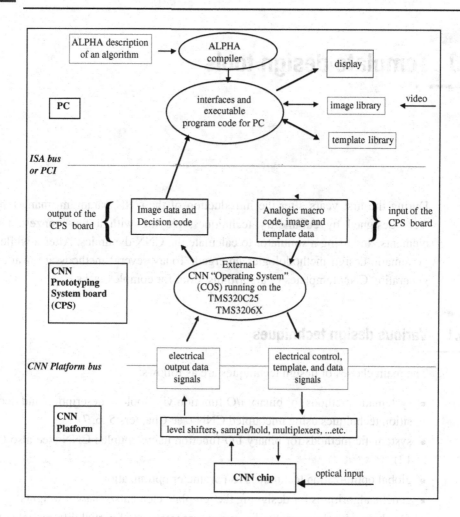

Fig. 9.14. The architecture of the CNN Chip Prototyping System (CCPS).

10 Template design tools

During the first years after the introduction of the CNN paradigm, many templates were designed by cut-and-try techniques, playing with a few nonzero template elements, and using a simulator to calculate the CNN dynamics. After a while, some systematic design methodologies emerged. Today several methods are available for generating CNN templates or algorithms, even for complex tasks.

10.1 Various design techniques

The main classes of design techniques are as follows:

- systematic methods for binary I/O function via Boolean description and decomposition techniques using uncoupled CNN (see Chapters 5, 6, 7)
- systematic methods for binary I/O function using coupled CNN (see also Chapter 12)
- global optimization techniques as parameter optimization
- genetic algorithms for designing the template elements/synaptic weights[1]
- matching with the spatially discrete representations of partial differential equations (PDEs)
- matching with some neuromorphic models of a living organism, typically the nervous system, in particular the visual pathway of vertebrates (see Chapter 16)
- fuzzy design techniques[2]
- neural network techniques[3]
- matching with existing 2D or 3D algorithms, including techniques in signal processing, telecommunications, adaptive control, nonlinear spatio-temporal dynamical systems, etc.

We have to emphasize, however, that, in spite of the many design techniques, new methods are emerging day by day based on the intuition and skill of the designers. A good example for this is a recent method[4] using active waves applied for a while and combining/colliding with other waves, as well as a method in which a wave metric is used[5] for complex pattern recognition tasks.

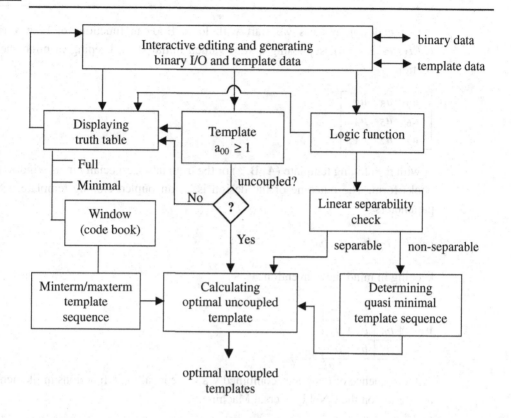

Fig. 10.1. The outline of the binary I/O CNN template or template sequence design.

In this chapter, referring to the results of Chapters 5, 6, and 7, we will demonstrate a systematic method for binary I/O functions. The outline of this design process is as follows (Fig. 10.1). This process is supported by the template design and optimization program TEMMASTER (Appendix C).

Logic truth tables are given by a {0, 1} code (white and black), however, we can code binary data as TRUE(1), FALSE(-1) and DON'T CARE(0) as well.

When designing CNN templates to implement a given logic function $F_k(\cdot)$, we are typically using uncoupled templates with the following description and coding:

$$\mathbf{A} = \begin{array}{|c|c|c|} \hline 0 & 0 & 0 \\ \hline 0 & a_{00} \geq 1 & 0 \\ \hline 0 & 0 & 0 \\ \hline \end{array} \quad \mathbf{B}_k = \begin{array}{|c|c|c|} \hline w_{-1-1} & w_{-10} & w_{-11} \\ \hline w_{0-1} & w_{00} & w_{01} \\ \hline w_{1-1} & w_{10} & w_{11} \\ \hline \end{array} \quad z \qquad (10.1)$$

In the design process we start with logic Boolean functions of nine variables $F_k(u_1, u_2, \ldots, u_9)$, supposing a zero valued initial state, keeping in mind the convention

$$\begin{bmatrix} u_9 & u_8 & u_7 \\ u_6 & u_5 & u_4 \\ u_3 & u_2 & u_1 \end{bmatrix}$$

or with the cloning template $(\mathbf{A}, \mathbf{B}, z)$ or the truth table, especially in its window (code book) form. The outcome of the design is an uncoupled cloning template with the parameters

$$a_{00}, b_1, b_2, b_3, \ldots, b_9, z$$

keeping in mind the convention

$$\mathbf{B}_k = \begin{array}{|c|c|c|} \hline b_9 & b_8 & b_7 \\ \hline b_6 & b_5 & b_4 \\ \hline b_3 & b_2 & b_1 \\ \hline \end{array}$$

or the sequence of templates combined via some local logic functions implemented as a program on the CNN Universal Machine.

10.2 Binary representation, linear separability, and simple decomposition

The Boolean representation of a local logic function of nine variables can be given in terms of the nine Boolean input variables $F(u_1, u_2, \ldots, u_9)$.

Given this function as a sum of products, we can directly apply a check to determine whether this function is linearly separable or not. If not, we have to decompose it into a sequence of linearly separable templates (see Section 10.3). The simplest method to generate this sequence, though it does not lead generally to the shortest sequence of templates, is via the window truth table. In this case, each window represents a minterm (or maxterm) related directly to an uncoupled template with the coding convention introduced in Chapter 5. For example, window #3 in Example 10.1 means a minterm $u_2 u_4 \bar{u}_5 u_6 u_8$ (x means DON'T CARE).

This term is implemented by a CNN with $x(0) = 0$ and the template parameters are: $a_{00} = 1$, $z = -4$ and $b_1, b_2, \ldots, b_9$ are directly coded by window #3.

Hence, window #3

$$u_2 \ u_4 \ \bar{u}_5 \ u_6 \ u_8$$

generates the input values

$$b_1 = 0, \quad b_2 = 1, \quad b_3 = 0, \quad b_4 = 1, \quad b_5 = -1, \quad b_6 = 1, \quad b_7 = 0, \quad b_8 = 1, \quad b_9 = 0$$

that is, the variables not appearing in the minterm (the DON'T CAREs) will get a value of 0 at the corresponding places.

Cascading the minterm Boolean functions $F_k(\cdot)$ represented by the appropriate templates by AND-ing the consecutive results, the Boolean function $F(\cdot)$ will be calculated.

EXAMPLE 10.1:

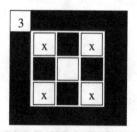

Suppose we have a binary image with one-pixel-wide lines. Detect those pixels where the line crossings are of 45° or 90°. Two examples are shown in Example 10.2 with few inputs and detected points. Indeed, we started with a blank Window Truth Table (all-white output) and "clicked" those windows black which contain the desired configurations to be detected. These are the following six places (simplest cases):

: 124, 186, 214, 313, 341, 403

The selected windows are shown in Examples 10.3–10.6.

To each configuration, we code a cloning template. For example, for the last one (#403)

$$a_{00} = 1 \quad \mathbf{B} = \begin{array}{|c|c|c|} \hline 1 & 1 & -1 \\ \hline -1 & 1 & -1 \\ \hline -1 & 1 & 1 \\ \hline \end{array} \quad z = -8$$

By AND-ing the six templates all the desired crossings will be detected.

EXAMPLE 10.2: Input images (a) and the corresponding detected crossing places (b).

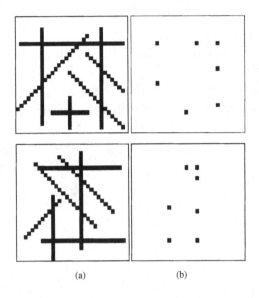

(a)　　　　　　　　(b)

EXAMPLE 10.3:

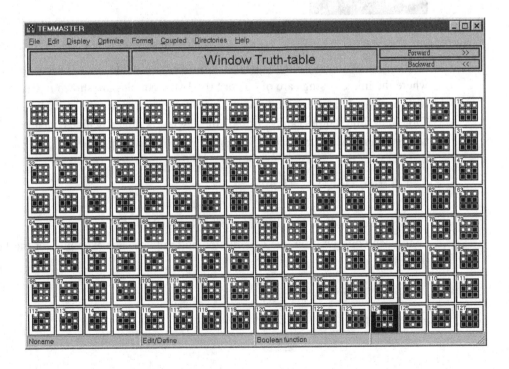

EXAMPLE 10.4:

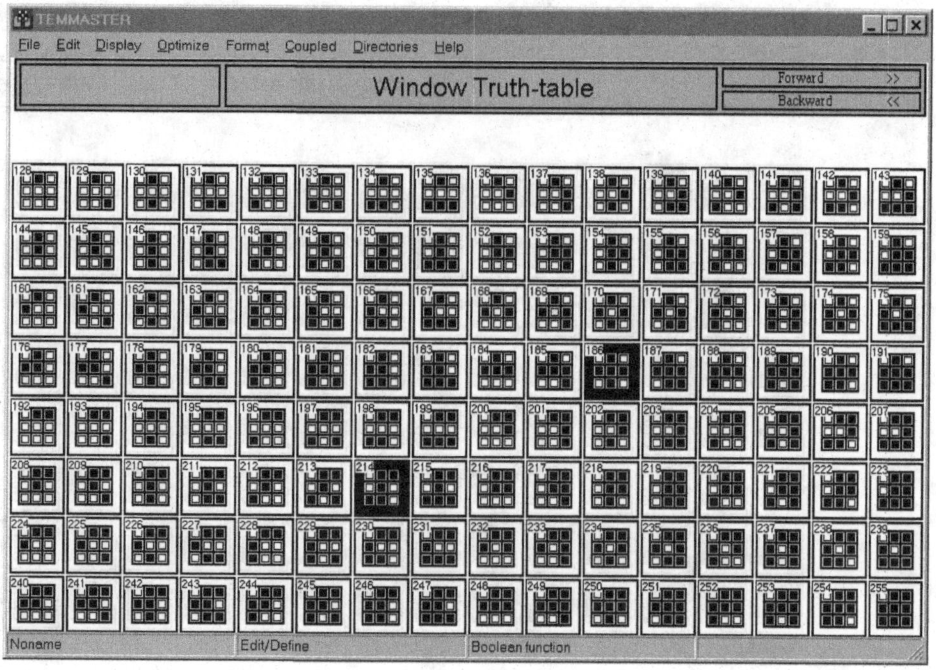

EXAMPLE 10.5:

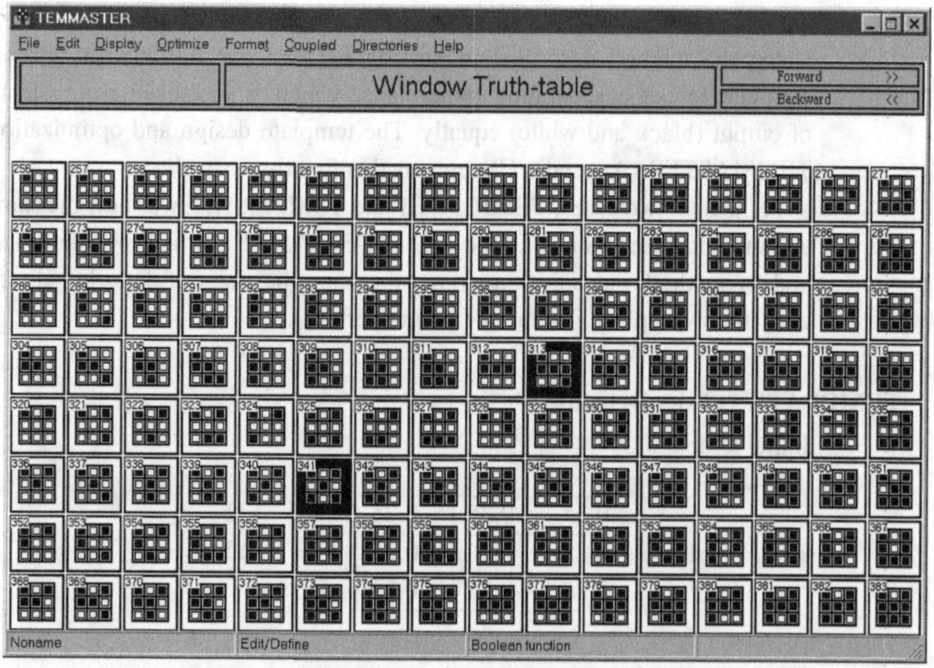

EXAMPLE 10.6:

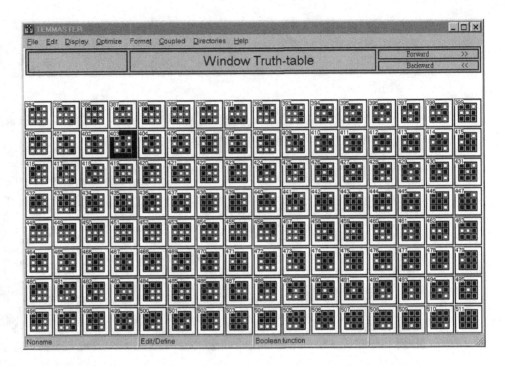

10.3 Template optimization

Once we get a template like the one just determined we can optimize it for robustness. Using the method described in Section 6.7, we can optimize a separable binary template to get a separating hyperplane, which is distanced from the two values of output (black and white) equally. The template design and optimization program TEMMASTER (Appendix C) contains this function as well.

In the next two cases, TEMPLATE1 and TEMPLATE2, we show the starting values and the optimized values. In the case of TEMPLATE1, which was designed by a cut-and-try method, indeed, it turned out that the robustness of the original template was zero (the hyperplane just hit one output vertex).

TEMPLATE 1: EdgeDetector

Initial template

$$a_{00} = 1 \quad \mathbf{B} = \begin{array}{|c|c|c|} \hline -0.25 & -0.25 & -0.25 \\ \hline -0.25 & 2 & -0.25 \\ \hline -0.25 & -0.25 & -0.25 \\ \hline \end{array} \quad z = -1.5$$

Optimized template

$$a_{00} = 1 \quad \mathbf{B} = \begin{array}{|c|c|c|} \hline -1 & -1 & -1 \\ \hline -1 & 8 & -1 \\ \hline -1 & -1 & -1 \\ \hline \end{array} \quad z = -1$$

TEMPLATE 2: LocalConcavePlaceDetector
Initial template

$$a_{00} = 1 \quad \mathbf{B} = \begin{array}{|c|c|c|} \hline 0 & 0 & 0 \\ \hline 1 & 2 & 1 \\ \hline 0.5 & -1 & 0.5 \\ \hline \end{array} \quad z = -5.5$$

Optimized template

$$a_{00} = 1 \quad \mathbf{B} = \begin{array}{|c|c|c|} \hline 0 & 0 & 0 \\ \hline 2 & 2 & 2 \\ \hline 1 & -2 & -1 \\ \hline \end{array} \quad z = -7$$

This template optimization is perfect if the CNN implementation is ideal. In a real situation with a given VLSI implementation, more complex optimization procedures are to be applied.

10.4 Template decomposition techniques

If the local Boolean function is not linearly separable then we can apply different decomposition techniques. Many of these techniques are based on some assumptions on the template values and the logic functions used for combining the consecutive templates. A method described in Section 7.6 and another "compact" decomposition method[6] are used in the TEMMASTER program (Appendix C). The determination of the minimal number of templates for any given $F(\cdot)$ is a computationally hard problem. For the example given in Section 10.2, the six templates of the minterm decomposition could not be reduced. At the same time, for the game-of-life problem both methods yielded a decomposition of two templates only. The sequences of the six templates of our example in Section 10.2 are as follows.
0.0

TEMPLATE 1

$$\mathbf{A} = \begin{array}{|c|c|c|} \hline 0.0 & 0.0 & 0.0 \\ \hline 0.0 & 1.0 & 0.0 \\ \hline 0.0 & 0.0 & 0.0 \\ \hline \end{array} \quad \mathbf{B} = \begin{array}{|c|c|c|} \hline -1.0 & -1.0 & 1.0 \\ \hline 1.0 & 1.0 & 1.0 \\ \hline 1.0 & -1.0 & -1.0 \\ \hline \end{array} \quad z = -8$$

XOR: TEMPLATE 2

$$\mathbf{A} = \begin{array}{|c|c|c|} \hline 0.0 & 0.0 & 0.0 \\ \hline 0.0 & 1.0 & 0.0 \\ \hline 0.0 & 0.0 & 0.0 \\ \hline \end{array} \quad \mathbf{B} = \begin{array}{|c|c|c|} \hline -1.0 & 1.0 & -1.0 \\ \hline 1.0 & 1.0 & 1.0 \\ \hline 1.0 & -1.0 & -1.0 \\ \hline \end{array} \quad z = -8$$

XOR: TEMPLATE 3

$$\mathbf{A} = \begin{array}{|c|c|c|} \hline 0.0 & 0.0 & 0.0 \\ \hline 0.0 & 1.0 & 0.0 \\ \hline 0.0 & 0.0 & 0.0 \\ \hline \end{array} \quad \mathbf{B} = \begin{array}{|c|c|c|} \hline -1.0 & 1.0 & 1.0 \\ \hline -1.0 & 1.0 & -1.0 \\ \hline 1.0 & 1.0 & -1.0 \\ \hline \end{array} \quad z = -8$$

XOR: TEMPLATE 4

$$\mathbf{A} = \begin{array}{|c|c|c|} \hline 0.0 & 0.0 & 0.0 \\ \hline 0.0 & 1.0 & 0.0 \\ \hline 0.0 & 0.0 & 0.0 \\ \hline \end{array} \quad \mathbf{B} = \begin{array}{|c|c|c|} \hline 1.0 & -1.0 & -1.0 \\ \hline 1.0 & 1.0 & 1.0 \\ \hline -1.0 & -1.0 & 1.0 \\ \hline \end{array} \quad z = -8$$

XOR: TEMPLATE 5

$$\mathbf{A} = \begin{array}{|c|c|c|} \hline 0.0 & 0.0 & 0.0 \\ \hline 0.0 & 1.0 & 0.0 \\ \hline 0.0 & 0.0 & 0.0 \\ \hline \end{array} \quad \mathbf{B} = \begin{array}{|c|c|c|} \hline 1.0 & -1.0 & 1.0 \\ \hline -1.0 & 1.0 & -1.0 \\ \hline 1.0 & -1.0 & 1.0 \\ \hline \end{array} \quad z = -8$$

XOR: TEMPLATE 6

$$\mathbf{A} = \begin{array}{|c|c|c|} \hline 0.0 & 0.0 & 0.0 \\ \hline 0.0 & 1.0 & 0.0 \\ \hline 0.0 & 0.0 & 0.0 \\ \hline \end{array} \quad \mathbf{B} = \begin{array}{|c|c|c|} \hline 1.0 & 1.0 & -1.0 \\ \hline -1.0 & 1.0 & -1.0 \\ \hline -1.0 & -1.0 & -1.0 \\ \hline \end{array} \quad z = -8$$

11 CNNs for linear image processing

11.1 Linear image processing with B templates is equivalent to spatial convolution with FIR kernels

Consider the class of *feed-forward (zero-feedback) CNNs* $C(0, \mathbf{B}, z)$ shown in Fig. 2.22 with zero threshold ($z = 0$).

The state equation of the CNN corresponding to a $(2\sigma + 1) \times (2\sigma + 1)$ **B** template is given by

$$
\begin{aligned}
\dot{x}_{ij} &= -x_{ij} + \sum_{k=-\sigma}^{\sigma} \sum_{l=-\sigma}^{\sigma} b_{kl} u_{i+k,j+l} \\
&= -x_{ij} + \sum_{k=\sigma}^{-\sigma} \sum_{l=\sigma}^{-\sigma} b_{-k,-l} u_{i-k,j-l} \\
&= -x_{ij} + \sum_{k=\sigma}^{-\sigma} \sum_{l=\sigma}^{-\sigma} h_{k,l} u_{i-k,j-l} \\
&= -x_{ij} + \sum_{k=\sigma}^{-\sigma} \sum_{l=\sigma}^{-\sigma} h_{k,l} u_{i-k,j-l}
\end{aligned}
\tag{11.1}
$$

where

$$
\begin{aligned}
h_{kl} &\overset{\Delta}{=} b_{-k,-l} \\
k, l &= -\sigma, -(\sigma - 1), \ldots, -1, 0, 1, \ldots, (\sigma - 1), \sigma
\end{aligned}
\tag{11.2}
$$

If we let **H** denote a template whose entries are h_{kl}, then the **H** template is simply related to the **B** template by a $180°$ rotation about the central element b_{00}. For example, the 3×3 ($\sigma = 1$) **B** and **H** templates are as follows

$$
\mathbf{B} =
\begin{array}{|c|c|c|}
\hline
b_{-1,-1} & b_{-1,0} & b_{-1,1} \\
\hline
b_{0,-1} & b_{0,0} & b_{0,1} \\
\hline
b_{1,-1} & b_{1,0} & b_{1,1} \\
\hline
\end{array}
\qquad
\mathbf{H} =
\begin{array}{|c|c|c|}
\hline
b_{1,1} & b_{1,0} & b_{1,-1} \\
\hline
b_{0,1} & b_{0,0} & b_{0,-1} \\
\hline
b_{-1,1} & b_{-1,0} & b_{-1,-1} \\
\hline
\end{array}
$$

Observe that

$$\mathbf{B} = \mathbf{H} \Leftrightarrow \mathbf{B} \text{ is symmetric}$$

The double summation series on the right-hand side of Eq. (11.1) is a *standard* numerical operation in signal processing called the *convolution operation* between the *impulse response kernel* h_{kl}, or the impulse response matrix $\mathbf{H}$, and the *input image* $\mathbf{U}_{ij}$, and denoted by an asterisk "$\star$"; namely:

$$\mathbf{H} \star \mathbf{U}_{ij} \triangleq \sum_{k=-\sigma}^{\sigma} \sum_{l=-\sigma}^{\sigma} h_{k,l} u_{i-k,j-l} \tag{11.3}$$

Observe that for a given $\mathbf{B}$ template, $\mathbf{H}$ is fixed but $\mathbf{U}_{ij}$ in general changes since it corresponds to the part of the input image exposed by a $\sigma \times \sigma$ "mask" whose "center" coincides with the pixel location $C(ij)$. Note that $\mathbf{H} \star \mathbf{U}_{ij}$ is a *scalar* even though both $\mathbf{H}$ and $\mathbf{U}_{ij}$ are $\sigma \times \sigma$ matrices. Observe also that we can replace "σ" by "∞" in Eq. (11.3), which we will occasionally do to simplify our discussion, by redefining $\mathbf{H}$ to be an infinite-dimensional matrix with zero entries except those associated with the $\mathbf{B}$ template. In terms of the convolution notation (11.3), Eq. (11.1) assumes the compact form:

$$\dot{x}_{ij} = -x_{ij} + \mathbf{H} \star \mathbf{U}_{ij} \tag{11.4}$$

Theorem 1: Feedforward CNN convolution property

Every *feedforward* CNN $C(0, \mathbf{B}, z)$ is *completely stable*. In particular, for *any* initial condition $x_{ij}(0)$, the state $x_{ij}(t)$ of state equation (11.4) converges to a constant equal to the *convolution* between $\mathbf{H}$ and the *static* input image $\mathbf{U}_{ij}$.

Proof:

Since Eq. (11.4) is a first-order linear differential equation, its solution is given by

$$x_{ij}(t) = x_{ij}(0)e^{-t} + (\mathbf{H} \star \mathbf{U}_{ij})(1 - e^{-t}), \quad t \geq 0 \tag{11.5}$$

As $t \to \infty$, we have

$$x_{ij}(\infty) \triangleq \lim_{t \to \infty} x_{ij}(t) = \mathbf{H} \star \mathbf{U}_{ij} \tag{11.6}$$

$\square$

Corollary:

The *state* $x_{ij}(\infty)$ of every feedforward ($\mathbf{A} = 0$) CNN with a *symmetric* $\mathbf{B}$ template and zero threshold is simply the *convolution* of the $\mathbf{B}$ template with any static input image.

The preceding theorem and corollary pertain to the *state* $x_{ij}(t)$ and not the output $y_{ij}(t) = f(x_{ij}(t))$, where $f(\cdot)$ is the standard nonlinear function shown in Fig. 2.4. In applications where "convolution" is the desired output, there are two options. For

CNN chips, where only the output $y_{ij}(t)$ is accessible, one can scale the **B** template so that

$$\sum_{k=-\sigma}^{\sigma} \sum_{l=-\sigma}^{\sigma} |b_{k,l}| < 1 \tag{11.7}$$

Since by our standing assumption, $|u_{ij}| \leq 1$, it follows from Eqs (11.1) and (11.7) that $|x_{ij}(\infty)| < 1$. Consequently,

$$y_{ij}(\infty) = x_{ij}(\infty) = \mathbf{H} \star \mathbf{U}_{ij}$$

The second option is to add one extra output pin in the CNN chips so that, by an internal multiplexing circuitry, the state $x_{ij}(t)$ of every cell is also accessible to the outside world.

It is important to observe that in *feedforward* CNNs, the *dynamics* is completely linear, regardless of the magnitude of the state $x_{ij}(t)$. The nonlinearity comes into play only in the *readout* map $y_{ij} = f(x_{ij})$ given by the standard piecewise-linear function $f(\cdot)$.

Finally, observe that a feedforward CNN $\mathcal{C}(0, \mathbf{B}, z)$ is a degenerate *special* case of the *uncoupled* class, which we have completely characterized in Fig. 6.8. In particular, this class corresponds to the origin in the Primary CNN Mosaic (Fig. 6.8) of Chapter 6 where $a_{00} = 0$. Observe that the output of such CNNs is given by

$$y_{ij}(\infty) = \frac{w_{ij}}{1 - a_{00}} = w_{ij}$$

where $|w_{ij}| = |\sum_{k=-\sigma}^{\sigma} \sum_{l=-\sigma}^{\sigma} b_{k,l} u_{k,l}| \leq 1$ in view of Eq. (11.7).

11.2   Spatial frequency characterization

Since *spatial convolution* is a *linear* equation, much insight and many analytical advantages can be gained by examining its corresponding *frequency domain* properties. Since the observable *physical* variables $x_{ij}(t)$, $y_{ij}(t)$, and $u_{ij}(t)$ as well as *the synaptic weights* a_{ij} and b_{ij}, $i = 1, 2, \ldots, M$ and $j = 1, 2, \ldots, N$, in a CNN are defined only at *discrete* points in space, at each instant "t" in time, we will use the notation

$$f_{n_1,n_2}(t) \leftrightarrow f_t(n_1, n_2)$$
$$x_{n_1,n_2}(t) \leftrightarrow x_t(n_1, n_2)$$
$$y_{n_1,n_2}(t) \leftrightarrow y_t(n_1, n_2)$$
$$u_{n_1,n_2}(t) \leftrightarrow u_t(n_1, n_2)$$
$$a_{n_1,n_2} \leftrightarrow a(n_1, n_2)$$
$$b_{n_1,n_2} \leftrightarrow b(n_1, n_2) \tag{11.8}$$

to denote *discrete spatial* variables or parameters, where "t" has been relegated to the subsidiary role of a *subscript* in order to emphasize the independent "discrete spatial domain" variables n_1 and n_2. Observe that "t" is deleted from the subscript of $a(n_1, n_2)$ and $b(n_1, n_2)$ in Eq. (11.8) because they vary only with space, but not with time. Corresponding to each "discrete" spatial dependent variable or parameter $f_t(n_1, n_2)$, let ω_1 and ω_2 denote the *independent* "continuous" frequency domain variables and choose the corresponding *capital* letter with a *tilde* superscript $\tilde{F}_t(\omega_1, \omega_2)$ to denote the *Fourier transform* of $f_t(n_1, n_2)$; namely

$$
\begin{array}{ccc}
\text{discrete-spatial domain} & & \text{continuous frequency domain} \\
f_t(n_1, n_2) & \leftrightarrow & \tilde{F}_t(\omega_1, \omega_2)
\end{array}
\tag{11.9}
$$

Let us define the relationship between these variables at any *fixed time t* in the two domains as follows

$$
\tilde{F}(\omega_1, \omega_2) = \sum_{n_1=-\infty}^{\infty} \sum_{n_2=-\infty}^{\infty} f_t(n_1, n_1) e^{-j\omega_1 n_1} \cdot e^{-j\omega_2 n_2}
\tag{11.10}
$$

$$
f_t(n_1, n_2) = \frac{1}{(2\pi)^2} \int_{-\pi}^{\pi} \int_{-\pi}^{\pi} \tilde{F}_t(\omega_1, \omega_2) e^{j\omega_1 n_1} \cdot e^{j\omega_2 n_2} d\omega_1 d\omega_2
\tag{11.11}
$$

We will henceforth refer to Eqs (11.10)–(11.11) as the two-dimensional *discrete Spatial Fourier Transform* (DSFT) between $f_t(n_1, n_2)$ and $\tilde{F}_t(\omega_1, \omega_2)$.

To verify that the above definitions are consistent, let us substitute Eq. (11.10) for $\tilde{F}_t(\omega_1, \omega_2)$ in Eq. (11.11):[1]

$$
\frac{1}{(2\pi)^2} \int_{-\pi}^{\pi} \int_{-\pi}^{\pi} \sum_{n_1=-\infty}^{\infty} \sum_{n_2=-\infty}^{\infty} f_t(n_1, n_2) e^{-j\omega_1 n_1} \cdot e^{-j\omega_2 n_2} \cdot e^{j\omega_1 n_1} \cdot e^{j\omega_1 n_2} d\omega_1 d\omega_2
$$

$$
= f_t(n_1, n_2) \left[\frac{1}{(2\pi)^2} \int_{-\pi}^{\pi} \int_{-\pi}^{\pi} d\omega_1 d\omega_2 \right] = f_t(n_1, n_2)
\tag{11.12}
$$

which is identical to the left-hand side of Eq. (11.11).

Observe that the independent spatial variables "n_1" and "n_2" in the double summation series in Eq. (11.1) range from $-\infty$ to ∞ which corresponds to the limiting case of an *infinite* CNN array where $M \to \infty$ and $N \to \infty$. To avoid clutter, the following derivations will be based on an infinite CNN array. In most cases of practical interest, the results to be derived in this section are also applicable to the practical situation where the CNN array has only a finite number of cells, namely $M \times N$. In such cases, we simply set $f_t(n_1, n_2) = 0$ for all $|n_1| > M$ and $|n_2| > N$.

Observe next that the integration limits in Eq. (11.11) range only from $-\pi$ to π because $\tilde{F}_t(\omega_1, \omega_2)$ is a 2π-periodic function of ω_1 and ω_2; namely

$$
\tilde{F}_t(\omega_1 + 2\pi p, \omega_2 + 2\pi q)
$$

$$
= \sum_{n_1=-\infty}^{\infty} \sum_{n_2=-\infty}^{\infty} f_1(n_1, n_2) e^{-j(\omega_1 + 2\pi p)n_1} \cdot e^{-j(\omega_2 + 2\pi q)n_2}
$$

$$= \sum_{n_1=-\infty}^{\infty} \sum_{n_2=-\infty}^{\infty} f_1(n_1, n_2) e^{-j\omega_1 n_1} \cdot e^{-j\omega_2 n_2} \cdot e^{j(2\pi p n_1 + 2\pi q n_2)}$$

$$= \tilde{F}_t(\omega_1, \omega_2), \quad \text{for any integers } p \text{ and } q.$$

Observe also that if $f_t(n_1, n_2)$ is a symmetric function of n_1 and n_2, i.e.,

$$f_t(n_1, n_2) = f_t(-n_1, -n_2) \tag{11.13}$$

then its Fourier transform $\tilde{F}_t(\omega_1, \omega_2)$ is a real function of ω_1 and ω_2. Indeed, Eqs (11.11) and (11.12) imply

$$\tilde{F}_t(\omega_1, \omega_2)^* = \tilde{F}_t(\omega_1, \omega_2) \tag{11.14}$$

where the superscript "*" denotes *complex conjugation*. Equation (11.14) is usually referred to as the *zero phase shift* property of the Fourier transform even though a 180° phase shift occurs whenever $\tilde{F}_t(\omega_1, \omega_2) < 0$.

Observe next that Eqs (11.10) and (11.11) imply the following two useful properties:

dc (average) value property

$$\tilde{F}_t(0, 0) = \sum_{n_1=-\infty}^{\infty} \sum_{n_2=-\infty}^{\infty} f_t(n_1, n_2) \tag{11.15}$$

offset level property

$$f_t(0, 0) = \frac{1}{(2\pi)^2} \int_{-\pi}^{\pi} \int_{-\pi}^{\pi} \tilde{F}_t(\omega_1, \omega_2) d\omega_1 d\omega_2 \tag{11.16}$$

Finally, we state without proof the following standard result

$$f_t(n_1, n_2) \star g_t(n_1, n_2) \quad \leftrightarrow \quad \tilde{F}_t(\omega_1, \omega_2) \tilde{G}_t(\omega_1, \omega_2) \tag{11.17}$$

Stated in words, Eq. (11.17) asserts

| Convolution in discrete spatial domain | $\leftrightarrow$ | Multiplication in continuous frequency domain |

Applying the DSFT to both sides of Eq. (11.4) and making use of Eq. (11.17), we obtain

$$\frac{d\tilde{x}_t(\omega_1, \omega_2)}{dt} = -\tilde{\mathbf{X}}_t(\omega_1, \omega_2) + \tilde{\mathbf{H}}(\omega_1, \omega_2) \tilde{\mathbf{U}}(\omega_1, \omega_2) \tag{11.18}$$

Eq. (11.18) is a scalar first-order linear ordinary differential equation in the transformed state variable $\tilde{\mathbf{X}}_t(\omega_1, \omega_2)$, and has the solution

$$\tilde{\mathbf{X}}_t(\omega_1, \omega_2) = \tilde{\mathbf{X}}_0(\omega_1, \omega_2) e^{-t} + \tilde{\mathbf{H}}(\omega_1, \omega_2) \tilde{\mathbf{U}}(\omega_1, \omega_2)[1 - e^{-t}], \quad t \geq 0 \tag{11.19}$$

As $t \to \infty$, we have

$$\tilde{\mathbf{X}}_\infty(\omega_1, \omega_2) \triangleq \lim_{t \to \infty} \tilde{\mathbf{X}}_t(\omega_1, \omega_2) = \tilde{\mathbf{H}}(\omega_1, \omega_2) \tilde{\mathbf{U}}(\omega_1, \omega_2) \tag{11.20}$$

where

$$\tilde{\mathbf{H}}(\omega_1, \omega_2) = \tilde{\mathbf{B}}(\omega_1, \omega_2) \tag{11.21}$$

is the DSFT of the space-varying (but time-invariant) **B** template of the *feedforward* CNN, which *we assume henceforth to be symmetric.*

It is important to remember that unlike in *digital signal processing* (DSP) where the DSFT is calculated using a digital processor, the DSFT $\tilde{\mathbf{X}}_{\infty}(\omega_1, \omega_2)$ in a CNN evolves from the initial DSFT $\tilde{\mathbf{X}}_0(\omega_1, \omega_2)$ at $t = 0$ until it converges to $\tilde{\mathbf{X}}_{\infty}(\omega_1, \omega_2)$ after the *settling time* of the CNN, which is typically less than 100 nanosecond in a CNN chip. However, it must be remembered that in a CNN, the output is a *spatial* pattern $\tilde{\mathbf{X}}_{\infty}(n_1, n_2)$, and *not* its DSFT $\tilde{\mathbf{X}}_{\infty}(\omega_1, \omega_2)$. Hence, the results in this section are mainly for *conceptual* purposes to help the reader understand the image processing capabilities of a CNN, and to allow the CNN image-processing designers to exploit the large body of design tools and techniques from the digital signal processing arsenal. Indeed, we will see in the next section that every "convolution" or "spatial filtering" DSP operation can be implemented in a CNN at a much higher speed which depends only on the *settling time* of the CNN, and *does not depend on the array size.*

In general, a speed advantage of 1000 times over conventional DSP image processing techniques can be realized by CNN chips using current one-micron CMOS technology. The extreme high speed, low power, and small size of the CNN makes it an attractive if not indispensable tool in many real-time signal and video-processing applications.

11.3 A primer on properties and applications of discrete-space Fourier transform (DSFT)

For ease of reference, the following table lists some of the properties of the discrete-space Fourier transform derived in the preceding section, as well as others whose proofs can be easily derived from Eqs (11.10)–(11.11). Reader already familiar with two-dimensional digital signal processing techniques and principles may skip this section.

11.4 Linear image processing with A and B templates is equivalent to spatial convolution with IIR kernels

It is a well-known fact in digital image processing that the more stringent a filter specification (e.g., very steep filter characteristics) is, the larger must be the size of the *impulse response* kernel, or, in the case of a *feedforward* CNN implementation, the larger must be the size of the **B** template. In particular, many complex filter specifications can only be realized by *infinite impulse response* (IIR) kernels. A corresponding feedforward CNN realization in this case would require a **B** template of infinite extent, i.e., $M \to \infty$, $N \to \infty$. Our objective in this section is to show that if we use the *general* CNN (with non-zero **A** and **B** templates) shown in Fig. 2.21, when $z = 0$, then even very stringent filter characteristics can be realized with relatively "small" **A** and **B** templates. Since all cells in the CNNs considered in this chapter for linear image processing *are assumed* to operate in the central linear region of the piecewise-linear characteristic $y_{ij} = f(x_{ij})$, we can substitute $y_{ij} = x_{ij}$ in Eq. (2.36) of Chapter 2 and write the state equation associated with the CNN $\mathcal{C}(\mathbf{A}, \mathbf{B}, 0)$ with a $\sigma \times \sigma$ ($\sigma = 2r + 1$) **A** and **B** templates, and a *zero threshold* ($z = 0$), as follows

$$\dot{X}_{ij} = -x_{ij} + \sum_{k=-\sigma}^{\sigma} \sum_{l=-\sigma}^{\sigma} a_{kl} x_{i+k j+l} + \sum_{k=-\sigma}^{\sigma} \sum_{l=-\sigma}^{\sigma} b_{kl} u_{i+k j+l} \tag{11.22}$$

Using the discrete-space notation of Eq. (11.8), we can recast Eq. (11.22) into the following standard *convolution* form

$$\frac{d}{dt} x_t(n_1, n_2) = \alpha(n_1, n_2) \star x_t(n_1, n_2) + \beta(n_1, n_2) \star u_t(n_1, n_2) \tag{11.23}$$

where

$$\begin{aligned}
\alpha(n_1, n_2) &= A_{00} - 1, &&\text{if } (n_1, n_2) = (0, 0) \\
&= A_{-n_1, -n_2}, &&\text{if } |n_1| \le \sigma, |n_2| \le \sigma \\
&= 0, &&\text{otherwise}
\end{aligned} \tag{11.24}$$

$$\begin{aligned}
\beta(n_1, n_2) &= B_{-n_1, -n_2}, &&\text{if } |n_1| \le \sigma, |n_2| \le \sigma \\
&= 0, &&\text{otherwise}
\end{aligned}$$

Observe that we have deleted the subscript "t" from $\alpha(n_1, n_2)$ and $\beta(n_1, n_2)$ because they do *not* depend on time.

Under the *standing assumption* throughout this chapter that *both the* **A** *and* **B** *templates are symmetric*, the parameter $\alpha(n_1, n_2)$ in Eq. (11.23) is identical to the element A_{n_1, n_2} of the **A** template for all (n_1, n_2) except the central element A_{00} where we must *subtract* "1" from it in order to account for the first term $-x_{ij}$ in Eq. (11.22). Similarly, the parameter $\beta(n_1, n_2)$ in Eq. (11.23) is identical to the element B_{n_1, n_2} of the **B** template for all (n_1, n_2), including $n_1 = n_2 = 0$.

Observe that unlike the state equation (11.1) in the feedforward case, which consists of a system of $M \times N$ *uncoupled* linear ordinary differential equations, Eq. (11.22) consists of a system of $M \times N$ *coupled* linear ordinary differential equations. Although the solutions of Eq. (11.22) can be written explicitly, it is virtually impossible to analyze the effect of the neighboring cells on the dynamics of any particular cell. This difficulty fortunately can be overcome by taking the discrete-space Fourier transform (DSFT) of Eq. (11.23) to obtain the following equivalent system of *uncoupled* first-order linear ordinary differential equations in the frequency domain

$$\frac{d}{dt} \tilde{\mathbf{X}}_t(\omega_1, \omega_2) = \tilde{\mathbf{A}}(\omega_1, \omega_2) \tilde{\mathbf{X}}_t(\omega_1, \omega_2) + \tilde{\mathbf{B}}(\omega_1, \omega_2) \tilde{\mathbf{U}}_t(\omega_1, \omega_2) \tag{11.25}$$

Since Eq. (11.25) applies for *each* $\omega_1 \in (-\infty, \infty)$ and $\omega_2 \in (-\infty, \infty)$, we have in principle an *infinite* number of linear ordinary differential equations to solve. However, unlike the *spatial domain* differential Eq. (11.22), the *frequency domain* differential equations in Eq. (11.25) are *not coupled* to each other! Moreover, $\tilde{\mathbf{X}}_t(\omega_1, \omega_2)$, $\tilde{\mathbf{A}}(\omega_1, \omega_2)$, $\tilde{\mathbf{B}}(\omega_1, \omega_2)$, and $\tilde{\mathbf{U}}_t(\omega_1, \omega_2)$ are doubly periodic in ω_1 and ω_2 with a *period* equal to 2π. Consequently, we need only analyze the solution of $\tilde{\mathbf{X}}_t(\omega_1, \omega_2)$ over the region $-\pi \le \omega_1 \le \pi$ and $-\pi \le \omega_2 \le \pi$.

Assuming a *static* input image so that $\tilde{\mathbf{U}}_t(\omega_1, \omega_2) = \tilde{\mathbf{U}}(\omega_1, \omega_2)$ does not depend on time, the solution of the *scalar* linear differential Eq. (11.25) in the frequency domain is given simply by

When $\tilde{\mathbf{A}}(\omega_1, \omega_2) \ne 0$

$$
\begin{aligned}
\tilde{\mathbf{X}}_t(\omega_1, \omega_2) &= e^{\tilde{\mathbf{A}}(\omega_1, \omega_2)t}\tilde{\mathbf{X}}_0(\omega_1, \omega_2) \\
&+ \frac{1}{\tilde{\mathbf{A}}(\omega_1, \omega_2)}\left[e^{\tilde{\mathbf{A}}(\omega_1, \omega_2)t} - 1\right] \cdot \tilde{\mathbf{B}}(\omega_1, \omega_2)\tilde{\mathbf{U}}(\omega_1, \omega_2)
\end{aligned}
\tag{11.26}
$$

When $\tilde{\mathbf{A}}(\omega_1, \omega_2) = 0$

$$
\tilde{\mathbf{X}}_t(\omega_1, \omega_2) = \tilde{\mathbf{X}}_0(\omega_1, \omega_2) + t\tilde{\mathbf{B}}(\omega_1, \omega_2)\tilde{\mathbf{U}}(\omega_1, \omega_2)
\tag{11.27}
$$

where $\tilde{\mathbf{X}}_0(\omega_1, \omega_2)$ is the initial state in the frequency domain at $t = 0$.

Consider now the important special case where

$$
\tilde{\mathbf{A}}(\omega_1, \omega_2) < 0
\tag{11.28}
$$

Under this condition,

$$
e^{\tilde{\mathbf{A}}(\omega_1, \omega_2)t} \to 0
$$

after a small *settling time* (less than 100 nanoseconds when implemented in one-micron CMOS technology), so that

$$
\tilde{\mathbf{X}}_\infty(\omega_1, \omega_2) \overset{\Delta}{=} \lim_{t \to \infty} \tilde{\mathbf{X}}_t(\omega_1, \omega_2) = -\left[\frac{\tilde{\mathbf{B}}(\omega_1, \omega_2)}{\tilde{\mathbf{A}}(\omega_1, \omega_2)}\right]\tilde{\mathbf{U}}(\omega_1, \omega_2)
\tag{11.29}
$$

Defining the *transfer function*

$$
\tilde{\mathbf{H}}(\omega_1, \omega_2) = -\frac{\tilde{\mathbf{B}}(\omega_1, \omega_2)}{\tilde{\mathbf{A}}(\omega_1, \omega_2)}
\tag{11.30}
$$

we obtain

$$
\tilde{\mathbf{X}}_\infty(\omega_1, \omega_2) = \tilde{\mathbf{H}}(\omega_1, \omega_2)\tilde{\mathbf{U}}(\omega_1, \omega_2)
\tag{11.31}
$$

Observe that even though Eq. (11.31) is identical to Eq. (11.20) in the *feedforward* case, the transfer function $\tilde{\mathbf{H}}(\omega_1, \omega_2)$ in Eq. (11.30) is different from that of Eq. (11.21). Here, $\tilde{\mathbf{H}}(\omega_1, \omega_2)$ is a *ratio* of two frequency domain functions. This gives us much more flexibility to "shape" the characteristics of $\tilde{\mathbf{H}}(\omega_1, \omega_2)$ using only relatively "small" **A** and **B** templates. In contrast, the *inverse* transform of $\tilde{\mathbf{H}}(\omega_1, \omega_2)$, namely, the two-dimensional impulse response kernel

$$h(n_1, n_2) \quad \leftrightarrow \quad \tilde{\mathbf{H}}(\omega_1, \omega_2) \tag{11.32}$$

is in general not zero for large n_1 and n_2. In other words, the two-dimensional *spatial domain kernel* $h(n_1, n_2)$ associated with the two-dimensional *frequency domain transfer function* $\tilde{\mathbf{H}}(\omega_1, \omega_2)$ is in general infinite in extent and corresponds to that of an *infinite impulse response* (IIR) two-dimensional filter.

12 Coupled CNN with linear synaptic weights

In this chapter we will consider single layer standard CNNs with linear synaptic weights. The feedback templates, however, could contain off-center nonzero elements as well. This class of standard CNN may result in more complex or even exotic dynamics. Two of the typical types of coupled CNN dynamics, a local non-equilibrium and a propagating wave-like, will be introduced first.

The standard CNN template shown below results in an *oscillatory CNN*[1] if there are three-pixel-wide vertical black stripes on the input and the white separation is at least three pixels wide (Fig. 12.1).

$$
A = \begin{array}{|c|c|c|} \hline 0 & 0 & 0 \\ \hline -1.5 & 2 & 1.5 \\ \hline 0 & 0 & 0 \\ \hline \end{array} \quad
B = \begin{array}{|c|c|c|} \hline 0 & 0 & 0 \\ \hline 3 & 0 & 3 \\ \hline 0 & 0 & 0 \\ \hline \end{array} \quad
z = -1.5
$$

The so-called *horizontal connected component detector* template (cited in Chapter 15) is shown below

$$
A = \begin{array}{|c|c|c|} \hline 0 & 0 & 0 \\ \hline 1 & 2 & -1 \\ \hline 0 & 0 & 0 \\ \hline \end{array} \quad
B = \begin{array}{|c|c|c|} \hline 0 & 0 & 0 \\ \hline 0 & 0 & 0 \\ \hline 0 & 0 & 0 \\ \hline \end{array} \quad
z = 0
$$

This template results in a propagating and then settling wave propagating from left to right. The process in each row is independent from the other rows. If the initial state is black and white, the output will result in a few distinct black pixels on the right-hand side, their number is equal to the number of connected black regions in the given row. A few initial state and output pairs of a row are shown in Fig. 12.2.

In general, it is very difficult to design coupled CNN templates, partly because of the enormous variety of the waveforms generated by these templates.

In what follows, to make our systems tractable for simpler design methods, we will restrict ourselves to the case when $a_{00} > 1$. This means that the cell cannot be at a STABLE equilibrium point in the linear region. That is the settled cell states are in one of the saturation regions, hence the output is $+1$ or -1. Moreover, we suppose that the dynamics of a cell is restricted to a switch type operation, i.e. if a cell leaves a saturation region (Q_+ or Q_-) then the cell flips to the other equilibrium point.

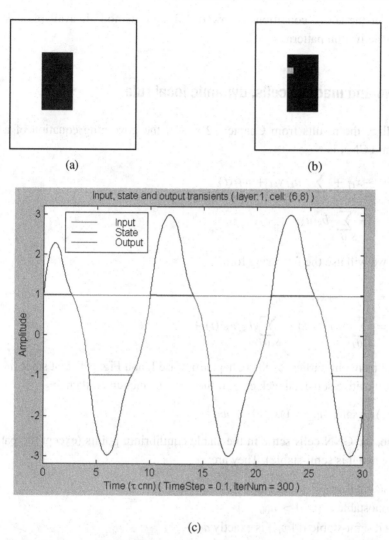

(a)   (b)

(c)

Fig. 12.1. Edge detection via oscillation. (a) 20×20 binary input image ($\mathbf{u} = \mathbf{x}(0)$), (b) the position of cell $C(6, 8)$ is marked, it is immediately to the left and right of a left sided edge, (c) state transient of the cell $C(6, 8)$ – non-edge cells will settle in $+1$ or -1.

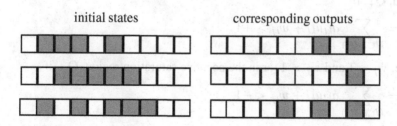

Fig. 12.2. A few initial state and output pairs.

Under the above conditions a powerful design method[2] is available based on the binary activation pattern.

12.1 Active and inactive cells, dynamic local rules

Recalling the results from Chapters 2 and 3, the governing equation of a cell in a standard CNN is

$$\frac{dx_{ij}}{dt} = -x_{ij} + \sum_{S_r(ij)} a_{kl} y_{kl} + w_{ij}(t) \tag{12.1}$$

$$w_{ij} = z + \sum_{S_r(ij)} b_{kl} u_{kl}$$

Here we will use the following form

$$\frac{dx_{ij}}{dt} = h_{ij} = -x_{ij} + w_{dij}$$

$$w_{dij} = \sum_{S_r(ij)} a_{kl} y_{kl}(t) + \sum_{S_r(ij)} b_{kl} u_{kl}(t) + z$$

Recall from our earlier results (Chapter 6, Case I, and Fig. 6.1) that since $a_{00} > 1$, the strong positive self-feedback case, if the CNN is uncoupled then

$$y_{ij}(\infty) = \text{sgn}\left[(a_{00} - 1)x_{ij}(0) + w_{ij}\right] \tag{12.2}$$

Hence, the CNN cells settle in the stable equilibrium points (except the pathological case when it is semi-stable). They are:

bistable if $|w_{ij}| < a_{00} - 1$
monostable if $|w_{ij}| > a_{00} - 1$
(and semi-stable if $|w_{ij}|$ is exactly $a_{00} - 1$)

However, now we have the effects of the feedback from the neighborhood cells and, hence, various propagation phenomena could occur.

If we examine Eq. (12.1) we can state that a cell is stable in the positive saturation region, $\mathbf{Q}_+$, if

$$w_{dij} = \sum_{kl \subset S_r(ij)} a_{kl} u_{kl} + w_{ij} > +1 \tag{12.3}$$

hence, $y_{ij} = 1$ and $x_{ij} > 1$, or in the negative saturation region, $\mathbf{Q}_-$, if

$$w_{dij} = \sum_{kl \subset S_r(ij)} a_{kl} u_{kl} + w_{ij} < -1 \tag{12.4}$$

hence, $y_{ij} = -1$ and $x_{ij} < -1$. This is clear when we take $dx_{ij}/dt = 0$ in Eq. (12.1), since $x_{ij}(\infty) = w_{dij}$, in case of non-oscillatory CNN.

From the above discussions it is also clear that, if $a_{00} > 1$, a cell can remain stable only in the saturation region and cannot remain stable in the linear (or active) region.

If all the neighborhood cells of a given cell are stable, then conditions (12.3) and (12.4) give the conditions for the regions of the stable outputs of the given cell. If, however, one of the *neighborhood cells changes* and therefore the changed new value of w_{dij} denoted by w_{dij}^+ goes to the linear region, then for $y_{ij} = 1$ and $w_{dij}^+ < 1$ or for $y_{ij} = -1$ and $w_{dij}^+ > -1$, the cell states will not remain in the saturation region.

Let us examine the case $y_{ij} = 1$ and $x_{ij}(t) > 1$ and $w_{dij}^+ < 1$. This means that $w_{dij}^+ < 1$ would be the new equilibrium point. But this point is not in the saturation region, hence, leaving now the $\mathbf{Q}_+$ region, $x_{ij}(t)$ and $y_{ij}(t)$ start decreasing. Since a_{00} is positive (indeed it is greater than $+1$), w_{dij} starts decreasing (the DP plot starts shifting down) and the cell goes into the negative saturation region. Moreover, we can prove[3] that under practically important conditions, ensuring *monotonic state transient property*, the cell will really go to the negative saturation region (see Proposition 1). Hence, once the state of a cell leaves a saturation region it goes into the opposite saturation region.

A cell is called *inactive* in a time instant if it is in the saturation region, and its state is not changing, otherwise it is called *active*.

Definition 1:
A CNN array has the *mono-activation property* if cells in $\mathbf{Q}_+$ only (respectively cells in $\mathbf{Q}_-$ only) can enter the linear region. Conditions for mono-activation property:

1 if cells can enter the linear region from $\mathbf{Q}_+$ only, then for those cells that are in $\mathbf{Q}_-$ condition $w_d(t) < -1$ should be satisfied. This condition guarantees that cells in $\mathbf{Q}_-$ never enter the linear region;

2 if cells can enter the linear region from $\mathbf{Q}_-$ only, then for those cells that are in $\mathbf{Q}_+$ condition $w_d(t) > 1$ should be satisfied. This condition guarantees that cells in $\mathbf{Q}_+$ never enter the linear region.

Proposition 1: Monotonic state transient property
Let a CNN be described by a linear template and consider that the following conditions are satisfied:

1 the CNN array has mono-activation property, i.e. only cells belonging to $\mathbf{Q}_-$ ($\mathbf{Q}_+$) can enter the linear region;
2 the **A** template is non-negative and $a_{00} > 1$;
3 the initial state values correspond to binary output values.

Under these conditions then, the state of each cell in the linear region is a non-decreasing (non-increasing) function of time; moreover, all the cells that enter the linear region change monotonically their state from -1 to $+1$ (from $+1$ to -1).

Proof:

We assume that, due to the mono-activation property, only cells belonging to $\mathbf{Q}_-$ can enter the linear region, whereas cells belonging to $\mathbf{Q}_+$ are not allowed to leave the positive saturation region (the opposite case can be dealt with in a dual way).

The proof is based on a fundamental result due to Kamke, on monotone flows. For the sake of completeness, we report here a corollary of Kamke's result that is more suitable for our purposes.   □

Kamke's theorem:

Let $\mathbf{F} : R^n \rightarrow R^n$ be a continuous map such that $\mathbf{F}_i(\mathbf{x}) = F_i(x_1, \ldots, x_n)$ is non-decreasing in x_k for all $k \neq i$. Let $\Phi_t(\mathbf{x}(0))$ be the solution of the autonomous differential equation $d\mathbf{x}/dt = \mathbf{F}(\mathbf{x})$ for a generic initial condition $\mathbf{x}(0)$, such that $\Phi_0(\mathbf{x}(0)) = \mathbf{x}(0)$. If $\mathbf{x}^a \leq \mathbf{x}^b$ then for all $t > 0$ we have $\Phi_t(\mathbf{x}^a) \leq \Phi_t(\mathbf{x}^b)$.

Proof:

See W. A. Coppel, "Stability and asymptotic behavior of differential equations," D.C. Heath, Boston, 1965.

The proof of Proposition 1 proceeds as follows:

1 By assumption, for $t = 0$ all the cells are in a saturation region, that is, they belong to $\mathbf{Q}_+ \cup \mathbf{Q}_-$. Due to the mono-activation property, all the active cells must belong to $\mathbf{Q}_-$; we denote the set of the active cells by $\mathbf{Q}^a$. The inactive cells may belong both to $\mathbf{Q}_+$ and to $\mathbf{Q}_-$: their set, for $t = 0$, is denoted by $\mathbf{Q}^i$.

2 Let us denote by $\mathbf{x}^a$ and $\mathbf{x}^i$ the vectors containing the state-values of the active ($\mathbf{Q}^a$) and inactive ($\mathbf{Q}^i$) cells, respectively. There exists $t_1 > 0$ such that in the interval $[0, t_1]$ the output voltages $\mathbf{y}^i$ corresponding to the inactive cells are constants. Hence the time-evolution of the active cells can be described by the following equation

$$\frac{dx^a}{dt} = -x^a + \mathbf{A}_a y^a + \mathbf{B}u + u_a + z \qquad (12.5)$$

where matrix $\mathbf{A}_a$ is obtained through the feedback template $\mathbf{A}$ by ordering the cells in some way and by considering only the active cells; matrix $\mathbf{B}$ is obtained by the input template $\mathbf{B}$, u_a represents the constant contribution due to the inactive cells, and z is a vector containing the bias terms. Since for the active cells $dx^a/dt\,(t = 0)$ is positive, there exists $t_2 \in [0\,t_1]$ such that $x^a(t_2) > x^a(0)$; due to the fact that all the non-diagonal elements of $\mathbf{A}_a$ are non-negative, the dynamical system (12.5) satisfies the assumptions of Kamke's theorem; therefore for all $0 < t < t_1$ the solution $x^a(t)$ is a non-decreasing function of t.

3 Due to the mono-activity property, it is not possible that cells belonging to $\mathbf{Q}_+$ enter the linear region. However it may occur that some inactive cells, belonging to $\mathbf{Q}_-$ (and not to $\mathbf{Q}^a$) become active. In such a case there exists a time instant $t = t_3 > t_1$

for which the state voltages of one or more originally inactive cells cross the value -1 (the set of these cells is denoted by $\mathbf{Q}^c$, whereas their state voltages are denoted by x^c). This means that Eq. (12.5) is valid in the whole interval $[0\ t_3]$ and that there exists $\varepsilon > 0$ such that

$$x^c(t_3 - 2\epsilon) \geq x^c(t_3 - \epsilon) \tag{12.6}$$

Now let us denote with x^{ac} the vector $x^{ac} = [(x^a)^t\ (x^c)^t]^t$ and with y^{ac} the corresponding outputs. The time evolution of x^{ac} in the interval $[0\ t_4]$ $(t_4 > t_3)$ is described by the equation:

$$\frac{dx^{ac}}{dt} = -x^{ac} + \mathbf{A}_{ac}y^{ac} + \mathbf{B}u + u_{ac} + I \tag{12.7}$$

where matrix $\mathbf{A}_{ac}$ is obtained through the feedback template $\mathbf{A}$ by considering only the cells whose state voltages belong to x^{ac}; u_{ac} represents the constant contribution due to the other cells. Now, since equation (12.5) is valid till $t = t_3$ the following relationship holds

$$x^a(t_3 - 2\epsilon) \geq x^a(t_3 - \epsilon) \tag{12.8}$$

From (12.6) and (12.8) we have

$$x^{ac}(t_3 - 2\epsilon) \geq x^{ac}(t_3 - \epsilon) \tag{12.9}$$

By applying Kamke's theorem two facts are readily proved: (a) the state voltages of the originally active cells $(\mathbf{Q}^a)$ continue to be a non-decreasing function of time; (b) the state voltages of the cells $(\mathbf{Q}^c)$ that cross -1 at $t = t_3$ are a non-decreasing function of time for $t \geq t_3$.

4 By increasing t, it is confirmed that no cell can leave the set $\mathbf{Q}_+$; if some cells of $\mathbf{Q}_-$ cross the value -1, then the same arguments used at point 3, can be applied. We can therefore conclude that: (a) the state voltages of the originally active cells $(\mathbf{Q}^a)$ continue to be non-decreasing functions of time for all $t > 0$; (b) the state voltages of the cells that cross -1 at a certain instant t_i are a non-decreasing function of time for $t \geq t_i$. It turns out that in the linear region the cell state voltages are a non-decreasing function of time. Since $a_{00} > 1$, the linear region exhibits at least one eigenvalue with positive real part and therefore it is unstable; hence with the exception of a set of initial conditions of measure zero, all the cells that enter the linear region change monotonically their state voltage from -1 to $+1$ (from $+1$ to -1, if the mono-activation property holds for cells in $\mathbf{Q}_+$). This proves the thesis of the proposition.

□

Here we show an example in which one of the conditions of the monotonic state transient is not satisfied, and the transient will not be monotonic.

Example 1

Templates **A** and **B** of (12.10) satisfy conditions (i) and (iii), but do not satisfy condition (ii) of the proposition. They activate only pixels in $\mathbf{Q}_+$, but never activate pixels in $\mathbf{Q}_-$. If a cell output is white, then $-2 \geq w_d \geq -8$, hence it is stable in the negative saturation region independently of its neighborhood configuration. Hence, template (12.10) is of mono-activation type

$$\mathbf{A} = \begin{bmatrix} 0 & -1 & 0 \\ 1 & 3 & 0 \\ 0 & -1 & 0 \end{bmatrix}, \quad B = \begin{bmatrix} 0 & 0 & 0 \\ 0 & 0 & 0 \\ 0 & 0 & 0 \end{bmatrix}, \quad z = -2 \tag{12.10}$$

However, the templates (12.10) have some negative values in the **A** template. We will show that the state of some cells in the linear region is *not* monotone increasing.

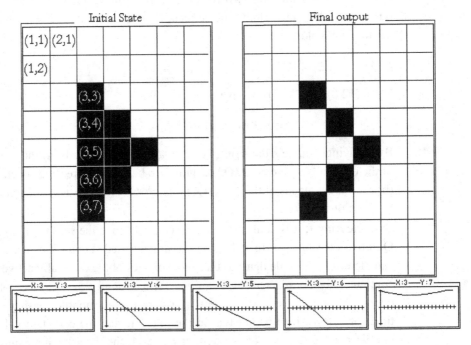

Fig. 12.3. Simulation results of Example 1. The initial state and the final output of the array are shown. The output signal transients of some cells are also given.

Fig. 12.3 shows an example. At $t = 0$ all the black cells are activated in the third column. As the time diagram shows, at the bottom the output signals of the cells in this column start to go toward the white saturation region (their rate of change differs from cell to cell). After a while, however, some of them turn back to the black saturation region (cells $(3, 3)$ and $(3, 7)$). Hence, this CNN array does not have the mono-activation property.

After this example we introduce some formal methods to decide which cell is (or becomes) active, and which is not.

Dynamic local rules (DLC)

In a standard CNN with a monotone state transient property the following four *local dynamic rules* govern the change of activity:

(i) $x_{ij}(t) > 1 \Rightarrow y_{ij}(t) = 1$ and $w_{dij}^{+} > 1$

    an inactive cell remains in the positive stable equilibrium ($\mathbf{Q}_{+}$) at $x_{ij} = w_{dij}^{+}$, hence the cell remains inactive and its output y_{ij} does not change

(ii) $x_{ij}(t) > 1 \Rightarrow y_{ij}(t) = 1$ and $w_{dij}^{+} < 1$

    an inactive cell in the positive stable equilibrium changes from region $\mathbf{Q}_{+}$ to region $\mathbf{Q}_{-}$, meanwhile it will be active and settles in $\mathbf{Q}_{-}$

(iii) $x_{ij}(t) < -1 \Rightarrow y_{ij}(t) = -1$ and $w_{dij}^{+} < -1$

    an inactive cell remains in the negative stable saturation region ($\mathbf{Q}_{-}$) at $x_{ij} = w_{dij}^{+}$, hence the cell remains inactive and its output $\mathbf{Q}_{+}$ does not change

(iv) $x_{ij}(t) < -1 \Rightarrow y_{ij}(t) = -1$ and $w_{dij}^{+} > -1$

    an inactive cell in the negative stable equilibrium changes from $\mathbf{Q}_{-}$ to $\mathbf{Q}_{+}$ region, meanwhile it will be active and settles in $\mathbf{Q}_{+}$.

12.2 Binary activation pattern and template format

Now, we are in a position to define the binary activation pattern, which will trigger unidirectional changes in a propagating wave.

Consider now a standard CNN with $a_{00} \gg 1$, fixed boundary (-1), and a given initial state and input. At the beginning and all along the possibly propagating transient process, the inactive and active cells define an activity pattern of the whole cell space. Suppose the whole propagation process will meet the following conditions:

- At the end, all cells belong to the inactive cell set.
- At the beginning, there exist at least one active cell in the active cell set. (Otherwise, there would not be any change, all the cells would remain in their stable inactive state.)
- During the transient process, an inactive cell becomes active if at least one of its neighborhood cells becomes active and the activity pattern of the neighborhood, called activity configuration, satisfies some conditions (then this configuration is called activator configuration).

Definition 2:
The *binary activation pattern* is defined within an $S_r(ij)$ neighborhood. It consists of two template-sized patterns, having a black, or white, or don't care value in each position. In addition to these two, *input related* and *current output related*, local activation patterns called *activator configurations*, a limit number (L) is also given. A cell c_{ij} will be activated (go to active state from an inactive state) if the actual local activity pattern is an activator configuration, i.e. in $S_r(ij)$ it matches at most or at least L black-and-white positions of the binary activation pattern (the don't cares do not count!). Hence, the local dynamic rule is given by the activator configurations and L.

Definition 3:
If the activation pattern is input independent, that is the input related part contains don't cares only, we call this situation *unconstrained propagation* and the **B** template is zero (otherwise it is called *constrained propagation*).

Definition 4:
The propagation rule, i.e. the activator configuration, is called *B/W (black and white) symmetric* if the rule is symmetric to the color (black/white). This means that the role of black pixels and the role of white pixels are interchangeable. In this case the *bias term of the template, (z), equals zero.*

12.3   A simple propagating type example with B/W symmetrical rule

In the next example we generate the left to right horizontal shadow of a black object on a binary image.

12.3.1   Global task

The task can be defined in each row, independently. In a black and white image, in each row, all the pixels right from the left-most black pixel should become black. An example is shown in Fig. 12.4.

12.3.2   Local rules and binary activation pattern

In this task, we have to find the left-most black pixel in each row, and change all white pixels black which are right of it. This can be done by starting a black propagation front moving right from each black pixel. Hence, the local rules are: (i) a white pixel where the direct left neighbor is black, change to black; (ii) the rest of the pixels should be unchanged.

The activation pattern and the local rule are shown in Fig. 12.5.

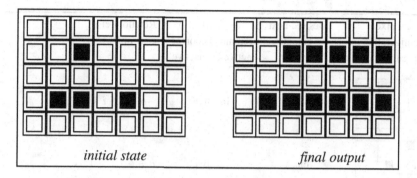

Fig. 12.4. Example for the left to right shadow generation.

Input dependency	Current output dependency	Limit number	Rule
(3×3 grid, all dashes)	(3×3 grid: top row dashes, middle row filled black, white, dash, bottom row dashes)	2	In the case of two matches the central white pixel in the output should change to black

Fig. 12.5. Binary activation pattern and local rule (shadow template).

12.3.3 Template type and template form

The propagation is unconstrained, because it is not effected by the input. (It starts from the left-most black pixel and goes along to the boundary.) It is asymmetric, because the black objects get shadows, the white ones (here the background) do not.

The template form can be derived from the activation pattern and the classifications. The center element of the **A** template (a_{00}) is the first free parameter. There is only one non-zero off-center in the activation pattern, which is the second free parameter. The **B** template is zero, because the propagation is unconstrained. The current (z) is the third free parameter, because the propagation is asymmetric. The template is sought in the following form:

$$\mathbf{A} = \begin{bmatrix} 0 & 0 & 0 \\ b & a & 0 \\ 0 & 0 & 0 \end{bmatrix}, \quad \mathbf{B} = \begin{bmatrix} 0 & 0 & 0 \\ 0 & 0 & 0 \\ 0 & 0 & 0 \end{bmatrix}, \quad z = i \tag{12.11}$$

12.3.4 System of inequalities and optimal solution

The relation system generation is based on *Dynamic Local Rules (DLC)*. Since two pixels affect the propagation, we have to examine four cases only. These cases are shown in Fig. 12.6.

Local pixel configuration in the current output	Desired next output	Cell remains/becomes active or inactive	Relation ref w_d case in DLC
	white	inactive	$-a - b + i < -1$ (iii)
	black	inactive	$a - b + i > 1$ (i)
	black	inactive	$a + b + i > 1$ (i)
	black	active	$-a + b + i > -1$ (iv)

Fig. 12.6. Binary activation pattern and local rule (shadow template).

We do not deal here with the solving of the system of inequalities and the template optimization for robustness. The optimized final template is the following:

$$\mathbf{A} = \begin{bmatrix} 0 & 0 & 0 \\ 1 & 2 & 0 \\ 0 & 0 & 0 \end{bmatrix}, \quad \mathbf{B} = \begin{bmatrix} 0 & 0 & 0 \\ 0 & 0 & 0 \\ 0 & 0 & 0 \end{bmatrix}, \quad z = 1 \tag{12.12}$$

12.4   The connectivity problem

The goal here is to delete all pixels which are part of a connected object defined by black pixels on a white background. Consider Fig. 12.7.

Two binary images are given. The first contains some black objects against a white background. The second is derived from the first one by changing some black pixels to white. Those objects are considered to be marked which have some deleted pixels. Design a template which deletes the marked objects and does not affect the rest of the image. If we delete a single pixel of a black object and apply this template, all the black pixels consisting of the object will change to white.

12.4.1   Global task

This is a 2D problem. All connected black pixels of the marked objects should change to white, and the rest of the pixels should remain unchanged. An example can be seen in Fig. 12.7.

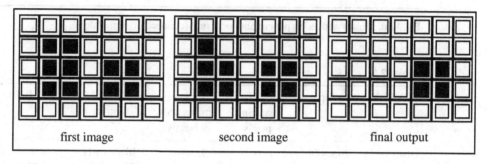

first image   second image   final output

Fig. 12.7. Example for the connectivity template.

12.4.2   Local rules and binary activation pattern

In this task, first, we have to find those pixels which are black in the first image and white in the second image. From these points we have to start propagation wave-fronts to all directions. The front should propagate on the black pixels only and change them to white. Since the wave-front moves on the second image it will be the initial state and the first image will be the input. Hence, the local rules are the following: (i) change those black pixels white which have at least one neighboring cell with white output and black input, and (ii) do not change the rest of the pixels. At the same time, it is clear from the task specification that if a pixel is black in the second image (current output), it must be black in the first image (input) also. From this it follows that here the difference of the output and the input counts instead of simply the output value of the neighboring cells.

We introduce a new sign in the activation pattern. The delta sign (Δ) means that the particular neighbor activates the cell if and only if its output and its input are different. Note that the definition of the task excludes those situations when the output are black and the input is white. So, here the delta sign (the match) means that the current output is white and the input is black in a particular position. A cell becomes active if both its central input and central current output are black, and if it has at least one matching neighbor. For simplicity we used four neighborhoods. The activation pattern is shown in Fig. 12.8.

Input dependency	Current output dependency	Limit number	Rule
(3×3 pattern)	(3×3 pattern)	1	If the central input and central current output are black, and there are one or more matches, the central black pixel in the output should change to white

Fig. 12.8. Binary activation pattern and local rule (connectivity template).

Table 12.1.

Output	Input	# of matching pixels	Becomes/ remains active or inactive	Desired output	Relation
Black (+1)	Black (+1)	0	Inactive	Black (+1)	$a + c + I > 1$
Black (+1)	Black (+1)	1	Active	White (−1)	$a - 2b + c + i < 1$
Black (+1)	Black (+1)	2	Active	White (−1)	$a - 4b + c + i < 1$
Black (+1)	Black (+1)	3	Active	White (−1)	$a - 6b + c + i < 1$
Black (+1)	Black (+1)	4	Active	White (−1)	$a - 8b + c + i < 1$
White (−1)	Black (+1)	0	Inactive	White (−1)	$-a + c + I < -1$
White (−1)	Black (+1)	1	Inactive	White (−1)	$-a - 2b + c + i < -1$
White (−1)	Black (+1)	2	Inactive	White (−1)	$-a - 4b + c + i < -1$
White (−1)	Black (+1)	3	Inactive	White (−1)	$-a - 6b + c + i < -1$
White (−1)	Black (+1)	4	Inactive	White (−1)	$-a - 8b + c + i < -1$
White (−1)	White (−1)	0	Inactive	White (−1)	$-a - c + i < -1$
White (−1)	White (−1)	1	Inactive	White (−1)	$-a - 2b - c - i < -1$
White (−1)	White (−1)	2	Inactive	White (−1)	$-a - 4b - c + i < -1$
White (−1)	White (−1)	3	Inactive	White (−1)	$-a - 6b - c + i < -1$
White (−1)	White (−1)	4	Inactive	White (−1)	$-a - 8b - c + i < -1$

12.4.3 Template type and template form

The propagation is constrained, because it can go over the black areas only. It is asymmetric, because it deals with the black objects, the originally white pixels are unchanged.

As usual the template form can be derived from the activation pattern and the classifications. The center element of the **A** template (a_{00}) is the first free parameter. The delta operators in the neighborhood affect both the **A** template and the **B** template. A neighbor which has the same input and output (both can be black or white) does not affect the cell. But if it has black input and white output it activates the cell. Hence, the second free parameter appears in the neighborhood in both the **A** and the **B** template, but with opposite sign. The center element of the **B** template is the third free parameter. Since the propagation is asymmetric, the bias (z) is the fourth free parameter. The template is sought in the following form:

$$A = \begin{bmatrix} 0 & b & 0 \\ b & a & b \\ 0 & b & 0 \end{bmatrix}, \quad B = \begin{bmatrix} 0 & -b & 0 \\ -b & c & -b \\ 0 & -b & 0 \end{bmatrix}, \quad z = i \tag{12.13}$$

12.4.4 System of inequalities and optimal solution

The relation system generation is based on *Dynamic Local Rules*. Since there are only three valid binary input–output combinations here, and five matching possibilities, there are 15 different cases. All cases yield a relation. The relation set is shown in Table 12.1.

We do not detail the solution of the relation system and the optimization here. The optimized final template is the following

$$A = \begin{bmatrix} 0 & 1 & 0 \\ 1 & 3 & 1 \\ 0 & 1 & 0 \end{bmatrix}, \quad B = \begin{bmatrix} 0 & -1 & 0 \\ -1 & 3 & -1 \\ 0 & -1 & 0 \end{bmatrix}, \quad z = -4 \tag{12.14}$$

Fig. 12.9 shows an example for the operation of the connectivity template.

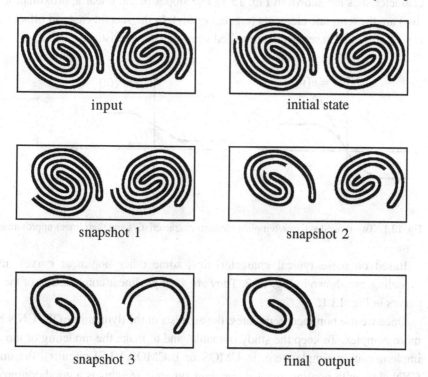

input   initial state

snapshot 1   snapshot 2

snapshot 3   final output

Fig. 12.9. Consecutive snapshots of the propagation of the connectivity template.

13 Uncoupled standard CNNs with nonlinear synaptic weights

So far, we have studied CNNs with linear synaptic weights (linear templates) described by the class 1 standard CNN dynamic equations (Eq. (2.2)). This means that the characteristics of a simple synapse or template element are linear. In many practical cases, these elements are voltage controlled (gated) current sources (conductances or transconductances). Indeed, in practice, they are never completely linear. We are approximating them on a well-defined domain, around an operating region (point). CNNs with nonlinear templates were introduced in the early years.[1] Two typical characteristics are shown in Fig. 13.1. The slopes of the linear approximation (dotted line) are the template elements (e.g. a_{kl} or b_{kl}). In the second case, an offset value (i_0) is also present. These curves are called sigmoid characteristics.

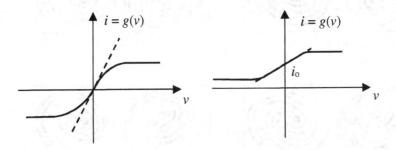

Fig. 13.1. Two typical synapse/template element characteristics and their linear approximation.

Based on these typical characteristics, some other nonlinear curves, useful in modeling, are shown in Fig. 13.2. They are a simple linear combination of the original curves in Fig. 13.1.

Once we use nonlinear templates, the analysis of the dynamics of the CNN becomes more complex. To keep the study tractable, and to make the modeling or the physical implementation simpler (e.g. in CMOS or BiCMOS VLSI circuits), the uncoupled CNN class with nonlinear space invariant synaptic weights is a good compromise. A simple framework with a_{00}, z, and a nonlinear **B** template are studied next. In this case, the DP plot technique described in Chapter 3 can still be used.

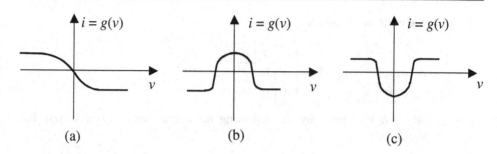

Fig. 13.2. Inverse sigmoid (a), bell-shape (Gaussian) (b), and inverse bell-shape characteristics (c).

13.1 Dynamic equations and DP plot

Restricting the class of nonlinear templates, consider the following cloning template:

$$\mathbf{A} = \begin{array}{|c|c|c|} \hline 0 & 0 & 0 \\ \hline 0 & a_{00} & 0 \\ \hline 0 & 0 & 0 \\ \hline \end{array} \quad \mathbf{B} = \begin{array}{|c|c|c|} \hline b_9 & b_8 & b_7 \\ \hline b_6 & b_5 & b_4 \\ \hline b_3 & b_2 & b_1 \\ \hline \end{array} \quad \boxed{z} \quad b_5 = b_{00}$$

The **B** template is, in general, nonlinear. This means that the template elements $(b_1, \ldots, b_9)$ are nonlinear functions of either the inputs or the input differences $(u_{kl} - u_{ij})$. Hence, the dynamics is described by the following state equation

$$\dot{x}_{ij} = -x_{ij} + a_{00} f(x_{ij}) + z + \sum_{C(kl) \in S_r(ij)} B(ij; kl) \cdot u_{kl} \tag{13.1}$$

where $B(ij; kl) \cdot u_{kl}$ has two types of forms: difference controlled,[2] i.e. the controlling variable of a template element is $u_{kl} - u_{ij}$, or value controlled, i.e. the controlling variable is u_{kl}. Note that in our case the nonlinearity is in the **B** template only, hence the state dynamic route Γ_x and the shifted DP plot $\Gamma_x(w_{ij})$ technique can still be applied (see Section 3.2). Following this technique, the standard forms of the state and output equations will be

$$\dot{x}_{ij} = g(x_{ij}) + w_{ij} = -x_{ij} + a_{00} f(x_{ij}) + w_{ij}$$
$$w_{ij} = z + \sum_{C(kl) \in S_r(ij)} B(ij; kl) \cdot u_{kl} \tag{13.2}$$
$$y_{ij} = f(x_{ij})$$

When drawing the shifted DP plot, we can determine the values and ranges of the shift w_{ij}. The basic structure of the DP plot remains the same as in Section 3.2.

Gray-scale contour detector

$$A = \begin{array}{|c|c|c|} \hline 0 & 0 & 0 \\ \hline 0 & 2 & 0 \\ \hline 0 & 0 & 0 \\ \hline \end{array} \quad B = \begin{array}{|c|c|c|} \hline a & a & a \\ \hline a & 0 & a \\ \hline a & a & a \\ \hline \end{array} \quad z = \boxed{0.7}$$

where a is defined by the following nonlinear function (piece-wise linear inverse bellshape)

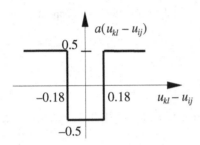

Fig. 13.3.

I Global task

Given: static gray-scale image $\mathbf{P}$

Input: $\mathbf{U}(t) = \mathbf{P}$

Initial state: $\mathbf{X}(0) = \mathbf{P}$

Boundary conditions: Fixed type, $u_{ij} = 0$ for all virtual cells, denoted by $[U] = 0^3$

Output: $\mathbf{Y}(t) \Rightarrow \mathbf{Y}(\infty) =$ Binary image where black pixels represent the contours of the objects in $\mathbf{P}$.

II Local rules

$u_{kl} - u_{ij} \rightarrow Y_{ij}(\infty)$

1 White local area (all nearest neighbors) → White

2 Black local area (all nearest neighbors) → White

3 White or black central pixel in a black or white neighborhood, respectively → Black

4 Straight white line with three neighbors against six blacks → Black

5 Straight black line with three neighbors against six whites → White

6 Substantial change in gray level between a central line and neighboring pixels → Black

Remark:

Substantial change may seem a loose term. However, it is far from trivial, mathematically. Unlike sophisticated PDE templates and algorithms, this simple template, by controlling the height and width of the inverse bell-shape (Gaussian-type) nonlinearity, can give a good estimate for our visual perception of a contour.

III Example:

Image name: madonna.bmp, image size: 59×59; template name: contour.tem.

input   output

IV Mathematical analysis

Suppose

$$w_{ij} = z + w_{ijB}$$

Then, in view of $a_{00} = 2$, the DP plot with w_{ijB} will be as shown in Fig. 13.4.

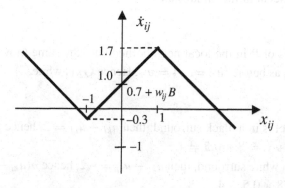

Fig. 13.4. The DP plot with $w_{ijB} = 0$.

Consider now the six local rules. The values of w_{ijB} to the six cases will be denoted by $w_1, w_2, \ldots, w_6$, respectively.

The DP plots for these cases are shown in Fig. 13.5.

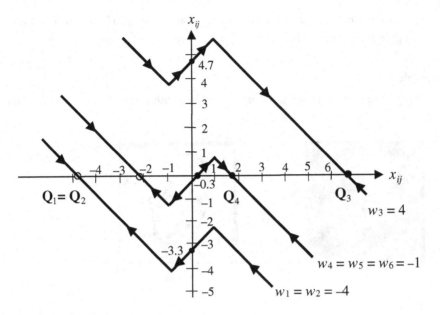

Fig. 13.5. The DP plots for the six local rules.

Local rule 1

Since all the pixel values of **P** in the local neighborhood are the same, $u_{kl} - u_{ij} = 0$ for $\forall C(kl) \in S_r(ij)$, that is $b(u_{kl} - u_{ij}) = b(0) = -0.5$. Hence, following equation (13.2)

$$w_{ijB} = w_1 = \sum B(ij; kl) \cdot u_{kl} = 8b(u_{kl} - u_{ij}) = 8b(\cdot) = -4$$

that is, $\mathbf{Q}_1$: white (independent of the initial state).

Local rule 2

Again, all the pixel values of **P** in the local neighborhood are the same (now black), hence $u_{kl} - u_{ij} = 0$, and, as before, $w_2 = -4 = w_1$. Hence $\mathbf{Q}_2$ is white.

Local rule 3

(a) If a white central pixel is in a black surround, then $u_{kl} - u_{ij} = 2$, hence $b(u_{kl} - u_{ij}) = 0.5$, therefore $w_{3a} = 8 \times 0.5 = 4$.

(b) If a black pixel is in a white surround, then $u_{kl} - u_{ij} = -2$, hence $b(u_{kl} - u_{ij}) = 0.5$, therefore $w_{3b} = 8 \times 0.5 = 4$.

In both cases, $w_3 = w_{3a} = w_{3b} = 4$. Following the DP plot for $w_3 = 4$, the equilibrium point $\mathbf{Q}_3$ is black (independent of the initial state).

Local rule 4

An example of a typical configuration referring to Local rule 4 is shown in Fig. 13.6.

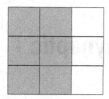

Fig. 13.6.

The straight white line with three neighbors against six blacks could be placed in other directions as well. In all cases, since $b_{00} = 0$

$$w_4 = \sum B(ij; kl) \cdot u_{kl} = 5 \cdot b(0) + 3 \cdot b(-2) = 5(-0.5) + 3(0.5) = -1.0$$

The DP plot for $w_4 = -1.0$ settles in $\mathbf{Q}_4$ since the initial state is black $(+1)$. $\mathbf{Q}_4$ is black $(>+1)$.

Local rule 5

In this case, a typical configuration related to Local rule 5 is shown in Fig. 13.7.

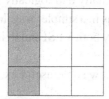

Fig. 13.7.

Hence, the reasoning follows as in Local rule 4,

$$w_5 = 5b(0) + 5b(2) = 5(-0.5) + 3 \cdot 0.5 = -1.0$$

However, since the initial state is white (-1) the stable state $\mathbf{Q}_5$ will be white.

Local rule 6

In this case the local rule is given in a fuzzy way: substantial changes occur in the gray level between the central line and neighboring pixels.

Indeed, this means that basically the DP plot will follow the plots for Local rules 4 and 5. The reason is that the inverse bell-shaped function has the same value if $|u_{kl} - u_{ij}| > 0.18$.

14 Standard CNNs with delayed synaptic weights and motion analysis

Modeling living neural networks, a typical construct is a so-called interneuron. This means a time-delayed action, sometimes a delayed excitation, sometimes a delayed inhibition. The introduction of ideal delaying template elements in cellular neural networks[1] was motivated by this fact. Later, the synapse delay in general neural networks became widely used. Although, in the VLSI implementation, the ideal delay in not easily implemented, and physiologically faithful models of living neural networks did not contain ideal time delay either, conceptually and logically the delay template is useful in explaining complex wave-like actions in a simpler way. Moreover, delayed synapse functions can be and are approximated by both VLSI and living neural implementations, respectively.

Motion analysis is one typical application. We will show some useful examples as well.

14.1 Dynamic equations

Following the original paper,[1] and referring to the notations used in Chapter 2, a class 1 standard CNN with space invariant templates with and without time delays is described by the following state and output equations

$$
\dot{x}_{ij} = -x_{ij} + z + \sum_{k=-1}^{1}\sum_{l=-1}^{1} a_{kl} y_{i+k,j+l(t)} + \sum_{k=-1}^{1}\sum_{l=-1}^{1} b_{kl} u_{i+k,j+l(t)}
$$

$$
+ \sum_{k=-1}^{1}\sum_{l=-1}^{1} a_{kl}^{\tau} y_{i+k,j+l(t-\tau)} + \sum_{k=-1}^{1}\sum_{l=-1}^{1} b_{kl}^{\tau} u_{i+k,j+l(t-\tau)}
$$

$$
\mathbf{A}: a_{kl}; \mathbf{A}^{\tau}: a_{kl}^{\tau}; \mathbf{B}: b_{kl}; \mathbf{B}^{\tau}: b_{kl}^{\tau} \tag{14.1}
$$

The delayed template values $a_{kl}^{\tau}, b_{kl}^{\tau}$ are given in the same way as the $\mathbf{A}$ and $\mathbf{B}$ templates (3×3, 5×5, 7×7, etc. matrices).

There are a few theoretical challenges when introducing delayed templates.[2] One can be formulated as follows.

Suppose, we have two different templates. We are combining them as a non-delayed and as a delayed template. What would be the function of the combined template?

An example is shown below.

Given a connected component detector and a vertical line detector template, suppose we are combining them as follows

$$\text{TEMCCD}: \quad \mathbf{A}_c = \begin{array}{|c|c|c|} \hline 0 & 0 & 0 \\ \hline 1 & 2 & -1 \\ \hline 0 & 0 & 0 \\ \hline \end{array} \quad \mathbf{B}_c = 0 \quad z_c = 0$$

$$\text{TEMVEDGE}: \quad \mathbf{A}_v = \begin{array}{|c|c|c|} \hline 0 & 1 & 0 \\ \hline 0 & -1 & 0 \\ \hline 0 & 1 & 0 \\ \hline \end{array} \quad \mathbf{B}_v = 0 \quad z_v = 0$$

The combined template:

$$\mathbf{A} = \mathbf{A}_c; \quad \mathbf{A}^\tau = \mathbf{A}_v; \quad \mathbf{B} = \mathbf{B}_c = 0; \quad \mathbf{B}^\tau = \mathbf{B}_v = 0; \quad z = z_c + z_v = 0$$

An original image, the output using the CCD template and the output using the combined template are shown in Examples 14.1(a), 14.1(b), and 14.1(c), respectively. It is instructive how the two different functions are combined: a CCD-like wave is vertically stopped at the various vertical edges of the input image.

EXAMPLE 14.1: An original picture (a), the output using CCD template (b), and the result when the combined template is applied (c).

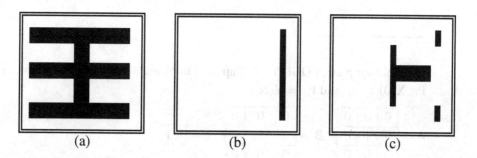

(a)   (b)   (c)

14.2 Motion analysis – discrete time and continuous time image acquisition

Motion detection and estimation is an evergreen problem. In this section we will consider a special problem and some related aspects. In a famous discovery by Hubel and Wiesel,[3] it was shown that if a bar was moving across a particular region of a cat's visual field in a certain direction and if the speed was around a given value, then some cortical neurons would fire (detecting this event). How can we imitate this detection task using a CNN template or a sequence of a few templates? In what follows, a simple solution will be shown. First, using a standard CNN with conventional templates acting on a sequence of snapshots; second, using also delay type templates in a continuous time mode of the image acquisition.[4]

Problem 1

Given a moving bar with a constant speed in a given direction (horizontal, to right), detect the object if it moves with a given speed.

Solving Problem 1, suppose that the given velocity is $v = \Delta x / \Delta t$. Adjust the sampling rate of this image sequence in such a way that at this velocity the movement of an object will be one pixel per sample. Now, to solve our problem, first we take the difference image between two consecutive snapshots and then examine whether the difference is one pixel wide.

To take the difference picture $\mathbf{P}_d$ of two consecutive snapshots $\mathbf{P}_0$ and $\mathbf{P}_1$, the truth table of Table 14.1 is to be realized. $\mathbf{P}_d = \mathbf{P}_1 \setminus \mathbf{P}_0$.

Table 14.1. *Truth table for the subtraction $\mathbf{P}_d = \mathbf{P}_1 \setminus \mathbf{P}_0$.*

$\mathbf{P}_0$	$\mathbf{P}_1$	$\mathbf{P}_d$
u_{ij}	$x_{ij}(0)$	$y_{ij}(\infty)$
-1	-1	-1
-1	1	1
1	-1	-1
1	1	-1

A simple template, LOGDIF of Chapter 3, implements the logical difference if $u_{ij} = \mathbf{P}_0, \mathbf{X}(0) = \mathbf{P}_1$, and $\mathbf{P}_d = \mathbf{Y}(\infty)$

$$A = \begin{bmatrix} 0 & 0 & 0 \\ 0 & 1 & 0 \\ 0 & 0 & 0 \end{bmatrix} \quad B = \begin{bmatrix} 0 & 0 & 0 \\ 0 & -1 & 0 \\ 0 & 0 & 0 \end{bmatrix} \quad z = \boxed{-1}$$

The *speed detection* means that the difference picture has a one-pixel wide object with a left neighbor in $\mathbf{P}_0$. This means that we have to delete every black pixel in $\mathbf{P}_d$ which has no left neighbor in $\mathbf{P}_0$. This is the basic idea of direct neighbor detection. The next template is completing this task

$$A = \boxed{\begin{array}{c|c|c} 0 & 2.1 & 0 \end{array}} \quad B = \boxed{\begin{array}{c|c|c} 2 & 0 & 0 \end{array}} \quad z = \boxed{-2}$$

$U = \mathbf{P}_0; \quad \mathbf{X}(0) = \mathbf{P}_d, \quad \text{and} \quad \mathbf{Y}(\infty) = \mathbf{P}_s$

where $\mathbf{P}_s$ is the output.

This can be proved, as an exercise, using the DP plot technique.

Suppose that $\mathbf{P}_0$ and $\mathbf{P}_1$, shown is Example 14.2(a) and (b), are the two consecutive samples of a moving object (taken at t_0 and t_1). $v = \Delta x / \Delta t$, $\Delta t = t_1 - t_0$, Δx is equal to the pixel size. All the pixels of the difference image $\mathbf{P}_d$, shown in Example 14.2(c), have a left neighbor in $\mathbf{P}_0$. If we delete all the black pixels in $\mathbf{P}_d$ having a left black neighbor in $\mathbf{P}_0$ implemented with template DWLB (delete with left black) shown below, then the resulting screen $\mathbf{P}_s$ will be empty (full white). This detects the event we are looking for.

EXAMPLE 14.2: The two consecutive snapshots $\mathbf{P}_0$ (a), $\mathbf{P}_1$ (b), and the difference image $\mathbf{P}_d$ (c).

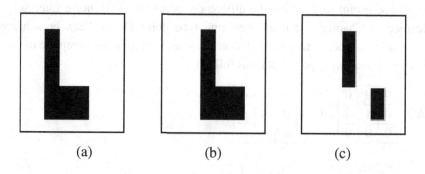

| (a) | (b) | (c) |

The template DWLB is as follows:

$$\mathbf{A} = \boxed{0 \mid 2 \mid 0} \quad \mathbf{B} = \boxed{2 \mid 0 \mid 0} \quad z = \boxed{-2}$$
$$U = \mathbf{P}_0; \quad \mathbf{X}(0) = \mathbf{P}_d, \quad \text{and} \quad \mathbf{Y}(\infty) = \mathbf{P}_s$$

This can be proved, as an exercise, using the DP plot technique.

In some cases, if the object is larger, some pixels might remain in $\mathbf{P}_s$, even if the displacement of the whole image is one pixel. Then, another template, which is, however, coupled, solves the problem. This template is

$$\mathbf{A} = \boxed{1 \mid 2.1 \mid -2} \quad \mathbf{B} = \boxed{2 \mid 0 \mid 0} \quad z = \boxed{-4}$$

Generating the difference picture in continuous time mode

If the image flow is continuous we cannot use the initial state as an independent input port (in the LOGDIF template). In order to take the difference of the actual sample and some proceeding sample of the motion picture, without receiving consecutive samples, we can use a delay-type template.

The simplest possible solution is a combination of a $\mathbf{B}$ and a $\mathbf{B}^t$ template with only central elements b_{00}, and b_{00}^τ, respectively. The output, in the linear domain, is

$$y(t) = b_{00} u_{ij} + b_{00}^\tau u_{ij}(t - \tau) \tag{14.2}$$

If $b_{00} = -b_{00}^\tau = b_0$ then

$$y(t) = b_0(u_{ij} - u_{ij}(t - \tau))$$

If we include a self-coupling (a_{00}) and bias term z, the template calculating the logic difference will be

$$\mathbf{A} = [a_{00}], \quad \mathbf{B} = [b_0], \quad \mathbf{A}^\tau = [0], \quad \mathbf{B}^\tau = [-b_0], \quad z \qquad (14.3)$$

It is supposed that the rate of change of $\mathbf{P}(t)$ is significantly slower than the time constant of the CNN (τ_{CNN}). Likewise, the delay time is also bigger than τ_{CNN}. For example, $\tau \geq 5\tau_{\mathrm{CNN}}$.

In most practical cases the extracted difference picture is corrupted by noise, due to light reflections and slight changes in the environment during motion. Therefore, it would be useful to combine the difference calculation with noise filtering. We have learned in Chapter 3 that an averaging type noise filtering can be achieved by a circularly symmetric template. Hence, we would combine the template in (14.3) with such an averaging type template as follows

$$\mathbf{A} = \begin{array}{|c|c|c|} \hline 0 & 0 & 0 \\ \hline 0 & 1 & 0 \\ \hline 0 & 0 & 0 \\ \hline \end{array} \quad \mathbf{B} = \begin{array}{|c|c|c|} \hline a & a & a \\ \hline a & b & a \\ \hline a & a & a \\ \hline \end{array} \quad z$$

$$(14.4)$$

$$\mathbf{A}^\tau = \begin{array}{|c|c|c|} \hline 0 & 0 & 0 \\ \hline 0 & 0 & 0 \\ \hline 0 & 0 & 0 \\ \hline \end{array} \quad \mathbf{B}^\tau = \begin{array}{|c|c|c|} \hline c & c & c \\ \hline c & d & c \\ \hline c & c & c \\ \hline \end{array}$$

As before, we propose that $b = -d$.

Then, $a, b, c,$ and z are the constants we want to determine. Under this conditions the transients are monotone in time[2] (prove it as an exercise). This means that each state variable is strictly increasing or strictly decreasing.

Since $\mathbf{A}$ is uncoupled with $a_{00} \geq 1$ and $\mathbf{A}^\tau = [0]$, the CNN is completely stable.

The truth table of the logical subtraction is shown in Table 14.1. In our case now, however, the first column belongs to the delayed input image, the second column represents the actual input image, while the third column represents the output (the difference image).

The first row of Table 14.1 states that if a certain pixel is white, in both the actual and the delayed input pictures, then the steady state of the corresponding state variable should be smaller than -1, independently of the neighboring cells. Due to the monotonicity property, just mentioned, a negative sign of the slope ($\dot{x}_{ij}$) is enough to fulfill the latter condition.

Since $u = u^2 = 1$, using the template (14.4), this condition means

$$\dot{x}_{ij}(t) = -x_{ij}(t) + y_{ij}(t) + z - b \pm 8a - d \pm 8c < 0$$

The terms $\pm 8a$ and $\pm 8c$ mean that any combinations of the neighbors are allowed. At $t = 0$, $x_{ij}(0) = y_{ij}(0)$, hence

$$z - b \pm 8a - d \pm 8c < 0 \tag{14.5}$$

Due to monotonicity, this condition will ensure the negative slope during the transient. With similar reasoning, using the third and fourth row in Table 14.1 we get

$$z - b \pm 8a + d \pm 8c < 0 \tag{14.6}$$
$$z + b \pm 8a + d \pm 8c < 0 \tag{14.7}$$

The second row of the truth table requires additional investigation. It states that if a specific pixel is black in the actual input picture and white in the delayed input picture, then the pixel should be black at the end of the transient. This is the normal operation for generating the logical difference (subtraction). However, we want to make also noise filtering. This means that if a pixel in the delayed input has less than two black neighbors, then it is considered to be noise and the output will tend to be white (even if all the pixels in the actual neighbors are black). These two cases, that is a zero black neighbor and one black neighbor in the delayed input, are represented by the following two inequalities, respectively

$$z + b + 8a - d + 8c < 0 \tag{14.8}$$
$$z + b + 8a - d + 6c < 0 \tag{14.9}$$

Finally, if there are two black neighbors then the state and output turns black and then the condition will be

$$z + b + 8a - d + 4c > 0 \tag{14.10}$$

If $c < 0$, then in case of more than two black neighbors the inequality (14.10) automatically ensures the condition for turning black.

Now, we have six inequalities (14.5)–(14.10) for four independent parameters (a, b, c, z). A suitable choice, inside the polyhedron, is

$$a = 0.25, \quad b = 2, \quad c = -0.25, \quad d = -2, \quad z = -4.75$$

This means that our template for taking the difference and, at the same time, making noise filtering, is

$$\mathbf{A} = \begin{array}{|c|c|c|} \hline 0 & 0 & 0 \\ \hline 0 & 1 & 0 \\ \hline 0 & 0 & 0 \\ \hline \end{array} \quad \mathbf{B} = \begin{array}{|c|c|c|} \hline 0.25 & 0.25 & 0.25 \\ \hline 0.25 & 2 & 0.25 \\ \hline 0.25 & 0.25 & 0.25 \\ \hline \end{array} \quad z = -4.75$$

$$\tag{14.11}$$

$$\mathbf{A}^\tau = \begin{array}{|c|c|c|} \hline 0 & 0 & 0 \\ \hline 0 & 0 & 0 \\ \hline 0 & 0 & 0 \\ \hline \end{array} \quad \mathbf{B}^\tau = \begin{array}{|c|c|c|} \hline -0.25 & -0.25 & -0.25 \\ \hline -0.25 & -2 & -0.25 \\ \hline -0.25 & -0.25 & -0.25 \\ \hline \end{array} \quad \tau \geq 5\tau_{cnn}$$

The performance of the template on an image flow showing a running clock with a rotating hand is shown in Example 14.3. Observe that in the center (kernel) part of the hand there is no change.

EXAMPLE 14.3: Snapshots in processing the image flow of a running clock with rotating hand. One snapshot of the input flow (a), a calculated difference image without noise filtering using template (14.3) (b), and the result using template (14.11) with noise filtering (c).

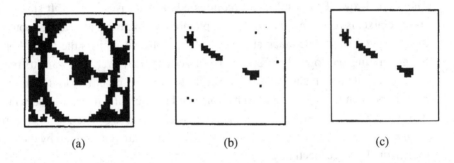

       (a)   (b)   (c)

15 Visual microprocessors – analog and digital VLSI implementation of the CNN Universal Machine

Digital technology has the key advantage that if *a few building blocks* are implemented then any complex system can be built from these by

- *wiring* and
- *programming*.

Moreover, most of the digital building blocks are placed in a regular arrangement: a simple block is repeated many times in a matrix arrangement (e.g. memories, PLAs, etc.).

The CNN core and the CNN Universal Machine architecture, containing also analog building blocks, possess the very same properties. Due to their special nature, however, they have orders of magnitude advantages in speed, power, and area (SPA) in some standard physical implementations. In many applications, like image flow computing, this advantage might be mission critical.

As a revolutionary feature, stored programmability can be introduced in the analog domain as well. This makes it possible to fabricate visual microprocessors.

In what follows, first, we show the building blocks and their simple CMOS implementation examples, without going into the details of their design issues.[1] The emulated digital implementation will be only briefly reviewed. As to this and the optical implementation, we refer to the literature.[2]

As a summary: using only six simple circuit building blocks, namely:

- resistor,
- capacitor,
- switch,
- VCCS (Voltage Controlled Current Source),
- logic register, and
- logic gate,

the most complex CNN array computer chip can be built in a VLSI friendly, regular structure.

Next, the visual microprocessor and its computational infrastructure is described. At first, it seems unusual to combine analog spatio-temporal dynamics with logic, programmability, and software. Indeed, in the CNN-UM and in the visual microprocessor, when the sensor array is integrated with the CNN-UM array processor, the most difficult digital task (solving a nonlinear wave equation) is selected as an elementary instruction. But this is exactly the task a CNN array can solve most easily.

Finally, some realistic measures are shown to compare the computing power of different architectures for array signal processing, especially for image flow processing.

15.1   The analog CNN core

There are only three building blocks in the core cell: a capacitor and a VCCS (voltage controlled current source) the latter may have a linear and a saturation region (Fig. 15.1), and a resistor.

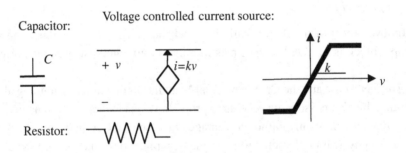

Fig. 15.1. The three building blocks of the CNN core.

The CMOS implementation of a capacitor is straightforward, though its smallest value is limited by the stray capacitors (sometimes this is exactly the capacitor of a CNN cell). The resistor is implemented by a transistor. The VCCS is implemented in many ways, the Operational Transconductance Amplifiers (OTAs) are the usual solutions with their many different circuit designs. One possible circuit, the recently invented "one transistor synapse,"[3] is shown, in its transistor level description, in Fig. 15.2. Indeed these OTAs, sometimes called synapse circuits, are the protagonists of the CNN CMOS implementations. The CNN core, is composed of a capacitor, a resistor, and a VCCS. The cell interactions between the cells are also implemented by VCCS blocks. The circuit model of such an interacting core cell is shown in Fig. 15.3.

The cell model in Fig. 15.3 is the so-called Chua–Yang model. In some cases, from an implementation point of view, the so-called full-range model is more convenient.[4]

In the full-range model, the state and input are connected and the circuit in the dashed line area is composed of a capacitor, a nonlinear resistor and a current source. In the CNN universal cell model in Fig. 15.6, the full range cell model is shown.

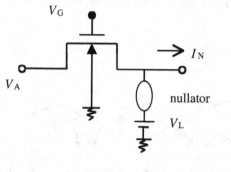

$$I_N = \beta(V_A - V_L)V_G - \beta\left(V_T + \frac{V_A + V_L}{2}\right)(V_A - V_L)$$

Fig. 15.2. A transistor level description of a "one transistor synapse" implementing a VCCS.

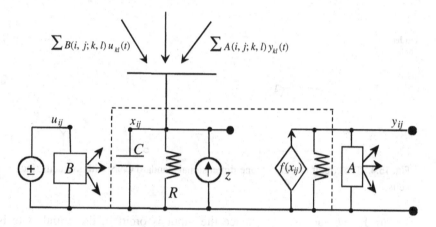

Fig. 15.3. A circuit model of a standard CNN cell.

The circuit model of a very simple CNN array, a one-dimensional CNN array with three inner cells and two border cells, having the simplest interconnections, just one to each neighbor, and self-feedback, is shown in Fig. 15.4.

This circuit has been used sometimes to test the circuit robustness as well as for implementing the simplest propagating template. In addition to its own useful function, the CCD template became an ubiquitous CNN test circuit.

It is instructive to show the transient signals in the consecutive cells. Indeed, the time constant of the cell can be determined, approximately, from the measured delay time of the propagation along the whole line.

As an exercise, after reviewing the cell transient, we will determine the method of how to measure the cell time constant of a five-cell CNN (three cells plus the two border cells).

Five-cell (three cells plus border cells) CNN with a connected component detector (CCD) template:

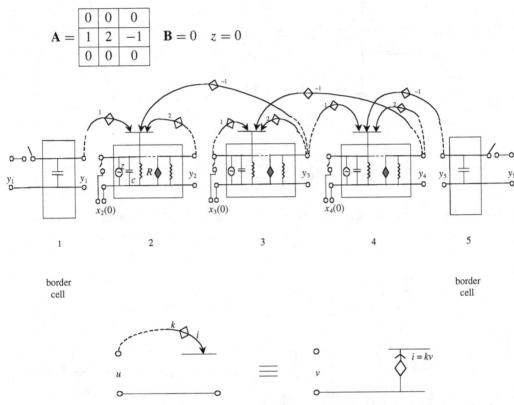

$$\mathbf{A} = \begin{array}{|c|c|c|} \hline 0 & 0 & 0 \\ \hline 1 & 2 & -1 \\ \hline 0 & 0 & 0 \\ \hline \end{array} \quad \mathbf{B} = 0 \quad z = 0$$

Fig. 15.4. The circuit model of a one-dimensional standard CNN with five cells (incl. two border cells).

The **B** template is zero, hence the input is omitted, the initial state is the only independent input information, the bias term is zero as well, and the feedback template is very simple: only a part of a border cell is shown, normally the border cell is the same as the intermediate cell.

The number of rows is 1, $m = 1$, the number of cells is five; we are not distinguishing here between border and inner cells, hence $n = 1, 2, 3, 4, 5$.

We show the signal transient of the circuit model for all the five cells ($m = 1, n = 1$; $m = 1, n = 2$; $m = 1, n = 3$; $m = 1, n = 4$; and $m = 1, n = 5$) in Fig. 15.5 (first five parts). There is a wave from left to right. An axonometric view of the signal transients for all the five cells is shown in the last part of Fig. 15.5.

Observing the cell signals, the fourth cell output reaches the positive saturation value about 1.6 (in terms of the time constant). Hence, if t_4^+ is the measured value of this time instant in an actual circuit, then the time constant is $t_4^+/1.6$.

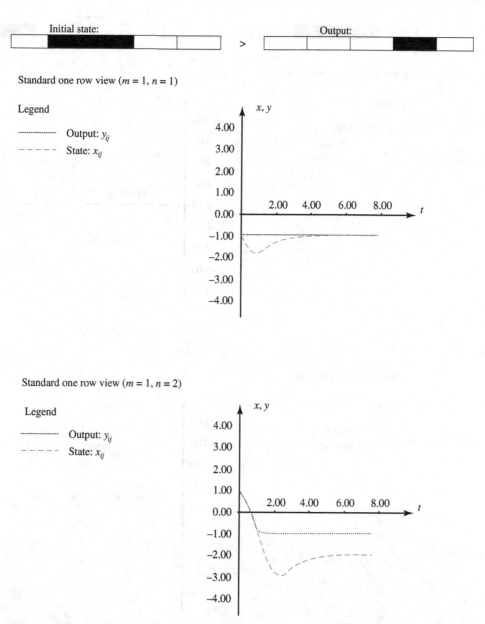

Fig. 15.5. Signal transient of the five cells (first two parts, see the consecutive parts on the next two pages).

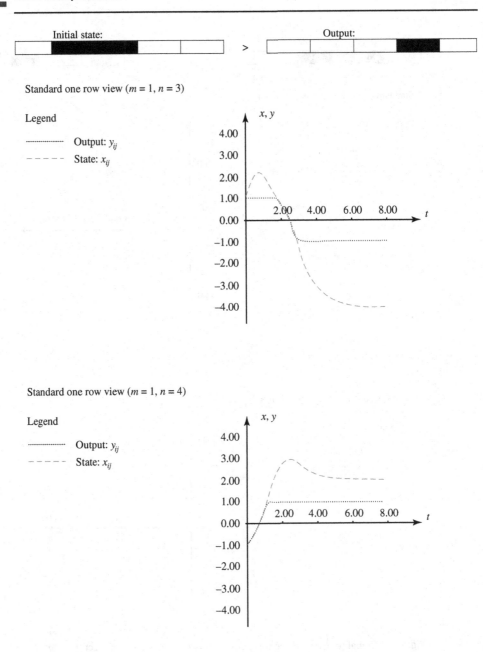

Fig. 15.5. Continued.

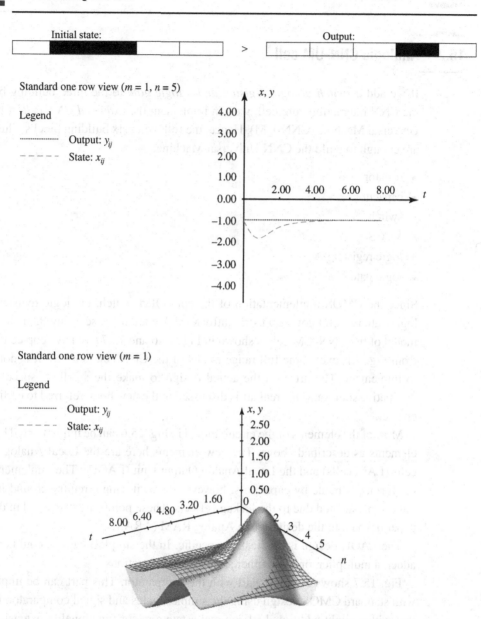

Fig. 15.5. Continued.

15.2   Analogic CNN-UM cell

If we add *a switch, a logic register, and a logic gate* to the three building blocks of the CNN interacting core cell, we can implement the *extended CNN cell* of the CNN Universal Machine (CNN-UM). Hence, the following six building blocks, plus wiring, are enough to build the CNN Universal Machine:

- resistor
- capacitor
- switch
- VCCS
- logic register
- logic gate

Since the CMOS implementation of the controlled switch, the logic register and the logic gate is well known and straightforward, we are not discussing them. The circuit model of the CNN-UM cell is shown in Figs 15.6 and 15.7 (we have copied them here from Fig. 9.1, except the full range model of the CNN cell is used). It is not difficult to implement. The art is in the actual design to make the smallest, speediest, least dissipative solution. This real art is discussed in the new book referred to earlier in this chapter.

Most of the elements of the circuit model in Fig. 15.6 can be implemented by CMOS elements as described above. The new elements here are the Local Analog Memory cells (LAM cells) and the Local Analog Output Unit (LAOU). The implementation of the former is made by capacitors, however the switching circuitry around it may be quite sophisticated due to the leakage effects. These points are discussed in detail in a paper devoted to the design of an Analog RAM (ARAM).[5]

The LAOU design is application specific. In the simplest case, it could contain an adder, a multiplier, or some other simple circuit functions.

Fig. 15.7 shows the logic part with the comparator. This part can be implemented with standard CMOS design using the simplest gates and signal comparator. It is clear that with a slight additional silicon real estate a major functionality extension can be made, fully parallel, for the whole array.

An up-to-date implementation[6] of such an extended cell in a 4096 processor cell CNN Universal Machine chip in a 64 × 64 configuration with optical input has the following main parameters:

Number of LAMs: 4
Number of LLMs: 4
Time constant in the linear domain: 200 nsec
Sphere of Influence, $r = 1$

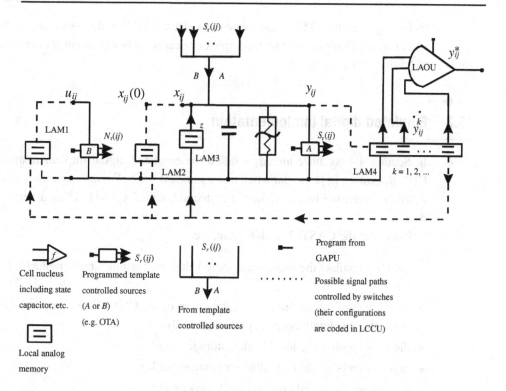

Fig. 15.6. The analog part of the analogic CNN universal cell.

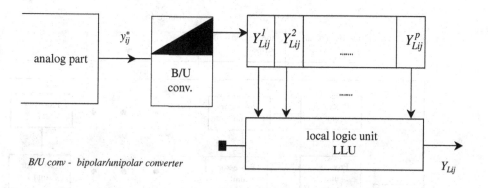

Fig. 15.7. The logic part of the CNN-UM cell with comparator.

Accuracy of the template elements: <1%

Range of the absolute value of the template elements: 4

Signal dynamics: 200 mV

Details of a former design are described in another paper.[7] The more sophisticated design with 64 × 64 extended cells cited above has a special calibration circuit and other tools to make it accurate and flexible enough. A new design, using 0.25 micron technology, can host 256×256 processing extended cells with optical input. A design with 128×128 processors with complex optical sensors has recently been completed (0.35 micron technology).

15.3   Emulated digital implementation

In Section 4.4 we have already studied the emulated digital implementation of the CNN dynamics, in particular when using standard DSPs. We have mentioned that later, in this chapter, we will introduce architecture, called CASTLE,[8] as a very efficient design.

Indeed, in the CASTLE architecture, we

- digitally emulate the analog and logic values by various word lengths $(1, 6, 12, \ldots$ bits),
- digitally emulate the numerical integration of the CNN spatio-temporal dynamics, using the absolutely necessary operators only,
- digitally emulate the local analog storage,
- digitally emulate some nonlinear operators, and
- implement the stored programmable processing.

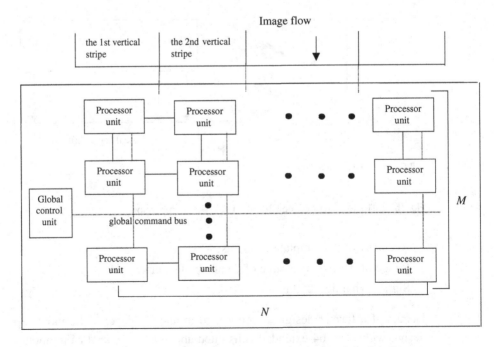

Fig. 15.8. M pieces of physical processors are processing a vertical stripe of the image.

Unlike in the DSP emulator discussed in Section 4.4 and shown in Fig. 4.10, here many (e.g. M) elementary emulated analogic processors process one vertical stripe of the image. The building block level schematic is shown in Fig. 15.8.

We suppose that the image flow is from top to bottom and after three horizontal lines are already read in, the next line of state variables is being read in a sequence following the move of the convolution window, one at a time (Fig. 15.9).

Since the number of parameters in the template is small, they can be stored in each processor. The state variables of the convolution terms in the sum related to the **A** template are read line by line and step by step as the convolution window is moving (see Fig. 15.9).

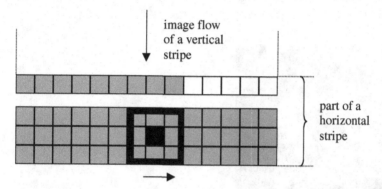

image flow
of a vertical
stripe

part of a
horizontal
stripe

Fig. 15.9. One horizontal stripe of 4 lines (in case of a 3 × 3 window) is stored on the CASTLE chip at a time. The downloading of the new state variable of an image is following the move of the convolution window. Updated values are shown in dark.

As to the division of labor among the M processors in a vertical stripe, many strategies can be organized. One possibility is the assignment of one processor per time step or one processor per stored row in the stripe.

Due to the fully custom-made design, as well as the scalable design, both in technology and in cascading many chips, the parameters are quite remarkable. One application area where this design is unique is the solution of 3D nonlinear spatio-temporal problems with propagating effects. This is the area where analogic chips, even if they are packed up on each other in a moderate number of layers in the third dimension, could not solve big and sophisticated problems, at present.

15.4   The visual microprocessor and its computational infrastructure

When the first microprocessor was designed and fabricated at Intel Corporation at the beginning of the 1970s, the goal was to make a calculator chip. The epoch-making microprocessor, however, proved to be a universal device. The key feature was:

stored programmability. For visual computing, especially when integrated with optical sensors, a single chip stored programmable device is the CNN-UM chip. The many types of "smart sensors" are, indeed, optical input CNN chips with fixed templates (or in some cases the templates are controllable). The qualitative breakthrough comes with stored programmability, resulting in the CNN-UM chips as visual microprocessors. The first, fully functional, optical input, analog I/O, fully stored programmable, *visual microprocessor*, with 64 × 64 processing cells, developed in Seville (cited earlier), is shown in Example 15.1.

EXAMPLE 15.1: One of the first fully functional visual microprocessors, code named cP 4000-O.

Similar to the classical microprocessors, however, stored programmability needs a complex computational infrastructure – high-level language, compiler, macro code, interpreter, operating system, physical code – to estimate the physical result and to interpret it for the human observer. The microprocessor development systems (sometimes called application development systems or chip prototyping systems) are doing just these jobs. For the visual microprocessors, the CNN Chip Prototyping System[9] (CCPS) has been developed.

The functional overview of the complete system is shown in Fig. 15.10. The CCPS consists of three parts:

- the *compiler and interpreter*,
- the *CNN Operating System* (COS) and *standard CNN Physical Interface* (CPI) hosted on a PC add-on board, called *CPS board* (CNN Prototyping System board), and
- *the Platform*, the only CNN-UM chip-dependent part, *hosting the actual visual microprocessor*.

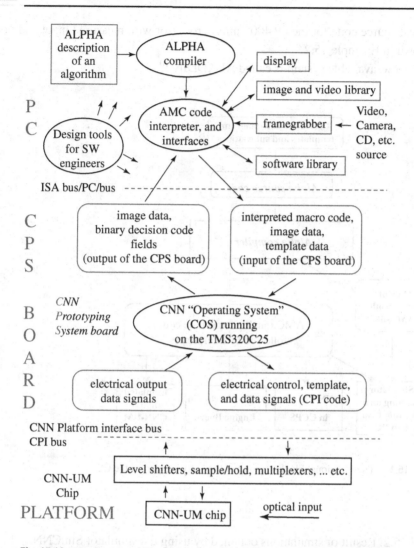

Fig. 15.10. The functional block diagram of the CNN Chip Prototyping System (CCPS).

Using this computational infrastructure, the visual microprocessors can be programmed: the programs can be downloaded on to the chips, as in the case of classical digital microprocessors. Hence, analogic CNN computer software can be developed without knowing how to make and embed the chips into the systems.

The functional block diagram of the software part (the first part of the CNN Chip Prototyping System) is shown in Fig. 15.11. Writing a program for an analogic CNN algorithm is as easy as writing a Basic program. We have used already parts of the Alpha language code in Chapter 9. When writing a complete source code for the closing operation (see Chapter 9 for details), the parameters of the actual visual microprocessor are stored in the Library (like the templates and subroutines). The actual source code for the cP 4000 microprocessor with measured input and output is shown in Example 15.2.

A new, available system is called ALADDIN.[10]

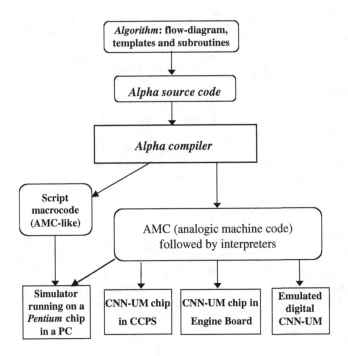

Fig. 15.11. The functional block diagram of the software part of the CCPS.

EXAMPLE 15.2: Result of simulations obtained by using the simulator SimCNN.

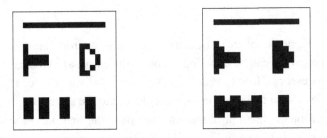

INPUT (image size: 20 x 22)   Result of the CLOSING operation

Table 15.1. *The Alpha source code and a measured input–output pair for the CLOSE operation.*

Alpha code	Description
`/* CLOSING.ALF */`	Performs the closing operation on a black and white image; developed for using on simulator;
`PROGRAM closing (in; out);`	*two logic names of parameters of the program are specified;*
`CONSTANT`	
`ONE = 1;`	*Definition of constants;*
`TWO = 2;`	
`WHITE = -1.0;`	
`TIME = 5;`	
`TIMESTEP = 0.5;`	
`ENDCONST;`	
`CHIP_SET simulator.eng;`	*Chip set definition section: the simulator.eng file serves as a system file for the compiler. It specifies the workspace;*
`A_CHIP`	*chip section starts here;*
`SCALARS`	*scalar variable definition section (chip);*
`IMAGES`	*image definition section (chip);*
`im1: BINARY;`	
`im2: BINARY;`	
`im3: BINARY;`	
`ENDCHIP;`	*end of chip section;*
`E_BOARD`	*board section starts here;*
`SCALARS`	*scalar variable definition section (board);*
`IMAGES`	*image definition section (board);*
`input: BINARY;`	
`output: BINARY; ENDBOARD;`	*end of board section;*
`OPERATIONS FROM closing.tms;`	definition of analog operation symbol table; the closing.tms file contains the template names of templates that will be used in the algorithm; *the core of the algorithm starts here;* *the specified templates will be used;*
`PROCESS closing;`	*time step specification;*
`USE (erosion, dilation);`	*loading the input image;*
`SwSetTimeStep (TIMESTEP);`	*displaying the input image;*
`HostLoadPic (in, input);`	
`HostDisplay (input, ONE);`	*loading the image from board to chip;* *executing the dilation template;*

Table 15.1. *Continued.*

Alpha code	Description

`im1:= input;`
`  dilation (im1, im1, im2, TIME,`
`    WHITE);`
`  erosion (im2, im2, im3, TIME,`
`    WHITE);`
	executing the erosion template using the result of "dilation";

`output:=im3;`	*the result is copied from chip to board;*
`HostDisplay (output, TWO);`	*displaying the output image;*
`ENDPROCESS;`	*the core of the algorithm ends here;*
`ENDPROG;`	*the end of the Alpha code;*

15.5 Computing power comparison

There are many different types and measures for computing power comparison. A simple type of comparison for the elementary template types (3×3) one-step convolution or **B** template, erosion–dilation or a_{00} and **B** template, and the Laplace operator or **A** and **B** templates). Clearly, the simple **B** template is the easiest one for a digital emulation and the last one is the most difficult.

In real life algorithms, several templates are to be computed to solve a complex problem. In Table 15.2 we show a type of comparison which considers two types of algorithms defined by a mix of different template types. Algorithm **A** has only one difficult template while Algorithm **B** has the same amount of simpler and more difficult templates. Clearly, in case of complex algorithms the computing power improvement is dramatic (about three orders of magnitude or more) in using similar technologies.

The task is to process an image of 128×128 pixels, including data transfer. If the task is complex, the data transfer time in the analogic CNN-UM chip is negligible. If the chip has an optical input with a capability of processing during image acquisition, the input data transfer time is even zero. This means, if the data downloading rate from a sensor is higher than the frame rate of the image flow, the problem is uncomputable with digital technologies using the standard method of downloading a snapshot and processing after it.

Table 15.2 shows that CNN computers offer an orders-of-magnitude speed advantage over conventional technology when the task is complex. There are also advantages in size, complexity, and power consumption. Very recent measurements on a 64×64 processor Visual Microprocessor show **an 8000 fold speed increase** over a 400 MHz Pentium when a **B** type algorithm with less erosions is used.

Table 15.2. *Comparison of digital and analogic image processing technology. Computing time in* μs *(data transfer included). Image size:* 128×128.

	Pentium II 0.25 μm, 400 MHz	TMS3206x 0.25 μm, 200 MHz 8 processors	CASTLE Emulated digital CNN 0.5 μm, 66 MHz 12 processors	CNN-UM chip 0.8 μm, τ_{CNN}: 250 ns	CNN-UM chip 0.5 μm τ_{CNN}: 200 ns
3×3 convolution					
B templates	1,000	427	32	$8/14.5^b$	$5.6/10.6^b$
$6\tau_{CNN}$ or 1 iteration		*2.34*	*31*	*125/69*	*89/47*
Erosion/dilation					
$a_{00} + \mathbf{B}$ templates	500	300	$2.7/32^a$	$8/14.5^b$	$5.6/10.6^b$
$6\tau_{CNN}$ or 1 iteration		*1.7*	*185/16^a*	*63/35*	*89/47*
Laplace					
$\mathbf{A} + \mathbf{B}$ templates	15,000	6,414	480	$10.3/16.8^b$	$6.5/11.5^b$
$15\tau_{CNN}$ or 15 iterations		*2.3*	*31*	*1456/892*	*2308/1304*
Algorithm A					
10 convolutions +	30,000	13,648	1,200	$40.3/46.8^b$	$18.5/23.5^b$
10 Erosions + 1 Laplace		*2.2*	*31*	*744/641*	*1622/1277*
Algorithm B					
10 convolutions +	165,000	77,788	5,440	$74/80.5^b$	$32/37^b$
10 Erosions + 10 Laplace		*2.12*	*31*	*2230/2050*	*5156/4459*

Notes: ^{a}binary/gray-scale.
^{b}optical input and electrical output/electrical input and output.
Figures *in italic* indicate the speed advantage compared to the Pentium II processor in the first column.

When an optical CNN computer is applied,[11] **B** templates can be computed with the speed of light. Then, the output data transfer is the only limiting factor in calculating the computing power.

16 CNN models in the visual pathway and the "Bionic Eye"

There is an on-going quest by engineers and specialists: compete with and imitate nature, especially some "smart" animals. Vision is one particular area computer engineers are interested in. Terms like "machine vision" and "computer vision" demonstrate this interest. Recently, modeling the living visual system has become a focus in science and technology. As the anatomy and physiology of the eye and other elements of the visual pathway are becoming more and more known, especially in the retinatopic part (Retina, Lateral Geniculate Nucleus (LGN), and the Visual Cortex), engineers have been trying to imitate these models. These studies have led to a better understanding of vision, overcoming the clear deficiencies of earlier, though useful, principles of computer vision before the mid 1980s.

Based on the ground-breaking studies of Barlow, Dowling, and Werblin on vertebrate retinas,[1,2,3] a very simple model[4] of the retina, a resistive grid, was implemented on silicon and demonstrated by simulation studies. In spite of the many "silicon retinas" built on this simple resistive grid model, it became clear that these models are too simple to explain even some practical qualitative effects related to higher-order spatio-temporal interactions in the retina. Attempts to address the more sophisticated retinal models led to descriptive[5] and network type[6] models. In the latter case, not only the retina, but a lot of other parts in the visual pathway had been first modeled by using a single paradigm: cellular neural networks. Soon after these results, the "Bionic Eye" architecture principle was invented,[7] which defines a formal framework of vision models and models of other spatio-temporal sensory modalities combined and implemented on the CNN Universal Machine. A tutorial description can be found in Werblin *et al.*[8] Recently, new discoveries[9,10,23] in retinal research have provided a deeper insight into spatio-temporal functions.

In this chapter, first, key notions, representations, and principles are introduced, which define the relation between studies of living visual organs and CNN models. Next, we show a couple of prototype CNN models for elementary functions in the visual pathway. In the third section, a simple qualitative CNN model of a "typical vertebrate retina" is introduced stressing the fact that, in general, this is an open field for research, and this mode is an "engineering understanding" of some facts

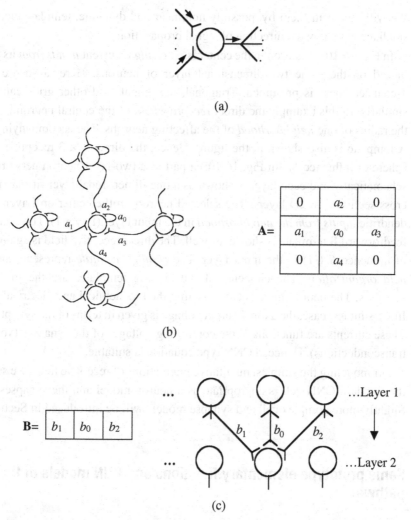

(a)

$$A= \begin{array}{|c|c|c|} \hline 0 & a_2 & 0 \\ \hline a_1 & a_0 & a_3 \\ \hline 0 & a_4 & 0 \\ \hline \end{array}$$

(b)

$$B= \begin{array}{|c|c|c|} \hline b_1 & b_0 & b_2 \\ \hline \end{array}$$

...Layer 1

...Layer 2

(c)

Fig. 16.1. A neuron with one axonal output and several dendritic synaptic inputs (a). A neuron network fragment with recurrent synapses and its **A** template (b). A one-dimensional two-layer neuron network with dendritic inputs from the preceding layer and its **B** template (c).

and measured results. A brief description of the "Bionic Eye" concept closes this chapter.

16.1   Receptive field organization, synaptic weights, and cloning template

A typical anatomical structure of the retina and the visual pathway is the receptive field organization. A schematic view of a receptive field organization is shown in Fig. 16.1. Fig. 16.1(a) shows a neuron with *one* axonal *output*, which may branch to several other neurons, and it has *several* dendritic *inputs*. The small gaps —⟨∘ denote the synapses.

We will represent them by, possibly nonlinear and dynamic, template elements. The small arrows show the direction of signal propagation.

In Fig. 16.1(b) a neuron in the center is *receiving* recurrent *inputs from* its *neighbors*, placed on the same two-dimensional layer of neurons. Here, a square grid with 4-connectedness is presumed. Triagonal, hexagonal, and other grids can be treated similarly. In this example the direct *receptive field* of the central neuron is defined by the radius of one *neighborhood* of the affecting neurons. The accompanying feedback **A** template is also shown in the figure. Hence, the direct 3×3 receptive field is the sphere of influence S_r. In Fig. 16.1(c) a part of a two-layer neuron network is shown schematically and each layer is shown as a one-dimensional layer (it may represent a cross section of a 2D layer). The selected neuron, in the center on Layer 2, *receives* dendritic *inputs from the neighborhood* in the input layer (Layer 1). The accompanying feedforward **B** template is shown, as well. The direct receptive field is again the sphere of influence $S_r(ij)$ in the input layer. The *cloning template* represents the *receptive field organization*. The elements of the cloning templates are the models of the synapses. The neuron models are reflecting the biochemical and electrical properties. In the simplest case, the axonal output voltage is given in terms of the synaptic currents. These currents are functions of the controlling voltages of the synapses (voltage gated transconductions). Hence, a CNN type equation is suitable.

For modeling the simplest qualitative interactions of receptive fields we suppose that the standard CNN cell is appropriate as a neuron model and the synapses are linear. Slightly more complex cell and synapse models will be introduced in Section 16.3.

16.2   Some prototype elementary functions and CNN models of the visual pathway

In Table 16.1, we list corresponding notions of neurobiology and the artificial CNN models related to spatio-temporal sensory information processing. This correspondence helps us in "translating" models of neuroanatomy and neurophysiology to CNN cloning templates.

For a one-dimensional (1D) model, the following cloning template is represented in Fig. 16.2

$$\mathbf{A} = \begin{array}{|c|c|c|} \hline x & x & x \\ \hline 3.1 & 2 & -2.5 \\ \hline x & x & x \\ \hline \end{array} \quad \mathbf{B} = \begin{array}{|c|c|c|} \hline x & x & x \\ \hline -0.7 & 0.5 & 1.5 \\ \hline x & x & x \\ \hline \end{array} \quad z = 1$$

It is clear from the figure that the elements of matrix **A** represent the feedback paths and the elements of **B** represent the feedforward path. The offset z is a local bias.

Table 16.1.

Neuroanatomy	CNN model	Notations/comments
neuron/cell	analog processor/cell	artificial living
signal : afferent : efferent	signal : input : output	
synapse	connection weight (template element)	
: inhibitory	: < 0	
: excitatory	: > 0	
: electrical	: without delay	
: chemical	: with delay	
signal path : feedforward/dendritic : feedback/recurrent	connection direction : feedforward : feedback	
stratum of neurons lamina/layer	layer	a 2D sheet of neurons/ processing elements
neural net	grid (regular geometrical grid); each node has the same local connectivity pattern	
receptive field with a given radius r	neighborhood of size r	each cell is locally connected within the neighborhood
receptive field organization (synapse strength pattern)	cloning template (CNNgene)	the local weight pattern
isotropy	all the off-center elements are the same in the cloning template	
isomorphism	space/plane invariance of the cloning template	the local weight pattern is the same everywhere

Table 16.1. *Continued.*

Neuroanatomy	CNN model	Notations/comments
center–surround antagonism	cloning template sign dichotomy	
ON-center OFF-surround	e.g. $\begin{bmatrix} - & - & - \\ - & + & - \\ - & - & - \end{bmatrix}$ $r = 1$	
OFF-center ON-surround	e.g. $\begin{bmatrix} + & + & + & + & + \\ + & - & - & - & + \\ + & - & - & - & + \\ + & - & - & - & + \\ + & + & + & + & + \end{bmatrix}$ $r = 2$	
tonic or phasic processing	sensitive to intensity values or intensity value changes	responsive to slow or fast input changes/low-pass or high-pass filtering
orientation	line or object position direction on a still image	
direction	direction of motion of an object in a moving scene	
orientation selectivity map	orientation selectivity map	
directional sensitivity map	directional sensitivity map	
"synapse on"	"effect to"	

The triad synapse action

The arrangement of the triad synapse is well known in neurobiology.[11] Its function is to sense changes in time. The arrangement is shown in Fig. 16.3. In the simplest model, the inhibitory interneuron, in the indirect path of signal transmission, introduces a delayed signal with sign reversal. The template realizing this action, with a unit time delay, is as follows.

$$\mathbf{A} = [0] \quad \mathbf{A}^\tau = [0] \quad \tau = 1.0$$

$$\mathbf{B} = \begin{array}{|c|c|c|} \hline 0 & 0 & 0 \\ \hline 0 & b_0 & b \\ \hline 0 & 0 & 0 \\ \hline \end{array} \quad \mathbf{B} = \begin{array}{|c|c|c|} \hline 0 & 0 & 0 \\ \hline 0 & -b_0 & 0 \\ \hline 0 & 0 & 0 \\ \hline \end{array} \quad z = 0$$

On the right-hand side of Fig. 16.3 an input signal and a corresponding output signal are shown. It shows clearly how changes in time are detected.

If the delay is not ideal but smooth, due to a first-order capacitive delay with a finite time constant, qualitatively the same task is solved.

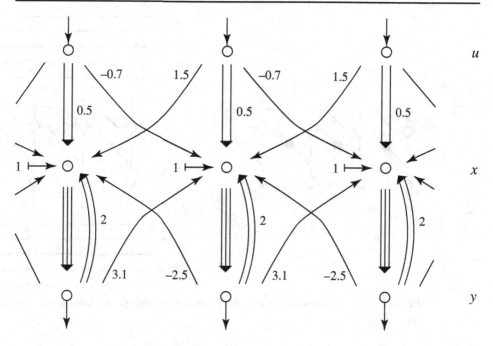

Fig. 16.2. Structure of a CNN model.

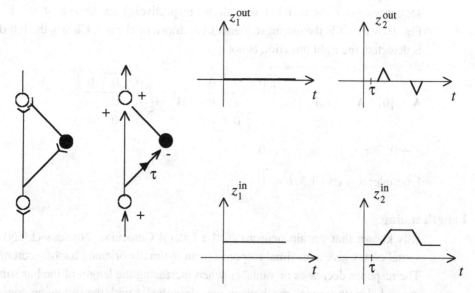

Fig. 16.3. (a) The triad synapse with living neurons. (b) The triad synapse model and its responses to two different input signals.

Directional selectivity

Directional selectivity is not a single-cell feature in the nervous system. Following its neuronal organization,[12] we have translated this architecture into a CNN architecture

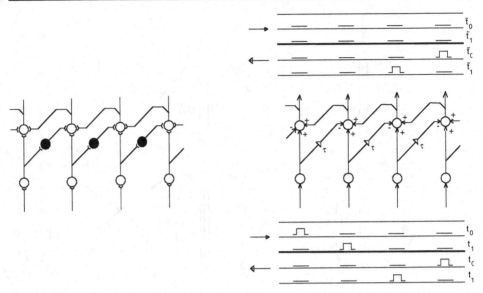

Fig. 16.4. (a) Direction-selective neuronal connection scheme. (b) Artificial neural representation of (a).

shown in Fig. 16.4. Putting reasonable parameters into the nonzero template elements, the template below was able to demonstrate the directional selectivity. The two input sequences (to right and left directions, respectively) are shown at the bottom of Fig. 16.4(b) while the output sequences are drawn on the top. Clearly the left direction is detected, the right direction is not.

$$\mathbf{A} = [0] \quad \mathbf{A}^\tau = [0] \quad \mathbf{B} = \begin{array}{|c|c|c|} \hline 0 & 0 & 0 \\ \hline 0 & a & b \\ \hline 0 & 0 & 0 \\ \hline \end{array} \quad \mathbf{B}^\tau = \begin{array}{|c|c|c|} \hline 0 & 0 & 0 \\ \hline -c & 0 & 0 \\ \hline 0 & 0 & 0 \\ \hline \end{array}$$

$z = 0; \quad \tau = 1; \quad a, b, c > 0$

Example: $a = c = 1.5, b = 1$

Length tuning

It is known that certain neurons in the Lateral Geniculate Nucleus (LGN) and the visual cortex give a maximal response to an optimally oriented bar of a certain length. The response decreases or vanishes when increasing the length of the bar stimulus. A general "length tuning" mechanism was described[12] with the following concept. In a bigger (5×5, 7×7, etc.) receptive field or radius of sphere of influence, a cell receives a moderate (say unity) excitatory (positive) stimulus from the near neighbor cell and a bigger inhibitory (negative) stimulus from a distant neighborhood. In addition, if there is a white spot in the center, the detection should also be prohibited. In this way all bars will be detected which are smaller than or equal to a length of $2r^+ + 1$, where r^+

is the neighborhood radius in a given direction with positive synapse weights. We also suppose that the negative weights are properly tuned to prohibit detection of longer bars. In the case of detecting bars in the basic directions (vertical, horizontal, and the two diagonals), the template shown in Fig. 16.5 performs the job.

$$A = [0]; \quad B = \begin{array}{|c|c|c|c|c|} \hline -3 & 0 & -3 & 0 & -3 \\ \hline 0 & 1 & 1 & 1 & 0 \\ \hline -3 & 1 & h & 1 & -3 \\ \hline 0 & 1 & 1 & 1 & 0 \\ \hline -3 & 0 & -3 & 0 & -3 \\ \hline \end{array} \quad z = -1; \quad x_{ij} = 0$$

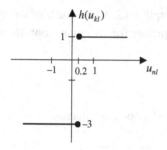

Fig. 16.5.

An input and output picture is shown on Example 16.1.

EXAMPLE 16.1: Length tuning. Detecting horizontal, vertical and diagonal bars with length not longer than three pixels.

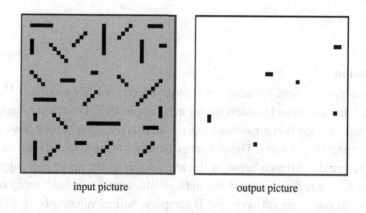

input picture   output picture

Orientation selectivity

Orientation selectivity is a well-known function in the visual cortex.[13] This means that light or dark bars with a given orientation will be detected. The uncoupled cloning template below detects bars with a $-45°$ slope. The geometry of the positive terms in the **B** template determines the enhancement of the derivative of the state variable and the positive feedback brings the values to black and white. The values of the template elements are determined based on the DP Plot. As a default, the initial state is zero.

$$
\mathbf{A} = \begin{array}{|c|c|c|} \hline 0 & 0 & 0 \\ \hline 0 & 2 & 0 \\ \hline 0 & 0 & 0 \\ \hline \end{array}
\qquad
\mathbf{B} = \begin{array}{|c|c|c|} \hline 0.25 & 0 & 0 \\ \hline 0 & 0 & 0 \\ \hline 0 & 0 & 0.25 \\ \hline \end{array}
\qquad z = -1
$$

An input–output picture pair is shown in Example 16.2. It is clear how easily we can hide information read out quickly by a CNN template (or, in a more sophisticated case, by analogic CNN algorithms).

EXAMPLE 16.2: Orientation selectivity. Bars with $-45°$ slope are detected.

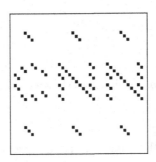

input picture   output picture

A simple visual illusion

Many, even complex, visual illusions can be reproduced via CNN models.[14,15] One of the simplest is the arrowhead illusion shown in Example 16.3. The effect is simple. On the input image we see two arrowhead pairs, one is converging (upper row) and the other is diverging (lower row). The distances between the arrowheads are the same. Still, we perceive the distance between the arrowheads in the upper row bigger than in the lower row. Keeping in mind the antagonistic center-surround receptive field organization, an on-center off-surround **B** template will eliminate pixels with more dense positive pixels nearby. Hence, it is not surprising that, if we put this type of **B** template in an uncoupled cloning template, the arrowhead illusion will be manifested, as shown on the output picture of Example 16.3.

$$
A = \begin{array}{|c|c|c|}
\hline
0 & 0 & 0 \\
\hline
0 & 1.3 & 0 \\
\hline
0 & 0 & 0 \\
\hline
\end{array}
\quad
B = \begin{array}{|c|c|c|c|c|}
\hline
-0.1 & -0.1 & -0.1 & -0.1 & -0.1 \\
\hline
-0.1 & -0.1 & -0.1 & -0.1 & -0.1 \\
\hline
-0.1 & -0.1 & 1.3 & -0.1 & -0.1 \\
\hline
-0.1 & -0.1 & -0.1 & -0.1 & -0.1 \\
\hline
-0.1 & -0.1 & -0.1 & -0.1 & -0.1 \\
\hline
\end{array}
\quad z = 0
$$

Needless to say, many other on-center off-surround-cloning templates can produce the same effect.

Using separate layers for the three colors, red, green, and blue (RGB), the basic single-opponent and double-opponent effects of color vision can be modeled[16] as well as some more complex phenomena.[17]

EXAMPLE 16.3: The arrowhead illusion. Input picture (a) and the simulated perceived illusion as an output (b).

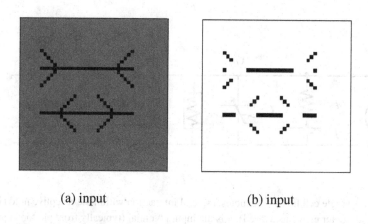

(a) input   (b) input

16.3   A simple qualitative "engineering" model of a vertebrate retina

In what follows, using a multi-layer CNN model, we present a qualitative model of a vertebrate retina. This is an "engineering" model compared to a neurobiology model. Still, it reflects many of the earlier and recent findings related to morphologically and physiologically faithful retinal models.[2,3,8,9,10,18,19,20,21,23] The aim and scope of this section is to make simpler CNN models with the same qualitative effects as measured in some vertebrate retinas.

First, we will introduce cell, synapse, and receptive field organization (template) prototypes as "Lego" elements for retina models.

The cell prototype

We usually use a simplified model which is able to take into account the most important physiology parameters. This is a first-order model of a CNN layer (Fig. 16.6):

$$C\dot{x}_{ij} = -\frac{1}{R}x_{ij} + \sum B_{ij,kl}u_{kl} + \sum D_{ij,kl}g(x_{ij}, x_{kl}, y_{kl}, u_{kl}, E_{revkl}) + z_{ij}$$

$$\tau = RC; \quad z_{ij} = I_L + \frac{E_r}{R} \tag{16.1}$$

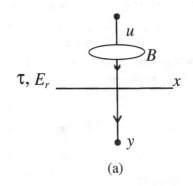

(a)

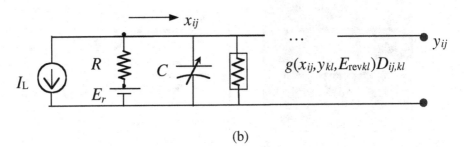

(b)

Fig. 16.6. (a) A single cell layer. ⊕ denotes a spatial interaction within the receptive field (**B** is a matrix with off-center elements as well), u is the input potential (typically from photoreceptors), $x(x_{ij})$ is the cell membrane potential, y is the output. (b) A simple core cell electrical equivalent circuit.

In this simplest case, we suppose an input receptive field ($S_r(ij)$) represented by a **B** template. All the other interactions are included in the last term (D). τ is the time constant, the product of the membrane capacitor (C) and the membrane resistance (R), I_L is the leakage current, E_r is the resting potential, E_{rev} is the reverse potential, and x_{ij} is the membrane potential. The last term contains a sum of voltage controlled/gated transconductances (VCCS: voltage controlled current sources). In this term, we take into account the voltage controlled interactions coming from the same and other layers. In the output equation, in its simpler form

$$y_{ij} = f(x_{ij}) \tag{16.2}$$

$f(\cdot)$ may be a simple linear term (e.g. $y_{ij} = x_{ij}$) or it may also be the various forms of the ubiquitous sigmoid functions. The unity gain threshold characteristics is:

$$y_{ij} = \tfrac{1}{2}(|x_{ij} + 1| - |x_{ij} - 1|) \tag{16.3}$$

By playing with a constant coefficient and changing the saturating signal levels, many different operation modes can be tuned in. In what follows we will use $y_{ij} = x_{ij}$.

As default, we use the following relative units: mV, msec, pA, GΩ, micron, pF.

Some synapse types (S)

The synapse conductance functions in the term $g(\cdot)$ are functions of the synapse voltage v; $i = g(v)$ or $i = g(v)(E_{\mathrm{rev}} - v)$. The form of $g(\cdot)$ could be linear or nonlinear. A few of these are shown in Fig. 16.7.

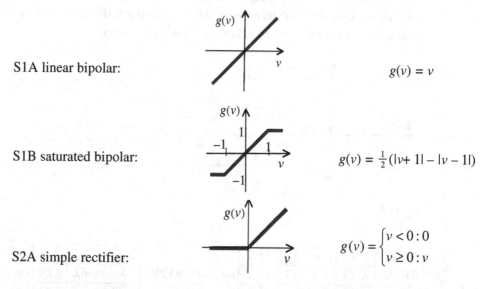

S1A linear bipolar: $g(v) = v$

S1B saturated bipolar: $g(v) = \tfrac{1}{2}(|v+1| - |v-1|)$

S2A simple rectifier: $g(v) = \begin{cases} v < 0 : 0 \\ v \geq 0 : v \end{cases}$

Fig. 16.7.

The S2A type rectifier curve can be shifted into the g or v direction (S2B).

To get the total synapse contribution, we have to multiply the synapse conductance function $g(\cdot)$ with the constant synapse weight. This synapse weight is defined as a template element, or a synaptic receptive field organization.

Receptive field organization types (RF)

The simplest receptive field organization, used mainly for a feedforward transfer to a layer either from an input (photoreceptor) or from a preceding layer output, is a **central**

gain type with a gain value G_0.

RF0:
0	0	0
0	G_0	0
0	0	0

$\cdot g$

A receptive field organization with **Gaussian weight** distribution of the weights in space is given as

RF1:
$G(\sqrt{2})$	$G(1)$	$G(\sqrt{2})$
$G(1)$	$G(0)$	$G(1)$
$G(\sqrt{2})$	$G(1)$	$G(\sqrt{2})$

$\cdot g$ where $G(p) = He^{-(p/\sigma)^2}$

p is the distance of the given cell from the center cell. RF1 is mainly used in interlayer feedforward interactions; σ is a parameter, its default value is 1.

Diffusion-type receptive field organization has spatial weighting defined below. This is mainly used in intra-layer interactions defining diffusion, by an antagonistic, OFF-center ON-surround receptive field. We use the following notation for a layer with diffusion-type receptive field of λ diffusion parameter.

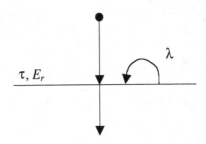

Fig. 16.8.

RF2A:
$\lambda^2/3$	$\lambda^2/3$	$\lambda^2/2$
$\lambda^2/3$	$-8\lambda^2/3$	$\lambda^2/2$
$\lambda^2/3$	$\lambda^2/3$	$\lambda^2/2$

$\cdot g$ or   RF2B:
$\lambda/2$	λ	$\lambda/2$
λ	-6λ	λ
$\lambda/2$	λ	$\lambda/2$

$\cdot g$

If the sign of the central element in RF2B is positive, (RF2C) we can generate trigger waves. As a default, we use RF2A.

General types of ON-center OFF-surround or OFF-center ON-surround receptive field organizations, even with larger radius (5×5, 7×7, etc.) or with other sign values can also be defined term by term.

In general, a receptive field organization is used in defining the templates.

Multilayer CNN for receptive field interactions

Modeling a retina, we need more layers. A transfer operator T_{pq} represents an interaction from the pth layer output to the qth layer state. This means we have a *state equation for the qth layer* in the same form as in (16.1), however, taking into account the interactions from other layers as well

$$C^q \dot{x}_{ij}^q = -\frac{1}{R^q} x_{ij}^q + \sum_{\substack{p=p_1,p_2,\ldots \\ p \neq q}} T_{pq} * y_p + \sum_{k=1,2,\ldots} T_{qq}^k * y_q + z^q \tag{16.4}$$

where the interlayer transfer template operator T_{pq} could come from several other layers ($p = p_1, p_2, \ldots$) and there may be several different intra-layer template operators, T_{qq}^k ($k = 1, 2, \ldots$), e.g. diffusion operators. The term z in the simple case is $z = I_L + E_r/R$.

If T_{pq} is an inter-layer transfer from one layer to another, then T_{pq} is typically a **B** template

$$T_{\substack{pq \\ p \neq q}} * y_p = \sum_{kl \in S_r^p(ij)} B_{ij,kl}^{pq} y_{kl}^p \tag{16.5}$$

where $S_r^p(ij)$ is the sphere of influence in the pth layer. If the pth layer is the generic input layer, then we get

$$T_{\substack{pq \\ p \neq q}} * u = \sum_{kl \in S_r^u(ij)} B_{ij,kl}^u u_{kl} \tag{16.6}$$

where $S_r^u(ij)$ is the sphere of influence in the generic input layer (u).

If T_{pq}^k is an intra-layer transfer, then T_{qq}^k is an **A** template

$$T_{qq}^k * y_q = \sum_{\substack{kl \in S_r^{kq}(ij) \\ k=1,2,\ldots}} A_{ij,kl}^{kq} y_{kl}^q \tag{16.7}$$

where A^{kq} is the kth **A** template in the qth layer and $S_r^{kq}(ij)$ is the sphere of influence in the qth layer for the kth **A** template.

Hence, as an example, a simple multilayer receptive field interaction prototype could be as follows (Fig. 16.9).

Suppose that RF0 is defined by linear synapses with $G_0 = 2$, RF1 is defined by linear synapses with $H = 1$ and $\sigma = 1$. RF0 and RF1 are **B** templates, representing inter-layer interactions. RF2B is an intra-layer interaction, a *diffusion-type* **A** template with $\lambda = 1.5$.

The following templates define these receptive field organizations:

RF0: $B = B_0 = $

0	0	0
0	2	0
0	0	0

RF1: $B = B_1 = $

0.13	0.37	0.13
0.37	1	0.37
0.13	0.37	0.13

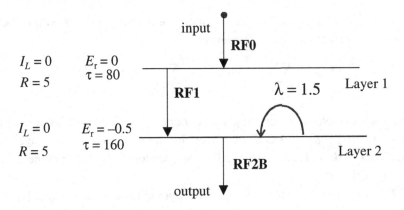

Fig. 16.9. A receptive field interaction prototype.

$$\text{RF1: } A = A_1 = \begin{array}{|c|c|c|} \hline 0.75 & 1.5 & 0.75 \\ \hline 1.5 & -9 & 1.5 \\ \hline 0.75 & 1.5 & 0.75 \\ \hline \end{array}$$

Hence, for the two layers the cloning templates are:

Layer 1:

$$A = [0], \quad B = B_0, \quad z = I_L + E_r/R = 0$$

Note that in the state equation $\tau = 80$.

Layer 2:

$$A = A_1, \quad B = B_1, \quad z = I_L + E_r/R = -0.1$$

In this state equation $\tau = 160$.
Let us now turn to some retinal models.

The structure of a prototype retinal model

Following the on-going and recent research results on retinal modeling[3,8,9,10,18,19,20,21,23], we condense the structure of the model into a one-dimensional cross section of the two-dimensional (2D) layers in Fig. 16.10 (also showing, in the middle, the branching of signal flow and later their converging).

The upper part of the model represents the so-called outer plexiform layer (OPL), the lower part the inner plexiform layer (IPL).

A more structured morphological model of the ON path using two types of amacrine cells is shown in Fig. 16.11.

A multilayer CNN model is shown in Fig. 16.12.

In this case, $E_r = 0$, and τ is controlled holding $R = 1$. Based on the values of the

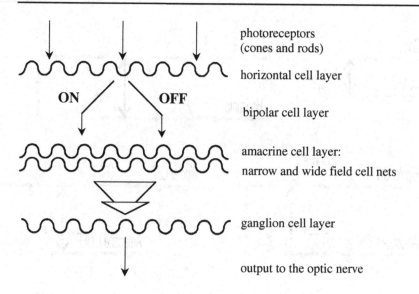

Fig. 16.10. A global structure of a retina model.

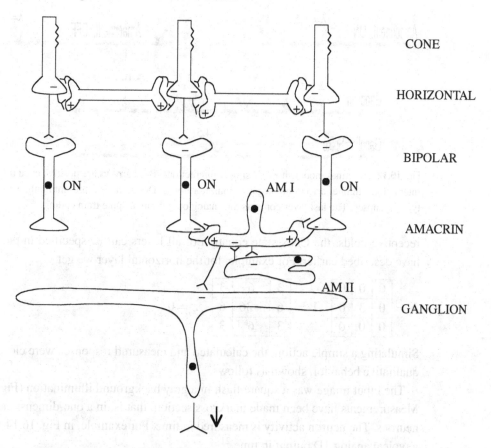

Fig. 16.11. An approximate interaction mechanism of the ON-path from a cone to a ganglion cell.

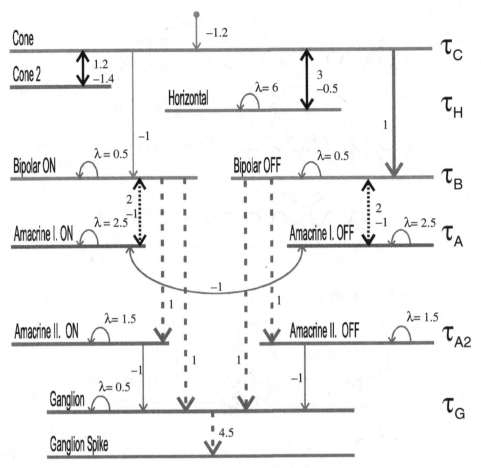

Fig. 16.12. A retinal model showing simple interactions. Bold arrows are positive excitatory interactions, thinner arrows are negative inhibitory ones. Dotted lines represent nonlinear (rectifier type) synapses. The last layer converts the analog output into a spike train coding.

receptive fields, the CNN state equation of all layers can be specified in the way we have described earlier. For example, for the horizontal layer we get

$$\mathbf{A} = \begin{array}{|c|c|c|} \hline 0 & 0 & 0 \\ \hline 0 & 3 & 0 \\ \hline 0 & 0 & 0 \\ \hline \end{array} \quad \mathbf{B} = \begin{array}{|c|c|c|} \hline 3 & 6 & 3 \\ \hline 6 & -36 & 6 \\ \hline 3 & 6 & 3 \\ \hline \end{array} \quad z = 0$$

Simulating a simple action, the calculated and measured responses were close in their qualitative behavior, shown as follows.

The input image was a square flash in a gray background illumination (Fig. 16.13). Measurements have been made in a cross section, that is, in a one-dimensional line of neurons. The neuron activity is measured in time. For example, in Fig. 16.14 we show a typical analog 1D output in time.[21]

Using the model of Fig. 16.12, two typical outputs, a two-tagged parameter setting,

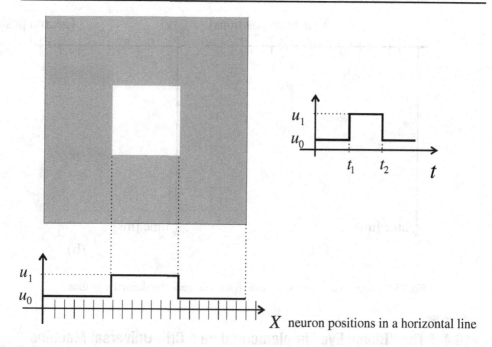

Fig. 16.13. The input is a square flash.

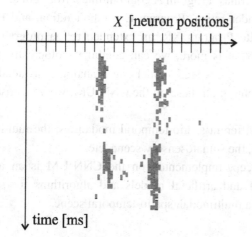

Fig. 16.14. 1D dynamics map: intensity is proportional to the darkness.

are shown in Fig. 16.15. Fig. 16.15(a) shows a derivative in space, and Fig. 16.15(b) shows a derivate in time. These results were in good agreement with the measurements.

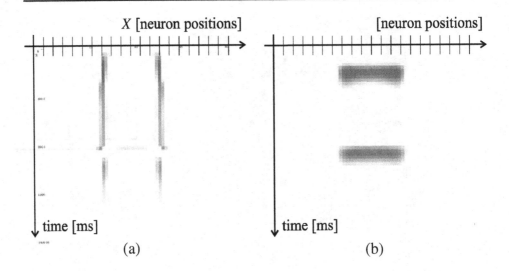

Fig. 16.15. Measured responses (a): derivative in space (b): derivative in time.

16.4   The "Bionic Eye" implemented on a CNN Universal Machine

The CNN Universal Machine (CNN-UM) architecture is ideal in implementing many spatio-temporal neuromorphic models. In a way, we can program, even stored program a CNN-UM to mimic different retinas. Program A could mimic a frog retina, Program B could mimic a tiger salamander retina, Program C a rabbit retina, and Program D an eagle retina. We can write Program XR, an extended retina program which could combine these retinas. What is more, we can combine biologically faithful, neuromorphic models, biologically inspired models, and analogic artificial image processing algorithms. Implementing all these on the CNN-UM, we are constructing a "Bionic Eye".[22]

Moreover we can combine different spatio-temporal modalities: the multispectral visual scene, the auditory scene, the somatosensory scene, etc.

Indeed the Bionic Eye concept implemented on the CNN-UM is an algorithmic combination of biological and artificial models and algorithms for sensing–computing–recognizing task in a multimodal, spatio-temporal scene.

Notes

1 Introduction

1 P. Saffo, "Sensors: the next wave of Infotech revolution," Institute for the Future, Menlo Park, 1999.

2 L.O. Chua and L. Yang, "Cellular Neural Networks: Theory and Applications," *IEEE Transactions on Circuits and Systems*, vol. 35, pp. 1257–1290, 1988.

3 T. Roska and L.O. Chua, "The CNN Universal Machine: An analogic array computer," *IEEE Transactions on Circuits and Systems*, Series II: Analog and Digital Signal Processing, vol. 40, pp. 163–173, 1993.

4 S. Espejo, R. Domínguez-Castro, G. Liñán, and A. Rodríguez-Vázquez, "A 64×64 CNN universal chip with analog and digital I/O," *Proc. 5th Int. Conf. on Electronics, Circuits and Systems* (ICECS-98), Lisbon, Portugal, pp. 203–206, 1998.

5 Á. Csurgay, W. Porod, and C. Lent, "Signal processing with near-neighbor-coupled time-varying quantum dot arrays," *IEEE Transactions on Circuits and Systems*, Series I, vol. 47, August 2000.

6 L.O. Chua, "Molecular devices, systems and computers," *Proc. IEEE International Symposium on Circuits and Systems*, ISCAS 2000, Geneva, 2000.

7 T. Roska, Á. Zarándy, S. Zöld, P. Földesy, and P. Szolgay, "The Computational Infrastructure of Analogic CNN Computing – Part I: The CNN-UM Chip Prototyping System," *IEEE Transactions on Circuits and Systems*, Series I, Special Issue on Bio-Inspired Processors and Cellular Neural Networks for Vision, vol. 46, pp. 261–268, 1999.

8 T. Roska, "Computer-sensors: spatial-temporal computers for analog array signals, dynamically integrated with sensors," *J. VLSI Signal Processing Systems*, vol. 23, pp. 221–237, 1999.

2 Notations, definitions, and mathematical foundation

1 There will be, in further chapters, more general nonlinearities.

2 P. Hartman, ODE, Birkhauser, 1982, p. 8.

3 The signal flow graph is a classical signal representation tool which is used in a slightly different context but with similar objectives. In Fig. 2.27, the bold edges coincide exactly with the classical definition of a signal flow graph. However, the light edges should not be interpreted as a part of the classical signal flow graph, but rather as a mnemonic aid for showing the degree of influence of the output of the center cell on its neighbors.

3 Characteristics and analysis of simple CNN templates

1 In the following, unless otherwise stated, we use this type of boundary condition.

2 Some common sources of noise include camera reflections and counting statistics in sensors, such as image detectors, due to a small number of incident photons, electrons, etc.

3 The *finiteness* property follows from the piecewise linearity of the shifted DP plot.

4 Courtesy of Professor Angel Rodríguez-Vázquez, from the University of Seville, Spain.

5 For simplicity so far, no boundary conditions have been specified in the previous examples since the features of interest (e.g., edges, corners, thresholds, etc.) are *local* and *static* (do not move) in nature, and hence are independent (except for the boundary cells) of the boundary conditions. The SHIFT template is our first example where it is essential to specify the boundary conditions.

6 The word "morphology" is of Greek origin meaning "form" or "structure." It is a branch of biology concerned with the study of the "shapes" and "structures" of living organisms and systems. It is used in image processing applications to denote any transformation or operation concerned with the "geometrical" shape and structure of patterns. The mathematical foundation is called mathematical morphology.

4 Simulation of the CNN dynamics

1 To run a simulation on the CANDY system, we use the graphical user interface called VisMouse Platform and the SimCNN multilayer CNN simulator.

2 Generally, $f(\cdot)$ may be any continuous function. In the literature, the most frequently used DTCNNs are using the two types of $f(\cdot)$ just introduced (being either a hard limiter or a unity gain piecewise linear saturation function).

5 Binary CNN characterization via Boolean functions

1 We have chosen here $\{0, 1\}$ instead of $\{-1, 1\}$ as our binary codes in order to exploit directly the immense literature and theory on Boolean functions, which are almost always couched in terms of "zeros" and "ones."

2 In order to appreciate how large the number Ω is, compare it to the following universal benchmarks:

Age of the universe $= 10^{30}$ picoseconds

Mass of the universe (calculated in units of mass of a hydrogen atom) $= 10^{80}$

Volume of the universe (calculated as a sphere with a diameter of 10 thousand million light-years) $= 10^{84}$ cm^3

3 Note that $\mathcal{C}(\mathbf{A}^0, \mathbf{B}, z)$ may generate non-Boolean maps as well.

4 This reclassification task is a *subjective* exercise since not everyone may agree on whether a particular pixel in fuzzy cases is a corner, or not a corner.

6 Uncoupled CNNs: unified theory and applications

1 Indeed, we will see later that even simple third-order circuits (containing two capacitors and an inductor) having only three equilibria can exhibit extremely complex oscillatory and non-periodic behaviors, called *chaos*.

2 This theorem can be easily extended to space-dependent CNNs as well.

3 The signum function is defined by:

$$\begin{aligned}\text{sgn}(x) &= 1, \quad \text{if } x > 0 \\ &= -1, \quad \text{if } x < 0\end{aligned}$$

4 Although Eq. (6.2) holds for both the *bistable* and the *monostable* cases, in the monostable case Eq. (6.2) can be replaced by the simpler formula

$$y_{ij}(\infty) = \text{sgn}[w_{ij} - (a_{00} - 1)]$$

which is independent of the initial state $x_{ij}(0)$.

5 We use the term *local* Boolean function to emphasize that each one of the 2^{512} *Boolean functions* constitutes a *complete set of local rules*.

6 The symbols **a**, **x**, and b in Eq. (6.45) are not related to the CNN templates. They are chosen here in order to conform to the common usage in the Boolean algebra literature.

7 To construct another example of a Boolean function of two variables which is not linearly separable, simply take the logic complement of β, i.e., change the pixels in Fig. 6.13(b) from "black" to "white," and vice versa. It is easy to verify that the XOR Boolean function β_4 and its complement $\beta_5 = \bar{\beta}_4$ are the only two Boolean functions of two variables which are not linearly separable.

8 To avoid clutter, we will often revert to a single-index notation u_i, instead of u_{kl}, whenever the context is obvious.

9 It is essential to use the CNN truth table here, *not* the Boolean truth table. A very common mistake, which the authors themselves have occasionally committed, is to apply the Boolean truth table directly to equations or numerics.

10 An inspection of the CNN template catalog will reveal that most **B** templates are sparse, usually less than five, in which case Eq. (78) consists only 32 linear inequalities.

11 Observe that the minimal truth table of each minterm CNN contains exactly one black pixel surrounded by a sea of white pixels. Since the minimal truth table for nine Boolean variables has 512 pixels, there are 512 distinct minterm CNNs, each one characterized by the location of its one and only *black* pixel.

12 In actual realization, it would be necessary to sandwich an interface circuitry for storing the output of each CNN over a time interval equal to at least the settling time of each CNN before applying it to the next CNN in the "chain." While this hard-wired CNN XOR can be mass produced as an ASIC (Application Specific Integrated Circuit) and sold as a CNN logic array building block, it would be more practical to "program" a CNN universal chip (to be presented in Chapter 7) if the application calls for only a small quantity of this component.

13 We have deleted the AND operators $\wedge$ in the input product terms $u_1^{\alpha_{k_1}} \wedge u_2^{\alpha_{k_2}} \wedge \cdots \wedge u_l^{\alpha_{k_{kl}}} \wedge \cdots \wedge u_9^{\alpha_{k_{N_9}}}$ in Eq. (6.85) to avoid clutter.

14 The minimal truth table for each maxterm CNN contains exactly one white pixel surrounded by a sea of black pixels. Clearly, for nine Boolean variables, there are 512 distinct maxterm CNNs, each one characterized by the location of the one and only "white" pixel in the minimal truth table.

7 Introduction to the CNN universal machine

1 E.R. Daugherty, Introduction to morphological image processing, SPIE, 1992.

2 A function b defined by weights $w_1, w_2, \ldots, w_9$ and is denoted by $b(w_1, w_2, \ldots, w_9), z$.

3 K.R. Crounse, E.L. Fung, and L.O. Chua, "Efficient implementation of neighborhood logic for cellular automata via the cellular neural network universal machine," *IEEE Trans.*, CAS-I, Vol. 44, 1997, pp. 355–361.

8 Back to basics: Nonlinear dynamics and complete stability

1 For a rigorous statement and proof of the Poincaré–Bendixon theorem, see P. Hartman, *Ordinary Differential Equations*, p. 151.

2 F. Zou and J.A. Nossek, "A chaotic attractor with cellular neural network," *IEEE Trans. on Circuits and Systems*, Vol. 38, no. 7, 1991, pp. 811–812.

3 F. Zou, G. Seiler, A.J. Schuler, B. Eppinger and J.A. Nossek, "Experimental confirmation of the lady's shoe attractor," *IEEE Trans. on Circuits and Systems*, Vol. 39, no. 10, 1992, pp. 844–846.

4 An equilibrium point $\mathbf{x}_Q$ of $\dot{x} = f(x)$ is said to be *isolated* if and only if there are no other equilibrium points in a sufficiently small neighborhood of $\mathbf{x}_Q$.

5 In the nonlinearity f we have been using, we can choose $\theta = 0$, since $f(-\infty) = -1, f(\infty) = 1$. For the sake of generality, the hypothesis on f does not require that the values of f lie between -1 and 1.

6 J.P. LaSalle, "An invariant principle in the theory of stability," in J.K. Hale and J.P. Salle, Editors, *Differential Equations and Dynamical Systems*, Academic Press, 1967.

7 A set $M \subset R^n$ is called an invariant set of Eq. (8.10) if any trajectory starting from a point $x_0 \in M$ at $t = 0$ remains in M for all $t > 0$. Since M in this case contains only equilibrium points, it is clearly an invariant set.

8 We have already encountered such a situation in Example 8.1(c) of Chapter 6.

9 This is, in fact, the *only general* tool currently available to prove complete stability of Eq. (24).

10 To be more precise, for theorems 2–4 (and the corollaries to these theorems) in this section, we should add that the complete stability property, unlike in theorem 1, applies to all initial conditions except for a set of measure zero. For example, there may exist (possibly rare) such completely stable CNNs where there is an unstable limit cycle.

11 In this section, it is useful to think of each directed branch as a *one-way street* and a node as an intersection between two or more one-way streets. Hence for each nonzero entry in $\mathbf{A}$ ($a_{kl} \neq 0$), there are two connecting one-way streets in the same direction which allows one to travel from node (k, l) to node $(\bar{k}, \bar{l})$. Two or more such branches in a directed graph are said to be *similarly directed*.

As an example, the signal flow graph $\mathcal{G}_A$ associated with the $\mathbf{A}$ template in Fig. 8.10(a) is shown in Fig. 8.10(b). Observe that $\mathcal{G}_A$ has six directed branches (not counting the self-loop) since there are only three non-zero non-central entries in the $\mathbf{A}$ template; namely, $a_{-1,-1} = -2.6$, $a_{-1,0} = 1.5$, and $a_{1,1} = 3.2$. Observe that for each zero entry ($a_{k,l} = 0, k \neq l$) in the $\mathbf{A}$ template, the corresponding node (k, l) in $\mathcal{G}_A$ has no branches attached to it. Observe also that the "sign" of $a_{kl} \neq 0$ is *irrelevant* in so far as the *direction* of the associated branch is concerned, which always goes from node (k, l) to the center node (i, j), and its reflected "twin" branch always goes from the center node (i, j) to node $(\bar{k}, \bar{l})$.

In the signal flow graph $\mathcal{G}_A$ shown in Fig. 8.10(b), we also write the synaptic weight a_{kl} next to the pair of directed branches associated with each entry of the $\mathbf{A}$ template where $a_{kl} \neq 0$. For completeness, we also draw a self-loop at node (i, j) with the self-feedback synaptic weight $a_{ij} = 4.7$ written next to it. For the purpose of this section, however, both the synaptic weights and the self-loop are irrelevant to the following complete stability theorem and will therefore be deleted from $\mathcal{G}_A$.

12 A similarly directed path from node (k_1, l_1) to node (k_2, l_2) is defined as a sequence of *directed* branches (one-way streets) which allows one to travel from an *initial* node (k_1, l_1) to a destination node (k_2, l_2).

13 Since N is an odd integer, the geometric center of $\mathcal{G}_A(N \times N)$ is a node of $\mathcal{G}_A(N \times N)$.

14 Two nodes (k, l) and $(\bar{k}, \bar{l})$ are said to be rotationally symmetric if and only if the position of (k, l) coincides with that of $(\bar{k}, \bar{l})$ upon rotating the CNN by $180°$ about its center position.

15 For the proof of the complete stability Theorem 3, see L.O. Chua and C.W. Wu, "On the Universe of Stable Cellular Neural Networks," *International Journal of Circuit Theory and Applications*, Vol. 20, 1992, pp. 497–517.

16 M.W. Hirsch, "System of differential equations that are competitive or cooperative II: Convergence almost everywhere," *SIAM Math. Anal.*, Vol. 16, no 3, May 1985, pp. 423–439.

17 L.O. Chua and T. Roska, "Stability of a class of nonreciprocal Cellular Neural Networks," *IEEE Trans. on Circuits and Systems*, Vol. 37, 1990, pp. 1520–1527.

18 L.O. Chua and C.W. Wu, "On the universe of stable Cellular Neural Networks," *International Journal of Circuit Theory and Applications*, Vol. 20, 1992, pp. 497–512.

19 M.W. Hirsch, "System of differential equations that are competitive or cooperative, II: Convergence almost everywhere," *SIAM Math. Anal.*, Vol. 16, no 3, May 1985, pp. 423–439.

20 A *permutation* matrix $\mathbf{P}$ is a matrix whose entries consists of 0 or 1 such that each row or column contains only one "1." A matrix $\mathbf{D}$ is *irreducible* if there exists a *permutation* matrix $\mathbf{P}$ such that $\mathbf{PDP}^T$ is of the form

where "$\circ$" denotes a matrix with all zero entries, "$\times$" denotes a nonzero matrix, and "$\otimes$" denotes any matrix.

9 The CNN universal machine (CNN-UM)

1 An operator $y(t) = \hat{y}(u_1(t), u_2(t), \ldots, u_n(t))$ is of fading memory if $\Delta y(t)|_{t=t_0} \to 0$ as $\Delta u_i(t - \tau)$ is bounded and $\tau \to \infty$.

2 T. Roska, "The CNN chip set, engine board and the visual mouse," *Proc. IEEE*, CNNA-96, pp. 487–492, Seville, 1996.

10 Template design tools

1 E.g. T. Kozek, T. Roska, and L.O. Chua, "Genetic algorithm for CNN template learning," *IEEE Trans. on Circuits and Systems, I: Fundamental Theory and Applications* (CAS-I), Vol. 40, No. 6, 1993, pp. 392–402.

2 E.g. Cs. Rekeczky, A. Tahy, Z. Végh, and T. Roska, "CNN based spatio-temporal nonlinear filtering and endocardial boundary detection in echocardiography," *Int. J. Circuit Theory and Applications: Special Issue: Theory, Design and Applications of Cellular Neural Networks, II: Design and Applications*, Vol. 27, No. 1, 1999, pp. 171–207.

3 E.g. P. Földesy, L. Kék, Á. Zarándy, T. Roska, and G. Bártfai, "Fault tolerant design of analogic CNN templates and algorithms, part I: The binary output case," *IEEE Trans. on Circuits and Systems I: Special Issue on Bio-Inspired Processors and Cellular Neural Networks for Vision*, Vol. 46, No. 2, 1999, pp. 312–322.

4 Cs. Rekeczky and L.O. Chua, "Computing with front propagation: Active contour and skeleton models in continuous-time CNN," *Journal of VLSI Signal Processing, Special Issue: Spatiotemporal Signal Processing with Analogic CNN Visual Microprocessors*, Vol. 23, No. 2/3, 1999, pp. 373–402, Kluwer.

5 I. Szatmári, Cs. Rekeczky and T. Roska, "A nonlinear wave metric and its CNN implementation for object classification," *Journal of VLSI Signal Processing, Special Issue: Spatiotemporal Signal Processing with Analogic CNN Visual Microprocessors*, Vol. 23, No. 2/3, 1999, pp. 437–448, Kluwer.

6 L. Nemes, L.O. Chua, and T. Roska, "Implementation of Arbitrary Boolean Functions on a CNN Universal Machine," *International Journal of Circuit Theory and Applications*, Vol. 26, 1998, pp. 593–610.

11 CNNs for linear image processing

1 It follows from Eq. (11.12) that an alternate definition of Eqs (11.10)–(11.11) can be made by choosing a common scaling factor equal to $\frac{1}{2\pi}$ in both equations.

12 Coupled CNN with linear synaptic weights

1 C.-W. Wu, T. Roska, and L.O. Chua, "Cellular Neural Networks operating in oscillatory modes," Memorandum No. UCB/ERL M94/5, Electronics Research Laboratory, University of California at Berkeley, 1994.

2 Á. Zarándy, "The art of template design," *International Journal of Circuit Theory and Applications*, Vol. 26, Nov.–Dec. 1998.

3 Á. Zarándy, "On conditions a propagation is of unidirectional change in coupled CNN," Technical Report DNS-11-1998, Computer and Automation Institute, Budapest, 1998.

13 Uncoupled standard CNNs with nonlinear synaptic weights

1 T. Roska and L.O. Chua, "Cellular Neural Networks, with non-linear and delay-type template elements and non-uniform grids," *International Journal of Circuit Theory and Applications*, Vol. 20, 1992, pp. 469–481.

2 Cs. Rekeczky, T. Roska, and A. Ushida, "CNN based difference-controlled adaptive nonlinear image filters," *International Journal of Circuit Theory and Applications*, Vol. 26, 1998, pp. 375–423.

3 Zero-flux would be better since this will generate non-existing edges at the boundary.

14 Standard CNNs with delayed synaptic weights and motion analysis

1 T. Roska, and L.O. Chua, "Cellular Neural Networks, with non-linear and delay-type template elements and non-uniform grids," *International Journal of Circuit Theory and Applications*, Vol. 20, 1992, pp. 469–481.

2 T. Roska, C.W. Wu, M. Balsi, and L.O. Chua, "Stablity and dynamics of delay-type general and Cellular Neural Networks," *IEEE Transactions on Circuits and Systems-I*, Vol. 39, 1992, pp. 487–490.

3 D.H. Hubel, and T.N. Wiesel, "Receptive fields, binocular, interaction and functional architecture in the cat's visual cortex," *J. Physiology*, Vol. 160, 1962, pp. 106–154.

4 T. Roska, T. Boros, and A. Radványi, "Detecting moving and standing objects using Cellular Neural Networks," *CTA*, Vol. 20, 1992, pp. 613–628.

15 Visual microprocessors – analog and digital VLSI implementation of the CNN universal machine

1 The interested reader can consult the many papers on this subject or the new book devoted to the design of CNN-UM visual microprocessors [T. Roska, and A. Rodríguez-Vázquez (eds), J. Wiley, 2000, in press].

2 N. Frühauf, E. Lüder, and G. Bader, "Fourier optical realization of Cellular Neural Networks," *IEEE Transactions on Circuits and Systems, Series II*, Vol. 40, 1993, pp. 156–162.

3 R. Domínguez-Castro, A. Rodríguez-Vázquez, S. Espejo, and R. Carmona, "Four-quadrant one transistor-synapse for high-density CNN implementations," *Proc. IEEE CNNA-98*, 1998, pp. 243–248.

4 A. Rodríguez-Vázquez *et al.*, "Current mode techniques for the implementation of continuous- and discrete-time cellular neural networks," *IEEE Transactions on Circuits and Systems, II*, Vol. 40, No 3, 1993, pp. 132–146.

5 R. Carmona-Galán, A. Rodríguez-Vázquez, S. Espejo-Meana, R. Domínguez-Castro, T. Roska, T. Kozek, and L.O. Chua, "An 0.5-μm CMOS analog random access memory chip for TeraOPS speed multimedia video processing," *IEEE Transactions on Multimedia*, Vol. 1, No 2, 1999, pp. 121–135.

6 G. Linán, S. Espejo, R. Domínguez-Castro, E. Roca, and A. Rodríguez-Vázquez, "CNNUC3: A mixed-signal 64 × 64 CNN universal chip," Proceedings of Seventh Int. Conf. on Microelectronics for Neural, Fuzzy and Bio-Inspired Systems (MicroNeuro'99), 1999, pp. 61–68, Granada.

7 R. Dominguez-Castro *et al.*, "A 0.8 μm CMOS 2-D programmable mixed-signal focal-plane array processor with on-chip binary imaging and instructions storage, *IEEE Solid State Circuits Journal*, Vol. 32, 1997, pp. 1013–1026.

8 P. Keresztes, Á. Zarándy, T. Roska, P. Szolgay, T. Bezák, T. Hídvégi, P. Jónás, and A. Katona, "An emulated digital CNN implementation," *Journal of VLSI Signal Processing, Special Issue: Spatiotemporal Signal Processing with Analogic CNN Visual Microprocessors*, Vol. 23, No 2/3, 1999, pp. 291–304.

9 T. Roska, Á. Zarándy, S. Zöld, P. Földesy, and P. Szolgay, "The computational infrastructure of analogic CNN computing, Part I: The CNN-UM chip prototyping system," *IEEE Trans. on Circuits and Systems*, I, Vol. 46, No 2, 1999, pp. 261–268.

10 ALADDIN, http://lab.analogic.sztaki.hu

11 Sz. Tőkés, L. Orzó, Cs. Rekeczky, T. Roska, and Á. Zarándy, "An optical CNN implementation with stored programmability," Proc. IEEE ISCAS-2000, Vol. 2, 2000, pp. 136–139.

16 CNN models in the visual pathway and the "Bionic Eye"

1 H.B. Barlow, "Sumation and inhibition in the frog's retina," *J. Physiology*, Vol. 119, 1953, pp. 69–88.

2   J.E. Dowling, *The Retina: An Approachable Part of the Brain*, Harvard University Press, Cambridge, MA, 1987.

3   F.S. Werblin, "Synaptic connections, receptive fields, and pattern of activity in the tiger salamander retina," *Investigative Ophthalmology and Visual Science*, Vol. 32, 1991, pp. 459–483.

4   C. Mead, *Analog VLSI and Neural Systems*, Addison Wesley, Reading, MA, 1989.

5   J. Teeters, and F.S. Werblin, "Real-time simulation of the retina allowing visualization of each processing stage," *SPIE*, Vol. 1472, Image Understanding and the Man–Machine Interface III, 1991.

6   T. Roska, J. Hámori, E. Lábos, K. Lotz, L. Orzó, J. Takács, P. Venetianer, Z. Vidnyánszky, and Á. Zarándy, "The use of CNN models in the subcortical visual pathway," *IEEE Trans. Circuits and Systems, I*, Vol. 40, 1993, pp. 182–195 (Report DNS-10-1991, MTA SZTAKI, Budapest, 1991).

7   F.S. Werblin, T. Roska, and L.O. Chua, "The analogic Cellular Neural Network as a bionic eye," *International Journal of Circuit Theory and Applications*, Vol. 23, 1995, pp. 541–569.

8   F.S. Werblin, A. Jacobs, and J. Teeters, "The computational Eye," *IEEE Spectrum*, Vol. 33, May 1996, pp. 30–37.

9   B. Roska, E. Nemeth, and F.S. Werblin, "Response to change is facilitated by a 3-neuron disinhibitory path-way in the Tiger Salamander Retina," *J. Neuroscience*, Vol. 18, 1998, pp. 3451–3459.

10   B. Roska, E. Nemeth, L. Orzó, and F.S. Werblin, "Analysis of retinal space-time patterns reveals image sharpening," *J. Neuroscience*, Vol. 20, 2000, pp. 1941–1951.

11   J. Hámori, T. Pasik, P. Pasik, and J. Szentágothai, "Triadic synaptic arrangements and their possible significance in the lateral geniculate nucleus of the monkey," *Brain Research*, Vol. 80, 1974, pp. 379–393.

12   A.M. Sillito, and P.C. Murphy, "GABAergic processes in the central visual system," *Neurotransmitters and Cortical Functions*, R.W. Dykes and P. Gloor, Plenum Press, 1988.

13   E.R. Kandel, J.H. Schwartz, and T.M. Jessel, *Principles of Neural Science*, 3rd edition, Elsevier, New York, 1991.

14   T. Roska, J. Hámori, E. Lábos, K. Lotz, L. Orzó, J. Takács, P. Venetianer, Z. Vidnyánszky, and Á. Zarándy, "The use of CNN models in the subcortical visual pathway," *IEEE Trans. Circuits and Systems, I*, Vol. 40, 1993, pp. 182–195 (Report DNS-10-1991, MTA SZTAKI, Budapest, 1991).

15   Á. Zarándy, L. Orzó, E. Grawes, and F. Werblin, "CNN based early vision models for color vision and visual illusions," *IEEE Trans. on Circuits and Systems, I: Special Issue on Bio-Inspired Processors and Cellular Neural Networks for Vision* (CAS-I Special Issue), Vol. 46, No 2, 1999, pp. 229–238.

16   L.O. Chua, and T. Roska, "The CNN paradigm," *IEEE Trans. on Circuits and Systems, I: Fundamental Theory and Applications*, Vol. 40, No 3, 1993, pp. 147–156.

17   T. Roska, Á. Zarándy, and L.O. Chua, "Color image processing by CNN," *Proceedings of 11 European Conference on Circuit Theory and Design* (ECCTD'93), 1993, pp. 57–62, Davos.

18   A. Jacobs, T. Roska, and F.S. Werblin, "Methods for constructing physiologically motivated neuromorphic models in CNNs," *International Journal of Circuit Theory and Applications*, Vol. 24, 1996, pp. 315–339.

19   K. Lotz, A. Jacobs, J. Vandewalle, F. Werblin, T. Roska, L. Vidnyánszky, and J. Hámori, "Cellular Neural Network realizations of neuron models with diverse spiking patterns," *International Journal of Circuit Theory and Applications*, Vol. 24, 1996, pp. 301–314.

20 Cs. Rekeczky, B. Roska, E. Nemeth, and F. Werblin "Neuromorphic CNN models for spatio-temporal effects measured in the inner and outer retina of Tiger Salamander, Proc. IEEE CNNA-2000, pp. 165–170.

21 D. Bálya, B. Roska, T. Roska, and F. Werblin, "A qualitative model-framework for spatio-temporal effects in vertebrate retinas," Proc. IEEE CNNA-2000, pp. 165–170.

22 F.S. Werblin, T. Roska, and L.O. Chua, "The analogic cellular neural network as a bionic eye," Memorandum No UCB/ERL M94/70, U.C. at Berkeley (1994), *International Journal of Circuit Theory and Applications*, Vol. 23, No 6, 1995, pp. 541–569.

23 B. Roska, and F.S. Werblin, "Vertical interactions across ten parallel, stacked representations in the mammalian retina," *Nature*, Vol. 410, 2001, pp. 583–587.

Bibliography

1988–1990

Chua, L.O. and T. Roska (1990), Stability of a class of nonreciprocal Cellular Neural Networks, *IEEE Transactions on Circuits and Systems*, **37**, 1520–7.

Chua, L.O. and L. Yang (1988a), Cellular Neural Networks: Theory, *IEEE Transactions on Circuits and Systems*, **35**, 1257–72.

Chua, L.O. and L. Yang (1988b), Cellular Neural Networks: Applications, *IEEE Transactions on Circuits and Systems*, **35**, 1273–90.

Frühauf, N. and E. Lüder (1990), Realization of CNNs by optical parallel processing with spatial light valves, Proceedings of IEEE International Workshop on Cellular Neural Networks and Their Applications (CNNA'90), pp. 281–90, Budapest.

Konishi, M. *et al.* (1988), Neurophysiological and anatomical substrates of sound localization in the owl, in G.M. Edelman, W.E. Gall, and W.M. Cowan (eds.), *Auditory Function*, Wiley, New York, pp. 721–45.

Matsumoto, T., L.O. Chua, and R. Furukawa (1990), CNN cloning template: Hole filler, *IEEE Transactions on Circuits and Systems*, **37**, 635–8.

Matsumoto, T., L.O. Chua, and H. Suzuki (1990a), CNN cloning template: Connected component detector, *IEEE Transactions on Circuits and Systems*, **37**, 633–5.

Matsumoto, T., L.O. Chua, and H. Suzuki (1990b), CNN cloning template: Shadow detector, *IEEE Transactions on Circuits and Systems*, **37**, 1070–3.

Mead, C. (1989) Analog VLSI implementation of neural systems, in C. Mead and M. Ismail (eds.), *Analog VLSI Implementation of Neural Systems*, Kluwer, Boston.

Rodriguez-Vázquez, Á., R. Domínguez-Castro, and J.L. Huertas (1990), Accurate design of analog CNN in CMOS digital technologies, Proceedings of IEEE International Workshop on Cellular Neural Networks and Their Applications (CNNA'90), pp. 273–80, Budapest.

Roska, T. (1988), Analog events and a dual computing structure using analog and digital circuits and operators, in P. Varaiya and A.B. Kurzhanski (eds.), *Discrete Event Systems: Models and Applications*, Springer Verlag, New York, pp. 225–38.

Roska, T., G. Bártfay, P. Szolgay, T. Szirányi, A. Radványi, T. Kozek, and Zs. Ugray (1990), A hardware accelerator board for Cellular Neural Networks: CNN-HAC, Proceedings of IEEE International Workshop on Cellular Neural Networks and Their Applications (CNNA'90), pp. 160–8, Budapest.

Varrientos, J.E., J. Ramírez-Angulo, and Sánchez-Sinencio (1990), Cellular Neural Networks implementation: A current-mode approach, Proceedings of IEEE International Workshop on Cellular Neural Networks and Their Applications (CNNA'90), pp. 216–25, Budapest.

1991–1992

Chua, L.A. and P. Thiran (1991), An analytic method for designing simple Cellular Neural Networks, *IEEE Transactions on Circuits and Systems*, **38**, 1332–41.

Chua, L.A. and T. Roska (1992), A two-layer radon transform Cellular Neural Network, *IEEE Transactions on Circuits and Systems, II: Analog and Digital Signal Processing*, **39**, 488–9.

Chua, L.A. and C.W. Wu (1992), On the universe of stable Cellular Neural Networks, *International Journal of Circuit Theory and Applications*, **20**, 497–518.

Cruz, J.M. and L.O. Chua (1991), A CNN chip for connected component detection, *IEEE Transactions on Circuits and Systems*, **38**, 812–17.

Cruz, J.M. and L.O. Chua (1992), Design of high-speed, high-density CNNs in CMOS technology, *International Journal of Circuit Theory and Applications*, **20**, 555–72.

Halonen, K., V. Porra, T. Roska, and L.O. Chua (1992), Programmable analogue VLSI CNN chip with local digital logic, *International Journal of Circuit Theory and Applications*, **20**, 573–82.

Harrer, H. and J.A. Nossek (1992), Discrete-time Cellular Neural Networks, *International Journal of Circuit Theory and Applications*, **20**, 453–67.

Harrer, H., J.A. Nossek, and R. Stelzl (1992), An analog implementation of discrete-time Cellular Neural Networks, *IEEE Transactions on Neural Networks*, **3**, 466–77.

Henseler, J. and P.J. Braspenning (1992), Membrain: A Cellular Neural Network model based on a vibrating membrane, *International Journal of Circuit Theory and Applications*, **20**, 483–96.

Huertas, J.L. and Á. Rodriguez-Vásquez (1992), Invited lecture: VLSI-implementation of CNN, Proceedings of IEEE International Workshop on Cellular Neural Networks and Their Applications (CNNA'92), pp. 141–50, Munich.

Kandel, E.R., J.H. Schwarz, and T.M. Jessel (1991), *Principles of Neural Science*, Elsevier, Amsterdam.

Krinsky, V.I., V.N. Biktashev, and I.R. Efimov (1991), Autowave principles for parallel image processing, *Physica D*, **49**, 247–53.

Mahowald, M. and C. Mead (1991), The silicon retina, *Scientific American*, **264**, 76–82.

Nossek, J.A., G. Seiler, T. Roska, and L.O. Chua (1992), Cellular Neural Networks: Theory and circuit design, *International Journal of Circuit Theory and Applications*, **20**, 533–53.

Roska, T., G. Bártfay, P. Szolgay, T. Szirányi, A. Radványi, T. Kozek, Zs. Ugray, and Á. Zarándy (1992), A digital multiprocessor hardware accelerator board for Cellular Neural Networks: CNN-HAC, *International Journal of Circuit Theory and Applications*, **20**, 589–99.

Roska, T., T. Boros, A. Radványi, P. Thiran, and L.O. Chua (1992), Detecting simple motion using Cellular Neural Networks, *International Journal of Circuit Theory and Applications*, **20**, 613–28.

Roska, T. and L.O. Chua (1992), Cellular Neural Networks with nonlinear and delay-type template elements and non-uniform grids, *International Journal of Circuit Theory and Applications*, **20**, 469–81.

Roska, T., K. Lotz, J. Hámori, E. Lábos, and J. Takács (1991), The CNN model in the visual system, Part 1: The CNN-retina and some direction and length-selective mechanisms, Research Report of the Analogic (Dual) and Neural Computing Systems Laboratory (DNS-8-1991), Budapest, MTA SZTAKI.

Roska, T. and J. Vandewalle (eds.) (1992), Guest editorial, *International Journal of Circuit Theory and Applications*, **20**(5), 449–51.

Roska, T., C.W. Wu, M. Balsi, and L.O. Chua (1992), Stability and dynamics of delay-type general and Cellular Neural Networks, *IEEE Transactions on Circuits and Systems, I: Fundamental Theory and Applications*, **39**, 487–90.

Rueda, A. and J.L. Huertas (1992), Testability in analogue Cellular Neural Networks, *International Journal of Circuit Theory and Applications*, **20**, 583–7.

Slot, K. (1992), Cellular Neural Network design for solving specific image-processing problems, *International Journal of Circuit Theory and Applications*, **20**, 629–637.

Slot, K., T. Roska, and L.O. Chua (1992), Optically realized feedforward-only Cellular Neural Networks, *Archiv für Elektronik und Übertragungstechnik* (AEÜ), **46**, 158–67.

Teeters, J.L. and F.S. Werblin (1991), Real-time simulation of the retina allowing visualization of each processing stage, SPIE, 1472.

Vandenberghe, L. and J. Vandewalle (1992), A path-following method for finding multiple equilibrium points in Cellular Neural Networks, *International Journal of Circuit Theory and Applications*, **20**, 519–31.

Werblin, F.S. (1991), Synaptic connections, receptive fields, and pattern of activity in the tiger salamander retina, *Investigative Ophthalmology and Visual Science*, **32**, 459–83.

Wu, C.W., L.O. Chua, and T. Roska (1992), A two-layer radon transform Cellular Neural Network, *IEEE Transactions on Circuits and Systems, II: Analog and Digital Signal Processing*, **39**, 488–9.

Zou, F. and J.A. Nossek (1991), A chaotic attractor with cellular neural networks, *IEEE Transactions on Circuits and Systems*, **38**, 811–12.

1993–1994

Anguita, M., F.J. Pelayo, A. Prieto, and J. Ortega (1993), Analog CMOS implementation of a discrete time CNN with programmable cloning templates, *IEEE Transactions on Circuits and Systems, II: Analog and Digital Signal Processing*, **41**(3), 215–18.

Balsi, M. (1993), Stability of Cellular Neural Networks with one-dimensional templates, *International Journal of Circuit Theory and Applications*, **21**(4), 293–7.

Bouzerdoum, A. and R.B. Pinter (1993), Shunting inhibitory Cellular Neural Networks: Derivation and stability analysis, *IEEE Transactions on Circuits and Systems, I: Fundamental Theory and Applications*, **40**(3), 215–21.

Chua, L.A. and T. Roska (1993), The CNN paradigm, *IEEE Transactions on Circuits and Systems, I: Fundamental Theory and Applications*, **40**(3), 147–56.

Chua, L.A., T. Roska, T. Kozek, and Á. Zarándy (1993), The CNN paradigm – a short tutorial, in T. Roska and J. Vandewalle (eds.), *Cellular Neural Networks*, Wiley & Sons, Chichester, pp. 1–14.

Chua, L.A., T. Roska, and P.L. Venetianer (1993), The CNN is universal as the Turing machine, *IEEE Transactions on Circuits and Systems, I: Fundamental Theory and Applications*, **40**(4), 289–91.

Cimagalli, V., M. Bobbi, and M. Balsi (1993), MODA: Moving object detecting architecture, *IEEE Transactions on Circuits and Systems, II: Analog and Digital Signal Processing*, **40**(3), 174–83.

Civalleri, P. and M. Gilli (1993), On dynamic behaviour of CNN with delay, Proceedings of 11 European Conference on Circuit Theory and Design, (ECCTD'93), Davos, pp. 687–91.

Civalleri, P.P. and M. Gilli (1994), Some dynamic phenomena in delayed Cellular Neural Networks, *International Journal of Circuit Theory and Applications*, **22**, 77–105.

Civalleri, P.P., M. Gilli, and L. Pandolfi (1993), On stability of Cellular Neural Networks with delay, *IEEE Transactions on Circuits and Systems, I: Fundamental Theory and Applications*, **40**(3), 157–65.

Crounse, K.R., T. Roska, and L.O. Chua (1993), Image halftoning with Cellular Neural Networks, *IEEE Transactions on Circuits and Systems, II: Analog and Digital Signal Processing*, **40**(4), 267–83.

Dalla Betta, G.F., S. Graffi, Zs.M. Kovács, and G. Masetti (1993), CMOS Implementation of an analogically programmable Cellular Neural Network, *IEEE Transactions on Circuits and Systems, II: Analog and Digital Signal Processing*, **40**(3), 206–14.

Forti, M., S. Manetti, and M. Marini, Necessary and sufficient condition for absolute stability of neural networks, *IEEE Transactions on Circuits and Systems, I: Fundamental Theory and Applications*, **41**, 241–4.

Fruehauf, N., E. Lueder, and G. Bader (1993), Fourier optical realization of Cellular Neural Networks, *IEEE Transactions on Circuits and Systems, II: Analog and Digital Signal Processing*, **40**(3), 156–62.

Galias, Z. (1993), Designing Cellular Neural Networks for the evaluation of local Boolean functions, *IEEE Transactions on Circuits and Systems, II: Analog and Digital Signal Processing*, **40**(3), 219–22.

Gilli, M. (1994), Stability of Cellular Neural Networks and delayed Cellular Neural Networks with nonpositive templates and nonmonotonic output functions, *IEEE Transactions on Circuits and Systems, I: Fundamental Theory and Applications*, **41**(8), 518–28.

Guzelis, C. and L.O. Chua (1993), Stability analysis of generalized Cellular Neural Networks, *International Journal of Circuit Theory and Applications*, **21**, 1–33.

Halonen, K., V. Porra, T. Roska, and L.O. Chua (1993), Programmable analogue VLSI CNN chip with local digital logic, in T. Roska and J. Vandewalle (eds.), *Cellular Neural Networks*, Wiley & Sons, Chichester.

Harrer, H. (1993), Multiple-layer discrete-time Cellular Neural Networks using time-variant templates, *IEEE Transactions on Circuits and Systems, II: Analog and Digital Signal Processing*, **40**(3), 191–9.

Harrer, H., Z. Galias, and J.A. Nossek (1993), On the convergence of discrete-time neural networks, *International Journal of Circuit Theory and Applications*, **21**(2), 191–5.

Heiligenberg, W. and T. Roska (1993), On biological sensory information processing principles relevant to Cellular Neural Networks, in T. Roska and J. Vandewalle (eds.), *Cellular Neural Networks*, Special issue of the *International Journal of Circuit Theory and Applications*, Wiley & Sons, Chichester, pp. 201–11.

Jankowski, St, C. Mazur, and R. Wanczuk (1993), Some problems of molecular physics solved by CNN, Proceedings of International Symposium on Nonlinear Theory and Applications (NOLTA'93), 1, Honolulu, pp. 17–22.

Joy, M.P. and V. Tavsanoglu (1993), A new parameter range for stability of opposite-sign Cellular Neural Networks, *IEEE Transactions on Circuits and Systems, I: Fundamental Theory and Applications*, **40**(3), 204–6.

Kaszkurewicz, E. and A. Bhaya (1994), On a class of globally stable neural circuits, *IEEE Transactions on Circuits and Systems, I: Fundamental Theory and Applications*, **41**(2), 171–4.

Kozek, T., T. Roska, and L.O. Chua (1993), Genetic algorithm for CNN template learning, *IEEE Transactions on Circuits and Systems, I: Fundamental Theory and Applications*, **40**(6), 392–402.

Martinelli, G. and R. Prefetti (1994), Generalized Cellular Neural Network for novelty detection, *IEEE Transactions on Circuits and Systems, I: Fundamental Theory and Applications*, **41**(2), 187–90.

Nossek, J.A. and T. Roska (eds.) (1993), Special Issue on Cellular Neural Networks, *IEEE Transactions on Circuits and Systems, II: Analog and Digital Signal Processing*, **40**(3).

Osuna, J.O., G.S. Moschytz, and T. Roska (1993), A framework for the classification of auditory signals with Cellular Neural Networks, Proceedings of 11 European Conference on Circuit Theory and Design (ECCTD'93), Davos, pp. 51–6.

Paul, S., K. Hüper, J.A. Nossek, and L.O. Chua (1993), Mapping nonlinear lattice equations on to Cellular Neural Networks, *IEEE Transactions on Circuits and Systems, I: Fundamental Theory and Applications*, **40**(3), 196–203.

Pérez-Munuzuri, V., V. Pérez-Villar, and L.O. Chua (1993), Autowaves for image processing on a two-dimensional CNN array of Chua's circuits: flat and wrinkled labyrinths, *IEEE Transactions on Circuits and Systems, I: Fundamental Theory and Applications*, **40**(3), 174–81.

Prefetti, R. (1993), CNN for fast adaptive equalization, *International Journal of Circuit Theory and Applications*, **21**(2), 165–75.

Rodriguez-Vázquez, Á., S. Espejo, R. Domínguez-Castro, J.L. Huertas, and E. Sánchez-Sinencio (1993), Current-mode techniques for the implementation of continuous- and discrete-time Cellular Neural Networks, *IEEE Transactions on Circuits and Systems, II: Analog and Digital Signal Processing*, **40**(3), 132–46.

Roska, T. and L.O. Chua (1993), The CNN universal machine: An analogic array computer, *IEEE Transactions on Circuits and Systems, II: Analog and Digital Signal Processing*, **40**(3), 163–73.

Roska, T., J. Hámori, E. Lábos, K. Lotz, L. Orzo, J. Takács, P. Venetianer, Z. Vidnyánszky, and A. Zarándy (1993), The use of CNN models in the subcortical visual pathway, *IEEE Transactions on Circuits and Systems, I: Fundamental Theory Applications*, **40**(3), 182–95.

Roska, T., C.W. Wu, and L.O. Chua (1993), Stability of Cellular Neural Networks with dominant nonlinear and delay-type templates, *IEEE Transactions on Circuits and Systems, I: Fundamental Theory and Applications*, **40**(4), 270–2.

Savaci, F.A. and J. Vandewalle (1993), On the stability analysis of Cellular Neural Networks, *IEEE Transactions on Circuits and Systems, I: Fundamental Theory and Applications*, **40**(3), 213–14.

Seiler, G. and J.A. Nossek (1993), Winner-take-all Cellular Neural Networks, *IEEE Transactions on Circuits and Systems, II: Analog and Digital Signal Processing*, **40**(3), 184–90.

Shi, B.E., T. Roska, and L.O. Chua (1993), Design of linear Cellular Neural Networks for motion sensitive filtering, *IEEE Transactions on Circuits and Systems, II: Analog and Digital Signal Processing*, **40**, 320–31.

Szirányi, T. and J. Csicsvári (1993), High-speed character recognition using a dual Cellular Neural Network architecture (CNND), *IEEE Transactions on Circuits and Systems, II: Analog and Digital Signal Processing*, **40**(3), 223–31.

Szolgay, P., G. Vörös, and G. Erőss (1993), On the applications of the Cellular Neural Network paradigm in mechanical vibrating systems, *IEEE Transactions on Circuits and Systems, I: Fundamental Theory and Applications*, **40**(3), 222–7.

Tanaka, M., C. Crounse, and T. Roska (1994), Parallel analog image coding and decoding by using Cellular Neural Networks, *IEICE (Japan) Transactions on Fundamentals of Electronics, Communications and Computer Sciences* (IEICE), E77-A, No. 8, 1387–95.

Thiran, P. (1993), Influence of boundary conditions on the behavior of Cellular Neural Networks, *IEEE Transactions on Circuits and Systems, I: Fundamental Theory and Applications*, **40**(3), 207–12.

Varrientos, J.E., E. Sánchez-Sinencio, and J. Ramirez-Angulo (1993), A current-mode cellular network implementation, *IEEE Transactions on Circuits and Systems, II: Analog and Digital Signal Processing*, **40**(3), 147–55.

Willis, J. and J. Pineda de Gyvez (1993), Functional testing for Cellular Neural Networks, *IEE Electronics Letters* (IEE EL), **29**(25), 2206–8.

Yang, T. (1994), Blind signal separation using Cellular Neural Networks, *International Journal of Circuit Theory and Applications*, **22**(5), 399–408.

Zou, F. and J.A. Nossek (1993a), Hopf-like bifurcation in Cellular Neural Networks, Proceedings of IEEE International Symposium on Circuits and Systems (ISCAS'93), 4, Chicago, pp. 2391–2394.

Zou, F. and J.A. Nossek (1993b), Bifurcation and chaos in Cellular Neural Networks, *IEEE Transactions on Circuits and Systems, I: Fundamental Theory and Applications*, **40**(3), 166–73.

1995–1996

Arena, P., S. Baglio, L. Fortuna, and G. Manganaro (1995), Chua's circuit can be generated by CNN cells, *IEEE Transactions on Circuits and Systems, I: Fundamental Theory and Applications*, **42**(2), 123–5.

Arena, P., S. Baglio, L. Fortuna, and G. Manganaro (1996), Generation of n-double scrolls via Cellular Neural Networks, *International Journal of Circuit Theory and Applications*, **24**(3), 241–52.

Arik, S. and V. Tavsanoglu (1996), Equilibrium analysis of non-symmetric CNNs, *International Journal of Circuit Theory and Applications*, **24**(3), 269–74.

Balsi, M., V. Cimagalli, and F. Galluzzi (1996), A proposal to implement optoelectronic CNN systems by amorphous silicon thin film technology, *International Journal of Circuit Theory and Applications*, **24**(1), 121–6.

Chua, L.A., M. Hasler, G.S. Moschytz, and J. Neirynck, Autonomous Cellular Neural Networks: A unified paradigm for pattern formation and active wave propagation, *IEEE Transactions on Circuits and Systems, I: Fundamental Theory and Applications*, **42**(10), 559–77.

Chua, L.A., T. Roska, T. Kozek, and Á. Zarándy (1996), CNN universal chips crank up the computing power, *IEEE Circuits and Devices* (IEEE C&D), **12**(4), 18–28.

Civalleri, P.P. and M. Gilli (1996), A spectral approach to the study of propagation phenomena in CNNs, *International Journal of Circuit Theory and Applications*, **24**(1), 37–48.

Crounse, K.R. and L.O. Chua (1995), Methods for image processing and pattern formation in Cellular Neural Networks: A tutorial, *IEEE Transactions on Circuits and Systems I: Fundamental Theory and Applications*, **42**(10), 583–601.

Cruz, J.M. and L.O. Chua (1995), Application of Cellular Neural Networks to model population dynamics, *IEEE Transactions on Circuits and Systems, I: Fundamental Theory and Applications*, **42**(10), 715–20.

Csapody, M. and T. Roska (1996), Dynamic analogic CNN algorithms for a complex recognition task – a first step towards a bionic eyeglass, *International Journal of Circuit Theory and Applications*, **24**(1), 127–44.

Espejo, S., R. Carmona, R. Domínguez-Castro, and Á. Rogriguez-Vázquez (1996a), A CNN universal chip in CMOS technology, *International Journal of Circuit Theory and Applications*, **24**(1), 93–110.

Espejo, S., R. Carmona, R. Domínguez-Castro, and Á. Rodriguez-Vázquez (1996b), A VLSI-oriented continuous-time CNN model, *International Journal of Circuit Theory and Applications*, **24**(3), 341–56.

Forti, M. and A. Tesi (1995), New conditions for global stability of neural networks with application to linear and quadratic programming problems, *IEEE Transactions on Circuits and Systems I: Fundamental Theory and Applications*, **42**(7), 354–66.

Jacobs, A., T. Roska, and F. Werblin (1996), Methods for constructing physiologically motivated neuromorphic models in CNNs, *International Journal of Circuit Theory and Applications*, **24**, 315–39.

Joy, M.P. and V. Tavsanoglu (1996), Circulant matrices and the stability of a class of CNNs, *International Journal of Circuit Theory and Applications*, **24**(1), 7–14.

Kinget, P. and M. Steyaert (1995), A programmable analog Cellular Neural Network (CMOS) chip for high speed image processing, *IEEE Journal of Solid State Circuits* (JSC), **30**, 235–43.

Kozek, T., L.O. Chua, T. Roska, D. Wolf, R. Tetzlaff, F. Puffer, and K. Lotz, Simulating nonlinear waves and partial differential equations via CNN – Part II. Typical Examples, *IEEE Transactions on Circuits and Systems, I: Fundamental Theory and Applications*, **42**(10), 816–20.

Kozek, T. and T. Roska (1996), A double time-scale CNN for solving two-dimensional Navier–Stokes equations, *International Journal of Circuit Theory and Applications*, **24**, 49–56.

Liszka, G., T. Roska, Á. Zarándy, J. Hegyesi, L. Kék, and Cs. Rekeczky (1995), Mammogram analysis using CNN algorithms, Proceedings SPIE Medical Imaging (SPIE Medical Imaging), 2434, pp. 461–470, San Diego.

Lotz, K., A. Jacobs, J. Vandewalle, F. Werblin, T. Roska, L. Vidnyánszky, and J. Hámori (1996), Cellular Neural Network realizations of neuron models with diverse spiking patterns, *International Journal of Circuit Theory and Applications*, **24**, 301–14.

Nemes, L. and T. Roska (1995), A CNN model of oscillation and chaos in ant colonies: A case study, *IEEE Transactions on Circuits and Systems, I: Fundamental Theory and Applications*, **42**(10), 741–5.

Nemes, L., G. Tóth, T. Roska, and A. Radványi (1996), Analogic CNN algorithms for 3D interpolation-approximation and object rotation using controlled switched templates, *International Journal of Circuit Theory and Applications*, **24**, 409–24.

Nossek, J.A. (1996), Design and learning with Cellular Neural Networks, *International Journal of Circuit Theory and Applications*, **24**(1), 15–24.

Ogorzalek, M.J., Z. Galias, W. Dabrowski, and A .Dabrowski (1996), Spatio-temporal co-operative phenomena in CNN arrays composed of chaotic circuits – simulation experiments, *International Journal of Circuit Theory and Applications*, **24**(3), 261–8.

Osuna, J.A. and G.S. Moschytz (1996), On the separating capability of Cellular Neural Networks, *International Journal of Circuit Theory and Applications*, **24**(3), 253–60.

Radványi, A.G. (1996), Spatial depth extraction using random stereograms in analogic CNN framework, *International Journal of Circuit Theory and Applications*, **24**, 69–92.

Rekeczky, C., A. Ushida, and T. Roska (1995), Rotation invariant detection of moving and standing objects using analogic Cellular Neural Network algorithms based on ring codes, *IEICE Transactions on Fundamentals of Electronics, Communications and Computer Sciences*, E-78, 1316–30.

Roska, T., L.O. Chua, D. Wolf, T. Kozek, R. Tetzlaff, and F. Puffer (1995), Simulating nonlinear waves and partial differential equations via CNN – Part I. Basic Techniques, *IEEE*

Transactions on Circuits and Systems, I: Fundamental Theory and Applications, **42**(10), 807–15.

Sargeni, F. and V. Bonaiuto (1996), A 3 × 3 digitally programmable CNN chip, *International Journal of Circuit Theory and Applications*, **24**(3), 369–80.

Stoffels, A., T. Roska, and L.O. Chua (1996), On object-oriented video coding using the CNN universal machine, *IEEE Transactions on Circuits and Systems, I: Fundamental Theory and Applications*, **43**, 948–52.

Suykens, J.A. and J. Vandewalle (1996), Discrete time interconnected Cellular Neural Networks within NLq theory, *International Journal of Circuit Theory and Applications*, **24**(1), 25–36.

Szirányi, S. (1996), Robustness of Cellular Neural Networks in image deblurring and texture segmentation, *International Journal of Circuit Theory and Applications*, **24**, 381–96.

Thiran, P., K.R. Crounse, L.O. Chua, and M. Hasler (1995), Pattern formation properties of autonomous Cellular Neural Networks, *IEEE Transactions on Circuits and Systems, I: Fundamental Theory and Applications*, **42**(10), 757–74.

Thiran, P. and M. Hasler (1996), Information storage using stable and unstable oscillations: An overview, *International Journal of Circuit Theory and Applications*, **24**(1), 57–68.

Vandewalle, J. and T. Roska (eds.) (1996), CTA Special Issue: Cellular Neural Networks II: Part 1, *International Journal of Circuit Theory and Applications*, **24**(1).

Venetianer, P.L., P. Szolgay, K.R. Crounse, T. Roska, and L.O. Chua (1996), Analogue combinatorics and cellular automata – key algorithms and layout design, *International Journal of Circuit Theory and Applications*, **24**, 145–64.

Venetianer, P.L., F. Werblin, T. Roska, and L.O. Chua (1996), Analogic CNN algorithms for some image compression and restoration tasks, *IEEE Transactions on Circuits and Systems, I: Fundamental Theory and Applications*, **42**(5), 278–84.

Werblin, F., T. Roska, and L.O. Chua (1995), The analogic Cellular Neural Network as a bionic eye, *International Journal of Circuit Theory and Applications*, **23**(6), 541–69.

Zarándy, I., F. Werblin, T. Roska, and L.O. Chua (1996), Spatial logic algorithm using basic morphological analogic CNN operations, *International Journal of Circuit Theory and Applications*, **24**, 283–300.

1997–1998

Anguita, M., F.J. Pelayo, F.J. Fernandez, and A. Prieto (1997), A low-power CMOS implementation of programmable CNNs with embedded photosensors, *IEEE Transactions on Circuits and Systems, I: Fundamental Theory and Applications*, **44**(2), 149–53.

Anguita, M., F.J. Pelayo, I. Rojas, and A. Prieto (1998), Area efficient implementations of fixed-template CNNs, *IEEE Transactions on Circuits and Systems, I: Fundamental Theory and Applications*, **45**(9), 968–73.

Arena, P., S. Baglio, L. Fortuna, and G. Manganaro (1998), Self-organization in a two-layer CNN, *IEEE Transactions on Circuits and Systems, I: Fundamental Theory and Applications*, **45**(2), 157–62.

Arena, P., M. Branciforte, and L. Fortuna (1998), A CNN based experimental frame for patterns and autowaves, *International Journal of Circuit Theory and Applications*, **26**(6), 635–50.

Arik, S. and V. Tavsanoglu (1998), Equilibrium analysis of delayed CNNs, *IEEE Transactions on Circuits and Systems, I: Fundamental Theory and Applications*, **45**(2), 168–71.

Brucoli, M., L. Carnimeo, and G. Grassi (1998), Heteroassociative memories via Cellular Neural Networks, *International Journal of Circuit Theory and Applications*, **26**(3), 231–41.

Brugge, M.H. ter, J.A.G. Nijhuis, and L. Spaanenburg (1998), Transformational DT-CNN design from morphological specifications, *IEEE Transactions on Circuits and Systems, I: Fundamental Theory and Applications*, **45**(9), 879–88.

Chua, L.O. (1997), A vision of complexity, *International Journal of Bifurcation and Chaos*, 7, No. 10, 2219–2425, World Scientific Publishing Company.

Csapodi, M., J. Vandewalle, and T. Roska (1998), Invertible operations on a Cellular Neural Network universal machine – based on the implementation of two-dimensional cellular automata, *International Journal of Circuit Theory and Applications*, **26**(6), 611–34.

Dogaru, R. and L.O. Chua (1998a), Edge of chaos and local activity domain of FitzHugh–Nagumo equation, *International Journal of Bifurcation and Chaos*, **8**(2), 211–57.

Dogaru, R. and L.O. Chua (1998b), Edge of chaos and local activity domain of the brusselator CNN, *International Journal of Bifurcation and Chaos*, **8**(6), 1107–30.

Dogaru, R. and L.O. Chua (1998c), CNN genes for one-dimensional cellular automata: A multi-nested piecewise-linear approach, *International Journal of Bifurcation and Chaos*, **8**(10), 1987–2001.

Dogaru, R., L.O. Chua, and K. Crounse (1998a), An extended class of synaptic operators with application for efficient VLSI implementation of cellular neural networks, *IEEE Transactions on Circuits and Systems, I: Fundamental Theory and Applications*, **45**(7), 745–53.

Dogaru, R., L.O. Chua, and K. Crounse (1998b), Piramidal cells: A novel class of adaptive coupling cells and their applications for cellular neural networks, *IEEE Transactions on Circuits and Systems, I: Fundamental Theory and Applications*, **45**(10), 1077–90.

Espejo, J., Á. Rodriguez-Vázquez, R.A. Carmona, P. Földesy, Á. Zarándy, P. Szolgay, T. Szirányi, and T. Roska (1997), 0.8 μm CMOS two dimensional programmable mixed-signal social-plane array processor with on-chip binary imaging and instruction storage, *IEEE Journal of Solid State Circuits* (JSC), **32**(7), 1013–26.

Fajfar, I., F. Bratkovic, T. Tuma, and J. Puhan (1998), A rigorous design method for binary Cellular Neural Networks, *International Journal of Circuit Theory and Applications*, **26**(4), 365–73.

Finger, L. and V. Tavsanoglu (1997), Mapping of one-dimensional Josephon function arrays onto Cellular Neural Networks and their dynamics, *International Journal of Circuit Theory and Applications*, **44**(5), 438–45.

Gilli, M., P.P. Civalleri, T. Roska, and L.O. Chua (1998), Analysis of time-varying Cellular Neural Networks for quadratic global optimatization, *International Journal of Circuit Theory and Applications*, **26**(2), 109–26.

Grimaila, M.R., J. Pineda de Gyvez, and G. Han (1997), Robust functional testing for VLSI Cellular Neural Network implementation, *IEEE Transactions on Circuits and Systems, I: Fundamental Theory and Applications*, **44**(2), 161–6.

Hirakawa, S., Cs. Rekeczky, Y. Nishio, A. Ushida, T. Roska, J. Endo, I. Kasem, and H. Nishitani (1997), Detecting lung cancer symptoms with analogic CNN algorithms based on a constrained diffusion template, *IEICE (Japan) Transactions on Fundamentals of Electronics, Communications and Computer Sciences*, E80-A. No. 7, 1340–1344.

Ikegana, T. and T. Ogura (1998), A DTCNN universal machine based on highly parallel 2-D cellular automata CAM2, *IEEE Transactions on Circuits and Systems, I: Fundamental Theory and Applications*, **45**(5), 538–46.

Joy, M.P. and V. Tavsanoglu (1998), An equilibrium analysis of CNNs, *IEEE Transactions on Circuits and Systems, I: Fundamental Theory and Applications*, **45**(1), 94–8.

Kék, L. and Á. Zarándy (1998), Implementation of large neighborhood nonlinear templates on the CNN universal machine, *International Journal of Circuit Theory and Applications*, **26**(6), 551–66.

Kinget, P. and M. Steyaert (1998), Analog VLSI design constraints of programmable Cellular Neural Networks, *Analog Integrated Circuits and Signal Processing*, **15**(3), 251–62.

Kozek, T., C.W. Wu, Á. Zarándy, Hua Chen, and T. Roska (1997), New results and measurements related to some tasks in object-oriented dynamic image coding using CNN universal chips, *IEEE Transactions on Circuits and Systems for Video Technology*, **7**(4), 606–14.

Liu, D. (1997), Cloning template design of Cellular Neural Networks for associative memories, *IEEE Transactions on Circuits and Systems, I: Fundamental Theory and Applications*, **44**(7), 646–50.

Majorana, S. and L.O. Chua (1998), A unified framework for multilayer high order CNN, *International Journal of Circuit Theory and Applications*, **26**(6), 567–92.

Mirzai, B. and G.S. Moschytz (1998), The influence of the boundary conditions on the robustness of a CNN, *IEEE Transactions on Circuits and Systems, I: Fundamental Theory and Applications*, **45**(4), 511–15.

Mladenov, V.M., D.M.W. Leenaerts, and F.H. Uhlmann (1998), Estimation of the basin of attractions in CNNs, *IEEE Transactions on Circuits and Systems, I: Fundamental Theory and Applications*, **45**(5), 571–4.

Nemes, L., L.O. Chua, and T. Roska (1998), Implementation of arbitrary Boolean functions on the CNN universal machine, *International Journal of Circuit Theory and Applications*, **26**(6), 593–610.

Paasio, A., A. Dawidziuk, K. Halonen, and V. Porra (1997), Fast and compact 16 by 16 CNN implementation, *Analog Integrated Circuits and Signal Processing* (AICASP), **12**, 59–70.

Parodi, M., M. Storace, and C. Regazzoni (1998), Circuit realization of Markov random fields for analog image processing, *International Journal of Circuit Theory and Applications*, **26**(5), 477–98.

Rekeczky, Cs., T. Roska, and A. Ushida (1998), CNN-based difference-controlled adaptive nonlinear image filters, *International Journal of Circuit Theory and Applications*, **26**, 375–423.

Salerno, M., F. Sargeni, and V. Bonaiuto (1998), A 6 × 6 cells interconnection-oriented programmable chip for CNN, *Analog Integrated Circuits and Signal Processing*, **15**(3), 239–50.

Shi, Bertram E. (1998), Gabor-type filtering in space and time with cellular neural networks, *IEEE Transactions on Circuits and Systems, I: Fundamental Theory and Applications*, **45**(2), 121–32.

Shi, B.E., T. Roska, and L.O. Chua (1998), Estimating optical flow with Cellular Neural Networks, *International Journal of Circuit Theory and Applications*, **26**(4), 343–64.

Slavova, A. (1998), Dynamic properties of Cellular Neural Networks with nonlinear output function, *IEEE Transactions on Circuits and Systems, I: Fundamental Theory and Applications*, **45**(5), 587–90.

Szirányi, T. (1997), Texture recognition using superfast Cellular Neural Network VLSI chip in real experimental environment, Proceedings of Pattern Recognition in Practice, in *Pattern Recognition Letters* Vol. 18, pp. 1329–1334, Vlieland.

Szirányi, T. and M. Csapodi (1998), Texture classification and segmentation by cellular Neural network using genetic learning, *Computer Vision and Image Understanding*, **71**(3), 255–70.

Szolgay, P., I. Szatmári, and K. László (1997), A fast fixed point learning method to implement associative memory on CNNs, *IEEE Transactions on Circuits and Systems, I: Fundamental Theory and Applications*, **44**, 362–6.

Venetianer, P.L. and T. Roska (1998), Image compression by cellular neural networks, *IEEE Transactions on Circuits and Systems, I: Fundamental Theory and Applications*, **45**(3), 205–15.

Yang, T., C-M. Yang, and L-B. Yang (1998), The differences between Cellular Neural Network based and fuzzy Cellular Neural Network based mathematical morphological operations, *International Journal of Circuit Theory and Applications*, **26**(1), 13–25.

Zarándy, I., A. Stoffels, T. Roska, and L.O. Chua (1998), Implementation of binary and grey-scale mathematical morphology on the CNN universal machine, *IEEE Transactions on Circuits and Systems, I: Fundamental Theory and Applications*, **45**(2), 163–8.

1999

Arena, P., L. Fortuna, and M. Branciforte (1999), Reaction-diffusion CNN algorithms to generate and control artificial locomotion, *IEEE Transactions on Circuits and Systems, I: Fundamental Theory and Applications*, **46**(2), 253–60.

Arena, P., L. Fortuna, and M. Branciforte (1999), Realization of a reaction–diffusion CNN algorithm for locomotion control in an hexapode robot, *Journal of VLSI Signal Processing*, **23**, 267–80.

Carmona-Galán, R., Á. Rodriguez-Vázquez, S. Espejo-Meana, R. Domínguez-Castro, T. Roska, T. Kozek , and L.O. Chua (1999), An 0.5 μm CMOS analog random access memory chip for teraOPS speed multimedia video processing, **1**(2), 121–35.

Carmona, R., G. Linan, R. Domínguez-Castro, S. Espejo, and Á. Rodriguez-Vázquez (1999), SIRENA: a CAD environment for behavioural modelling and simulation of VLSI Cellular Neural Network chips, *International Journal of Circuit Theory and Applications*, **27**(1), 43–76.

Cauwenberghs, G. and J. Waskiewicz (1999), Focal-plane analog VLSI cellular implementation of the boundary contour system, *IEEE Transactions on Circuits and Systems, I: Fundamental Theory and Applications*, **46**(2), 327–34.

Chandler, B., Cs. Rekeczky, Y. Nishio, and A. Ushida (1999), Adaptive simulated annealing in CNN template learning, *IEICE (Japan) Transactions on Fundamentals of Electronics, Communications and Computer Sciences* (IEICE), E82-A, No. 2, 398–402.

Földesy, P., L. Kék, T. Roska, Á. Zarándy, T. Roska, and G. Bártfai (1999), Fault tolerant design of analogic CNN templates and algorithms, part I: The binary output case, *IEEE Transactions on Circuits and Systems, I: Fundamental Theory and Applications*, **46**(2), 312–22.

Hanggi, M. and G.S. Moschytz (1999), An exact and direct analytical method for the design of optimally robust CNN templates, *IEEE Transactions on Circuits and Systems, I: Fundamental Theory and Applications*, **46**(2), 304–11.

Hiratsuka, M., T. Aoki, and T. Higuchi (1999), Enzyme transistor circuits for reaction–diffusion computing, *IEEE Transactions on Circuits and Systems, I: Fundamental Theory and Applications*, **46**(2), 294–303.

Keresztes, P., Á. Zarándy, T. Roska, P. Szolgay, T. Bezák, T. Hídvégi, P. Jónás, and A. Katona (1999), An emulated digital CNN implementation, *Journal of VLSI Signal Processing*, **23**, 291–303.

Kozek, T. and D.L. Vilarino (1999), An active contour algorithm for continuous-time Cellular Neural Networks, *Journal of VLSI Signal Processing*, **23**, 403–14.

Lotz, K., L. Bölöni, T. Roska, and J. Hámori (1999), Hiperacuity in time: a CNN model of a time-coding pathway of sound localization, *IEEE Transactions on Circuits and Systems I: Fundamental Theory and Applications*, **46**(8), 994–1002.

Luthon, F. and D. Dragomirescu (1999), A cellular analog network for MRF-based video motion detection, *IEEE Transactions on Circuits and Systems, I: Fundamental Theory and Applications*, **46**(2), 281–93.

Moreira-Tamayo, O. and J. Pineda de Gyvez (1999), Subband coding and image compression using CNN, *International Journal of Circuit Theory and Applications* **27**(1), 135–52.

Paasio A. and D. Dawidziuk (1999), CNN template robustness with different output nonlinearities, *International Journal of Circuit Theory and Applications*, **27**(1), 87–102.

Paasio, A., A. Kananen, K. Halonen, and V. Porra (1999), A QCIF resolution binary I/O CNN-UM chip, *Journal of VLSI Signal Processing*, **23**, 281–90.

Radványi, A.G. (1999), Structural analysis of sterograms for CNN depth detection, *IEEE Transactions on Circuits and Systems, I: Fundamental Theory and Applications*, **46**(2), 239–52.

Radványi, A.G., L. Gáspár, and G. Tóth (1999), CNNUM stereo architecture and 3D template design techniques, *International Journal of Circuit Theory and Applications*, **27**(1), 25–42.

Rekeczky, Cs. and L.O. Chua (1999), Computing with front propagation: Active contour and skeleton models in continuous-time CNN, *Journal of VLSI Signal Processing*, **23**, 373–402.

Rekeczky, Cs., A. Tahy, Z. Végh, and T. Roska (1999), CNN based spatio-temporal nonlinear filtering and endocardial boundary detection in echocardiography, *International Journal of Circuit Theory and Applications*, **27**(1), 171–207.

Roca, E., S. Espejo, R. Domínguez-Castro, G. Linan, and Á. Rodriguez-Vázquez (1999), A programmable imager for very high speed cellular signal processing, *Journal of VLSI Signal Processing*, **23**, 305–18.

Rodriguez-Vázquez, A., E. Roca, M. Delgado-Restituto, S. Espejo, and R. Domínguez-Castro (1999), MOST-based design and scaling of synaptic interconnections in VLSI analog array processing CNN chips, *Journal of VLSI Signal Processing*, **23**, 239–66.

Roska, T. (1999), Computer-sensors: Spatial-temporal computers for analog array signals, dynamically integrated with sensors, *Journal of VLSI Signal Processing*, **23**, 221–37.

Roska, T., Á. Zarándy, S. Zöld, P. Földesy, and P. Szolgay (1999), The computational infrastructure of analogic CNN computing – part I: The CNN-UM chip prototyping system, *IEEE Transactions on Circuits and Systems, I: Fundamental Theory and Applications*, **46**(2), 261–8.

Serrano-Gotarredona, T. and Á. Rodriguez-Vázquez (1999), On the design of second order dynamics reaction–diffusion CNNs, *Journal of VLSI Signal Processing*, **23**, 351–371.

Shi, B.E. (1999), Focal plane implementation of 2D steerable and scalable gabor-type filters, *Journal of VLSI Signal Processing*, **23**, pp. 319–334.

Shi, B.E. (1999), A one-dimensional CMOS focal plane array for gabor-type image filtering, *IEEE Transactions on Circuits and Systems, I: Fundamental Theory and Applications*, **46**(2), 323–326.

Slot, K., L.O. Chua, and T. Roska (1999), Very low bit-rate video coding using Cellular Neural Network universal machine, *International Journal of Circuit Theory and Applications*, **27**(1), 153–170.

Szirányi, T. and L. Czúni (1999), Image compression by orthogonal decomposition using Cellular Neural Network chips, *International Journal of Circuit Theory and Applications*, No. 1, 117–134.

Szolgay, P. and K. Tömördi (1999), Analogic algorithms for optical detection of breaks and short circuits on the layouts of printed circuits boards using CNN, *International Journal of Circuit Theory and Applications*, **27**(1), 103–116.

Tetzlaff, R., R. Kunz, and D. Wolf (1999), Minimizing the effects of parameter deviations on Cellular Neural Networks, *International Journal of Circuit Theory and Applications*, **27**(1), 77–86.

Torralba, A.B. and J. Hérault (1999), An efficient neuromorphic analog network for motion estimation, *IEEE Transactions on Circuits and Systems, I: Fundamental Theory and Applications*, **46**(2), 269–80.

Wang, J-S., Q. Gan, Y. Wei, and L. Xie (1999), Cellular Neural Networks with opposite-sign templates for image thinning, *International Journal of Circuit Theory and Applications*, **27**(2), 229–40.

Zarándy, I. (1999), The art of CNN template design, *International Journal of Circuit Theory and Applications*, **17**(1), 5–24.

Zarándy, I., L. Orzó, E. Grawes, and F. Werblin (1999), CNN based models for color vision and visual illusions, *IEEE Transactions on Circuits and Systems, I: Fundamental Theory and Applications*, **46**(2), 229–38.

Additional references can be found at
http://www.ieee-cas.org/~cnnactc
and
http://lab.analogic.sztaki.hu

Exercises

Chapter 2

Exercise 2.1 (Simple morph)

Given: two gray-scale images: **P1** and **P2**

Input: $\mathbf{U}(t) = \mathbf{P}1$

Initial state: $\mathbf{X}(0) = \mathbf{P}2$

Boundary conditions: *white frame*

Output: $\mathbf{Y}(t) = $ a transition from **P2** to **P1**.

Task

Design a single template, which implements this transition.

Example

Exercise 2.2 (Hexagonal neighborhood)

The standard CNN definition specifies that the cells form a rectangular grid. Anther feasible form could be a hexagonal grid.

Task

Give a formula for the side length and the area of a hexagon (measured in cells) in the case of a hexagonal cell grid, when the sphere of influence equals r.

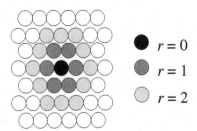

Exercise 2.3 (Triangular neighborhood)

The standard CNN definition specifies that the cells form a rectangular grid. There are only three possibilities to cover the plane. These are rectangular, hexagonal, and triangular.

Task
Give a formula for the area of a triangle in the case of a triangular cell grid, when the sphere of influence equals r.

Chapter 3

Exercise 3.1 (Separate connected objects)

The problem to be solved is to separate connected objects. The example shows a test image where objects are all similar in size. All objects should be separated but their sizes must be preserved.

Task
Design an algorithm which will separate objects, preserving their original properties, such as width, height, size, etc.

Example

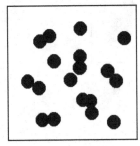

Input (200 × 200)

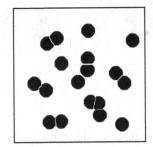

Desired output

Hint
- The combination of an EROSION followed by a DILATION is called an opening, referring to the ability of this combination to open up spaces between just-touching objects.

- The quasi-inverse operation of CLOSE is OPEN. The templates used for erosion and dilation are sufficient to solve this problem.

- It is necessary to use a mask image which prohibits dilation at boundaries of touching objects. This mask image is constructed from a skeleton of an inverse binary image of objects.

Exercise 3.2 (EDGE–CORNERDETECTION comparison)

There are two similar templates, the EDGE and the CornerDetection templates. The first one detects edges on binary images, and the second one detects corners. The templates are of the following form:

$$
A = \begin{array}{|c|c|c|} \hline 0 & 0 & 0 \\ \hline 0 & 1 & 0 \\ \hline 0 & 0 & 0 \\ \hline \end{array} \quad
B = \begin{array}{|c|c|c|} \hline -1 & -1 & -1 \\ \hline -1 & 8 & -1 \\ \hline -1 & -1 & -1 \\ \hline \end{array} \quad z
$$

where $z = -1$ in the EDGE template and $z = -8.5$ in the CornerDetection template. The mathematical analysis shows that the final output of a pixel is the sign of w_{ij}, where

$$
w_{ij} = z + 8u_{ij} - \sum_{(k,l) \in S(i,j) \wedge (k,l) \neq (i,j)} u_{kl}
$$

Let p_b and p_w denote the total number of black and white surround pixels respectively. Let us consider the case where $u_{ij} = 1$.

Question

What is the criterion of $w_{ij} > 0$? What is the role of z?

Example

Input

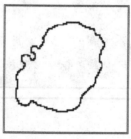

$z = -1 \ (p_b < 7.5)$

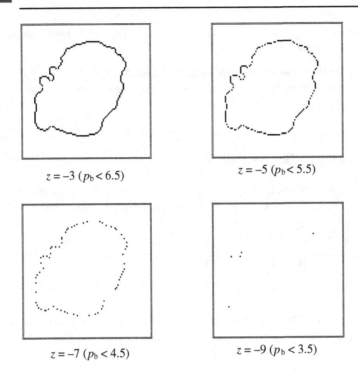

$z = -3 \; (p_b < 6.5)$

$z = -5 \; (p_b < 5.5)$

$z = -7 \; (p_b < 4.5)$

$z = -9 \; (p_b < 3.5)$

Exercise 3.3 (Main group of points)

Task

Given an image similar to the one below, locate the main groups of points.

Example

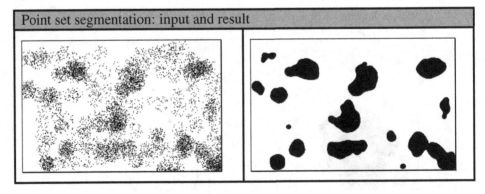

Point set segmentation: input and result

Hint

To solve this problem non-local information is needed. We have to use the propagating property of the **A** template. Where the average pixel number is large enough there is a group. Apply blurring, then some kind of thresholding method.

Chapter 5

Exercise 5.1 (Truth table)

Question

What is the difference between the Minimal Truth Table and the Optimized Minimal Truth Table, and what is the reason for having these two distinct truth tables?

Exercise 5.2 (Boolean function)

Question

Which class of Boolean functions can be implemented by the uncoupled binary CNN?

Chapter 6

Exercise 6.1 (Crossword puzzle endings)

Crossword puzzle is a table, in which white squares represent empty places for the letters, while black squares denote invalid positions. A word must be written in the white squares vertically and/or horizontally. There are specifications for the vertical and horizontal words as well. Closed squares are those squares which are members of one word only. The boundary cells count as black squares.

Task

Design a template which detects the closed squares.

Given: static binary image $\mathbf{P}$

Input: $\mathbf{U}(t) = \mathbf{P}$

Initial state: $\mathbf{X}(0) = 0$

Boundary conditions: 1

Output: $\mathbf{Y}(t) \rightarrow \mathbf{Y}(\infty) =$ a binary image, which represents the closed squares.

Example

Input   Output

Chapter 8

Exercise 8.1 (Dynamic construction of a grid)

Task

Construct dynamically a grid.

Given: nothing

Input: $\mathbf{U}(t) = 0$

Initial state: $\mathbf{X}(0) = 0$

Boundary conditions: 1

Output: $\mathbf{Y}(t) \rightarrow \mathbf{Y}(\infty) =$ a binary image, with a 3×3 grid

Example

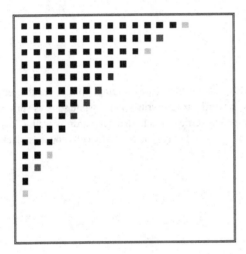

Hint

The grid grows from the upper left corner to the lower right corner. Use a similarly structured template.

$$\mathbf{A} = \begin{array}{|c|c|c|} \hline -a & -a & 0 \\ \hline -a & 0 & 0 \\ \hline 0 & 0 & 0 \\ \hline \end{array} \; , \quad \mathbf{B} = \begin{array}{|c|c|c|} \hline 0 & 0 & 0 \\ \hline 0 & 0 & 0 \\ \hline 0 & 0 & 0 \\ \hline \end{array} \; , \quad z$$

Exercise 8.2 (Reaction–diffusion equations)

Task

Design the templates of a double-layer, one-dimensional CNN realizing the following reaction–diffusion equations

$$\frac{dA}{dt} = c_1 A + c_2 I + c_3 + D_A \frac{d^2 A}{dx} - g_A A \quad \text{and} \quad \frac{dI}{dt} = c_4 A + c_5 + D_I \frac{d^2 I}{dx^2} - g_I I$$

where x is the coordinate for the one-dimensional space, A and I are the concentrations of the two so-called *morphogens*, the Activator and Inhibitor molecules. Parameters c_i, g_i, *and* D_i are constants. The equations describe the generation of the so-called Turing patterns.

Start with a random initial state, and, after a periodic pattern appears, increase the size of the cell array by one and wait for the steady state pattern. Continue increasing the size and look at the steady state solution several times. How does the periodicity of the pattern change?

Input: $\mathbf{U}(t)$ = not used

Initial state: random

Boundary conditions: periodic

Output: $\mathbf{Y}(t) \rightarrow \mathbf{Y}(\infty)$ = sine waves with $L = 10$ periodicity

Example

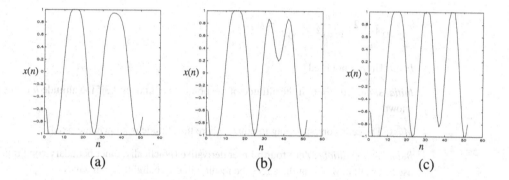

(a)　　　　　　　　　(b)　　　　　　　　　(c)

Fig. 1. Three snapshots of generating Turing patterns in an increasing cell array. The vertical axis shows the output of the cells. (a) The array of 51 cells has already reached its settled state. (b–c) After increasing the array size to 52, a new peak appears.

Hint

The first layer corresponds to the quantity A, the second one to I. The second-order derivatives with respect to x must be discretized. The CNN cell equations are

$$\frac{dA_i}{dt} = aA_i + bI_i + c + \mu(A_{i-1} - 2A_i + A_{i+1}),$$

$$\frac{dI_i}{dt} = dA_i + eI_i + f + \nu(I_{i-1} - 2I_i + I_{i+1})$$

where parameters a, b, c, d, e, f, μ, and v can be easily expressed in terms of c_i, g_i, and D_i. The templates describing the two-layer circuits are

$$\mathbf{A}_{1\,\text{to}\,1} = [\mu \;\; (a - 2\mu + 1) \;\; \mu], \quad \mathbf{A}_{2\,\text{to}\,1} = [0 \;\; b \;\; 0], \quad I_1 = c;$$
$$\mathbf{A}_{1\,\text{to}\,2} = [0 \;\; d \;\; 0], \quad \mathbf{A}_{2\,\text{to}\,2} = [v \;\; (e - 2v + 1) \;\; v], \quad \text{and} \quad I_2 = f.$$

Determine suitable values.

Exercise 8.3 (Surface interpolation)

Task

Design a CNN for surface interpolation. The altitude of the surface is given at some of the grid points; however, it is unknown in most of the grid points. The $v(x, y)$ interpolated surface must satisfy

$$\nabla^4 v = \frac{\partial^4 v}{\partial x^4} + 2 \frac{\partial^4 v}{\partial x^2 \partial y^2} + \frac{\partial^4 v}{\partial y^4} = 0$$

Input: $\mathbf{U}(t) = $ not used

Initial state: $\mathbf{X}(0) = 0$, if the altitude of the point is not known; h, if the altitude h of the point is known

Mask: The cells corresponding to points where the altitude is known, are fixed.

Boundary conditions: Zero fourth-order derivative (practically, other boundary conditions can be used as well; however, at the edges the result will differ slightly from what we expect).

Output: $\mathbf{Y}(t) \to \mathbf{Y}(\infty) = $ the interpolated surface

Example

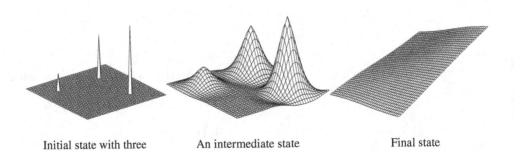

Initial state with three   An intermediate state   Final state

Hint

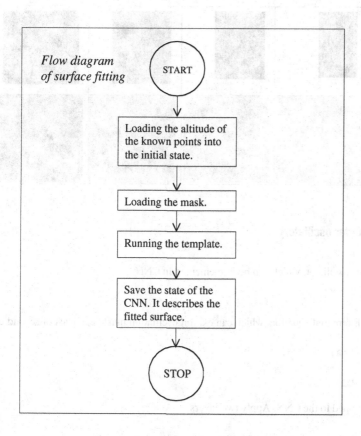

Flow diagram of surface fitting

START

Loading the altitude of the known points into the initial state.

Loading the mask.

Running the template.

Save the state of the CNN. It describes the fitted surface.

STOP

Exercise 8.4 (Black pixel count)

Task

In some more complicated tasks it is necessary to count the number of all black pixels in a result, or the number relative to the full area. This can easily be done through a serial algorithm, but this is not the most effective CNN application. In such a serial algorithm the principle of full CNN solution is necessary for implementing this interesting task. Give a simpler, parallel solution.

Given: static binary image $\mathbf{P}$

Input: $\mathbf{U}(t)$ = arbitrary

Initial state: $\mathbf{X}(0) = \mathbf{P}$

Boundary conditions: Periodic or 0 (periodic is supposed to be faster)

Output: $\mathbf{Y}(t) \rightarrow \mathbf{Y}(\infty)$ = uniform gray-scale image, which is equal in value to the rate of the total number of black pixels relative to the total area.

Hint

It can be carried out through a diffusion, which retains the sum of the state values.

Example

Input

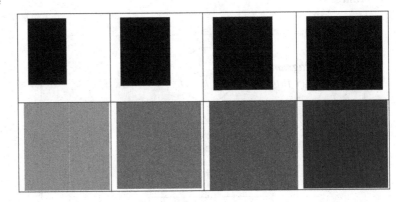

Output

Exercise 8.5 (Second-order oscillator)

Task

Design a simple oscillator, which can be implemented in CNN.

Hint

The simplest differential equation, which can exhibit oscillation must be at least of second order

$$\dot{x}_1 = a_{11}x_1 + a_{12}x_1$$

$$\dot{x}_2 = a_{21}x_1 + a_{22}x_2$$

This can be mapped to the CNN. Apply two layers.

Example

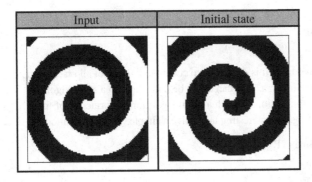

Input	Initial state

Chapter 9

Exercise 9.1 (Roughness measurement)

Task

Design a simple algorithm which measures the roughness of an object.

Hint

The basic idea here is to find the concave parts of objects. First the gray-scale image is converted into a binary image via the threshold operation. Next, pixels which are located at concave places are driven to black, using the "ConcaveLocationFiller" template. This template turns black all those white pixels which have at least four black direct neighbors. Next we extract concavities of objects using the logical XOR operation between the threshold image and the filled image.

Example

The following example shows the detected concave parts of an object.

INPUT PICTURE   OUTPUT_PICTURE

Hint – block diagram of the algorithm

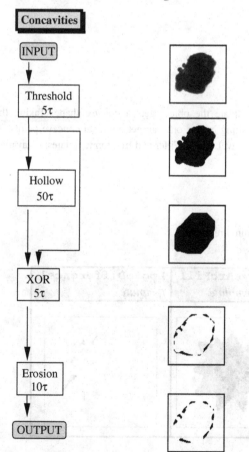

Templates can be found in the CNN Software Library v7.1 [1] as Threshold, ConcaveLocationFiller, and Erosion respectively.

Exercise 9.2 (Local concavity)

Task
Find the local concavities of an image.

Example

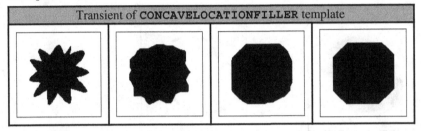

Hint
Using the ConcaveLocationFiller template the object gets a convex shape. Taking the logical difference of the original and the resulting image, one can get the local concave points. The result can be improved by Erosion. The ConcaveLocationFiller and Erosion templates are available in the template library.

Exercise 9.3 (Concavity orientation)

Task
Find the local concavities in one certain direction.

Example

Input image	**ConcaveArcFill er65** *template*	**LogicDifference1** *template*

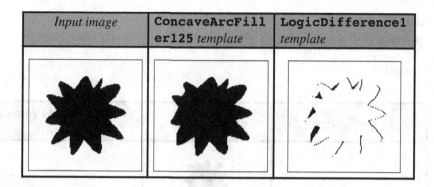

Input image	ConcaveArcFill er125 *template*	LogicDifference1 *template*

Hint

Use the ConcaveArcFiller templates, which are similar to the ConcaveLocationFiller template but, due to symmetry distortion, the wave propagation is direction selective. These templates result in directed shadows originating from concave locations.

To enhance the results the SmallObjectRemover template can be applied:

Example

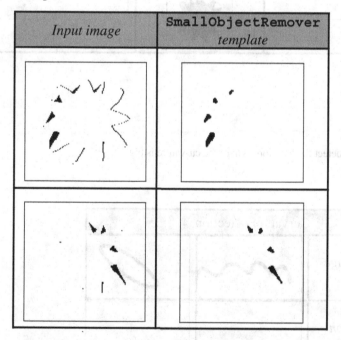

Input image	SmallObjectRemover *template*

Exercise 9.4 (Improved concavity orientation)

Task

Improve the selectivity of the direction-selective local concavity templates. Local concavity finder templates result in many patches over a wide range of angles. In some applications this range should probably be more precisely defined.

Hint

Use logical AND operation after applying three or four local concavity finder templates.

Example

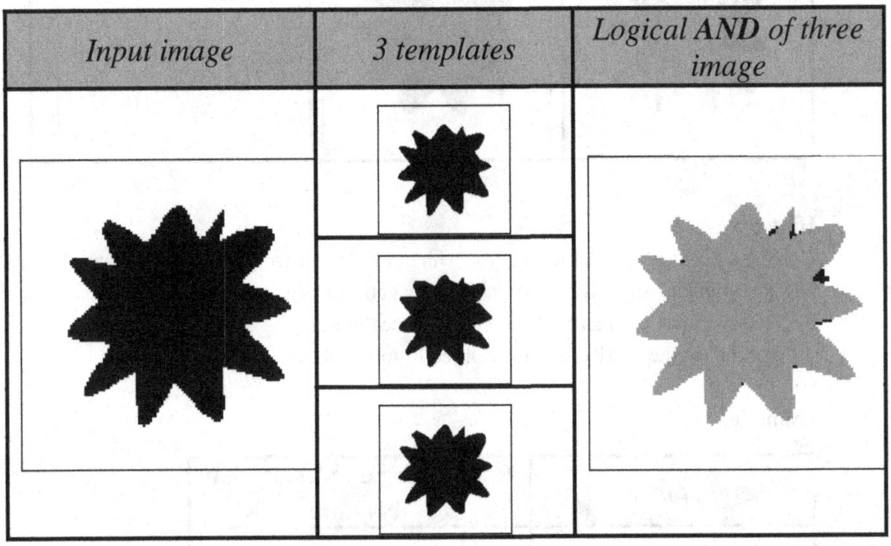

Input image	3 templates	Logical **AND** of three image

Exercise 9.5 (Curvature)

Task

Given an image, detect the locations where the curvature is big.

Example

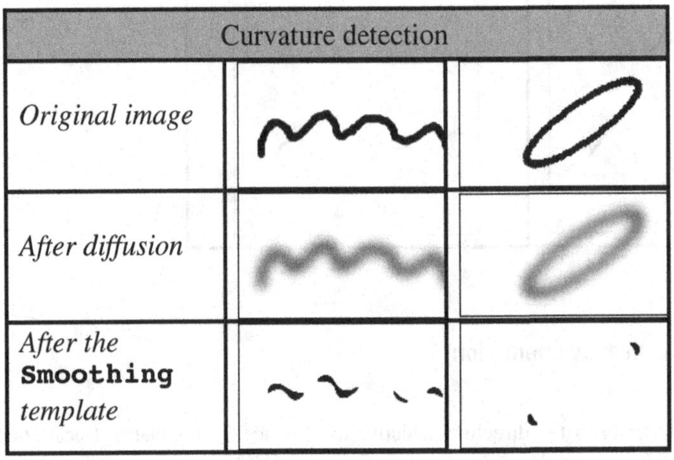

Curvature detection		
Original image		
After diffusion		
After the **Smoothing** *template*		

Hint

This property needs non-local information. Use the diffusion template. The image is brighter where the average pixel count is less.

Exercise 9.6 (Absolute value)

Task

Write an algorithm which implements the absolute value function of an image.

Hint

The absolute value can be computed using the nonlinearity of the CNN:

$$\text{abs}(I_{ij}) = f(f(i_{ij} - 1) + 1) - f(f(I_{ij} + 1) - 1)$$

where $f(\cdot)$ denotes the piecewise linear function:

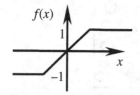

Example

Absolute value function
Original image
$f(I+1), f(I-1)$
$f(f(I+1)-1),$ $f(f(I-1)+1)$
$-f(f(I-1)+1)$
Two image subtracted $f(f(I+1)-1)$ $-f(f(I-1)+1)$

Exercise 9.7 (X and O segmentation)

Task

Given a black and white image with two types of textons, segment the image.

Hint

First detect some characteristic points of one of the textons. Then segment based on the resulting points. To solve this problem non-local information is needed. We have to use the propagating property of the **A** template. Use blur, then some kind of thresholding method. In this case the point set is rather sparse. To enhance the effect of blur, use a *fixed state* map.

Example

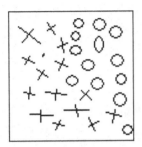

Input image

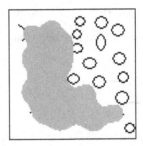

Segmented image

Algorithm frame

Texture segmentation		
Original image	![X and O input image]	*Result of the* `Junction` `Extractor` *template*
		![points result]
Skeletonized image		![skeletonized X and O image]
Result of the `Junction` `Extractor` *template*	![points]	*Its inverse created for fixed state mask*
		![black fixed state mask]

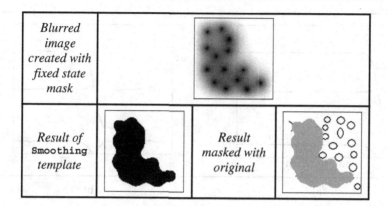

| Blurred image created with fixed state mask | |
| Result of Smoothing template | Result masked with original |

Exercise 9.8 (QCA simulation)

Task

Design a one-dimensional three-layer CNN simulating the behavior of a Quantum-dot Cellular Automata (QCA) cell line of 30 cells. The equation giving the dynamics of a QCA cell is

$$\hbar \frac{d}{dt} \begin{bmatrix} u_{ij} \\ v_{ij} \\ w_{ij} \end{bmatrix} = E_k \begin{bmatrix} 0 & -E_k w_{\Sigma ij} & 0 \\ w_{\Sigma ij} & 0 & 2\gamma \\ 0 & -2\gamma & 0 \end{bmatrix} \cdot \begin{bmatrix} u_{ij} \\ v_{ij} \\ w_{ij} \end{bmatrix}$$

where

$$w_{\Sigma ij} = E_k (w_{i,j-1} + w_{i,j+1} + w_{i-1,j} + w_{i+1,j}$$
$$- \frac{1}{4}(w_{i-1,j-1} + w_{i+1,j+1} + w_{i-1,j+1} + w_{i+1,j-1}))$$

Here γ and E_k are constants, characterizing the cell, and "*hbar*" is the Planck constant divided by 2π. For simplicity, take $\gamma = 0.3$, $E_k = 1$, and "*hbar*" = 1. The three-element vector (u_{ij}, v_{ij}, w_{ij}) gives the state of the ith cell.

As initial values for the columns of three layers use:

u: $-0.0156, 0, 0.0234, 0.703, 0.0234, 0, 0, \ldots, 0$

v: $-0.8047, 0.8047, -0.9063, -1.0, -0.8984, -0.8281, -0.8047, \ldots, -0.8047$

w: $-0.6094, -0.6016, -0.4375, 0.0234, 0.4453, 0.5703, 0.5938, \ldots, 0.5938$

> Input: $\mathbf{U}(t)$ = not used
> Initial state: a wave front starting to propagate
> Boundary conditions: doubling; the first and the last column are fixed
> Output: $\mathbf{Y}(t)$: state of the cell line after state t

Example

The propagation of a wave front from the left to the right in an array of QCA cells. All the cells contain the same value in a column, thus only a 1D section is shown. (a) The initial state and (b) an intermediate state.

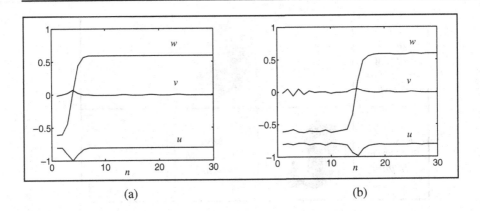

(a)   (b)

Chapter 10

Exercise 10.1 (Template design)

Task

Design a template which can detect one-pixel-wide line endings! Use the TEMMASTER application!

Hint

We restrict the solution to a 3×3 neighborhood and a one-pixel-wide line. Possible cases (eight neighbors):

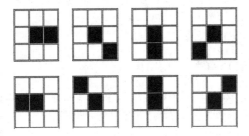

This problem is linearly not separable, therefore it must be decomposed into a sequence of templates. These templates must apply to the initial image, then the results must be XOR-ed to get the final result.

Example

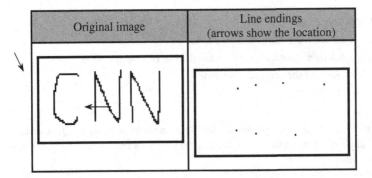

Chapter 12

Exercise 12.1 (Distance classification)

Task

Design an algorithm which can select those points whose distance from each other is less than a certain value along a given direction.

Example

Input image	Result of DirectedGrowing Shadow0	Result of Peel0 masked with original
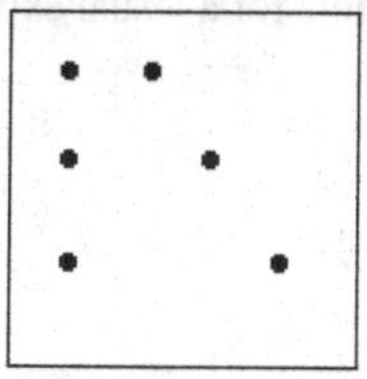	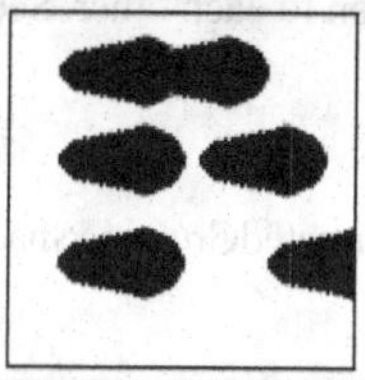	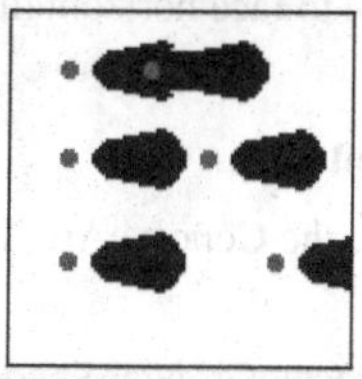

Input image	Result of DirectedGrowing Shadow45	Result of Peel45 masked with original
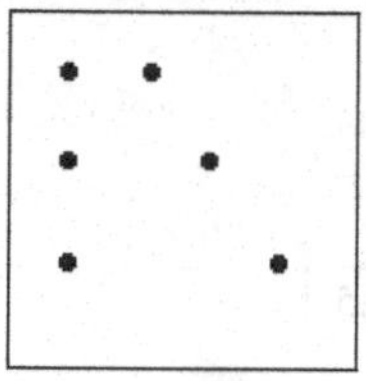		

Hint

Create growing shadows and then remove the starting points. The remaining points are those which are inside the shadow. The length of the shadow is proportional to the iteration number. Use the following templates:

DirectedGrowingShadow0

$$\mathbf{A} = \begin{array}{|c|c|c|} \hline 0.4 & 0.3 & 0 \\ \hline 1 & 2 & -1 \\ \hline 0.4 & 0.3 & 0 \\ \hline \end{array}, \quad \mathbf{B} = \begin{array}{|c|c|c|} \hline 0 & 0 & 0 \\ \hline 0 & 1.4 & 0 \\ \hline 0 & 0 & 0 \\ \hline \end{array}, \quad z = \boxed{2.5}$$

DirectedGrowingShadow

$$\mathbf{A} = \begin{array}{|c|c|c|} \hline 0 & 0 & -1 \\ \hline 1 & 2 & 0 \\ \hline 1 & 1 & 0 \\ \hline \end{array}, \quad \mathbf{B} = \begin{array}{|c|c|c|} \hline 0 & 0 & 0 \\ \hline 0 & 1.4 & 0 \\ \hline 0 & 0 & 0 \\ \hline \end{array}, \quad z = \boxed{2.5}$$

LeftPeeler

$$A = \begin{array}{|c|c|c|} \hline 0 & 0 & 0 \\ \hline 2 & 2 & 0 \\ \hline 0 & 0 & 0 \\ \hline \end{array}, \quad B = \begin{array}{|c|c|c|} \hline 0 & 0 & 0 \\ \hline 0 & 0 & 0 \\ \hline 0 & 0 & 0 \\ \hline \end{array}, \quad z = \boxed{-2}$$

Other directions can be gained by appropriate rotation. The effect of templates can be seen above.

Exercise 12.2 (Arc detection)

Task

Design an algorithm that selects those arcs for the input image of which concave sides are positioned face to face horizontally in relation to each other. See the Example for a visual explanation.

Hint

Use the ConcaveArcFiller and DirectedGrowingShadow templates:

DirectedGrowingShadow0

$$A = \begin{array}{|c|c|c|} \hline 0.4 & 0.3 & 0 \\ \hline 1 & 2 & -1 \\ \hline 0.4 & 0.3 & 0 \\ \hline \end{array}, \quad B = \begin{array}{|c|c|c|} \hline 0 & 0 & 0 \\ \hline 0 & 1.4 & 0 \\ \hline 0 & 0 & 0 \\ \hline \end{array}, \quad z = \boxed{2.5}$$

DirectedGrowingShadow180

$$A = \begin{array}{|c|c|c|} \hline 0 & 0.3 & 0.4 \\ \hline 1 & 2 & -1 \\ \hline 0 & 0.3 & 0.4 \\ \hline \end{array}, \quad B = \begin{array}{|c|c|c|} \hline 0 & 0 & 0 \\ \hline 0 & 1.4 & 0 \\ \hline 0 & 0 & 0 \\ \hline \end{array}, \quad z = \boxed{2.5}$$

ConcaveArcFiller35

$$A = \begin{array}{|c|c|c|} \hline 1 & 0 & 1 \\ \hline 0 & 2 & 0 \\ \hline 1 & 1 & 0 \\ \hline \end{array}, \quad B = \begin{array}{|c|c|c|} \hline 0 & 0 & 0 \\ \hline 0 & 1 & 0 \\ \hline 0 & 0 & 0 \\ \hline \end{array}, \quad z = \boxed{2}$$

ConcaveArcFiller−155

$$A = \begin{array}{|c|c|c|} \hline 0 & 1 & 1 \\ \hline 0 & 2 & 0 \\ \hline 1 & 0 & 1 \\ \hline \end{array}, \quad B = \begin{array}{|c|c|c|} \hline 0 & 0 & 0 \\ \hline 0 & 1 & 0 \\ \hline 0 & 0 & 0 \\ \hline \end{array}, \quad z = \boxed{2}$$

To get the desired result, use the logical AND, XOR operation (or LogicDifference1 template) and the SmallObjectRemover template to remove small objects. The LogicDifference1 and SmallObject-Remover templates are available in the template library. The ConcaveArcFiller* templates result in directed shadows originating from concave locations.

Example

Arc detection result images	
Input image	

`ConcaveArc`
`Filler-155`
and
`ConcaveArc`
`Filler35`	

After **XOR** *operation* *and* `SmallObject` `Remover` *template* 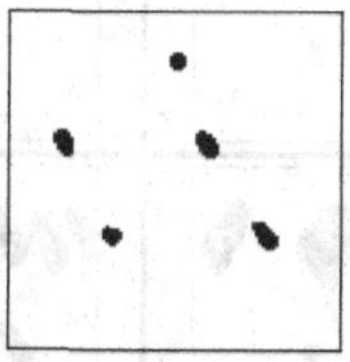 	

Masked result of
`DirectedGrowingS`
`hadow0` *and*
`DirectedGrowingS`
`hadow180`
templates	

The locations	

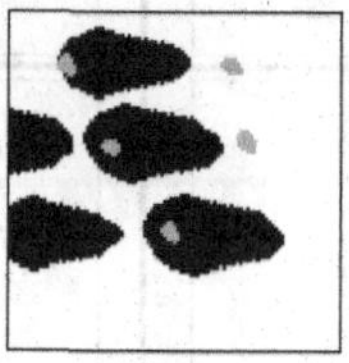

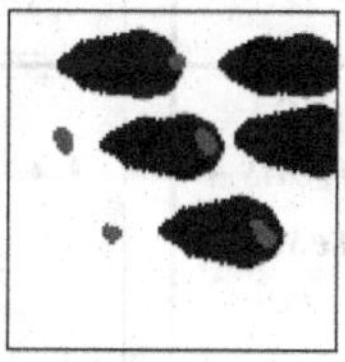

Exercise 12.3 (Detect forks)

Task

Given the following picture, detect the fork.

Hint

We have to find characteristic features of the object and then try to extract them. Such features are arcs or endings and the position of them in relation to each other. Some post- and intermediate processing is needed; for example, small object removing.

Object detection result images		
Input image		
ConcaveArc Filler65 *and* **ConcaveArc Filler-65**		
After **XOR** *operation and* **SmallObject Remover** *template*		
After **DirectedGrowing Shadow315** *and* **DirectedGrowing Shadow225**		
The result of logic **AND** *of the previous 4 image and the result of* **PatchMaker**		
The result of the **SelectedObjects Extraction** *template with the previous and the original image*		

Use the ConcaveArcFiller and DirectedGrowingShadow templates:

ConcaveArcFiller65

$$\mathbf{A} = \begin{array}{|c|c|c|} \hline 1 & 0 & 0 \\ \hline 1 & 2 & 0 \\ \hline 0 & 0 & 2 \\ \hline \end{array} \, , \quad \mathbf{B} = \begin{array}{|c|c|c|} \hline 0 & 2 & 0 \\ \hline 0 & 0 & 0 \\ \hline 0 & 0 & 0 \\ \hline \end{array} \, , \quad z = \boxed{3}$$

ConcaveArcFiller−65

$$\mathbf{A} = \begin{array}{|c|c|c|} \hline 1 & 0 & 1 \\ \hline 1 & 2 & 0 \\ \hline 0 & 0 & 1 \\ \hline \end{array}, \quad \mathbf{B} = \begin{array}{|c|c|c|} \hline 0 & 0 & 0 \\ \hline 0 & 1 & 0 \\ \hline 0 & 0 & 0 \\ \hline \end{array}, \quad z = \boxed{2}$$

DirectedGrowingShadow315

$$\mathbf{A} = \begin{array}{|c|c|c|} \hline 1 & 1 & 0 \\ \hline 1 & 2 & 0 \\ \hline 0 & 0 & -1 \\ \hline \end{array}, \quad \mathbf{B} = \begin{array}{|c|c|c|} \hline 0 & 0 & 0 \\ \hline 0 & 1.4 & 0 \\ \hline 0 & 0 & 0 \\ \hline \end{array}, \quad z = \boxed{2.5}$$

DirectedGrowingShadow225

$$\mathbf{A} = \begin{array}{|c|c|c|} \hline 0 & 1 & 1 \\ \hline 0 & 2 & 1 \\ \hline -1 & 0 & 0 \\ \hline \end{array}, \quad \mathbf{B} = \begin{array}{|c|c|c|} \hline 0 & 0 & 0 \\ \hline 0 & 1.4 & 0 \\ \hline 0 & 0 & 0 \\ \hline \end{array}, \quad z = \boxed{2.5}$$

The SelectedObjectsExtraction template reconstructs the image starting from one point. The SmallObjectRemover template removes the small objects. The SelectedObjectsExtraction, SmallObjectRemover and the PatchMaker templates are available in the template library. The ConcaveArcFiller* templates result in directed shadows originating from concave locations.

Exercise 12.4 (Locate small ellipses)

Task

Design an algorithm which can locate small circles and small ellipses.

Hint

Use the filling property of the local concavity detector template (ConcaveArcFiller*). Fill the objects on image from two opposite directions. The small objects are filled in both cases. The next step is to find those objects which are not filled completely in both images and then remove them from the original image.

Example

Algorithm for detecting small circles and ellipses		
Input image	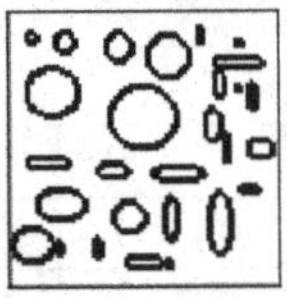	
ConcaveArc Filler-155 *and* **ConcaveArc Filler35**		
After logic **AND** *of the previous images and the* **ConcaveLocation Filler** *template*	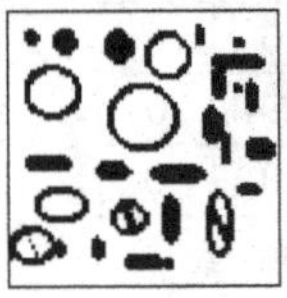	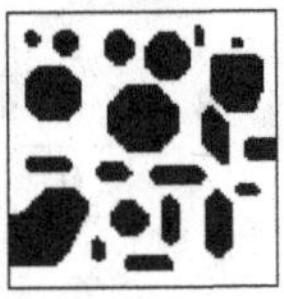
After local **hole** *filling*	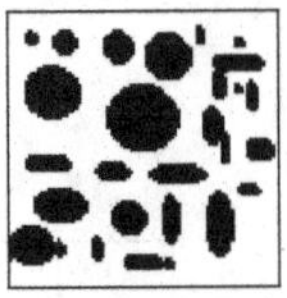	
The logic difference of the two previous image, and applying the **PatchMaker** *template*		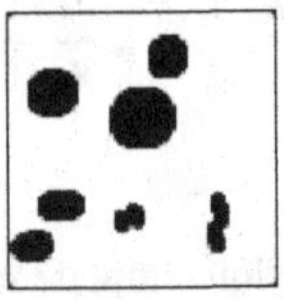
Result of **SelectedObjects Extraction** *template applied to the original and the previous image and its inverse*	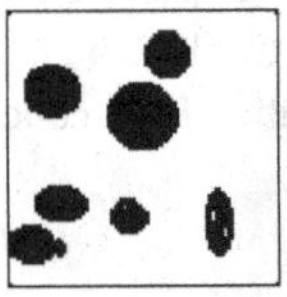	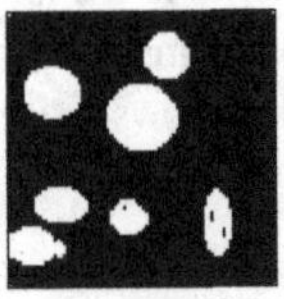
The logic difference of the original and the previous (inverted) image	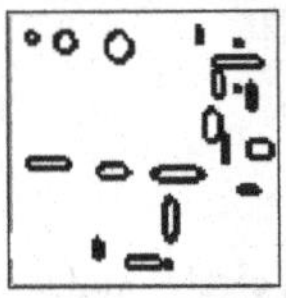	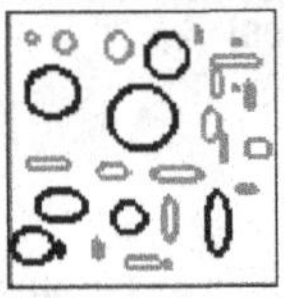

Use the following ConcaveArcFiller templates:

ConcaveArcFiller35

$$\mathbf{A} = \begin{array}{|c|c|c|} \hline 1 & 0 & 1 \\ \hline 0 & 2 & 0 \\ \hline 1 & 1 & 0 \\ \hline \end{array}, \quad \mathbf{B} = \begin{array}{|c|c|c|} \hline 0 & 0 & 0 \\ \hline 0 & 1 & 0 \\ \hline 0 & 0 & 0 \\ \hline \end{array}, \quad z = \boxed{2}$$

ConcaveArcFiller—155

$$\mathbf{A} = \begin{array}{|c|c|c|} \hline 0 & 1 & 1 \\ \hline 0 & 2 & 0 \\ \hline 1 & 0 & 1 \\ \hline \end{array}, \quad \mathbf{B} = \begin{array}{|c|c|c|} \hline 0 & 0 & 0 \\ \hline 0 & 1 & 0 \\ \hline 0 & 0 & 0 \\ \hline \end{array}, \quad z = \boxed{2}$$

The SelectedObjectsExtraction, ConcaveLocationFiller, HoleFilling, and PatchMaker templates are available in the template library. The ConcaveArcFiller* templates result in directed shadows originating from concave locations.

Chapter 13

Exercise 13.1 (Linear morph)

Given: two gray-scale images **P**1 and **P**2

Input: $\mathbf{U}(t) = \mathbf{P}1$

Initial state: $\mathbf{X}(0) = \mathbf{P}2$

Boundary conditions: -1

Output: $\mathbf{Y}(t) = $ a transition from **P**2 to **P**1. The transition has to be linear:

$$\mathbf{Y}(t) = \lambda(t)\mathbf{P}1 + (1 - \lambda(t))\mathbf{P}2$$

Task

Design a D type template which accomplishes a linear transition from image **P**2 to **P**1.

Hint

The solution is basically a three-layer model, where the first two layers compute λ and $1 - \lambda$ and on the third layer the output image is computed. Try to solve the exercise without looking at the following solution.

```
%MORPH
NRLAYERS 3
LAYER 1
Neighborhood: 0
FEEDBACK FROM 1
1
CURRENT −0.1
LAYER 2
Neighborhood: 0
FEEDBACK FROM 2
1
CURRENT 0.1
LAYER 3
nonlin_d
u#y
1#1
1
nonlin_d
u#y
2#2
1
```

Example

Exercise 13.2 (Parity check)

Parity check is an important task of computing; it is well known that it is used in error detection of memories. A nonlinear solution already exists in the CNN Software library. Now solve it using a D type template.

Task

A binary input picture is given. The task is to produce an output picture which represents the parity of the input picture defined as follows. A particular pixel in the output is black, if an even number of black pixels can be found at the left of that particular pixel (including the position of the pixel itself).

Given: static binary image $\mathbf{P}$

Input: $\mathbf{U}(t) = \mathbf{P}$

Initial state: $\mathbf{X}(0) = \mathbf{P}$

Boundary conditions: -1

Output: $\mathbf{Y}(t) \rightarrow \mathbf{Y}(\infty) = $ a binary image, which represents the row parity calculated from the left side of the image

Example

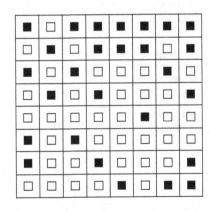

Input   Output

Hint

The applied template realizes the following network equations:

$$\dot{x}_{ij} = -x_{ij} + y_{(i-1)j} * u_{ij}$$
$$y_{ij} = f(x_{ij})$$

where f is the usual sigmoid function.

Exercise 13.3 (Limit set)

Task

In mathematical set theory the limit point is a well-known notion. Can we define a discrete notion and detect the limit point of a discrete binary set?

> Given: static binary image $\mathbf{P}$
> Input: $\mathbf{U}(t) = \mathbf{P}$
> Initial state: $\mathbf{X}(0) = $ arbitrary (0)
> Boundary conditions: 0
> Output: $\mathbf{Y}(t) \rightarrow \mathbf{Y}(\infty) = $ binary image, the limit points of the set defined as those white points, which has at least one black point neighborhood

Example

Pictures are taken from the picture library. The last case shows how the template behaves in the gray-scale case.

Question

This exercise is very similar to the Edge template. Why? What is the difference?

Exercise 13.4 (Chaotic cell)

A chaotic function with one cell and $\mathbf{D}$ template.

Task

Design a template which implements the following so-called "logistic equation" in the range $[-1, 1]$ as a DT-CNN.

The logistic map is known as $f(x) = \lambda x(1 - x)$. It is known that the iteration of this function becomes chaotic if λ is greater than ~ 3.56. The discrete iteration is

$$x(n + 1) = \lambda x(n)(1 - x(n))$$

Example

The following picture shows a transient with starting value $x(1) = 0.7$.

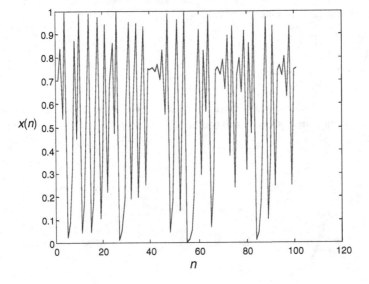

Appendices

Appendix A: TEMLIB, a CNN Template Library

Under the name TEMLIB, within the Software Library for analogic cellular (CNN) computers, a set of fairly standard types of CNN template data are contained. The template names in TEMLIB can be used in the template and algorithm simulators defined in Appendix B.

Appendix B: TEMPO, template optimization tools

Under the name TEMMASTER, a student version of a program for template optimization and design is available. It is used mainly for Boolean CNN and for robust template design.

Appendix C: CANDY, a simulator for CNN templates and analogic CNN algorithms

Under the name CANDY (CNN Analogic Dynamics), a student version of a software simulator system is available. Multi-layer CNN templates as well as analogic CNN algorithms (defined on the CNN Universal Machine having a one layer, first-order dynamics CNN core) can be simulated. An easy to use Template Runner program as well as a high-level language compiler (Alpha) help the user to analyze complex spatial-temporal dynamics easily and with expressive visualization tools.

Index

Printed in the United States
By Bookmasters